Rick

VENICE

Rick Steves & Gene Openshaw

CONTENTS

Area of Detail

TRONCHETTO

STAZIONE MARITTIMA

GHETTO

CANNAREGIO

Grand Canal

TRAIN STATION

SANTA CROCE

PIAZZALE ROMA

SAN POLO

FRARI

RIALTO

CASTELLO

SAN MARCO

SAN MARCO

DORSODURO

ACCADEMIA

PUBLIC GARDENS

ARSENALE

SAN GIORGIO

GIUDECCA

Lagoon

To Mainland

SANTA LUCIA TRAIN STATION (FERROVIA)

To Tronchetto & Mainland

SCALZI

Ferrovia

SAN SIMEONE PICCOLO

SCALZI BRIDGE

SCALZI W

Piazzale Roma

CALATRAVA BRIDGE

GARAGE

PEOPLE MOVER

Piazzale Roma BUS STATION

To Stazione Marittima (Cruise Port) & Tronchetto (Parking)

Giardini Papadopoli

SCUOLA SAN ROCCO

SAN TOMÀ

PALAZZO BALBI

San Tomà

Campo Santa Margarita

CA' FOSCARI

CA' REZZONICO

PALAZZO GRASSI

San Samuele

Campo San Barnaba

Campo San Trovaso

ACCADEMIA

ACCADEMIA BRIDGE

Campo S. Agnese

DORSODURO

To Stazione Marittima (Main Cruise Port), San Basilio Dock, & Santa Marta Dock

Zattere

Giudecca

GHETTO

Campo de Gheto Novo

CANNARE

Guglie

Campo San Geremia

SAN MARCUOLA

San Marcuola

Riva de Biasio

SANTA CROCE

Campo San Giacomo de l'Orio

Campo S. Maria M. Domi

SAN

FRARI

Campo San Stin

Campo San Polo

SAN POLO

Sant'Angelo

PALAZZO MOCENIGO

Campo San Stefano

SIGHTS

1. Accademia Gallery
2. Bridge of Sighs
3. Ca' d'Oro
4. Ca' Pesaro Internat'l Gallery of Modern Art
5. Ca' Rezzonico
6. Campanile
7. Clock Tower
8. Correr Museum
9. Doge's Palace
10. Frari Church
11. Jewish Ghetto & Museum
12. La Fenice Opera House
13. La Salute Church
14. Palazzo Grassi
15. Palazzo Mocenigo Costume Museum
16. Peggy Guggenheim Collection
17. Piazzale Roma
18. Punta della Dogana Museum
19. Rialto Bridge & Fondaco dei Tedeschi Mall
20. St. Mark's Basilica
21. St. Mark's Square
22. San Giorgio Maggiore Church
23. San Polo Church
24. San Zaccaria Church
25. Santa Maria Formosa Church
26. Scala Contarini del Bovolo
27. To Scuola Dalmata di San Giorgio
28. Scuola San Rocco
29. Train Station

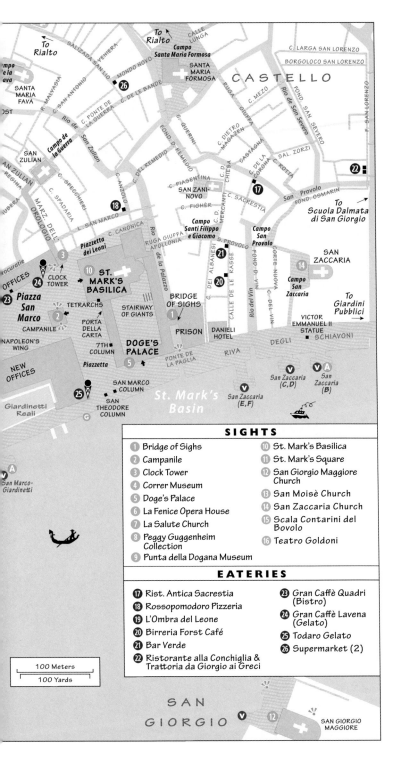

To Rialto

CALLE LUNGA

SALIZADA SAN VENIERA

Campo Santa Maria Formosa

C. LARGA SAN LORENZO

BORGOLOCO SAN LORENZO

To Rialto

MONDO NOVO

SANTA MARIA FORMOSA

CASTELLO

mpo e la ava

SANTA MARIA FAVA

C. MALVASIA

C. SAN ANTONIO

C. PONTE DE LA GUERRA

C. DE LE BANDE

RUGA GIUFFA

C. MEZO

FOND. SAN SEVERO

Rio de San Severo

OST

Campo de la Guerra

Rio de San Zulian

C. QUERINI

C. DIETRO MAGAZEN

F. SAN LORENZO

SAN ZULIAN

AN ZULIAN REGINA

C. SPADARIA

C. SPECCHIERI

C. DEL REMEDIO

FOND. D. REMEDIO

C. PIASENTINA

C. D. CHIESA

C. D. LA CASTAGNA

CORONA

C. DE LA SAL. ZORZI

C. ROTTA

22

UBERA

MARZ. DELL OROLOGIO

L. SAN MARCO

18

C. ANZOLO

SAN ZANI-NOVO

C. FIGHER

C. D. MERCANTI

C. SACRESTIA

17

San Provolo

FOND. OSMARIN

To Scuola Dalmata di San Giorgio

crie

OFFICES

23

Piazza San Marco

24

CLOCK TOWER

3

Piazzetta dei Leoni

10 ST. MARK'S BASILICA

C. CANONICA

Rio de Palazzo

RUGA GIUFFA APOLLONIA

Campo Santi Filippo e Giacomo

21

S. PROVOLO

20

Campo San Provolo

CORTE NUOVA

14

SAN ZACCARIA

C. DEI ALBANESI

CALLE DE LE RASSE

FOND. D. VIN

Campo San Zaccaria

To Giardini Pubblici

2

CAMPANILE

TETRARCHS

PORTA DELLA CARTA

STAIRWAY OF GIANTS

BRIDGE OF SIGHS

1

VICTOR EMMANUEL II STATUE

NAPOLEON'S WING

7TH COLUMN

Piazzetta

DOGE'S PALACE

5

PRISON

DANIELI HOTEL

Rio del Vin

C. DEL VIN

SCHIAVONI

NEW OFFICES

25

SAN MARCO COLUMN

PONTE DE LA PAGLIA

RIVA

DEGLI

Giardinetti Reali

G

SAN THEODORE COLUMN

St. Mark's Basin

San Zaccaria (E,F)

San Zaccaria (C,D)

San Zaccaria (B)

V

V A

A

San Marco-Giardinetti

SIGHTS

1 Bridge of Sighs
2 Campanile
3 Clock Tower
4 Correr Museum
5 Doge's Palace
6 La Fenice Opera House
7 La Salute Church
8 Peggy Guggenheim Collection
9 Punta della Dogana Museum

10 St. Mark's Basilica
11 St. Mark's Square
12 San Giorgio Maggiore Church
13 San Moisè Church
14 San Zaccaria Church
15 Scala Contarini del Bovolo
16 Teatro Goldoni

EATERIES

17 Rist. Antica Sacrestia
18 Rossopomodoro Pizzeria
19 L'Ombra del Leone
20 Birreria Forst Café
21 Bar Verde
22 Ristorante alla Conchiglia & Trattoria da Giorgio ai Greci

23 Gran Caffè Quadri (Bistro)
24 Gran Caffè Lavena (Gelato)
25 Todaro Gelato
26 Supermarket (2)

100 Meters
100 Yards

SAN GIORGIO

V

12

SAN GIORGIO MAGGIORE

EATERIES & NIGHTLIFE

7 Trattoria da Bepi
8 La Cantina
9 Vini da Gigio
10 Bacarando Bar
11 Osteria al Portego & Cioccolateria VizioVirtù
12 Osteria da Alberto
13 "Cicchetti Strip"
14 "Bancogiro Stretch"
15 Al Mercà Bar
16 Ristorante Vini da Pinto
17 Osteria al Ponte Storto
18 Trattoria Antiche Carampane
19 Antica Birraria la Corte
20 Osteria alle Testiere
21 Osteria al Mascaron
22 Peter Pan Kebabs & Pizza
23 La Boutique del Gelato
24 Gelatoteca Suso
25 Supermarket (3)
26 Devil's Forest Pub
27 Inishark Pub

100 Meters
100 Yards

To Fondamenta Nove

CANNAREGIO

CASTELLO

SAN MARCO

To San Marco

To San Marco

SIGHTS

1 Ca' d'Oro
2 Ca' Pesaro International Gallery of Modern Art
3 Palazzo Mocenigo Costume Museum
4 Rialto Bridge
5 Santa Maria Formosa Church
6 Teatro Goldoni

Italy

Venice's lagoon, Roman Bridge in Verona, Venetian masks, St. Mark's Square

Rick Steves®

VENICE

Welcome to Rick Steves' Europe

Travel is intensified living—maximum thrills per minute and one of the last great sources of legal adventure. Travel is freedom. It's recess, and we need it.

I discovered a passion for European travel as a teen and have been sharing it ever since—through my tours, public television and radio shows, and travel guidebooks. Over the years, I've taught millions of travelers how to best enjoy Europe's blockbuster sights—and experience "Back Door" discoveries that most tourists miss.

Written with my talented co-author, Gene Openshaw, this book offers you a balanced mix of Venice's artistic splendors and backstreet charm, from its impressive museums to its tranquil and colorful canals. It's selective: Rather than listing dozens of glassblowing demonstrations, we recommend only the best. And it's in-depth: Our self-guided museum tours and city walks provide insight into the city's vibrant history and today's living, breathing culture.

We advocate traveling simply and smartly. Take advantage of our money- and time-saving tips on sightseeing, transportation, and more. Try local, characteristic alternatives to expensive hotels and restaurants. In many ways, spending more money only builds a thicker wall between you and what you traveled so far to see.

We visit Venice to experience it—to become temporary locals. Thoughtful travel engages us with the world, as we learn to appreciate other cultures and new ways to measure quality of life.

Judging by the positive feedback we receive from our readers, this book will help you enjoy a fun, affordable, and rewarding vacation—whether it's your first trip or your tenth.

Buon viaggio! Happy travels!

Rick Steves

INTRODUCTION

Engineers love Venice—a completely man-made environment rising from the sea, with no visible means of support. Romantics revel in its atmosphere of elegant decay, seeing the peeling plaster and seaweed-covered stairs as a metaphor for beauty in decline. And first-time visitors are often stirred deeply, awaking from their ordinary lives to a fantasy world unlike anything they've ever experienced before.

Those are strong reactions, considering that Venice today, frankly, can also be an overcrowded, prepackaged, tacky tourist trap. But Venice is unique. Built on a hundred islands with wealth from trade with the East, its exotic-looking palaces are laced together by sun-speckled canals. It can seem to the visitor like one giant amusement park for grown-ups, centuries in the making. And yet, the longer you're here—and the more you explore its back streets—the clearer it becomes that this is also a real, living town, with its own personality and challenges.

By day, Venice is a city of museums and churches, packed with great art. Everything's within a half-hour walk. Cruise the canals on a vaporetto water bus. Climb towers for stunning seascape views. Shop for Venetian crafts (such as glass and lace), high fashions, or tacky souvenirs. Linger over lunch, trying to crack a crustacean with weird legs and antennae. Sip a *spritz* at a café on St. Mark's Square while the orchestra plays "New York, New York."

At night, when the hordes of day-trippers have gone, another Venice appears. Dance across a floodlit square. Glide in a gondola through quiet canals while music echoes across the water. Pretend it's Carnevale time, don a mask—or just a fresh shirt—and become someone else for a night.

Planning Your Trip

This section will help you get started planning your trip—with advice on trip costs, when to go, and what you should know before you take off.

TRIP COSTS

Six components make up your trip costs: airfare to Europe, transportation in Europe, room and board, sightseeing/entertainment, shopping/miscellany, and gelato.

Airfare to Europe: A basic round-trip flight from the US to Venice (or even cheaper, Milan) can cost, on average, about $900-1,500 total, depending on where you fly from and when (cheaper in winter). If Venice is part of a longer trip, consider saving time and money by flying into one city and out of another; for instance, into Venice and out of Dubrovnik. Overall, Kayak.com is the best place to start searching for flights on a combination of mainstream and budget carriers.

Transportation in Europe: Venice's sights are within walking distance of each other, but vaporetto boat rides are fun and save time. Most visitors buy a vaporetto pass (figure about $24/day). For a one-way trip between Venice's airport and the city, allow about $10 by bus, $18 by Alilaguna water bus, or $130 by water taxi (can be shared by up to 4 people).

Round-trip, second-class train transportation to day-trip destinations is affordable as long as you avoid express trains (about $5 each way to Padua and $10 to Verona by local train). For more on public transportation and driving, see "Transportation" in the Practicalities chapter.

Room and Board: You can manage comfortably in Venice on $135 a day per person for room and board. This allows $15 for lunch, $25 for dinner, and $90 for lodging (based on two people splitting the cost of a $180 double room that includes breakfast). That leaves you $5 for gelato. Students and tightwads can enjoy Venice for as little as $70 a day ($40 for a bed, $30 for meals and snacks).

Sightseeing and Entertainment: Figure about $15-20 per major sight (Accademia, Doge's Palace, Guggenheim), $8-12 for minor ones (climbing church towers), and $30-35 for splurge expe-

Venice Almanac

Population: While there are approximately 270,000 people in greater Venice, fewer than 55,000 people live on the actual islands.

Nicknames: La Serenissima and The Queen of the Adriatic

City Layout: The city of Venice is built on more than 100 small islands in the Venetian Lagoon along the Adriatic Sea. The historic center is broken up into six districts *(sestieri):* Cannaregio, Castello, Dorsoduro, San Polo, Santa Croce, and San Marco.

Tallest Structure: The Campanile on St. Mark's Square reaches 325 feet and offers a beautiful view of the city. Good news: It has an elevator.

Tourist Tracks: Roughly 28 million tourists flock to Venice each year, with at least 30,000 roaming the streets each day of the Carnevale festival. St. Mark's Square is the most popular sight and the Rialto Bridge is the top photo spot.

Culture Count: Venice's population has long been almost entirely Italian—but that's changing. You'll notice lots of Asians working in shops and restaurants, as well as lots of Senegalese on the streets selling knockoff bags. While Italian is the official language of Italy, most of the Veneto region's 2 million people speak the Venetian dialect among themselves (you might notice how they don't roll their r's). The vast majority of native Venetians are Roman Catholics.

Fun Food Facts: Venice is known for its wine bars (*bacari* or *enoteche*) that serve small bite-sized snacks called *cicchetti,* which are similar to Spanish tapas.

Most Venerable Café: Caffè Florian, on the south side of St. Mark's Square, opened in 1720. Famous visitors have included Lord Byron and Charles Dickens.

Average Venetian: The average Venetian is 46 years old, has 1.4 children, and will live until the age of 82. Half of the Venetian population works in some sector of the tourism industry. Venetians are more likely to have a gondolier license than a driver's license, and many go weeks without seeing a car.

riences (such as walking tours and concerts). A gondola ride costs roughly $100; split the cost by going with a pal—or six. An overall average of $40 a day works for most people. Don't skimp here. After all, this category is the driving force behind your trip—you came to sightsee, enjoy, and experience Venice.

Shopping and Miscellany: Figure $3 per coffee, soft drink, or gelato. Shopping can vary in cost from nearly nothing to a small fortune. Good budget travelers find that this category has little to do with assembling a trip full of lifelong and wonderful memories.

WHEN TO GO

Venice's best travel months (also its busiest and most expensive) are April, May, June, September, and October.

Summer in Venice is more temperate (high 70s and 80s) than in Italy's scorching inland cities. Most Venetian hotels come with air-conditioning—important in the summer—but it's usually available only from May (at the earliest) through September. Spring and fall can be cool, and many hotels—thanks to a national interest in not wasting energy—are not allowed to turn on their heat until winter.

Between November and March you can usually expect mild winter weather (with lows in the 30s and 40s), occasional flooding, shorter lines, lower prices, and fewer tourists (except during the Carnevale festival—see the sidebar). March offers a good balance of low-season prices and reasonable weather. (For specifics, see the climate chart in the appendix.)

Venice has two main weather patterns: Wind from the southeast (the Balkans) brings cold and dry weather, while the sirocco wind from the south (north Africa) brings warm and wet weather, pushing more water into the lagoon and causing flooding *(acqua alta)*. This shouldn't greatly affect your sightseeing plans. *Tabacchi* (tobacco shops) and some souvenir shops sell boots to keep your feet dry. Elevated wooden walkways are sometimes set up in the busier, more flooded squares to keep you above the water. And it's worth a trip to St. Mark's Square to see waiters in fancy tuxes and rubber boots.

Off-Season Travel Tips: Off-season has none of the sweat and stress of the tourist season, but sights may have shorter hours, lunchtime breaks, and fewer activities. Here are several things to keep in mind if you visit Venice off-season, roughly November through March.

• Most sights close early, often at 17:00.

• The orchestras in St. Mark's Square may stop playing at 18:00 (and may not play at all in bad weather or during their annual vacations, usually in March).

• Vaporetto #2 (the Grand Canal fast boat) terminates at the Rialto stop before 9:00 and after 20:00, which means no stops at San Marco and Accademia early in the morning and late in the evening (you can take the slow boat, vaporetto #1, instead).

• Expect occasional flooding, particularly at St. Mark's Square.

• Room prices can be about 25-50 percent lower.

BEFORE YOU GO

You'll have a smoother trip if you tackle a few things ahead of time. For more information on these topics, see the Practicalities chapter (and www.ricksteves.com, which has helpful travel tips and talks).

Unmasking Venice's Carnevale

Every February, Venice celebrates its own version of Mardi Gras with an extravagant festival of costumes, food, drink, and entertainment—an entire city purging itself of winter in masked celebration. Carnevale, which means "farewell to meat," originated centuries ago as a wild, two-month-long party. In pagan times, it was an end-of-winter festival of feasting on leftover winter stock to celebrate the onset of spring.

With the arrival of Christianity, Carnevale evolved into the final debauchery before the restrictions of Lent. Aristocrats from all over Europe, Africa, and the Middle East came here to revel in the hedonism. Today, the festival is still an international affair, with revelers donning ornate, outrageous costumes and colorful masks (for more on Venetian masks, see the sidebar on page 294).

The 18-day celebration kicks off sometime in February, culminating on Shrove Tuesday—the night before Ash Wednesday (so dates vary from year to year). The festival begins with a centuries-old ritual: the Flight of the Angel. A young costumed woman is harnessed and hoisted down from St. Mark's Basilica to greet the thousands gathered in the square below. In the weeks following, parties, dinners, and themed parades fill Venice's streets and canals. At the "Festa delle Marie," 12 selected women parade through town to honor the rescue of 12 brides captured during the reign of Doge Pietro III Candiano in the 10th century. The festivities end with a huge dance lit with fireworks on St. Mark's Square.

European tourists descend en masse during Carnevale, spending hundreds of euros on costumes and attending fanciful events. It's most festive on weekends, but can be quiet during the first week. The energy ramps up as Fat Tuesday approaches. If you plan to visit during Carnevale, book accommodations as soon as your dates are finalized (prepare for high prices). If Venice is all booked up, consider staying in nearby Padua (30 minutes away by train). To really get into the spirit of Carnevale, rent a costume and consider participating in some of the fun, from intimate dinners and masquerade balls to cabaret shows and cruises (book in advance at www.venice-carnival-italy.com).

Make sure your travel documents are valid. If your passport is due to expire within six months of your ticketed date of return, you need to renew it. Allow up to six weeks to renew or get a passport (www.travel.state.gov). Beginning in 2021, you may also need to register with the European Travel Information and Authorization System (ETIAS).

Arrange your transportation. Book your international flights. You won't want a car in Venice, but if Venice is part of a longer trip, figure out your main form of transportation: bus or train (and either a rail pass or individual train tickets), rental car, or a cheap flight. (You can wing it in Europe, but it may cost more.) Drivers: Consider bringing an International Driving Permit (sold at AAA offices in the US, www.aaa.com) along with your license.

Book rooms well in advance, especially if your trip falls during peak season or any major holidays or festivals.

Make reservations or buy tickets in advance for major sights. In Padua, **reservations** are mandatory to visit the Scrovegni Chapel, famous for its frescoes by Giotto, so book well in advance (easily done online; see page 330). Also consider reserving an entry slot for St. Mark's Basilica in Venice (see page 32).

Consider travel insurance. Compare the cost of the insurance to the cost of your potential loss. Check whether your existing insurance (health, homeowners, or renters) covers you and your possessions overseas.

Call your bank. Alert your bank that you'll be using your debit and credit cards in Europe. Ask about transaction fees, and get the PIN number for your credit card. You don't need to bring euros for your trip; you can withdraw euros from cash machines in Europe.

Use your smartphone smartly. Sign up for an international service plan to reduce your costs, or rely on Wi-Fi in Europe instead. Download any apps you'll want on the road, such as maps, translators, transit schedules, and Rick Steves Audio Europe (see sidebar).

Pack light. You'll walk with your luggage more than you think. I travel for weeks with a single carry-on bag and a daypack. Use the packing checklist in the appendix as a guide.

Travel Smart

If you have a positive attitude, equip yourself with good information (this book), and expect to travel smart, you will.

Read—and reread—this book. To have an "A" trip, be an "A" student. Note opening hours of sights, closed days, crowd-beating tips, and whether reservations are required or advisable. Check the latest at www.ricksteves.com/update.

Be your own tour guide. As you travel, get up-to-date info

INTRODUCTION

Free Video Clips and Audio Tours from Rick Steves

Travel smarter with these free, fun resources:

Rick Steves Classroom Europe, a powerful tool for teachers, is also useful for travelers. This video library contains over 400 three- to five-minute clips excerpted from my public television series. Enjoy these videos as you sort through options for your trip and to better understand what you'll see in Europe. Just enter a topic (city name, historical event, etc.) into the search bar for a list of everything I've filmed on a subject. Check it out at http://classroom.ricksteves.com.

Rick Steves Audio Europe, an app for Apple and Android mobile devices, makes it easy to download my audio tours and listen to them offline as you travel. For Venice, these audio tours include my Grand Canal Cruise and tours of the Frari Church, St. Mark's Basilica, and St. Mark's Square (look for the 🎧 in this book). The app also offers insightful travel interviews from my public radio show with experts from Europe and around the globe. Find it in your app store or at www.ricksteves.com/audioeurope.

on sights, reserve tickets and tours, reconfirm hotels and travel arrangements, and check transit connections. Visit local tourist information offices (TIs). Upon arrival in a new town, lay the groundwork for a smooth departure; confirm the train, bus, boat, or road you'll take when you leave.

Outsmart thieves. Pickpockets abound in crowded places where tourists congregate. Treat commotions as smokescreens for theft. Keep your cash, credit cards, and passport secure in a money belt tucked under your clothes; carry only a day's spending money in your front pocket. Don't set valuable items down on counters or café tabletops, where they can be quickly stolen or easily forgotten.

Minimize potential loss. Keep expensive gear to a minimum. Bring photocopies or take photos of important documents (passport and cards) to aid in replacement if they're lost or stolen. Back up photos and files frequently.

Beat the summer heat. If you wilt easily, choose a hotel with air-conditioning, start your day early, take a midday siesta at your hotel, and resume your sightseeing later. Churches offer a cool haven (though dress modestly—no bare shoulders or shorts). Take frequent gelato breaks. Join the *passeggiata*, when locals stroll in the cool of the evening.

Guard your time and energy. Taking a water taxi can be a good value if it saves you an exhausting walk across town. To avoid long lines, follow my crowd-beating tips, such as making advance reservations, or sightseeing early or late. If you save St. Mark's Basilica for Sunday morning (when it's closed), you've missed the gondola. You can sweat in line at the Doge's Palace, or you can buy your pass at the nearby Correr Museum and zip right through the palace turnstile. Day-tripping to Verona on a Monday, when sights tend to only be open in the afternoon, is not a great idea.

Be flexible. Even if you have a well-planned itinerary, expect changes, strikes, closures, sore feet, bad weather, and so on. Your Plan B could turn out to be even better.

Attempt the language. Many Italians—especially in the tourist trade and in cit-ies—speak English, but if you learn some Italian, even just a few phrases, you'll get more smiles and make more friends. Prac-tice the survival phrases near the end of this book, and even better, bring a phrase book.

Connect with the culture. Interacting with locals carbonates your experience. Enjoy the friendliness of the Italian people. Ask questions; most locals are happy to point you in their idea of the right direction. Set up your own quest for the best little square, vaporetto ride, or gelato. When an opportunity pops up, make it a habit to say "yes."

Italy...here you come!

ORIENTATION TO VENICE

The island city of Venice is shaped like a fish. Its major thorough-fares are canals. The Grand Canal winds through the middle of the fish, starting at the mouth where all the people and food enter, passing under the Rialto Bridge, and ending at St. Mark's Square (Piazza San Marco). Park your 21st-century perspective at the mouth and let Venice swallow you whole.

VENICE: A VERBAL MAP

Venice is a car-less kaleidoscope of people, bridges, and odorless canals. It's made up of more than a hundred small islands—but for simplicity, I refer to the whole shebang as "the island."

Venice has six districts known as *sestieri:* **San Marco** (from St. Mark's Square to the Accademia Bridge), **Castello** (the area east of St. Mark's Square—the "tail" of the fish), **Dorsoduro** (the "belly," on the far side of the Accademia Bridge), **Cannaregio** (between the train station and the Rialto Bridge), **San Polo** (west of the Rialto Bridge), and **Santa Croce** (the "eye" of the fish, across the canal from the train station).

The easiest way to navigate is by landmarks. Many street corners have a sign pointing you to *(per)* the nearest major land-mark, such as San Marco, Accademia, Rialto, and Ferrovia (train station). Obedient visitors stick to the main thoroughfares as directed by these signs...and miss the charm of back-street Venice.

Beyond the city's core lie several other islands, including San

Giorgio (with great views of Venice), Giudecca (more views), San Michele (old cemetery), Murano (famous for glass), Burano (lace-making), Torcello (old church), and the skinny Lido (with Venice's beach).

PLANNING YOUR TIME

Venice is small. You can walk across it, from head to tail, in about an hour. Nearly all of your sightseeing is within a 20-minute walk of the Rialto Bridge or St. Mark's Square. Remember that Venice itself is its greatest sight. Make time to wander, explore, shop, and simply be. When you cross a bridge, look both ways—you may be hit with a lovely view. Venice has what's considered one of the highest concentrations of art anywhere in the world. Art lovers need to be particularly well organized to get the most out of their visit.

Key considerations: Ninety percent of tourists congregate in a very narrow zone in the center. But even the most touristy stretches of the city are almost ghostly peaceful early and late. Maximize your evening magic, and avoid the midday crowds around St. Mark's Basilica and the Doge's Palace. If you arrive in Venice late in the day, try taking my Grand Canal Cruise and St. Mark's Square Tour. These sights are more romantic and much less crowded after dark—and they provide a wonderful welcome to the city.

Depending on when you visit, you may have to juggle the itineraries provided, as sights' visiting hours will vary by season and day of the week.

Venice in One Brutal Day (Plus the Night Before)

On the night before, walk or boat to the train station and then, aboard an empty vaporetto #1, take my self-guided Grand Canal

Cruise to St. Mark's Square (which is much more enjoyable as an audio tour from my app—see page 8).

Day 1

9:00 Take my self-guided St. Mark's to Rialto Loop Walk as far as the Rialto Bridge.

10:00 Enjoy the action at the Rialto Bridge and Rialto Market.

11:00 Follow my Rialto to Frari Church Walk.

12:00 Tour the Frari Church.

13:00 Wander into the Dorsoduro district toward the Accademia museum, exploring and enjoying lunch along the way. Stroll across the Accademia Bridge (tour the Accademia only if you're an art lover—and really energetic) and back to St. Mark's Square.

15:30 Tour St. Mark's Basilica.

17:00 Visit the Doge's Palace.

18:30 Take my St. Mark's Square Tour.

19:30 Dinner and a gondola ride (or vice versa, as a gondola ride at sunset is best).

22:00 Enjoy a drink with the orchestras on St. Mark's Square.

Venice in Two or More Days (Plus the Night Before)

On the night before, walk or boat to the train station and then, aboard an empty vaporetto #1, take my self-guided Grand Canal Cruise to St. Mark's Square.

Day 1

9:00 Ride to the top of the Campanile.

10:00 Take my self-guided St. Mark's Square Tour. Pop into a glass shop for a glass-blowing demo.

11:00 Take my St. Mark's to Rialto Loop Walk.

13:00 Lunch.

14:00 Tour the Correr Museum (ticket purchased here includes Doge's Palace).

15:30 Tour St. Mark's Basilica.

17:00 Visit the Doge's Palace.

19:00 Dinner and maybe a gondola ride (or vice versa, as a gondola ride at sunset is best).

22:00 Enjoy a drink with the orchestras on St. Mark's Square.

Day 2

9:00 Enjoy the action at the Rialto Bridge and Rialto Market.

10:00	Follow my Rialto to Frari Church Walk.
11:00	Tour the Frari Church.
12:00	Wander into the Dorsoduro district toward Ca' Rezzonico, exploring and enjoying lunch along the way. (Visit Scuola San Rocco only if you're an art lover.)
14:00	Tour Ca' Rezzonico (Museum of 18th-Century Venice).
16:00	Tour the Accademia museum (only if you're an art lover), then stroll across the Accademia Bridge and back to St. Mark's Square.
18:00	Commence pub crawl for dinner (consider taking Alessandro's Classic Venice Bars Tour; see "Tours in Venice," later).
20:00	Evening free for a concert or gondola ride.

Day 3: Lagoon Tour

10:00	Catch boat at Fondamente Nove to San Michele (old cemetery), then continue to Murano.
11:00	Tour Murano.
13:00	Boat to Burano for lunch and browsing.
15:00	Boat to Torcello, tour church, back to Burano.
18:00	Zip back to Fondamente Nove in 45 minutes, or—if you'd like to see more of the lagoon—take the long way back by boat via the mainland peninsula of Cavallino and the Lido (no need to stop there—just enjoy the cruise).
20:00	Dinner and/or concert in Venice.

Day 4 and Beyond

Shop and browse some of Venice's more characteristic areas (such as the zone between Campo Santa Margarita and Campo San Barnaba; the back lanes of Cannaregio, near the Jewish Ghetto; or the sleepy part of Dorsoduro behind the Accademia and Guggenheim). Or, stroll the harborside promenade—the Riva—to the "tail of the fish" and enjoy the neighborhood action along Via Garibaldi.

Or consider these options: Take a guided or theme tour (such as a food tour), visit the Church of San Giorgio Maggiore, or side-trip to Padua (30-50 minutes away by train).

Overview

TOURIST INFORMATION

With this book, a free city map from your hotel, and the events schedule on the TI's website, there's little need to make an in-person visit to a Venice TI. That's fortunate, because though the city's TIs try to help, they're understaffed and have few free printed ma-

ORIENTATION

Daily Reminder

Sunday: While anyone is welcome to worship, most churches are closed to sightseers on Sunday morning. They reopen in the afternoon: St. Mark's Basilica (14:00-17:00, until 16:30 Nov-Easter), Frari Church (13:00-18:00), and the Church of San Zaccaria (16:00-18:00). The Church of San Polo is closed all day, and the Rialto open-air market consists mainly of souvenir stalls (fish and produce sections closed). It's a bad day for a pub crawl, as most pubs are closed.

Monday: All sights are open except the Rialto fish market, Ca' Pesaro, Palazzo Mocenigo Costume Museum, Lace Museum (on the island of Burano), and Torcello church museum (on the island of Torcello). The Accademia and Ca' d'Oro close at 14:00. Don't side-trip to Verona today, as most sights there are closed in the morning.

Tuesday: All sights are open except the Peggy Guggenheim Collection, Ca' Rezzonico (Museum of 18th-Century Venice), and Punta della Dogana.

Wednesday/Thursday/Friday: All sights are open.

Saturday: All sights are open except the Jewish Museum.

terials to hand out. To check or confirm something, try phoning the TI information line at 041-2424 or visit www.veneziaunica.it; this website can be more helpful than the actual TI office. Other useful websites are www.visitmuve.it (city-run museums in Venice), www.unospitedivenezia.it/en (sights and events), www.venicexplorer.net (detailed maps), www.veniceforvisitors.com (general travel advice), www.venicelink.com (travel agent selling public and private transportation tickets), and www.theveniceinsider.com (transportation tips and current events).

If you must visit a TI, you'll find four convenient branches (all are open daily): **St. Mark's Square** (in the far-left corner with your back to the basilica), **airport, bus station** (inside the huge white Autorimessa Comunale parking garage), and **train station** (across from track 2).

Be wary of the travel agencies or special information services that masquerade as TIs but serve fancy hotels and tour companies. They're in the business of selling things you don't need.

Maps: Of all places, Venice demands a good map. Hotels give away freebies (similar in quality to the small color ones at the front of this book). TIs and vaporetto ticket booths sell decent €3 maps—but you can find a wider range at bookshops, newsstands, and postcard stands. The cheap maps are pretty bad, but if you spend €5, you'll get a map that shows all the tiny alleys. It may be the best money you spend in Venice. But know you'll still spend some time "exploring" (read: lost).

Also consider a mapping **app** for your mobile phone. To avoid data-roaming charges, look for an offline map that can be downloaded in its entirety before your trip. (**City Maps 2Go** and **Google Maps** cover Venice well.) In some areas of Venice, cell phone coverage is weak and your mapping app won't work; ask a local for general directions to a major monument or *piazza,* then try calling up your map again.

ARRIVAL IN VENICE

For a rundown on Venice's train station, bus station, airport, and cruise terminal, and tips for drivers, see the Venice Connections chapter.

HELPFUL HINTS

Sightseeing Tips: Venice offers plenty of sightseeing passes, but only a few—like the Doge's Palace and Correr Museum combo-ticket—are worth the money. For more on passes and other sightseeing advice, see page 28.

Theft Alert: The dark, late-night streets of Venice are generally safe. Even so, pickpockets (often elegantly dressed) work the crowded main streets, docks, and vaporetti. Your biggest risk of pickpockets is inside St. Mark's Basilica, near the Accademia or Rialto bridges (especially if you're preoccupied with snapping photos), or on a tightly packed vaporetto.

A handy *polizia* station is on the right side of St. Mark's Square as you face the basilica (at #63, near Caffè Florian). To call the police, dial 113. The Venice TI handles complaints— which must be submitted in writing— about local crooks, including gondoliers, restaurants, and hotel rip-offs (complaint. apt@turismovenezia. it).

It's illegal for street vendors to sell knockoff handbags, and it's illegal for you to buy them; both you and the vendor can get big fines.

Medical Help: Venice's Santi Giovanni e Paolo hospital (tel. 118) is a 10-minute walk from both the Rialto and San Marco neighborhoods, located behind the big church of the same name on Fondamenta dei Mendicanti (toward Fondamente Nove). You can take vaporetto #4.1 from San Zaccaria, or #5.2 from the train station or Piazzale Roma, to the Ospedale stop. Also, a first-aid station staffed by English-speaking doctors is on St. Mark's Square, on the right-hand side as you face the basilica (at #63 next to Caffè Florian—same address as *polizia* station, daily 8:00-20:00, tel. 041-2960-784).

Behave in Venice: Remember that Venice is a community of about 50,000 people who welcome visitors but feel violated when tourists don't respect the city they love. The vast majority of visitors are day-trippers stampeding in, seeing the famous stuff, and stampeding out. Venetians ask a few simple rules are followed: Dress decently, don't swim in the canals, don't litter, stay on the right as you walk, and treat things as if they are both historic and fragile...because they are.

Be Prepared to Splurge: Venice is expensive for both residents and tourists, as everything must be shipped in and hand-trucked to its final destination. I find that the best way to enjoy Venice is just to succumb to its charms, accept that prices are 20 percent higher than on the mainland, and blow through a little money. It's a unique place that's worth paying a premium to fully experience.

Dress Modestly: When visiting St. Mark's Basilica or other major churches, men, women, and even children must cover their shoulders and knees. Remove hats when entering a church.

Picnics: Picnicking is illegal anywhere on St. Mark's Square, and offenders can be fined. The only place nearby for a legal picnic is in Giardinetti Reali, the small bench-filled park along the waterfront west of the Piazzetta near St. Mark's Square. Elsewhere in Venice, picnicking is no problem.

Bookstores: In keeping with its literary heritage, Venice has classy and inviting bookstores. The small **Libreria Studium,** a block behind St. Mark's Basilica, has a carefully chosen selection of new English books, including my guidebooks (Mon-Sat 9:00-19:30, shorter hours Sun, on Calle de la Canonica at #337, tel. 041-522-2382).

Used-bookstore lovers will appreciate the funky **Acqua Alta** ("high water") bookstore, whose quirky owner Luigi has prepared for the next flood by displaying his wares in a selection of vessels, including bathtubs and a gondola. Look for the "book stairs" in his back garden (daily 9:00-20:00, large and classically disorganized selection includes prints of Venice, just beyond Campo Santa Maria Formosa on Lunga Santa Maria Formosa, Castello 5176, tel. 041-296-0841). For a solid selection of used books in English, visit **Marco Polo**, on Calle del Teatro o de l'Opera, close to the St. Mark's side of the Rialto Bridge, behind the church (daily 9:30-19:30, Cannaregio 5886a, tel. 041-522-6343). For bookstore locations, see the map on page 292.

Public Toilets: Handy pay WCs are near major landmarks, including: St. Mark's Square (behind the Correr Museum and at the waterfront park, Giardinetti Reali), Rialto, and the Accademia Bridge. Or use free toilets at any museum you're visiting, or any café you're eating in.

Laundry: Across the Grand Canal from the train station is the coin-operated **Orange Self-Service Lavanderia** (daily 7:30-22:30, on Ramo de le Chioverete, Santa Croce 665b—see map on page 252, mobile 346-972-5446).

These laundry places are near St. Mark's Square (see page 242 for locations): Self-service **Effe Erre** is off Campo Santa Maria Formosa (daily 6:30-23:30, on Ruga Giuffa, Castello 4826, mobile 349-058-3881). **Lavanderia Gabriella** offers full-service laundry, a few streets north of St. Mark's Square (drop off Mon-Fri 8:00-12:30, closed Sat-Sun; pick up 2 hours later or next working day, on Rio Terà de le Colonne, San Marco 985, tel. 041-522-1758, friendly Elisabetta).

Travel Agencies: If you need help arranging train tickets, making seat reservations, or booking an overnight berth, you can avoid a time-consuming trip to Venice's crowded train station by using a downtown travel agency. Ask your hotel for the nearest one. Most trains between Venice, Florence, and Rome require reservations, even for rail-pass holders.

Best Views: A slow vaporetto ride down the **Grand Canal**—ideally very early or just before sunset—is a shutterbug's delight. On St. Mark's Square, enjoy views from the soaring **Campanile** or the **balcony of St. Mark's Basilica** (both require admission). The **Rialto and Accademia bridges** provide expansive views of the Grand Canal, along with a cooling breeze. The luxury mall **Fondaco dei Tedeschi**, just north of the Rialto Bridge, has even better views, especially around sunset (free but book a reservation; see details on page 43). Or get off the main island for a view of the Venetian skyline: Ascend **San Giorgio Maggiore's bell tower** (admission fee), or venture to Giudecca Island to visit the swanky bar of the **Molino Stucky Hilton Hotel** (the free-to-"customers" shuttle boat leaves from near the San Zaccaria-B vaporetto dock).

ORIENTATION

English Church Services: San Zulian Church offers a Mass in English (generally Mon-Fri at 9:30 and Sun at 11:30, Oct-April Sun at 10:30, 2 blocks toward Rialto off St. Mark's Square, tel. 041-523-5383). **St. George's Anglican Church** welcomes all to its English-language Eucharist (Sun at 10:30, located on Campo San Zio in Dorsoduro, midway between Accademia and Peggy Guggenheim Collection, www.stgeorgesvenice.com).

Water: I carry a water bottle to refill at public fountains. Venetians pride themselves on having pure, safe, and tasty tap water piped in from the foothills of the Alps. You can actually see the mountains from Venice's bell towers on crisp, clear winter days.

Pigeon Poop: If your head is bombed by a pigeon, resist the initial response to wipe it off immediately—it'll just smear into your hair. Wait until it dries, and it should flake off cleanly. But if the poop splatters on your clothes, wipe it off immediately to avoid a stain.

GETTING AROUND VENICE
On Foot

The city's "streets" are narrow pedestrian walkways connecting its docks, squares, bridges, and courtyards. To navigate, look for signs on street corners pointing you to *(per)* the nearest major landmark. The first landmarks you'll get to know are San Marco (St. Mark's Square), Rialto (the bridge), Accademia (another bridge), Ferrovia ("railroad," meaning the train station), and Piazzale Roma (the bus station). Determine whether your destination is in the direction of a major, signposted landmark, then follow the signs through the maze.

As you get more comfortable with the city, dare to disobey these signs, avoid the posted routes, and make your own discoveries. While 80 percent of Venice is, in fact, not touristy, 80 percent of the tourists never notice. Escape the crowds and explore on foot. Walk and walk to the far reaches of the town.

Don't worry about getting lost—in fact, get as lost as possible. Keep reminding yourself, "I'm on an island, and I can't get off." When it comes time to find your way, just follow the arrows on building corners or simply ask a local, *"Dov'è San Marco?"* ("Where is St. Mark's?") Most Venetians speak some English. If they don't, listen politely, watch where their hands point, say *"Grazie,"* and head off in that direction. In a few blocks, ask again. If you're lost, refer to a map, or pop into a hotel and ask for their business card—it probably comes with a map and a prominent "You are here."

Every building in Venice has a house number. The numbers relate to the district (each with about 6,000 address numbers), not the street. Therefore, if you need to find a specific address, it helps to know its district, street, house number, and nearby landmarks.

Some helpful street terminology: *Campo* means square, a *campiello* is a small square, *calle* (pronounced "KAH-lay" with an "L" sound) means "street," and a *ponte* is a bridge. A *fondamenta* is the embankment along a canal or the lagoon. A *rio terà* is a street that was once a canal and has been filled in. A *sotoportego* is a covered passageway. *Salizzada* literally means a paved area (usually a wide street). The abbreviations S. and SS. mean "saint" and "saints" respectively. Don't get hung up on the exact spelling of street and square names, which may sometimes appear in Venetian dialect (which uses *de la, novo,* and *vechio*) and other times in standard Italian (which uses *della, nuovo,* and *vecchio*).

By Vaporetto

Venice's public transit system, run by a company called ACTV, is a fleet of motorized bus-boats called vaporetti. They work like city buses except that they never get a flat, the stops are docks, and if you jump off between stops, you might drown. For the same prices, you can purchase tickets and passes at docks and from ACTV affiliate VèneziaUnica (ACTV-tel. 041-2424, www. actv.it; VèneziaUnica—www. veneziaunica.it).

Tickets and Passes

Individual Vaporetto Tickets: A single ticket costs €7.50 (kids under 6 travel free). Tickets are good for 75 minutes; you can hop on and off at stops and change boats during that time. Your ticket (a paper ticket embedded with a chip) is refillable—don't toss it after the first use. You can put more money on it at the kiosks and avoid waiting in line at the ticket window. It's also smart to keep your receipt (in case you're checked and your ticket is faulty).

Vaporetto Passes: You can buy a pass for unlimited use of vaporetti: €20/24 hours, €30/48 hours, €40/72 hours, €60/7-day pass (the clock starts ticking the first time you use it). Because single tickets are pricey, these passes pay for themselves in a hurry. Think through your Venice itinerary before you step up to the ticket booth to pay for your first vaporetto trip. The 48-hour pass pays for itself with five rides (for example: to your hotel on your arrival, on a Grand Canal joyride, into the lagoon and back, to the train sta-

Handy Vaporetti from San Zaccaria, near St. Mark's Square

Several vaporetti leave from the San Zaccaria docks, located 150 yards east of St. Mark's Square. The four docks are spaced about 70 yards apart, with six different berths, lettered A to F. Check the big electronic board (next to the C/D dock), which indicates the departure time, line number, destination, and berth letter of upcoming vaporetti. Once you've figured out which boat you want, go to that letter berth and hop on.

Line #1: This vaporetto goes up the Grand Canal, making all the stops, including San Marco, Rialto, Ferrovia (train station), and Piazzale Roma (but it does not go as far as Tronchetto). In the other direction, it goes from San Zaccaria to Arsenale and Giardini before ending on the Lido (dock E).

Line #2: This vaporetto zips over to San Giorgio Maggiore, the island church across from St. Mark's Square (5 minutes, €5 ride). From there, it continues on to stops on the island of Giudecca, the parking lot at Tronchetto, and then down the Grand Canal (dock B). Note: You cannot ride the #2 up the Grand Canal (for example, to Rialto or the train station) directly from this stop—you'll need to walk five minutes along the waterfront, past St. Mark's Square, to the San Marco-Giardinetti dock and hop the #2 from there.

Line #4.1: This boat goes to San Michele and Murano (45 minutes, dock D).

Line #7: This is the summertime express boat to Murano (25 minutes, dock D).

Molino Stucky Shuttle Boat: This takes even non-guests to the Hilton Hotel, with its popular view bar (20-minute ride, 3/hour, from its own dock near the San Zaccaria-B dock).

Lines #5.1 and **#5.2:** These are the *circulare* (cheer-koo-LAH-ray), making a loop around the perimeter of the island, with a stop at

tion...and that spur-of-the-moment moonlight cruise). It's fun to be able to hop on and off spontaneously, and avoid long ticket lines. Because some smaller and outlying stops are unstaffed, that's another reason to buy a pass.

Travelers ages 14-29 can get a 72-hour pass for €22 if they also buy a **Rolling Venice** discount card for €6 (see page 29). Those settling in for a much longer stay can ride like a local by buying the Vènezia Unica card (see www.veneziaunica.it for details).

Passes are also valid on some of ACTV's mainland buses, including bus #2 to Mestre (but not the #5 to the airport or the airport buses run by ATVO, a separate company). Pass holders get a discounted fare for all ACTV buses that originate or terminate at Marco Polo Airport (see page 310).

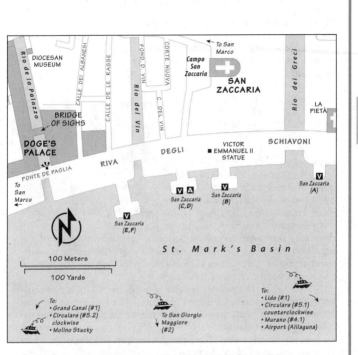

ORIENTATION

the Lido—perfect if you just like riding boats. Line #5.1 goes counterclockwise, and #5.2 goes clockwise. Both run less frequently in the evenings (#5.1 leaves from dock D, #5.2 from dock C).

Alilaguna Shuttle Boat: This runs to and from the airport (dock D).

Buying and Validating Tickets and Passes: Purchase tickets and passes from the machines at most stops (English-language option, major credit cards accepted), from ticket windows (at larger stops), or from the VèneziaUnica offices at the train station, bus station, and Tronchetto parking lot.

Before you board, validate your ticket or pass by touching it to the small white pad on the dock until you hear a pinging sound. With passes, you need to touch the pass each time you board a boat. The machine readout shows how long your ticket is valid—and inspectors do come by now and then to check tickets. If you're unable to purchase a ticket before boarding, seek out the conductor immediately to buy a single ticket (or risk a €60 fine).

ORIENTATION

Is Venice Sinking?

Venice has battled rising water levels since the fifth century. But today, the water seems to be winning. Several factors, both natural and man-made, cause Venice to flood dozens of times a year—usually from October until late winter—a phenomenon called the *acqua alta*.

On my last trip I asked a Venetian how much the city is sinking. He said, "Less than the sea is rising." Venice sits atop sediments deposited at the ancient mouth of the Po River, which are still compacting and settling. Early industrial projects, such as offshore piers and the railroad bridge to the mainland, affected the sea floor and tidal cycles in ways that made the city more vulnerable to flooding. Twentieth-century industry worsened things by pumping massive amounts of groundwater out of the aquifer beneath the lagoon for nearly 50 years before the government stopped the practice in the 1970s. In the last century, Venice has sunk by about nine inches.

Meanwhile, the waters around Venice are rising, a phenomenon that's especially apparent in winter. The highest so far was in November of 1966, when a huge storm (the same one that famously flooded Florence) raised Venice's water level to more than six feet above the norm. The notorious *acqua alta* happens when an unusually high tide combines with strong sirocco winds and a storm. Although tides are minuscule in the Mediterranean, the narrow, shallow Adriatic Sea has about a three-foot tidal range. When a storm—an area of low pressure—travels over a body of water, it pulls the surface of the water up into a dome. As strong sirocco winds from Africa blow storms north up the Adriatic, they push this high water ahead of the front, causing a surging storm tide. Add to that the worldwide sea-level rise that's resulted from recent climate change (melting ice caps, thermal expansion of the water, more frequent and more powerful storms) and it makes a high sea that much higher.

If the *acqua alta* appears during your visit, you'll see the first puddles in the center of paved squares, pooling around the lime-

Important Vaporetto Lines

For most travelers, only two vaporetto lines matter: **line #1** and **line #2**. These lines leave every 10 minutes or so and go up and down the Grand Canal, between the "mouth" of the fish at one end and St. Mark's Square at the other. Line #1 is the slow boat, taking 45 minutes and making every stop along the way. Line #2 is the fast boat that zips down the Grand Canal in 25 minutes, stopping only stone grates at the square's lowest point. These grates cover cisterns that long held Venice's only source of drinking water. That's right: Surrounded by the lagoon and beset by constant flooding, this city had no natural source of fresh water. For centuries, residents carried water from the mainland with much effort and risk. In the ninth century, they devised a way to collect rainwater by using paved, cleverly sloped squares as catchment systems, with limestone filters covering underground clay tubs. Venice's population grew markedly once citizens were able to access fresh water by simply dropping buckets down into these "wells." Hundreds of cisterns provided the city with drinking water up until 1884, when an aqueduct was built (paralleling the railroad bridge) to bring in water from nearby mountains. Now the wells are capped, the clay tubs are rotted out, and rain drains from squares into the lagoon—or up from it, as the case may be.

So, what is Venice doing about the flooding? After the 1966 flood, officials knew something had to be done, but it took about four decades to come up with a solution. In 2003, a consortium of engineering firms began construction on the MOSE Project. Named for the acronym of its Italian name, Modulo Sperimentale Elettromeccanico, it's also a nod to Moses and his (albeit temporary) mastery over the sea.

Underwater "mobile" gates are being installed on the floor of the sea at the three inlets where the open sea enters Venice's lagoon. When the seawater rises above a certain level, air will be pumped into the gates, causing them to rise and shut out the Adriatic. The first gates are already installed and on the verge of becoming operational. But, in good Italian fashion, greedy government officials were unable to resist the opportunity for personal enrichment and a corruption scandal has stranded the entire project for the foreseeable future.

at Tronchetto (parking lot), Piazzale Roma (bus station), Ferrovia (train station), Rialto Bridge, San Tomà (Frari Church), San Samuele (opposite Ca' Rezzonico), Accademia Bridge, and San Marco (west end of St. Mark's Square, end of the line).

Take time to study the maps at docks before you board. Some boats run on circular routes, in one direction only (for example, lines #5.1 and #5.2, plus the non-Murano sections of lines #4.1 and

#4.2). Line #2 runs in both directions and is almost, but not quite, a full loop. The #2 boat leaving from the San Marco stop goes in one direction (up the Grand Canal), while from the San Zaccaria stop—just a five-minute walk away—it goes in the opposite direction (around the "tail" of the fish). Make sure you use the correct stop to avoid taking the long way around to your destination.

To clear up any confusion, ask a ticket-seller or conductor for help (sometimes they're stationed on the dock to help confused tourists). Get a copy of the most current ACTV map and timetable (in English and Italian, download from www.actv.it, theoretically free at ticket booths but often unavailable). System maps are posted at stops, but it's smart to print out your own copy of the map from the ACTV website before your trip.

Boarding and Riding

Once you know which line you want, you need to find the right departure platform (many stops have more than one). At these larger stops, check the electronic departure board to see which boats are coming next, when, where they're going, and from which platform they leave (for example, "Line 2 to San Marco, from platform B"). At smaller stops without electronic

displays, signs on each platform show the vaporetto lines that stop there and the direction they are headed. Once you find your platform, be aware that other boats may also be leaving from the same platform. When the boat arrives, confirm the direction posted on the bow ("Line 2, San Marco"). To double-check, ask the conductor when you board ("San Marco?").

Crowd-Beating Tips

For fun, take the Grand Canal Cruise (see that chapter). But be warned: Grand Canal vaporetti can be absolutely jam-packed, especially during the tourist rush hour (during mornings heading in from Piazzale Roma, and in evenings heading out to Piazzale Roma). Riding at night, with nearly empty boats and chandelier-lit palace interiors viewable from the Grand Canal, can be a highlight of your Venetian experience.

By *Traghetto*

Only four bridges cross the Grand Canal, but *traghetti* (shuttle gondolas) ferry locals and in-the-know tourists across the Grand Canal at three additional locations (see the map on page 54). Just step in, hand the gondolier €2, and enjoy the ride—standing or sitting. Some *traghetti* are seasonal, some stop running as early as 12:30, and all stop by 18:00. *Traghetti* are not covered by any transit pass.

By Water Taxi

Venetian taxis, like speedboat limos, hang out at busy points along the Grand Canal. Prices are regulated: €15 for pickup, then €2 per minute; €5 per person for more than four passengers (boats can carry around 10 people); and €10 between 22:00 and 6:00. If you have more bags than passengers, the extra ones cost €5 apiece. (For information on taking the water taxi to/from the airport, see the Venice Connections chapter.) Despite regulation, prices can be soft; negotiate and settle on the price or rate before stepping in. For travelers with lots of luggage or small groups who can split the cost, taxi-boat rides can be a worthwhile and time-saving convenience—and skipping across the lagoon in a classic wooden motorboat is a cool indulgence. For about €120 an hour, you can have a private, unguided taxi-boat tour. You may find more competitive rates if you prebook through the Consorzio Motoscafi water taxi association (tel. 041-522-2303, www.motoscafivenezia.it).

By Gondola

If you're interested in hiring a gondolier for your own private cruise, see the Nightlife in Venice chapter.

Tours in Venice

Local guides and tour companies offer plenty of walking tours that cater to a variety of interests.

　∩ To sightsee on your own, download my series of **free audio tours** that illuminate some of Venice's top sights and neighborhoods (see the sidebar on page 8 for details).

Avventure Bellissime Venice Tours

This company offers several small-group, English-only tours, including a basic two-hour St. Mark's Square introduction called the "Original Venice Walking Tour" (€25, includes church entry, most days at 11:00, Sun at 14:00), a 65-minute boat tour of the Grand Canal (€48, daily at 16:00, 10 people maximum), a Rialto Market-area food-and-wine tour (€69, in summer 3/week at 11:15), and mainland excursions (RS%—10 percent discount, contact them before booking for a promo code; details at www.tours-italy.com, tel. 041-970-499, info@tours-italy.com).

ORIENTATION

Alessandro's Classic Venice Bars Backstreets Tours

Alessandro Schezzini is a connoisseur of Venetian *bacari*—classic old bars serving wine and traditional *cicchetti* snacks. He organizes two-hour Venetian bar tours (€35/person, most nights at 18:00) that include sampling *cicchetti* with wines at three *bacari*. (If you think of this tour as a light dinner with a local friend, it's a particularly good value.)

Alessandro is not a licensed guide, so he can't take you into sights. But his 1.5-hour Backstreets Tour gets you into offbeat Venice (€20/person, most nights at 16:30).

Both tours depart almost daily in season when six or more sign up. They meet 50 yards north of the Rialto Bridge under the big clock on Campo San Giacomo. (Book via email, alessandro@schezzini.it, or by phone at 335-530-9024; www.schezzini.it.)

Venice Bites Food Tours

Adam and Maya Stonecastle are expats from Los Angeles who enjoy sharing their adopted community and their love for *cicchetti* culture with travelers. Their two 3.5-hour food tours—usually led by both Adam and Maya—include lots of walking and fun insights. On their lunch tour, you'll munch and drink at 7 spots from the Accademia to the Rialto Bridge (€105/person, most days at 11:00, 10 people maximum). The dinner walk loops out and back from the Rialto Bridge, stopping at 5 or 6 places (€112/person, RS%—€15 off if you book online with discount code "RICKSTEVES"; tours run most nights at 18:00, 8 people maximum, tel. 800-656-0713, www.venicebitesfoodtours.com).

Venicescapes

Michael Broderick's private, themed tours of Venice are intellectually demanding and engrossing for history buffs. Michael, a passionate teacher, has spent nearly 30 years living and studying in Venice. He's an instinctive "dot connector," so his tours intertwine history, art, politics, economics, culture, and religion (various 4- to 6-hour itineraries, 2 people—$280-320 or the euro equivalent, $60/person after that, admissions and transport extra, tel. 041-850-5742, mobile 349-479-7406, www.venicescapes.org, info@venicescapes.org).

Local Guides

Plenty of licensed, trained guides are available (figure on €75/hour with a 2-hour minimum). I've enjoyed working with the following guides and groups:

Walks Inside Venice is enthusiastic

about teaching (€280/3 hours per group of up to 6, RS%; Roberta: mobile 347-253-0560; Sara: mobile 335-522-9714; www.walksinsidevenice.com, info@walksinsidevenice.com).

Elisabetta Morelli and Corine Govi, who run **2Guides-4Venice,** are informative and reliable (Elisabetta: mobile 328-753-5220, bettamorelli@inwind.it; Corine: mobile 347-966-8346, corine_g@libero.it; www.2guides4venice.com).

Venice with a Guide, a co-op of eight good Venetian guides, offers a range of tours (€75/hour, www.venicewithaguide.com).

BestVeniceGuides.it offers a smartly organized online catalog of about 100 local guides, with information to help you pick the right guide for you. Note that Italy allows all licensed guides to lead tours anywhere in the country, so it behooves the thoughtful traveler to book a Venetian guide for the best Venetian experience (family-friendly guides, shared group tours available, most guides about €75/hour, www.bestveniceguides.it). Guides also contribute to the site's blog about Italian art and culture.

Tour Leader Venice, a.k.a. **Treviso Car Service,** specializes in getting you outside of Venice by car or minivan—to countryside villas, prosecco wine-and-cheese tastings, and the Dolomites—but also offers guided walks in Venice (mobile 348-900-0700 or 333-411-2840; www.trevisocarservice.com, tvcarservice@gmail.com; for Venice tours also see www.tourleadervenice.com, info@tourleadervenice.com; Igor, Andrea, and Marta). They also provide transfer services to Venice's airport and cruise terminal (see page 310).

SIGHTS IN VENICE

Venice's greatest sight is the city itself. As well as seeing world-class museums and buildings, make time to wander narrow lanes, linger over a meal, or enjoy evening magic on St. Mark's Square. One of Venice's most delightful experiences—a gondola ride, worth ▲▲▲—is covered in the Nightlife in Venice chapter.

When you see a 📖 in a listing, it means the sight is described in greater detail in one of my self-guided walks or tours. A 🎧 means the walk or tour is also available as a free audio tour (via my Rick Steves Audio Europe app—see page 8). Some walks and tours are available in both formats—take your pick. This is why some of Venice's most important sights get the least coverage in this chapter—we'll explore them in greater depth elsewhere in this book.

SIGHTSEEING STRATEGIES
Avoiding Lines and Crowds
The city is inundated with cruise-ship passengers and tours from mainland hotels daily from 10:00 to about 16:00. Major sights are busiest in the late morning, making this a smart time to explore the back lanes. Sights that have crowd problems get even more packed when it rains.

To avoid the worst of the crowds at **St. Mark's Basilica,** go early or late. To bypass the ticket line, reserve a time online—or if you have a large day bag, you can usually avoid the line by checking it (see the St. Mark's Basilica Tour chapter for details). For the **Doge's Palace,** purchase your ticket at the Correr Museum across St. Mark's Square (see next page). You can also visit later in the day, when crowds thin out. For the **Campanile,** ascend first thing in the morning or go late, or skip it entirely if you're going to the similar San Giorgio Maggiore bell tower.

State museums in Italy are free to enter once or twice a month.

The specific day varies in peak season (in low season, it's the first Sun). Free days are actually bad news—they attract crowds. In peak season, I'd check state museum websites in advance and make a point to avoid their free days. In Venice, these include the Accademia and Ca' d'Oro museums.

Sightseeing Passes

Venice offers a dizzying array of combo-tickets and sightseeing passes. For most people, the two best options are the combo-ticket for the Doge's Palace and Correr Museum or the Museum Pass (which covers those two plus more). Note that many of the most visit-worthy sights in town (the Accademia, Peggy Guggenheim Collection, Scuola San Rocco, Campanile, and the three sights within St. Mark's Basilica that charge admission) are not covered by any pass.

All the passes described here are sold at the TI (except for the combo-ticket). Most are also available at participating sights.

Doge's Palace/Correr Museum Combo-Ticket: A €25 combo-ticket covers both of these sights. To bypass the long line at the Doge's Palace, buy your combo-ticket at the never-crowded Correr Museum (or online—€1 surcharge). The two sights are also covered by the Museum Pass and Venice Card.

Museum Pass: Busy sightseers may prefer this more expensive pass, which covers these city-run museums: the Doge's Palace; Correr Museum; Ca' Rezzonico (Museum of 18th-Century Venice); Palazzo Mocenigo Costume Museum; Casa Goldoni (home of the Italian playwright); Ca' Pesaro (modern art); Museum of Natural History in the Santa Croce district; the Glass Museum on the island of Murano; and the Lace Museum on the island of Burano. At €35, this pass is the best value if you plan to see the Doge's Palace, Correr Museum, and one or two of the other covered museums. You can buy it at any participating museum or via their websites (€1 surcharge).

Chorus Pass: This pass gives church lovers admission to 17 of Venice's churches and their art (generally €3 each) for €12 (www.chorusvenezia.org). The Frari Church is included, but not St. Mark's. The typical tourist is unlikely to see more than the four churches needed to recoup the cost of the pass.

Venice Card: This pass (also called a "Silver City Pass") includes the city-run museums and the churches covered by the Chorus Pass, plus the Jewish Museum and a few minor discounts, for €40. A cheaper variation, St. Mark's City Pass, is more selective: It covers the Correr Museum, Doge's Palace, and your choice of any three churches for €29. But it's hard to make either of these passes pay off on a short stay (valid for 7 days, www.veneziaunica.it).

Rolling Venice: If you're under 30, this youth pass offers

SIGHTS

Venice

To Mestre & Mainland

Canale de Cannaregio

GHETTO

CANNA

Campo de Gheto Novo

GUGLIE BRIDGE

SAN LEONARDO

SAN GEREMIA

SAN MARCUOLA

SANTA LUCIA STATION (FERROVIA)

SCALZI

LISTA DI SPAGNA

Grand Canal

SAN ZAN DEGOLA

BEMBO

To Tronchetto & Mainland

SCALZI BRIDGE

SAN SIMEONE GRANDE

SAN SIMEONE PICCOLO

SAN GIACOMO

Campo S.Giacomo de l'Orio

GROCERY

SANTA CROCE

CALATRAVA BRIDGE

SAN

PEOPLE MOVER

GARAGE

P

Piazzale Roma

To Stazione Marittima (Cruise Port) & Tronchetto (Parking)

BUS STATION

CA'AMAI

SAN NICOLO DA TOLENTINO

Campo San Stin

SAN ROCCO

FRARI

Campo dei Frari

SAN POLO

TINTORETTO

SCUOLA SAN ROCCO

Campo San Rocco

LARGA

SAONERI

NOMBOLI

T

RIO TERA DEI PENSIERI

FOND. DEL RIO NOVO

SAN PANTALON

SAN TOMA

C. LARGA FOSCARI

SANTA MARGARITA

CA' FOSCARI

PALAZZO GRASSI

CAR. S. SAM.

BALL

FONDAMENTA FOSCARINI

Campo Santa Margarita

R. TERA CANAL

CA' REZZONICO

SAN BARNABA

SANTA MARIA DEI CARMINI

Campo San Barnaba

Grand

SAN SEBASTIAN

AVOGARIA

C. LUNGA S. BARNABA

CORFU

ACCADEMIA BRIDGE

SALIZADA SAN BASEGIO

FOND. S. SEBASTIAN

Campo San Basegio

OGNISANTI

TOLETTA

ACCADEMIA GALLERY

SAN TROVASO

AGNESE

FONDAMENTA ZATTERE AL PONTE LONGO

RIO TERA FOSCARINI

DORSO

A

N

200 Meters
200 Yards

Giudecca Canal

discounts at dozens of sights and shops, but its best deal is for transit. It lets you buy a 72-hour transit pass for just €22—about half price (€6 pass for ages 14-29; sold at TIs, vaporetto ticket offices, and VeneziaUnica shops).

SAN MARCO DISTRICT
▲▲▲St. Mark's Square (Piazza San Marco)

This grand square is surrounded by splashy, historic buildings and sights: St. Mark's Basilica, the Doge's Palace, the Campanile bell

tower, the Clock Tower, and the Correr Museum. The square is filled with music, lovers, pigeons, and tourists by day, and is your private rendezvous with the Venetian past late at night, when Europe's most magnificent dance floor is *the* romantic place to be.

For a slow and pricey evening thrill, invest €15 or so (including service and cover charge for the music) for a drink at one of the elegant cafés with the dueling orchestras (see "Cafés on St. Mark's Square" on page 72). For an unmatched experience that offers the best people-watching, it's worth the splurge.

For more on the square, the Clock Tower, the Campanile, and other sights on the square, see the 📖 St. Mark's Square Tour chapter or download my free 🎧 audio tour.

▲▲▲St. Mark's Basilica (Basilica di San Marco)

Built in the 11th century to replace an earlier church, this basilica's distinctly Eastern-style architecture underlines Venice's connec-

tion with Byzantium (which protected it from the ambition of Charlemagne and his Holy Roman Empire). It's decorated with booty from returning sea captains—a kind of architectural Venetian trophy chest. The interior glows mysteriously with gold mosaics and colored marble. Since about AD 830, the saint's bones have been housed

on this site. The San Marco Museum within holds the original bronze horses (copies of these overlook the square), and a balcony offering a remarkable view over St. Mark's Square.

Cost and Hours: Basilica entry is free, though you can pay €3 for an online reservation that lets you skip the line. Three separate exhibits within the church charge admission: the Treasury—€3, Golden Altarpiece—€2, and San Marco Museum—€5. Church and all exhibits open Mon-Sat 9:30-17:00, Sun 14:00-17:00 (Sun until 16:30 Nov-Easter), interior brilliantly lit Mon-Sat 11:30-12:45. Tel. 041-270-8311, www.basilicasanmarco.it.

See the ☐ St. Mark's Basilica Tour chapter or download my free ◯ audio tour.

▲▲▲Doge's Palace (Palazzo Ducale)

The seat of the Venetian government and home of its ruling duke, or doge, this was the most powerful half-acre in Europe for 400 years. The Doge's Palace was built to show off the power and wealth of the Republic. The doge lived with his family on the first floor up, near the halls of power. From his once-lav- ish (now sparse) quarters, you'll follow the one-way tour through the public rooms of the top floor, fin- ishing with the Bridge of Sighs and the prison. The place is wallpa- pered with masterpieces by Veronese and Tintoretto.

SIGHTS

Cost and Hours: €25 combo-ticket includes Correr Museum, also covered by Museum Pass; Sun-Thu 8:30-21:00, Fri-Sat until 23:00, Nov-March daily until 19:00; café, next to St. Mark's Ba- silica, just off St. Mark's Square, vaporetto stops: San Marco or San Zaccaria, tel. 041-271-5911, http://palazzoducale.visitmuve.it.

Avoiding Lines: If the line is long at the Doge's Palace, buy your combo-ticket at the Correr Museum across the square; then you can go directly through the Doge's turnstile without waiting in line. Or, you can buy your ticket online. Crowds tend to diminish after 16:00.

☐ See the Doge's Palace Tour chapter.

▲▲Correr Museum (Museo Correr)

This uncrowded museum gives you a good overview of Venetian history and art. The doge memorabilia, armor, banners, statues (by Canova), and paintings (by the Bellini family and others) re-create the festive days of the Venetian Republic. And it's all accompa- nied—throughout the museum—by English descriptions and views of St. Mark's Square.

Cost and Hours: €25 combo-ticket includes Doge's Palace, also covered by Museum Pass; daily 10:00-19:00, Nov-March

Venice at a Glance

▲▲▲**St. Mark's Square** Venice's grand main square. See page 32.

▲▲▲**St. Mark's Basilica** Cathedral with mosaics, saint's bones, treasury, museum, and viewpoint of square. **Hours:** Mon-Sat 9:30-17:00, Sun 14:00-17:00 (Sun until 16:30 Nov-Easter). See page 32.

▲▲▲**Doge's Palace** Art-splashed palace of former rulers, with prison accessible through Bridge of Sighs. **Hours:** Sun-Thu 8:30-21:00, Fri-Sat until 23:00, Nov-March daily until 19:00. See page 33.

▲▲▲**Rialto Bridge** Distinctive bridge spanning the Grand Canal, with a market nearby. **Hours:** Market—souvenir stalls open daily, produce market closed Sun, fish market closed Sun-Mon. See page 43.

▲▲**Correr Museum** Venetian history and art. **Hours:** Daily 10:00-19:00, Nov-March 10:30-17:00. See page 33.

▲▲**Accademia** Venice's top art museum. **Hours:** Tue-Sun 8:15-19:15, Mon until 14:00. See page 39.

▲▲**Peggy Guggenheim Collection** Popular display of 20th-century art. **Hours:** Wed-Mon 10:00-18:00, closed Tue. See page 40.

▲▲**Frari Church** Franciscan church featuring Renaissance masters. **Hours:** Mon-Sat 9:00-18:00, Sun from 13:00. See page 44.

▲▲**Scuola San Rocco** "Tintoretto's Sistine Chapel." **Hours:** Daily 9:30-17:30. See page 44.

▲▲**Ca' Rezzonico** Posh Grand Canal palazzo with 18th-century Venetian art. **Hours:** Wed-Mon 10:00-18:00, Nov-March until 17:00, closed Tue year-round. See page 41.

▲**Campanile** Dramatic bell tower on St. Mark's Square with elevator to the top. **Hours:** Daily 8:30-21:00, Sept-mid-Oct until sunset, mid-Oct-April 9:30-17:30. See page 36.

▲**Bridge of Sighs** Famous enclosed bridge, part of Doge's Palace, near St. Mark's Square. **Hours:** Always viewable. See page 37.

SIGHTS

▲**La Salute Church** Striking church dedicated to the Virgin Mary. **Hours:** Daily 9:30-12:00 & 15:00-17:30. See page 40.

▲**Punta della Dogana** Museum of contemporary art. **Hours:** Wed-Mon 10:00-19:00, closed Tue. See page 40.

▲**Ca' Pesaro International Gallery of Modern Art** Fine museum in a canalside palazzo. **Hours:** Tue-Sun 10:00-18:00, Nov-March until 17:00, closed Mon year-round. See page 41.

▲**Fondaco dei Tedeschi View Terrace** Rooftop terrace atop luxury mall, with views over the Grand Canal. **Hours:** Daily 10:15-19:30, June-Aug until 20:15, Nov-March until 19:15. See page 43.

▲**Scuola Dalmata di San Giorgio** Exquisite Renaissance meeting house. **Hours:** Mon 13:30-17:30, Tue-Sat 9:30-17:30, Sun 9:30-13:30. See page 47.

▲**Via Garibaldi** Walkable residential area with welcoming restaurants, parks, and shops. See page 49.

Church of San Zaccaria Final resting place of St. Zechariah, plus a Bellini altarpiece and an eerie crypt. **Hours:** Mon-Sat 10:00-12:00 & 16:00-18:00, Sun 16:00-18:00. See page 38.

Nearby Islands
▲▲**Burano** Sleepy island known for lacemaking and lace museum. **Hours:** Museum open Tue-Sun 10:30-17:00, Nov-March until 16:30, closed Mon year-round. See page 51.

▲**San Giorgio Maggiore** Island facing St. Mark's Square, featuring dreamy church and fine views back on Venice. **Hours:** Daily 9:00-19:00, Nov-March 8:30-18:00. See page 38.

▲**Murano** Island famous for glass factories and glassmaking museum. **Hours:** Glass Museum open daily 10:30-18:30, Nov-March until 16:30. See page 51.

▲**Torcello** Near-deserted island with old church, bell tower, and museum. **Hours:** Church open daily 10:30-18:00, Nov-Feb 10:00-17:00, museum closed Mon. See page 51.

SIGHTS

10:30-17:00; elegant café, enter at far end of square directly opposite basilica, tel. 041-240-5211, http://correr.visitmuve.it.

📖 See the Correr Museum Tour chapter.

Clock Tower (Torre dell'Orologio)

Built during the Renaissance in 1496, the Clock Tower marks the entry to the main shopping drag, called the Mercerie (or "Marzarie," in Venetian dialect), which connects St. Mark's Square with the Rialto Bridge. From the piazza, you can see the bronze men (Moors) swing their huge clappers at the top of each hour. In the 17th century, one of them knocked an unsuspecting worker off the top and to his death—probably the first ever killing by a robot. Notice one of the world's first "digital" clocks on the tower facing the square (with dramatic flips every five minutes).

You can go inside the Clock Tower with a pre-booked guided tour that takes you close to the clock's innards and out to a terrace with good views over the square and city rooftops.

Cost and Hours: €12 combo-ticket includes Correr Museum—where the 45-minute tour starts—but not Doge's Palace; €7 for the tour if you already have a Museum Pass or Correr/Doge's Palace combo-ticket; tours in English Mon-Wed at 11:00 and 12:00, Thu-Sun at 14:00 and 15:00; no kids under age 6.

Reservations: While reservations are required for the Clock Tower tour, you have a decent chance of being able to "reserve" on the spot—try dropping by the Correr Museum for same-day (or day-before) tickets. To ensure a spot in advance, reserve by calling 848-082-000, or book online at http://torreorologio.visitmuve.it.

▲Campanile (Campanile di San Marco)

This dramatic bell tower replaced a shorter tower, part of the original fortress that guarded the entry of the Grand Canal. That tower crumbled into a pile of bricks in 1902, a thousand years after it was built. Ride the elevator 325 feet to the top of the bell tower for the best view in Venice (especially at sunset). For an ear-shattering experience, be on top when the bells ring. The golden archangel Gabriel at the top always faces into the wind. Beat the crowds and enjoy the crisp morning air at 9:00 or the cool evening breeze at 18:00. Go inside to buy tickets; the kiosk in front only rents audioguides and is operated by a private company.

Cost and Hours: €8; daily 8:30-21:00, Sept-mid-Oct until sunset, mid-Oct-April 9:30-17:30, last entry 45 minutes before closing; may close during thunderstorms, audioguide—€3, tel. 041-522-4064, www.basilicasanmarco.it.

La Fenice Opera House (Gran Teatro alla Fenice)

During Venice's glorious decline in the 18th century, this was one of seven opera houses in the city, and one of the most famous in Europe. For 200 years, great operas and famous divas debuted here, applauded by ladies and gentlemen in their finery. Then in 1996, an arson fire completely gutted the theater. But La Fenice ("The Phoenix") rose from the ashes, thanks to an eight-year effort to rebuild the historic landmark according to photographic archives of the interior. To see the results at their most glorious, attend an evening **performance** (theater box office open daily 10:00-17:00, tel. 041-2424, www.teatrolafenice.it).

During the day, you can take an **audioguide tour** of the opera house. All you really see is the theater itself; there's no "backstage" tour of dressing rooms, or an opera museum, and the dry 45-minute guide mainly recounts two centuries of construction. But the auditorium, ringed with box seats, is impressive: pastel blue with sparkling gold filigree, muses depicted on the ceiling, and a starburst chandelier. It's also a bit saccharine and brings sadness to Venetians who remember the place before the fire. Other than a minor exhibit of opera scores and Maria Callas memorabilia, there's little to see from the world of opera. To save money and get just a peek at the place, walk into the entrance hall and browse the small bookshop.

For more on the opera house, see page 217 of the St. Mark's to Rialto Loop Walk chapter.

Cost and Hours: €10 audioguide tours, generally open daily 9:30-18:00, but can vary wildly depending on the performance schedule—to confirm, call box office number (listed above) or check www.festfenice.com. La Fenice is on Campo San Fantin, between St. Mark's Square and the Accademia Bridge.

Palazzo Grassi

This former palace, gleaming proudly on the San Marco side of the Grand Canal, holds a branch of the Punta della Dogana contemporary art museum (for details, see Punta della Dogana listing, later; www.palazzograssi.it).

BEHIND ST. MARK'S BASILICA
▲Bridge of Sighs

This much-photographed bridge connects the Doge's Palace with the prison. Travelers popularized this bridge in the Romantic 19th century. Supposedly, a condemned man would be led over this bridge on his way to the prison, take one last look at the glory of Venice, and sigh. Though overhyped, the Bridge of Sighs is undeniably tingle-worthy—especially after dark, when the crowds have dispersed and it's just you and floodlit Venice. In the middle of the day, however, being immersed in the pandemonium of global tourism (and selfie sticks) can be a fascinating experience in itself.

Getting There: The Bridge of Sighs is around the corner from the Doge's Palace. Walk toward the waterfront, turn left along the water, and look up the first canal on your left. You can walk across the bridge (from the inside) by visiting the Doge's Palace.

For more on the Bridge of Sighs, see the 🕮 St. Mark's to San Zaccaria Walk chapter and the 🕮 Doge's Palace Tour chapter.

Church of San Zaccaria

This historic church is home to a sometimes-waterlogged crypt, a Bellini altarpiece, a Tintoretto painting, and the final resting place of St. Zechariah, the father of John the Baptist.

Cost and Hours: Free, €1.50 to enter crypt, €0.50 coin to light up Bellini's altarpiece; Mon-Sat 10:00-12:00 & 16:00-18:00, Sun 16:00-18:00 only; two canals behind St. Mark's Basilica.

For details on visiting the church, see the 🕮 St. Mark's to San Zaccaria Walk chapter.

ACROSS THE LAGOON FROM ST. MARK'S SQUARE

▲San Giorgio Maggiore

This is the dreamy church-topped island you can see from the waterfront by St. Mark's Square. The striking church, designed by Palladio, features art by Tintoretto, a bell tower, and good views of Venice.

Cost and Hours: Church—free, open daily 9:00-19:00, Nov-March 8:30-18:00; bell tower elevator—€6, runs until 20 minutes before the church closes, does not run during Sun services; tel. 041-522-7827.

Getting There: To reach the island from St. Mark's Square,

> # Venice Early and Late
>
> Most sightseeing in Venice is restricted to the hours between 10:00 and 18:00. Here are some exceptions:
>
> ## Sights Open Early
> **Accademia:** Daily at 8:15
> **Doge's Palace:** Daily at 8:30
> **Campanile:** Daily at 8:30, mid-Oct-April at 9:30
> **Frari Church:** Mon-Sat at 9:00
> **La Salute Church:** Daily at 9:30
> **San Giorgio Maggiore:** Daily at 9:00, Nov-March at 8:30
> **Scuola Dalmata di San Giorgio:** Tue-Sun at 9:30
> **Scuola San Rocco:** Daily at 9:30
> **St. Mark's Basilica:** Mon-Sat at 9:30
>
> ## Sights Open Late
> **Doge's Palace:** Sun-Thu until 21:00, Fri-Sat until 23:00, Nov-March daily until 19:00
> **Correr Museum:** April-Oct daily until 19:00
> **Punta della Dogana:** Wed-Mon until 19:00
> **Campanile:** May-Sept daily until 21:00
> **Accademia:** Tue-Sun until 19:15
> **Ca' d'Oro:** Tue-Sun until 19:15
>
> ## Always Open
> St. Mark's Square and the Rialto Bridge are always open, uncrowded in the early morning, and magical at night.

SIGHTS

take the one-stop, five-minute ride on vaporetto #2 from San Zaccaria (€5 special vaporetto ticket, runs every 12 minutes from dock B, direction: Piazza Roma).

📖 See the San Giorgio Maggiore Tour chapter.

DORSODURO DISTRICT
▲▲Accademia (Galleria dell'Accademia)
Venice's top art museum, packed with highlights of the Venetian Renaissance, features paintings by the Bellini family, Titian, Tintoretto, Veronese, Tiepolo, Giorgione, Canaletto, and Testosterone. It's just over the wooden Accademia Bridge from the San Marco action.

Cost and Hours: €15; Tue-Sun 8:15-19:15, Mon until 14:00, last entry one hour before closing; dull audioguide—€6, vaporetto: Accademia, tel. 041-522-2247, www.gallerieaccademia.it.

📖 See the Accademia Tour chapter.

▲▲Peggy Guggenheim Collection

The popular museum of far-out art, housed in the American heiress' former retirement palazzo, offers one of Europe's best reviews of the art of the first half of the 20th century. Stroll through styles represented by artists whom Peggy knew personally—Cubism (Picasso, Braque), Surrealism (Dalí, Ernst), Futurism (Boccioni), American Abstract Expressionism (Pollock), and a sprinkling of Klee, Calder, and Chagall.

Cost and Hours: €15; Wed-Mon 10:00-18:00, closed Tue; audioguide—€7, pricey café, vaporetto: Accademia or Salute, tel. 041-240-5411, www.guggenheim-venice.it.

☐ See the Peggy Guggenheim Collection Tour chapter.

▲La Salute Church (Santa Maria della Salute)

This impressive church with a crown-shaped dome was built and dedicated to the Virgin Mary by grateful survivors of the 1630 plague.

Cost and Hours: Church—free; Sacristy—€4; both open daily 9:30-12:00 & 15:00-17:30; 10-minute walk from the Accademia Bridge, at vaporetto: Salute, tel. 041-274-3928, www.seminariovenezia.it.

☐ See the La Salute Church Tour chapter.

▲Punta della Dogana

This museum of contemporary art, opened in 2009, makes the Dorsoduro a major destination for art lovers. Housed in the former Customs House at the end of the Grand Canal, it features cutting-edge 21st-century art in spacious rooms. This isn't Picasso and Matisse, or even Pollock and Warhol—those guys are ancient history. But if you're into the likes of Jeff Koons, Cy Twombly, Rachel Whiteread, and a host of newer artists, the museum is world class. The dis-plays change completely about every year, drawn from the museum's large collection—so large it also fills Palazzo Grassi, farther up the Grand Canal.

Cost and Hours: €20 (varies depending on exhibit); Wed-Mon 10:00-19:00, closed Tue, last entry one hour before closing; small café, tel. 199-112-112 within Italy, 041-200-1057 from abroad, www.palazzograssi.it.

Getting There: Punta della Dogana is near La Salute Church (vaporetto: Salute). Palazzo Grassi is a bit upstream, on the east side of the Grand Canal (vaporetto #2: San Samuele).

▲▲Ca' Rezzonico (Museum of 18th-Century Venice)

This Grand Canal palazzo offers the most insightful look at the life of Venice's rich and famous in the 1700s. Wander under ceilings by Tiepolo, among furnishings from that most decadent century, enjoying views of the canal and paintings by Guardi, Canaletto, and Longhi.

Cost and Hours: €10; Wed-Mon 10:00-18:00, Nov-March until 17:00, closed Tue year-round; ticket office closes one hour before museum, audioguide—€5 or €6/2 people, café, at vaporetto: Ca' Rezzonico, tel. 041-241-0100, http://carezzonico.visitmuve.it.

📖 See the Ca' Rezzonico Tour chapter.

SANTA CROCE DISTRICT

▲Ca' Pesaro International Gallery of Modern Art

This museum features 19th- and early-20th-century art in a 17th-century canalside palazzo. The collection is strongest on Italian (especially Venetian) artists, but also presents a broad array of other well-known artists. While the Peggy Guggenheim Collection is undisputedly Venice's best modern collection, Ca' Pesaro comes in a clear second—and features a handful of recognizable masterpieces (most notably Klimt's *Judith II*, Kandinsky's *White Zig Zags*, and Chagall's *Rabbi #2*).

Cost and Hours: €10; Tue-Sun 10:00-18:00, Nov-March until 17:00, closed Mon year-round, last entry one hour before closing; 2-minute walk from vaporetto: San Stae, tel. 041-721-127, http://capesaro.visitmuve.it.

Visiting the Museum: After buying your tickets, head upstairs and make your way through the rooms. You'll start with 19th-century sculpture (Rodin and Medardo Rossi, Room 1), then Romanticism (Room 2), and then in Rooms 3-4, Impressionism and turn-of-the-century art, including Klimt's beautiful/creepy *Judith II,* with her eagle-talon fingers. Room 5 has more sculpture (including by the Milanese sculptor Adolfo Wildt), as well as Chagall's surprisingly realistic portrait of his hometown rabbi, *Rabbi #2* (a.k.a. *The Rabbi of Vitebsk*). Room 6 shows off Venetian Impressionism. Rooms 7-9 are devoted to Modernist art from the 1920s and 1930s, including Bonnard's colorful *Nude in the Mirror,* which flattens the 3-D scene into a 2-D pattern of rectangles. Room 10 moves on to the 1930s and 1940s, while Room 11 has big international names including Klee, Kandinsky, Picasso, Calder, and Ernst. Abstract art is in Rooms 12-14, and finally, Dada and Pop Art in Room 15. Forgotten on the top floor is the skippable Museum of Oriental Art.

A Dying City?

Venice's population (fewer than 55,000 in the historic city) is half what it was just 30 years ago, and people are leaving at a rate of a thousand a year. Of those who stay, 25 percent are 65 or older.

Sad, yes, but imagine raising a family here: Apartments are small, high up, and expensive. Humidity and occasional flooding make basic maintenance a pain. Home-improvement projects require navigating miles of red tape, and you must follow regulations intended to preserve the historical ambience. Everything is expensive because it has to be shipped in from the mainland. You can easily get glass and tourist trinkets, but it's hard to find groceries or get your shoes fixed. Running basic errands involves lots of walking and stairs—imagine crossing over arched bridges while pushing a child in a stroller and carrying a day's worth of groceries.

With millions of visitors a year (150,000 a day at peak times), on any given day Venetians are likely outnumbered by tourists. Despite government efforts to subsidize rents and build cheap housing, the city is losing its residents. The economy itself is thriving, thanks to tourist dollars and rich foreigners buying second homes. But the culture is dying.

Greedy residents could sink Venice long before the sea swallows it up. Locals happily rent apartments to tourists a few times a month rather than affordably to local families, and shopkeepers sell trinkets to tourists before pots and pans to the local population. Even the most hopeful city planners worry that in a few decades Venice will not be a city at all, but a museum, a cultural theme park, a decaying Disneyland for adults.

Palazzo Mocenigo Costume Museum (Museo di Palazzo Mocenigo)

This museum offers a pleasant walk through a dozen rooms in a fine 17th-century mansion. Besides viewing period clothing and accessories, you can sniff an array of perfumes and spices and watch a video about the history of perfume in Venice (runs in a loop in three languages). The rooms provide a sense of aristocratic life during Venice's Golden Age, with furnishings, family portraits, ceilings painted (c. 1790) with family triumphs (the Mocenigos produced seven doges), and Murano glass chandeliers in situ. English-language cards in each room give sparse descriptions.

Cost and Hours: €8; Tue-Sun 10:00-17:00, Nov-March until 16:00, closed Mon year-round; a block in from vaporetto: San Stae, tel. 041-721-798, http://mocenigo.visitmuve.it.

SAN POLO DISTRICT
▲▲▲Rialto Bridge

One of the world's most famous bridges, this distinctive and dramatic stone structure crosses the Grand Canal with a single confident span. The arcades along the top of the
bridge help reinforce the
structure...and offer some
enjoyable shopping diver-
sions, as does the **market**
surrounding the bridge
(produce market closed
Sun, fish market closed
Sun-Mon).

For more on the Rialto Bridge, see the 📖 St. Mark's to Rialto Loop Walk chapter. For more on the markets, see the 📖 Rialto to Frari Church Walk chapter.

▲Fondaco dei Tedeschi (German Exchange) View Terrace

In the Middle Ages, Venice was the world's trading center, host-ing scores of nationalities, each with its own caravanserai-like center. The most famous is the home of the Tedeschi (German) traders, just off the Rialto Bridge. Later on, the Fondaco dei Tede-schi served as the main post office of Venice before recently being purchased by the Benetton family and turned into a luxury mall designed strategically to cater to the shopping tastes of interna-tional tourists (big name, high-price brands with no association with Venice other than being sold here). The ground floor features gourmet food shops and ritzy cafés.

The mall's top floor terrace offers a unique perspective over the roofs of Venice and an unforgettable view of the big bend in the Grand Canal. Four times an hour, 80 people are allowed onto the roof for 15 minutes. As you ride the red-carpet elevator to the top floor, notice how the old architectural bones of the structure survive.

Cost and Hours: The terrace is free but access requires a reser-vation (15-minute timeslots, book online at www.dfs.com/en/info/t-fondaco-rooftop-terrace; you can attempt to show up and reserve, but no guarantees). Terrace open daily 10:15-19:30, June-Aug until 20:15; east side of Rialto Bridge, tel. 041-314-2000.

▲▲Frari Church (Basilica di Santa Maria Gloriosa dei Frari)

My favorite art experience in Venice is seeing art in the setting for which it was designed—as it is at the Frari Church. The Franciscan "Church of the Brothers" and the art that decorates it are warmed by the spirit of St. Francis. It features the work of three great Renaissance masters: Donatello, Giovanni Bellini, and Titian—each showing worshippers the glory of God in human terms.

Cost and Hours: €3; Mon-Sat 9:00-18:00, Sun from 13:00; audioguide—€2, modest dress recommended, on Campo dei Frari, near San Tomà vaporetto and *traghetto* stops, tel. 041-272-8611, www.basilicadeifrari.it.

See the 📖 Frari Church Tour chapter or download my free 🎧 audio tour.

▲▲Scuola San Rocco

Sometimes called "Tintoretto's Sistine Chapel," this lavish meeting hall (next to the Frari Church) has some 50 large, colorful Tintoretto paintings plastered to the walls and ceilings. The best paintings are upstairs, especially the *Crucifixion* in the smaller room. View the neck-breaking splendor with the mirrors available in the Grand Hall.

Cost and Hours: €10, daily 9:30-17:30, tel. 041-523-4864, www.scuolagrandesanrocco.org.

📖 See the Scuola San Rocco Tour chapter.

CANNAREGIO DISTRICT

Jewish Ghetto

Tucked away in the Cannaregio district is the ghetto where Venice's Jewish population once lived, segregated from their non-Jewish neighbors. While today's Jewish population is dwindling, the neighborhood still has centuries of history, Jewish-themed sights, and eateries.

Getting There: From the train station, walk five minutes to the Ponte de Guglie bridge over the Cannaregio Canal. Cross the bridge and turn left. About 50 yards north of the bridge, a small covered alleyway (Sotoportego del Gheto Vechio) leads between the *farmacia* and the

SIGHTS

Gam-Gam Kosher Restaurant, through a newer Jewish section, across a second bridge, and into the historic core of the ghetto at Campo de Gheto Novo.

Before you reach the second bridge and Campo de Gheto Novo, consider stopping at the **information point** run by the Jewish community, at #1222, where Anat Shriki answers questions about ghetto history in fluent English (open Sun-Fri 10:00-17:30 in Oct-May, closed Sat, on Calle del Gheto Vechio, tel. 041-523-7565, www.jvenice.org).

Visiting the Jewish Ghetto: Campo de Gheto Novo must have been quite a scene in the 17th century, ringed by 70 shops and with all of Venice's Jewish commerce compressed into this one spot. Today there are only about 500 Jews in all of Venice—and only a few dozen live in the actual ghetto. The square is still surrounded by the six-story "skyscrapers" that once made this a densely packed neighborhood.

Today the square, with its three cistern wells, is quiet. The Jewish people you may see here are likely tourists. Look for the large Jewish senior center/community center (Casa Israelitica di Riposo), flanked by two different Holocaust memorials by the Lithuanian artist Arbit Blatas. The barbed wire and bronze plaques remind us that it was on this spot that the Nazis rounded up 200 Jews for deportation (only 8 returned).

The **Jewish Museum** (Museo Ebraico), at #2902b, is small, but modern and well-presented—a worthwhile stop. Exhibits in-

Jews in Venice's Ghetto

In medieval times, Jews were grudgingly allowed to do business in Venice, but they weren't permitted to live here until 1385 (subject to strict laws and special taxes). Anti-Semitic forces tried to oust them from the city, but in 1516, the government compromised by restricting Jews to a special (undesirable) neighborhood. It was located on an easy-to-isolate island near the former foundry (geto). In time, the word "ghetto" caught on across Europe as a term for any segregated neighborhood.

The population swelled with immigrants from elsewhere in Europe, reaching 5,000 in the 1600s, the Golden Age of Venice's Jews. Restricted within their tiny neighborhood (the Gheto Novo—"New Ghetto"), they expanded upward, building six-story "skyscrapers" that still stand today. The community's five synagogues were built atop the high-rise tenements. (As space was very tight and you couldn't live above a house of worship, this was the most practical use of precious land.) Only two synagogues are still active. You can spot them (with their five windows) from the square, but to visit them you have to book a tour through the Jewish Museum.

Relations with the non-Jewish community were complex: While Jewish moneylenders were treated harshly, Jewish merchants were more valued and treated with more respect. The island's two bridges were locked at night, when only Jewish doctors—coming to the aid of Venetians—were allowed to come and go. Eventually the ghetto community was given more land and spread to adjacent blocks.

In 1797, Napoleon opened the ghetto gates and ended its isolation. Complete emancipation for Venice's Jews came with the founding of the Italian republic in the 1860s.

clude silver menorahs, cloth covers for Torah scrolls, and a concise bilingual exhibit on the Venetian Jewish community (€8, Sun-Fri 10:30-16:30, Oct-May closes at 17:00, closed Jewish holidays and Sat year-round, modest dress required, bookstore, small café, Campo de Gheto Novo, tel. 041-715-359, www.museoebraico.it). You can see three of the ghetto's five **synagogues** with the 40-minute English tour (€12, includes museum admission, frequent tours Sun-Fri, no tours Sat and Jewish holidays). Group sizes are limited (the 11:30 and 12:30 tours are the most popular), so show up 30 minutes early to be sure you get in—or reserve online or by phone (generally necessary only for groups of 15 or more).

After visiting, exit through Sotoportego del Gheto Novo for the best view of the "fortress ghetto," with tall tenement buildings rising from the canal and an easy-to-lock-up little bridge and gateway.

Calatrava Bridge (a.k.a. Ponte della Costituzione)

This controversial bridge, designed by Spanish architect Santiago Calatrava, is just upstream from the train station. Only the fourth bridge to cross the Grand Canal, it carries foot traffic between the train station and bus terminal at Piazzale Roma.

The bridge draws snorts from Venetians. Its modern design is a sore point for a city with such rich medieval and Renaissance architecture. With an original price tag of €4 million, the cost rose to around €11 million by the time it finally opened, after lengthy delays, in 2008. Then someone noticed that people in wheelchairs couldn't cross, so the bridge was retrofitted with a special, orb-shaped carriage on a track. Today, this "egg cabin" is famously stuck, and those in wheelchairs still struggle. A bridge designed to look sleek and elegant, isn't. And, to add practical insult to aesthetic injury, critics say the heavy bridge is crushing the centuries-old foundations at either end, threatening nearby buildings.

Ca' d'Oro

This "House of Gold" palace, fronting the Grand Canal, is quintessential Venetian Gothic (Gothic seasoned with Byzantine and Islamic accents—see "Ca' d'Oro" on page 59). Inside, the permanent collection includes a few big names in Renaissance painting (Ghirlandaio, Signorelli, and Mantegna), a glimpse at a lush courtyard, and a grand view of the Grand Canal.

Cost and Hours: €6; Tue-Sun 8:15-19:15, Mon until 14:00; dry audioguide—€4, vaporetto: Ca' d'Oro, tel. 041-520-0345, www.cadoro.org.

CASTELLO DISTRICT
▲Scuola Dalmata di San Giorgio

This little-visited *scuola* (which, in this case, means a gild or fraternity) features an exquisite wood-paneled chapel decorated with the world's best collection of paintings by Vittorio Carpaccio (1465-1526).

The Scuola, a reminder that cosmopolitan Venice was once Europe's trade hub, was one of scores of such community centers for various ethnic, religious, and economic groups, supported by the government partly to keep an eye on foreigners. It was here that the Dalmatians (from a region of Croatia) worshiped in their own way, held neighborhood meetings, and preserved their culture. Your entry fee contributes to one of five such fraternities in Venice still active in this century.

Cost and Hours: €6; Tue-Sat 9:30-17:30, Sun 9:30-13:30, Mon 13:30-17:30; on Calle dei Furlani at Castello 3259a, tel. 041-522-8828.

Getting There: The Scuola is located midway between St. Mark's Square and the Arsenale. Go north from Campo San Provolo (by the Church of San Zaccaria), following the street as it changes names from L'Osmarin to St. George to Greci. At the second bridge, turn left on Fondamenta dei Furlani.

Visiting the Scuola: The chapel on the ground floor is one of the best-preserved Renaissance interiors in Venice. Ringing the room is the cycle of paintings that Carpaccio was hired to paint (1502-1507). For more information, you can buy an English booklet for €6.

The scenes run clockwise around the room, telling the story of St. George (Dalmatia's patron saint), who slew a dragon and metaphorically conquered paganism. In the first panel on the far left, George meets the dragon (each day given a sacrificial victim) on the barren plain. The ground is littered with corpses...and the princess is next. George heroically charges forward, and jams his lance through the dragon's skull, to the relief of the damsel in distress (in red). This is one of Carpaccio's masterpieces.

The story continues in the next panel, as George leads the bedraggled dragon (lance still in its head) before the thankful, wealthy pagan king and queen. Next, they kneel before George (now with a red sash, far right) as he holds a pan of water, baptizing them.

The rest of the panels (about St. Jerome and St. Tryphone) are also by Carpaccio. In the last panel on the right, St. Augustine pauses while writing. He hears something. The dog hears it, too. It's the encouraging voice of St. Jerome, echoing mysteriously through the spacious room. Carpaccio sweated small details like the scattered books and the shadow cast by the statue of Christ.

In the adjoining room, see the cross and censers (incense burners) used by the community in religious processions. Upstairs is another paneled room with more depictions of St. George (but not by Carpaccio).

Naval Museum, Arsenale, and Ship Pavilion

The mighty Republic of Venice was home to Europe's first great military-industrial complex: a state-of-the-art shipyard that could build a powerful warship of standardized parts in an assembly line (and did so to intimidate visiting heads of state).

Cost and Hours: €10 ticket covers museum and Ship Pavilion; daily 10:00-18:00, Nov-March until 17:00, last entry one hour before closing; off Riva San Biasio, Castello 2148, tel. 041-244-1399, www.visitmuve.it/en/museums.

Getting There: From the Doge's Palace, hike six bridges east along the waterfront to the Naval Museum.

Visiting the Complex: See the museum first, then (holding on to your museum ticket) walk down the canal to the Ship Pavilion, next to the Arsenale gate.

The **Naval Museum** (Museo Storico Navale) is old-school and military-run, but anyone into maritime history or sailing will find its several floors of exhibits interesting. With limited energy, focus on floors 1 and 3. The first floor features ships and instruments of the republic, including a model of the doge's ornate state barge. The third floor has gondolas (with hard tops and canopies, including Peggy Guggenheim's private gondola) and Venetian boats of the 19th century.

The **Arsenale** (which took up one-eighth of the city) is still a military base and is therefore closed to the public, but its massive and evocative gate, the Porta Magna, is worth a look. (To see the gate, turn left as you face the Naval Museum and follow the canal.) The Porta Magna (c. 1450) was one of the first Renaissance structures in Venice. The lions flanking the big doors were looted from Greece. Imagine newly constructed warships parading regally and ominously from the Arsenale down the canal, ready to defend the Venetian Republic.

The **Ship Pavilion** (Padiglione delle Navi) shows bigger Venetian boats from the 19th century. It's near the Arsenale gate, just across the Arsenale Bridge.

▲Via Garibaldi: A Neighborhood of Venetians

A 10-minute walk down the Riva from the Doge's Palace, past the Arsenale, in "the tail" of Venice is a delightful residential zone around Via Garibaldi. This street—big and wide—was once a canal. Today, it's the spine of a vital neighborhood—lively with locals, inviting restaurants, and *cicchetti* bars. Stroll the entire length of Via Garibaldi: You'll find real shops rather than souvenir shops, side lanes flanked with laundry flying like flags, children at play, and reasonable prices.

Midway on the right, you'll pass the grand, gated entry to Giardino Garibaldi (leading past a classic old flower shop with a café/bar and on toward the Giardini Pubblici park and its vaporetto stop). Continue on Via Garibaldi for about 50 yards to find a rare surviving produce boat moored at the end of the street (busy in the morning). From the bridge at the end of Via Garibaldi, look left to see the huge walls protecting the massive Arsenale shipyard.

Of the many eateries on this street, consider these two: **$$$ Ristorante Nevodi** is a local favorite named for a couple of nephews and run by Uncle Silvio (indoor and promenade seating, daily 12:00 until late, Castello 1788, tel. 041-241-1136). At the end of the promenade, just past the park gates, **$$ Hostaria All'Ombra** serves typical Venetian cuisine (Tue-Sun 12:00-22:00, closed Mon, Castello 1252, tel. 041-523-1179).

Sant'Elena

Farther from the action and even less touristy is the neighborhood of Sant'Elena, at the far end of the fish's tail. For a pleasant peek at this residential side of Venice, walk or catch vaporetto #1 from St. Mark's Square to the S. Elena stop. This 100-year-old suburb lives as if there were no tourism. You'll find a kid-friendly park, a few lazy restaurants, and beautiful sunsets over San Marco.

La Biennale

From roughly June through November, Venice hosts an annual world's fair—contemporary art in odd years, modern architecture in even years—in buildings and pavilions scattered throughout Giardini Pubblici park and the Arsenale. The festival is an excuse for temporary art exhibitions, concerts, and other cultural events around the city (for more information, see page 468; www.labiennale.org).

VENICE'S LAGOON

With more time, venture to some nearby islands in Venice's lagoon. While still touristy, they offer an escape from the crowds, a chance to get out on a boat, and some enjoyable diversions for fans of glass-making, lace, and sunbathing.

The first four islands are listed in order of proximity to Venice, from nearest to farthest. For more information, see the 📖 Venice's Lagoon Tour chapter. The fifth island has the beach.

San Michele (a.k.a. Cimitero)

This island is the final resting place of Venetians and a few foreign VIPs, from poet Ezra Pound to composer Igor Stravinsky (cemetery open daily 7:30-18:00, Oct-March until 16:30).

SIGHTS

▲Murano

Famous for its glassmak-
ing, this island is home
to several glass factories
and the **Glass Museum**
(Museo del Vetro), which
traces the history of this
delicate art (€14, daily
10:30-18:30, Nov-March
until 16:30, tel. 041-739-
586, http://museovetro.visitmuve.it).

▲▲Burano

This island's claim to fame is lacemaking, and (along with countless lace shops) it offers a delightful pastel village alternative to
big, bustling Venice. Its **Lace Museum** (Museo del Merletto di
Burano) shows the island's lace heritage (€5, Tue-Sun 10:30-17:00,
Nov-March until 16:30, closed Mon year-round, tel. 041-730-034,
http://museomerletto.visitmuve.it).

▲Torcello

This sparsely populated island features Venice's oldest church—
Santa Maria Assunta—with impressive mosaics, a climbable
bell tower, and a modest museum of Roman sculpture and medieval sculpture and manuscripts (€12 combo-ticket covers museum, church, and bell tower; museum only—€3; church and bell
tower—€5 each; church open daily 10:30-18:00, Nov-Feb 10:00-
17:00, museum and bell tower close 30 minutes earlier, museum
closed Mon year-round; museum tel. 041-730-761).

Lido Beach

Venice's nearest beach is the Lido, across the lagoon on an island
connected to the mainland (which means car traffic). The sandy
beach is pleasant, family-friendly, and good for swimming. You can
rent an umbrella, buy beach gear at the shop, get food at the self-
service café, or have a drink at the bar. Everything is affordable and
in the same building (vaporetto: Lido S.M.E., walk 10 minutes on
Gran Viale S. Maria Elisabetta to beach entry).

GRAND CANAL CRUISE

Canal Grande

Take a joyride and introduce yourself to Venice by boat. Cruise the Canal Grande all the way to St. Mark's Square, starting at the train station (Ferrovia) or the bus station (Piazzale Roma).

If it's your first trip down the Grand Canal, you might want to stow this book and just take it all in—Venice is a barrage on the senses that hardly needs narration. On the other hand, these notes give the cruise meaning and help orient you to this great city.

This tour is designed to be done on the slow boat #1. The express boat #2 travels the same route, but it skips many stops, making this tour hard to follow and hop-on, hop-off sightseeing impossible.

To help you enjoy the visual parade of canal wonders, the tour is keyed to each boat stop. I'll point out both what you can see from the current stop, and what to look forward to as you cruise to the next stop. Because it's hard to see everything in one go, you may want to do this tour twice (perhaps once in either direction).

If you download my 🎧 free audio tour, you can focus entirely on the view without having to look at the book.

Orientation

Length of This Tour: Allow 45 minutes.

Cost: €7.50 for a 75-minute vaporetto ticket, or covered by a pass—best choice if you want to hop on and off (see page 19).

When to Go: Boats run every 10 minutes or so. Enjoy the best light and the fewest crowds by riding late in the day. Avoid the morning rush hour (8:00-10:00), when local workers and tourists commute into town from Ferrovia to San Marco. In the evening, the crowds head the opposite way, and boats to San Marco are less crowded. Sunset bathes the buildings in gold (particularly on the left side, the San Marco side). After dark, boats are nearly empty as chandeliers light up building interiors. (Boat #1 goes 3/hour through the night, and is labeled "N.")

Seating Strategies: As the vaporetti can be jammed, strategize about where to sit—then, when the boat pulls up, make a beeline for your preference. You're more likely to find an empty seat if you catch the vaporetto at Piazzale Roma—the stop *before* Ferrovia.

A few remaining older vaporetti have seats in the bow (in front of the captain's bridge), the perfect vantage point for spotting sights left, right, and forward. With a standard boat and normal crowds, I'd head for the open-air section in the stern and grab the middle seat. While views directly ahead are obliterated by the boat's cabin, you'll have a good view of my described sights on both sides of the boat. If it's not crowded, you can hang out in the middle (loading zone) and bop from side to side (especially easy after dark). Your worst option is sitting inside and trying to look out the window.

Getting There: This tour starts at the Ferrovia vaporetto stop (at Santa Lucia train station). The #1 boat to San Marco generally leaves from dock E (far to the right).

Stops to Consider: You can break up the tour by hopping on and off at various sights—but remember, a single-fare vaporetto ticket is good for just 75 minutes (passes let you hop on and off all day). These stops are all worth considering: San Marcuola (Jewish Ghetto), Rialto Mercato (fish market and famous bridge), Ca' Rezzonico (Museum of 18th-Century Venice), Accademia (art museum and the nearby Peggy Guggenheim Collection), and Salute (huge and interesting church and nearby Punta della Dogana contemporary art museum).

Tours: ◯ Download my free Grand Canal Cruise audio tour.

Starring: Palaces, markets, boats, bridges—Venice.

BACKGROUND

The Grand Canal is Venice's "Main Street." At more than two miles long, nearly 150 feet wide, and nearly 15 feet deep, it's the city's largest canal, lined with its most impressive palaces. It's the remnant of a river that once spilled from the mainland into the Adriatic. The sediment it carried formed barrier islands that cut Venice off from the sea, forming a lagoon.

Venice was built on the marshy islands of the former delta, sitting on wood pilings driven nearly 15 feet into the clay (alder was the preferred wood). About 25 miles of canals drain the city, dumping like streams into the Grand Canal. Technically, Venice has only three canals: Grand, Giudecca, and Cannaregio. The 45

Grand Canal

Vaporetto Stops
1. Ferrovia
2. Riva de Biasio
3. San Marcuola
4. San Stae
5. Ca' d'Oro
6. Rialto Mercato
7. Rialto
8. San Silvestro
9. Sant'Angelo
10. San Tomà
11. Ca' Rezzonico
12. Accademia
13. Santa Maria del Giglio
14. Salute
15. San Marco
16. San Zaccaria

Traghetto Stops
- A. Traghetto Santa Sofia
- B. Traghetto San Tomà
- C. Traghetto Santa Maria del Giglio

GRAND CANAL

small waterways that dump into the Grand Canal are referred to as rivers (e.g., Rio Novo).

Venice is a city of palaces, dating from the days when the city was the world's richest. The most lavish palaces formed a grand architectural cancan along the Grand Canal. Once frescoed in reds and blues, with black-and-white borders and gold-leaf trim, they made Venice a city of dazzling color. This cruise is the only way to truly appreciate the palaces, approaching them at water level, where their main entrances were located. Today, strict laws prohibit any changes in these buildings, so while landowners gnash their teeth, we can enjoy Europe's best-preserved medieval/Renaissance city—slowly rotting. Many of the grand buildings are now vacant. Others harbor chandeliered elegance above mossy, empty (often flooded) ground floors.

The Tour Begins

❶ Ferrovia

This site has been the gateway into Venice since 1860, when the first train station was built. The **Santa Lucia station,** one of the few modern buildings in town, was built in 1954. The "F.S." logo above the entry stands for "Ferrovie dello Stato," the Italian state railway system. Consider that before the causeway was built in the mid-1800s, Venice was an island with no road or train access and no water system. With the causeway the city got a train line, an aqueduct, and a highway.

More than 20,000 people a day commute in from the mainland, making this the busiest part of Venice during rush hour. The nearby **Calatrava Bridge,** spanning the Grand Canal between the train station and Piazzale Roma upstream, was built in 2008 to alleviate some of the congestion.

Opposite the train station, atop the green dome of **San Simeon Piccolo** church, St. Simeon waves *ciao* to whoever enters or leaves the "old" city. The pink church with the white Carrara-marble facade, just beyond the station, is the **Church of the Scalzi** (Church of the Barefoot, named after the shoeless Carmelite monks), where the last doge (Venetian ruler) rests. It looks relatively new because it was partially rebuilt after being bombed in 1915 by Austrians aiming (poorly) at the train station. The stately Scalzi Bridge was rebuilt simply and elegantly under Mussolini.

❷ Riva de Biasio

Venice's main thoroughfare is busy with all kinds of **boats:** taxis, police boats, garbage boats, ambulances, construction cranes, and

even brown-and-white UPS boats. Somehow they all manage to share the canal in relative peace.

About 25 yards past the Riva de Biasio stop, look left down the broad Cannaregio Canal to see what was the Jewish Ghetto. The twin, pale-pink, six-story "skyscrap-ers"—the tallest buildings you'll see at this end of the canal—are reminders of how densely populated the world's original ghetto was. Set aside as the local Jewish quarter in 1516, this area became extremely crowded. This urban island developed into one of the most closely knit business and cultural quarters of all the Jewish communities in Italy, and gave us our word "ghetto" (from *geto,* the copper foundry located here).

❸ San Marcuola

At this stop, facing a tiny square just ahead, stands the unfinished Church of San Marcuola, one of only five churches fronting the

Grand Canal. Centuries ago, this canal was a com-mercial drag of expensive real estate in high demand by wealthy merchants. About 20 yards ahead on the right (across the Grand Canal) stands the stately gray **Turkish Exchange** (Fondaco dei Turchi), one of the oldest houses in

Venice. Its horseshoe arches and roofline of triangles and dingle balls are reminders of its Byzantine heritage. Turkish traders in turbans docked here, unloaded their goods into the warehouse on the bottom story, then went upstairs for a home-style meal and a place to sleep. Venice in the 1500s was very cosmopolitan, welcoming every religion and ethnicity, so long as they carried cash. (Today the building contains the city's Museum of Natural History—and Venice's only dinosaur skeleton.)

Just 100 yards ahead on the left (the tallest building with the red canopy), Venice's **Casinò** is housed in the palace where German composer Richard *(The Ring)* Wagner died in 1883. See his distinct, strong-jawed profile in the white plaque on the brick wall. In the 1700s, Venice was Europe's Vegas, with casinos and prostitutes everywhere. *Casinòs* ("little houses" in Venetian dialect) have long provided Italians with a handy escape from daily life. Today they're run by the state to keep Mafia influence at bay. Notice the fancy front porch, rolling out the red carpet for high rollers arriving by taxi or hotel boat. Across the canal, the plain brick 15th-century building was a granary. Now it's a grade school.

❹ San Stae

The San Stae Church sports a delightful Baroque facade. Opposite the San Stae stop is a little canal opening—on the second building to the right of that opening, look for the peeling plaster that once made up **frescoes** (you can barely distinguish the scant remains of little angels on the lower floors). Imagine the facades of the Grand Canal at their finest. Most of them would have been covered in frescoes by the best artists of the day. As colorful as the city is today, it's still only a faded, sepia-toned remnant of a long-gone era, a time of lavishly decorated, brilliantly colored palaces.

Just ahead (on the right, with blue posts) is the ornate white facade of **Ca' Pesaro** (which houses the International Gallery of

Modern Art). "*Ca'*" is short for *casa* (house). Because only the house of the doge (Venetian ruler) could be called a palace *(palazzo)*, all other Venetian palaces are technically "*Ca'*."

In this city of masks, notice how the rich marble facades along the Grand Canal mask what are generally just simple, no-nonsense brick buildings. Most merchants enjoyed showing off. However, being smart businessmen, they only decorated the sides of the buildings that would be seen and appreciated. But look back as you pass Ca' Pesaro. It's the only building you'll see with a fine side facade. Ahead (about 100 yards on the left) is Ca' d'Oro, with its glorious triple-decker medieval arcade (just before the next stop).

❺ Ca' d'Oro

The lacy Ca' d'Oro (House of Gold) is the best example of Venetian Gothic architecture on the canal. Although a simple brick construction, its facade is one of the city's finest. Its three stories offer different variations on balcony design, topped with a spiny white roofline. Venetian Gothic mixes traditional Gothic (pointed arches and round medallions stamped with a four-leaf clover) with Byzantine styles (tall, narrow arches atop thin columns), filled in with Islamic frills.

Like all the palaces, this was originally painted and gilded to make it even more glorious than it is now. Today the Ca' d'Oro is an art gallery.

Look at the Venetian chorus line of palaces in front of the boat. On the right is the arcade of the covered **fish market,** with the open-air **produce market** just beyond. It bustles in the morning but is quiet the rest of the day. This is a great scene to wander through—even though European Union hygiene standards have made it cleaner but less colorful than it once was.

Find the *traghetto* gondola ferrying shoppers—standing like Washington crossing the Delaware—back and forth. While once much more numerous, today only three *traghetto* crossings survive along the Grand Canal, each one marked by a classy low-key green-and-black sign. Piloting a *traghetto* isn't the normal day job of these gondoliers. As a public service, all gondoliers are obliged to row a *traghetto* a few days a month. Make a point to use them. At €2 a ride, *traghetti* offer the cheapest gon-

GRAND CANAL

dola ride in Venice (but at this price, don't expect them to sing to you).

❻ Rialto Mercato

This stop serves the busy market. The long, official-looking building at the stop is the Venice courthouse. Directly ahead (on the left),

is the Fondaco dei Tedeschi—the former German Exchange (a trading center for German merchants in the 16th century). Later the central post office, it's now a luxury shopping mall with great rooftop views. Rising above it is the tip of the Campanile (bell tower), crowned by its golden-angel weathervane at St. Mark's Square, where this tour will end.

You'll cruise by some trendy and beautifully situated wine bars on the right, but look ahead as you round the corner and see the impressive Rialto Bridge come into view.

A major landmark, the **Rialto Bridge** is lined with shops and tourists. Constructed in 1588, it's the third bridge built on

this spot. Until the 1850s, this was the only bridge crossing the Grand Canal. With a span of 160 feet and foundations stretching 650 feet on either side, the Rialto was an impressive engineering feat in its day. Earlier bridges here could open to let big ships in, but not this one. By the time it was completed in the 16th century, Venetian trading power was ebbing. After that, much of the Grand Canal was closed to shipping and became a canal of palaces.

When gondoliers pass under the fat arch of the Rialto Bridge, they take full advantage of its acoustics: *"Volare, oh, oh..."*

❼ Rialto

Rialto, a separate town in the early days of Venice, has always been the commercial district, while San Marco was the religious and governmental center. Today, a winding street called the Mercerie connects the two, providing travelers with human traffic jams and a mesmerizing gauntlet of shopping temptations. This is one of the only stretches of the historic Grand Canal with landings upon which you can walk. Boats unloaded the city's basic necessities here: oil, wine, charcoal, iron. Today, the quay is lined with tourist-trap restaurants.

Venice's sleek, black, graceful **gondolas** are a symbol of the city. With about 500 gondoliers joyriding amid the churning vaporetti, there's a lot of congestion on the Grand Canal. Pay attention—this is where most of the gondola and vaporetto accidents take place. While the Rialto is the highlight of many gondola rides, gondoliers understandably prefer the quieter small canals. Watch your vaporetto driver curse the better-paid gondoliers.

Ahead 100 yards on the left, two gray-colored **palaces** stand side by side (City Hall and the mayor's office). Their horseshoe-shaped, arched windows are similar and their stories are the same height, lining up to create the effect of one long balcony.

❽ San Silvestro

We now enter a long stretch of important **merchants' palaces,** each with proud and different facades. Because ships couldn't navigate beyond the Rialto Bridge, the biggest palaces—with the major shipping needs—line this last stretch of the navigable Grand Canal.

Palaces like these were multifunctional: ground floor for the warehouse, offices and showrooms upstairs, and living quarters above, on the "noble floors" (with big windows to allow in maximum light). Servants lived and worked on the very top floors (with the smallest windows). For fire-safety reasons, kitchens were also located on the top floors. Peek into the noble floors to catch a glimpse of their still-glorious chandeliers of Murano glass.

The **Palazzo Grimani** (across from the San Silvestro dock) sports a heavy white Roman-style facade—a reminder that the Grimani family included a cardinal and had strong Roman connections.

The **Palazzo Papadopoli,** with the two obelisks on its roof (50 yards beyond the San Silvestro stop on the right, with the blue posts), is the very fancy Aman Hotel where George and Amal Clooney were married in 2014.

❾ Sant'Angelo

Notice how many buildings have a foundation of waterproof white stone *(pietra d'Istria)* upon which the bricks sit high and dry. Many canal-level floors are abandoned as the rising water level takes its toll.

The **posts**—historically painted gaily with the equivalent of family coats of arms—don't rot underwater. But the wood at the waterline, where it's exposed to oxygen, does. On the smallest canals, little "no motor-boats" signs indicate that these canals are for gondolas only (no motorized craft, 5 kph speed limit, no wake).

⑩ San Tomà

Fifty yards ahead, on the right side (with twin obelisks on the rooftop) stands **Palazzo Balbi,** the palace of an early-17th-century captain general of the sea. These Venetian equivalents of five-star admirals were honored with twin obelisks decorating their palaces. This palace, like so many in the city, flies three flags: Italy (green-white-red), the European Union (blue with ring of stars), and Venice (a lion on a field of red and gold). Today it houses the administrative headquarters of the regional government.

Just past the admiral's palace, look immediately to the right, down a side canal. On the right side of that canal, before the bridge, see the traffic light and the **fire station** (the 1930s Mussolini-era building with four arches hiding fireboats parked and ready to go).

The impressive **Ca' Foscari,** with a classic Venetian facade (on the corner, across from the fire station), dominates the bend in the canal. This is the main building of the University of Venice, which has about 25,000 students. Notice the elegant lamp on the corner—needed in the old days to light this inter-section.

The grand, heavy, white **Ca' Rezzonico,** just before the stop of the same name, houses the Museum of 18th-Century Venice. Across the canal is the cleaner and leaner **Palazzo Grassi,** the last major palace built on the canal, erected in the late 1700s. It was purchased by a French tycoon and now displays part of Punta della Dogana's contemporary art collection.

⑪ Ca' Rezzonico

Up ahead, the Accademia Bridge leads over the Grand Canal to the **Accademia Gallery** (right side), filled with the best Venetian paintings. There was no bridge here until 1854, when a cast-iron one was built. It was replaced with this wooden bridge in 1933. While meant to be temporary, it still stands today, nearly a century later.

⑫ Accademia

From here, look through the graceful bridge and way ahead to enjoy a classic view of **La Salute Church,** topped by a crown-shaped

dome supported by scrolls. This Church of St. Mary of Good Health was built to ask God to deliver Venetians from the devastating plague of 1630 (which had killed about a third of the city's population).

The low, white building among greenery (100 yards ahead, on the right, between the Accademia Bridge and the church) is the **Peggy Guggenheim Collection.** The American heiress "retired" here, sprucing up a palace that had been abandoned in mid-construction. Peggy willed the city her fine collection of modern art.

As you approach the next stop, notice on the right how the fine line of higgledy-piggledy palaces evokes old-time Venice. Two

doors past the Guggenheim, Palazzo Dario has a great set of characteristic **funnel-shaped chimneys.** These forced embers through a loop-the-loop channel until they were dead—required in the days when stone palaces were surrounded by hum-

ble wooden buildings, and a live spark could make a merchant's workforce homeless. Notice this early Renaissance building's flat-feeling facade with "pasted-on" Renaissance motifs. Three doors later is the **Salviati building,** which once served as a glassworks. Its fine Art Nouveau mosaic, done in the early 20th century, features Venice as a queen being appreciated by the big shots of society.

⑬ Santa Maria del Giglio

Back on the left stands the fancy Gritti Palace hotel. Hemingway and Woody Allen both stayed here.

Take a deep whiff of Venice. What's all this nonsense about stinky canals? All I smell is my shirt. By the way, how's your captain? Smooth dockings?

⑭ Salute

The huge La Salute Church towers overhead as if squirted from a can of Catholic Reddi-wip. Like Venice itself, the church rests upon pilings. To build the foundation for the city, thousands of trees were piled together, reaching beneath the mud to the solid

clay. Much of the surrounding countryside was deforested by Venice. Trees were imported and consumed locally—to fuel the furnaces of Venice's booming glass industry, to build Europe's biggest merchant marine, to form light and flexible beams for nearly all the buildings in town, and to prop up this city in the mud.

As the Grand Canal opens up into the lagoon, the last building on the right with the golden ball is the 17th-century **Customs House,** which now houses the Punta della Dogana contemporary art museum. Its two bronze Atlases hold a statue of Fortune riding the ball. Arriving ships stopped here to pay their tolls.

⑮ San Marco

Up ahead on the left, the green pointed tip of the Campanile marks **St. Mark's Square,** the political and religious center of Venice...and the final destination of this tour. You could get off at the San Marco stop and go straight to St. Mark's Square.

But I'm staying on the boat for one more stop, just past St. Mark's Square (it's a quick walk back).

Survey the lagoon. Opposite St. Mark's Square, across the water, the ghostly white church with the pointy bell tower is San Giorgio Maggiore, with great views of Venice. Next to it is the residential island Giudecca, stretching from close to San Giorgio Maggiore past the Venice youth hostel (with a nice view, directly across) to the Hilton Hotel (good nighttime view, far right end of island).

Still on board? If you are, as we leave the San Marco stop look left and prepare for a drive-by view of St. Mark's Square. First comes the bold white facade of the old mint (in front of the bell tower) marked by a tiny cupola yet as sturdy as Fort Knox, where Venice's golden ducat, the "dollar" of the Venetian Republic, was made. Next door is the library, its facade just three windows wide. Then comes the city's ceremonial front door: twin columns topped by St. Theodore standing on a crocodile and the winged lion of St. Mark, who've welcomed visitors since the 15th century. Between the columns, catch a glimpse of two giant figures atop the **Clock Tower**—they've been whacking their clappers every hour since 1499. The domes of **St. Mark's Basilica** are soon eclipsed by the lacy facade of the **Doge's Palace.** Next you'll see many gondolas with their green breakwater buoys, the **Bridge of Sighs** (leading from the palace to the prison—check out the maximum-security bars), and finally the grand harborside promenade—the **Riva.**

Follow the Riva with your eye, past elegant hotels to the green area in the distance. This is the largest of Venice's few **parks,** which hosts the annual Biennale festival. Much farther in the distance is the **Lido,** the island with Venice's beach. Its sand and casinos are tempting, though given its car traffic, it lacks the medieval charm of Venice.

⑯ San Zaccaria

OK, you're at your last stop. Quick—muscle your way off this boat! (If you don't, you'll eventually end up at the Lido.)

At San Zaccaria, you're right in the thick of the action. A number of other vaporetti depart from here (see page 20). Otherwise, it's a short walk back along the Riva to St. Mark's Square. Ahoy!

ST. MARK'S SQUARE TOUR

Piazza San Marco

Venice was once Europe's richest city, and Piazza San Marco was its center. As middleman in the trade between Asia and Europe, wealthy Venice profited from both sides. In 1450, at its peak, Venice had 150,000 citizens (many more than London) and a gross "national" product that exceeded that of entire countries.

The rich Venetians taught the rest of Europe about the good life—silks, spices, and jewels from the East, crafts from northern Europe, good food and wine, fine architecture, music, theater, and laughter. Venice was a vibrant city full of painted palaces, glittering canals, and impressed visitors. Five centuries after its power began to decline, Venice still has all of these things, with the added charm of romantic decay. In this tour, we'll spend an hour in the heart of this Old World superpower.

Orientation

Getting There: Signs all over town point to *San Marco*—meaning both the square and the basilica—located where the Grand Canal spills out into the lagoon. Vaporetto stops: San Marco or San Zaccaria.

Campanile: €8 to ascend bell tower; daily 8:30-21:00, Sept-mid-Oct until sunset, mid-Oct-April 9:30-17:30.

Clock Tower: To see the interior, you need to book a spot on a tour (see page 36 for specifics).

Tours: ∩ Download my free St. Mark's Square **audio tour.**

Services: Pay WCs are behind the Correr Museum and also at the waterfront park, Giardinetti Reali (near San Marco-Vallaresso vaporetto dock).

Eating: Cafés with live music provide an engaging soundtrack for St. Mark's Square (see the "Cafés on St. Mark's Square" side-

St. Mark's Square

Eateries & Entertainment
1 Caffè Florian
2 Gran Caffè Quadri
3 Gran Caffè Lavena
4 Gran Caffè Chioggia
5 Eden Bar
6 Caffè Aurora

Other
7 Vetri d'Arte Glassblowing
8 Il Merletto Lace Shop
9 Libreria Studium Bookstore

bar, in this chapter). The Correr Museum (at the end of the square opposite the basilica) has a quiet upstairs coffee shop overlooking the crowded square. For a list of restaurants in the area, see page 268.

Nearby: For a free glassblowing demo, find the **Vetri d'Arte** showroom in Palazzo Rota (behind Gran Caffè Quadri on the square). For details, see page 291.

Starring: Byzantine domes, Gothic arches, Renaissance arches... and the wonderful, musical space they enclose.

The Tour Begins

• *For an overview of this grand square and the buildings that surround it, view it from the west end of the square (away from St. Mark's Basilica).*

The Piazza

Take in this spacious vista—ringed with historic buildings, lined with cafés and glitzy shops, and filled with tourists and pigeons.

St. Mark's Basilica dominates the square with its Eastern-style onion domes and glowing mosaics. Mark Twain said it looked like "a vast warty bug taking a meditative walk." (I say it looks like tiara-wearing ladybugs copulating.) To the right of the basilica is its 325-foot-tall Campanile. Behind the Campanile, you can catch a glimpse of the pale pink Doge's Palace. Lining the square are the former government offices *(procuratie)* that administered the Venetian empire's vast network of trading outposts, which stretched all the way to Turkey.

The square is big, but it feels intimate with its cafés and dueling orchestras. By day, it's great for people-watching and pigeon-chasing. By night, under lantern light, it transports you to another century, complete with its own romantic soundtrack. The piazza draws Indians in saris, English nobles in blue blazers, and Nebraskans in shorts. Napoleon called the piazza "the most beautiful living room in Europe." Napoleon himself added to the intimacy by building the final wing, opposite the basilica, that encloses the square.

For architecture buffs, here are three centuries of styles, bam, side by side, *uno-due-tre,* for easy comparison:

1. On the left (as you face the basilica) are the "old" offices, built about 1500 in solid, column-and-arch Renaissance style. Closed to the public for 500 years, the offices (called the Procuratie Vecchie) are being restored to host art exhibitions, installations, and seminars (may open in 2020).

2. The "new" offices (on the right), in a High Renaissance style from a century later (c. 1600), are a little heavier and more ornate. This wing mixes arches and the three orders of columns in layers from bottom to top—Doric, Ionic, and Corinthian.

3. Napoleon's wing, at the end opposite from the basilica, is later and designed to fit in. The dozen Roman emperors decorating the parapet were once joined by Napoleon in the middle, but today

the French emperor is gone. The Correr Museum is housed in this wing.

The arcade ringing the square provides an elegant promenade—complete with drapes to provide relief from the sun.

Imagine this square full of water. That happens every so often at very high tides *(acqua alta)*, a reminder that Venice and the sea are intertwined. (Now, as one sinks and the other rises, they are more intertwined than ever.)

Venice became Europe's richest city from its trade with northern Europeans, Ottoman Muslims, and Byzantine Christians. Here in St. Mark's Square, the exact center of this East-West axis, we see the luxury and cosmopolitan mix of East and West.

Watch out for pigeon speckle. Venetians don't like pigeons, but they do like seagulls—because they eat pigeons. In 2008, Venice outlawed the feeding of pigeons. But tourists—eager for a pigeon-clad photo op—haven't gotten that message.

• *Now approach the basilica. If it's hot and you're tired, grab a shady spot at the foot of the Campanile.*

St. Mark's Basilica

The facade is a wild mix of East and West, with round, Roman-style arches over the doorways, golden Byzantine mosaics, a roofline ringed with pointed Gothic pinnacles, and topped with Muslim-style onion domes (made of wood, covered with lead). The brick-structure building is blanketed in marble that came from Constantinople (in 1204), which had itself looted it from throughout the eastern Mediter-

ranean. There are columns from Alexandria, capitals from Sicily, and carvings from Anatolia. The columns flanking the doorways show the facade's variety—purple, green, gray, white, yellow, some speckled, some striped horizontally, some vertically, some fluted— all topped with a variety of different capitals.

What's amazing isn't so much the variety as the fact that the whole thing comes together in a bizarre sort of harmony. St. Mark's is simply the most interesting church in Europe, a church that (to paraphrase Goethe) "can only be compared with itself."

For more on the basilica, inside and out, see the 📖 St. Mark's Basilica Tour chapter.

• *Facing the basilica, turn 90 degrees to the left to see the...*

Clock Tower (Torre dell'Orologio)

Any proper Renaissance city wanted to have a prominent gate with a clock tower as its formal entrance. In Venice's case, its entry was visible from the sea. The Clock Tower retains some of its original blue and gold pigments, a reminder that, in centuries past, this city glowed with bright color.

Two bronze "Moors" stand atop the Clock Tower. Built originally in 1499 to be Caucasian giants, they only switched ethnicity when their metal darkened over the centuries. At the top of each hour they swing their giant clappers. The clock dial shows the 24 hours, the signs of the zodiac, and in the blue center, the phases of the moon—practical information, as a maritime city with a shallow lagoon needs to know the tides. Above the dial is the world's first digital clock (added in 1858), which changes every five minutes.

An alert winged lion, the symbol of St. Mark and the city, looks down on the crowded square. He opens a book that reads *"Pax Tibi Marce,"* or "Peace to you, Mark." As legend goes, these were the comforting words that an angel spoke to the stressed evangelist, assuring him he would find serenity during a stormy night that the saint spent here on the island. Eventually, St. Mark's body found its final resting place inside the basilica, and now his winged-lion symbol is everywhere. (Find four in 20 seconds. Go.)

Venice's many lions express the city's various mood swings through history—triumphant after a naval victory, sad when a favorite son has died, hollow-eyed after a plague, and smiling when the soccer team wins. Every Venetian child born since the dawn of cameras has probably been photographed riding one of the pair of lions squatting between the Clock Tower and the basilica.

Campanile

The original Campanile (bell tower) was an observation tower and a marvel of medieval and Renaissance architecture until 1902, when it toppled into the center of the piazza. It had groaned ominously the night before, sending people scurrying from the cafés. The next morning... crash! The golden angel on top landed right at the basilica's front door, standing up.

The Campanile was rebuilt 10 years later complete with its golden archangel Gabriel, who always faces the breeze. You can ride an elevator to the top for the best view of Venice. It's crowded at peak times, but well worth it.

Because St. Mark's Square is the first place in town to start flooding, there are tide gauges at the outside base of the Campanile (near the exit, facing the square) that show the current sea level *(livello marea)*. Find the stone plaque (near the exit door) that commemorates the high-water 77-inch level from the disastrous floods of 1966. In October 2018, Venice suffered another terrible high tide, cresting at 61 inches.

If the tide is mild (around 20 inches), the water merely seeps up through the drains. But when there's a strong tide (around 40 inches), it looks like someone's turned on a faucet down below. The water bubbles upward and flows like a river to the lowest points in the square, which can be covered with a few inches of water in an hour or so. When the water level rises one meter above mean sea level, a warning siren sounds, and it repeats if a serious flood is imminent.

Many doorways have three-foot-high wooden or metal barriers to block the high water *(acqua alta)*, but the seawater still seeps in through floors and drains, rendering the barriers nearly useless. (For background on what causes the flooding, see the sidebar on page 22.)

You might see stacked wooden benches in the square; during floods, the benches are placed end-to-end to create elevated sidewalks. If you think the square is crowded now, when it's flooded it turns into total gridlock, as all the people normally sharing the whole square jostle for space on the narrow, raised wooden walkways.

In 2006, the pavement around St. Mark's Square was taken up, and the entire height of the square was raised by adding a layer of sand and then replacing the stones. If the columns along the ground floor of the Doge's Palace look stubby, it's because this process has been carried out many times over the centuries, buying a little more time as the sea slowly swallows the city.

• *The small square between the basilica and the water is the...*

Cafés on St. Mark's Square

In Venice's heyday, it was said that the freedoms a gentleman could experience here went far beyond what any true gentleman would actually care to indulge in. But one extravagance all could enjoy was the ritual of publicly consuming coffee: showing off with an affordable luxury, doing something trendy, while sharing the ideas of the Enlightenment.

Exotic coffee was made to order for the fancy café scene. Traders introduced coffee, called the "wine of Islam," from the Middle East (the plant is native to Ethiopia). The first coffeehouses opened in the 17th century, and by 1750 there were dozens of cafés lining Piazza San Marco and 200 operating in Venice.

Today, several fine old cafés survive and still line the square. Those with live music feature similar food, prices, and a three- to five-piece combo playing a selection of classical and pop hits, from Brahms to "Bésame Mucho."

You can wander around the square listening to the different orchestras, or take a seat at a café. At any place with live music, it's perfectly acceptable to nurse a cappuccino for an hour—you're paying for the music with the cover charge. Or you can sip your coffee at the bar at a nearly normal price. The prices are clearly posted. If you sit outside and get just an espresso (your cheapest option), expect to pay €12.50—6.50 for the coffee and a €6 cover charge when the orchestra is playing (which is most of the day). Service is included (no need to tip).

Piazzetta

This "Little Square" is framed by the Doge's Palace on the left, the library on the right, and the waterfront of the lagoon. In former days, the Piazzetta was closed to the public for a few hours a day so that government officials and bigwigs could gather in the sun to strike shady deals.

The pale pink **Doge's Palace** is the epitome of the style known as Venetian Gothic. Columns support traditional, pointed Gothic arches, but with a Venetian flair—they're curved to a point, ornamented with a trefoil (three-leaf clover), and topped with a round medallion of a quatrefoil (four-leaf clover). The pat-

Caffè Florian (on the right as you face the church) is the most famous Venetian café and was one of the first places in Europe to serve coffee (daily 9:00-24:00, shorter hours in winter, www.caffeflorian.com). It was originally named "Triumphant Venice" (Venezia Triomfante). But under French occupation, in the early 19th century, that politically incorrect name was changed.

The Florian has been a popular spot for a discreet rendezvous in Venice since 1720. Each room has a historic or artistic theme. For example, the "Room of the Illustrious Men" features portraits of great Venetians from Marco Polo to Titian. The outside tables are the main action, but do walk inside through the richly decorated, old-time rooms where Casanova, Lord Byron, Charles Dickens, and Woody Allen have all paid too much for a drink. The café's orchestra—the most serious on the square—plays daily from 10:00 to 24:00. Each hour comes with a musical theme (operetta, Latin, Romantic, jazz, Venetian, and so on—you can ask for the program).

Gran Caffè Quadri, opposite the Florian and established in 1780, has another illustrious roster of famous clientele.

Gran Caffè Lavena, near the Clock Tower, is less storied—although it dates from 1750 and counts composer Richard Wagner as a former regular—so it's less intimidating than the more formal cafés here. It was the hangout of gondoliers and lantern bearers for local bigwigs. Drop in to check out its dazzling but politically incorrect chandelier.

Gran Caffè Chioggia, on the Piazzetta facing the Doge's Palace, charges no cover and has one or two musicians playing—usually a pianist (€7 cocktails, music from 10:30 to 23:00—jazz after 21:00).

Eden Bar and **Caffè Aurora** are less expensive and don't have live music.

tern is found on buildings all over Venice and on the formerly Venetian-controlled Croatian coast, but nowhere else in the world (except Las Vegas).

The two large 12th-century **columns** near the water were (like so much else) looted from Con-

stantinople. Mark's winged lion sits on top of one. The lion's body (nearly 15 feet long) predates the wings and is more than 2,000 years old. The other column holds St. Theodore (battling a crocodile), the former patron saint who was replaced by Mark. I guess

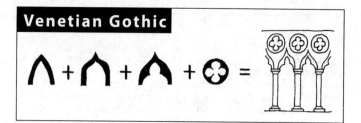

Venetian Gothic

$$\bigwedge + \bigcap + \bigcap + \clubsuit =$$

stabbing crocs in the back isn't classy enough for an upwardly mobile world power. After public ridicule, criminals were executed by being hung from these columns in the hope that the public could learn its lessons vicariously.

Venice was the "Bride of the Sea" because she depended on sea trading for her livelihood. This "marriage" was celebrated annually by the people on Ascension Day. The doge, in full regalia, boarded a ritual boat here at the edge of the Piazzetta and sailed out into the lagoon. There a vow was made, and he dropped a jeweled ring into the water to seal the marriage.

In the distance, on an island across the lagoon, is one of the grandest views in the city, of the Church of San Giorgio Maggiore. With its four tall columns as the entryway, the church, designed by the late-Renaissance architect Andrea Palladio, influenced the appearance of future government and bank buildings around the world.

Palladio's sober classical lines are pure and intellectual, but with their love of extravagance, Venetians wanted something more exuberant. More to local taste was the High Renaissance style of Jacopo Sansovino, who (around 1530) designed the library (here on the Piazzetta) and the delicate Loggetta at the base of the Campanile (destroyed by the collapse of the tower in 1902 and then pieced back together).

Tetrarchs and the Doge's Palace's Seventh Column

Where the basilica meets the Doge's Palace is the traditional entrance to the palace, decorated with an ancient Roman statue of the four **Tetrarchs.** This dates from the fourth century AD, after Rome was divided into two empires. It features the emperors of the east and west (bearded and wise), each with their younger (and not bearded) successors. It serves as a decorative cornerstone of a tower from the doges' fortress (which was destroyed in 976). I like to think they're the scared leaders of a divided Rome during its fall, holding

Escape from St. Mark's Square

Crowds getting to you? Here are some relatively quiet areas on or near St. Mark's Square.

Correr Museum Café: Sip a cappuccino in the café of this uncrowded history museum that overlooks St. Mark's Square (entrance at far end of the piazza, no museum ticket necessary). ☐ See the Correr Museum Tour chapter.

Giardinetti Reali: This small park along the waterfront is the only place near the square for a legal picnic (it's west of the Piazzetta—facing the water, turn right).

Il Merletto: This lace shop is in a small, decommissioned chapel near the northwest corner of St. Mark's Square (daily 10:00-17:00, go through Sotoportego del Cavalletto and across the little bridge on the right; for details, see page 295 of the Shopping in Venice chapter).

La Salute Church: This cool church in a quiet neighborhood is a short hop on vaporetto #1 from the San Marco-Vallaresso stop. ☐ See the La Salute Church Tour chapter.

Caffè Florian: The plush interior of this luxurious 18th-century café on St. Mark's Square is generally quiet and nearly empty. A coffee here can be a wonderful break (see the "Cafés on St. Mark's Square" sidebar in this chapter).

their swords and each other as all hell breaks loose around them. These statues—made of precious purple porphyry stone (quarried in Egypt)—are symbols of power. They were looted from Constantinople (1204), and then placed here proudly as spoils of war.

Nearby is more booty from the Crusades. The two square pillars to the left decorated a Genovese fortress in Palestine that was taken by the Venetians in the 13th century. And just beyond that, at the corner of the basilica, is a purple four-foot-tall column—a pedestal for the official government herald announcing decrees, laws, and news...more loot from Constantinople.

About two-thirds of the way down the Doge's Palace, look for a **column** that's slightly shorter and fatter than the rest (it's the seventh from the water). Its carved capital tells a story of love, romance, and tragedy: 1) In the first scene (the carving facing the Piazzetta), a woman on a balcony is wooed by her lover, who says, "Babe, I want *you!*" 2) She responds, "Why, little ol' *me?*" 3) They get married. 4) Kiss. 5) Hit the sack—pretty racy for 14th-century art. 6) Nine months later, guess what? 7) The baby takes its first steps. 8) And as was all too common in the 1300s...the child dies.

• *Continue down the Piazzetta to the waterfront. Turn left and walk (east) along the water. At the top of the first bridge, look inland at the...*

Bridge of Sighs

In the Doge's Palace (on your left), the government doled out justice. On your right are the prisons. (Don't let the palatial facade fool you—see the bars on the windows?) Prisoners sentenced in the palace crossed to the prisons by way of the covered bridge in front of you. This was called the Prisons' Bridge until the Romantic poet Lord Byron renamed it in the 19th century. From this bridge, the convicted got their final view of sunny, joyous Venice before entering the black and dank prisons. According to the Romantic legend, they sighed.

Venice has been a major tourist center for four centuries. Anyone who's ever come here has stood on this very spot, looking at the Bridge of Sighs. Lean on the railing leaned on by everyone from Casanova to Byron to Hemingway.

> *I stood in Venice, on the Bridge of Sighs;*
> *A palace and a prison on each hand:*
> *I saw from out the wave, her structures rise*
> *As from the stroke of the enchanter's wand:*
> *A thousand years their cloudy wings expand*
> *Around me, and a dying glory smiles*
> *O'er the far times when many a subject land*
> *Looked to the winged Lion's marble piles,*
> *Where Venice sat in state, throned on her hundred isles!*
> —Lord Byron, *Childe Harold's Pilgrimage*, Canto 4

ST. MARK'S SQUARE

ST. MARK'S BASILICA TOUR

Basilica di San Marco

Among Europe's churches, St. Mark's is peerless. From the outside, it's a riot of domes, columns, and statues, completely unlike the towering Gothic churches of northern Europe or the heavy Baroque of much of the rest of Italy. Inside is a decor of mosaics, colored marbles, and Byzantine treasures that's rarely seen elsewhere. The Christian symbolism is unfamiliar to Western eyes, done in the style of Byzantine icons and even Islamic designs. Older than most of Europe's churches, it feels like a remnant of a lost world. To truly say you've "seen" the basilica, plan to visit three paid-admission sights within it, which give an up-close look at the church's treasures. This is your best chance in Italy (outside of Ravenna) to glimpse a forgotten and somewhat mysterious part of the human story—Byzantium.

Orientation

Cost: Entering the church is free, though you can pay for a reservation that lets you skip the line (explained below). Three separate, optional sights inside require paid admission: the Treasury (€3), Golden Altarpiece (€2), and San Marco Museum (€5).

Hours: The church and its three museums are open Mon-Sat 9:30-17:00, Sun 14:00-17:00 (Sun until 16:30 Nov-Easter). The interior is brilliantly lit Mon-Sat from 11:30 to 12:45; although this is an especially busy time, the additional lighting brings the otherwise dim gold-leaf domes and mosaics to glowing life.

Information: Tel. 041-270-8311, www.basilicasanmarco.it.

Avoiding Lines: There's almost always a long line to get into St. Mark's, but you can avoid it. The easiest way is to reserve an entry time online, even for the same day (€3, April-Oct only, book at www.venetoinside.com). Or, if you have a large day bag (bigger than a purse), you can check it near the church, show your claim tag to the guard, and skip the line (see "Bag Check," below). For shorter lines and fewer crowds, visit early or late.

If you wind up in a long line, don't fret; it gives you time to enjoy one of Europe's finest squares as you read ahead in this chapter. Once inside, it can be packed, and you just have to shuffle through on a one-way system (another good reason to read this chapter before you enter). Be sure to step aside from the flow if you don't want to be rushed.

Dress Code: Modest dress (no bare knees or bare shoulders) is strictly enforced for men, women, and even kids. Shorts are OK if they cover the knees.

Theft Alert: St. Mark's Basilica is the most notorious place in Venice for pickpocketing—inside, it's always a crowded jostle.

Getting There: Signs throughout Venice point to *San Marco*, meaning both the square and the church (vaporetto: San Marco or San Zaccaria).

Church Services: Experience the church in its uncrowded glory at any Mass outside of visiting hours (e.g., daily at 8:00 or 18:45; see the website for the full schedule). Enter through the "worship only" door around the left side of the basilica.

Tours: Free, hour-long **English tours** (heavy on the mosaics' religious symbolism) are offered many days at 11:30 (meet in atrium, schedule varies, see schedule board just inside entrance). **Audioguides** are on sale as you enter.

∩ Download my free St. Mark's Basilica **audio tour.**

Length of This Tour: Allow one hour. If you have less time, forgo one (or all) of the basilica's three museums.

Bag Check (and Skipping the Line): Small purses and shoulder bags are usually allowed inside, but larger bags and backpacks are not. Unfortunately, what's allowed is up to the guard's discretion. If you're unsure, ask the guard before getting in line—("OK?"). Above-limit bags must be checked for free for up to one hour at the nearby church called Ateneo San Basso, 30 yards to the left of the basilica, down narrow Calle San Basso (see the map; daily 9:30-17:00). Note that you can't check small bags that would be allowed inside.

Once you've checked your bag, take your claim tag to the basilica's tourist entrance. Keep to the left of the railing where the line forms and show your tag to the gatekeeper. He'll generally let you in, ahead of the line—along with your companions (meaning about one or two others—keep it within reason).

Visitor Services: A WC is inside the San Marco Museum. For restaurant suggestions nearby, see page 268.

Starring: St. Mark, Byzantium, mosaics, and ancient bronze horses.

The Tour Begins

EXTERIOR

• *Start outside in the square, far enough back to take in the whole facade. Then zero in on the details.*

❶ Mosaic of Mark's Relics

St. Mark's Basilica is a treasure chest of booty that was looted during Venice's glory days. That's most appropriate for a church built on the stolen bones of a saint.

The **mosaic over the far left door** shows the theft that put Venice on the pilgrimage map. Two men (in the center, with crooked staffs) enter the church bearing a coffin with the body of St. Mark, who looks pretty grumpy from the long voyage.

St. Mark was the author of one of the Gospels, the four Bible books (Matthew, Mark, Luke, and John) telling the story of Jesus' life. Eight centuries after Mark's death, his holy body was in Muslim-occupied Alexandria,

Egypt. In AD 829, two visiting Venetian merchants "rescued" the body from the "infidels" and spirited it away to Venice.

The merchants presented the body—not to a pope or bishop—but to the doge (with white ermine collar, on the right) and his wife, the dogaressa (with entourage, on the left), giving instant status to Venice's budding secular state. They built a church here over Mark's bones and made him the patron saint of the city. You'll see his symbol, the winged lion, all over Venice.

The original church burned down in AD 976. Today's structure was begun in 1063. The mosaic, from 1260, shows that the church hasn't changed much since then—you can see the onion domes and famous bronze horses on the balcony.

The St. Mark's you see today, mostly from the 11th century,

St. Mark's Basilica

To San Zaccaria

CALLE DE LA CANONICA

Not to Scale

10 MAIN ALTAR (MARK'S BONES BENEATH)

8

6 CENTRAL **7**
NORTH TRANSEPT **5** SOUTH TRANSEPT
DOME

C. RIZZA

ENTRY (WORSHIP ONLY)

BAG CHECK
SAN BASSO

Piazzetta dei Leoni

NARTHEX

4 NAVE **3**

BAPTISTERY

TREASURY **9**

11 **2**
ATRIUM

To Rialto

MARZARIA OROLOGIO

CLOCK TOWER

LIONS

1

ENTRANCE

To Doge's Palace

Piazza San Marco

To Campanile

TOUR BEGINS

1 Mosaic of Mark's Relics
2 Atrium Mosaic of Noah's Ark & the Great Flood
3 Nave Mosaics
4 Pentecost Mosaic
5 Central Dome Ascension Mosaic
6 Rood Screen
7 Doge's Pulpit
8 Nicopeia Icon
9 Treasury
10 Golden Altarpiece
11 Stairs up to Museum

ST. MARK'S BASILICA

was modeled after a great fourth-century church in Constantinople/Istanbul (the long-gone Church of the Holy Apostles), giving the city deep (if faux) roots.

In subsequent centuries, the church was encrusted with materials looted from buildings throughout the Venetian empire (see the "Byzantium, the Fourth Crusade, and Venice" sidebar, later). The facade was decorated with a mishmash of plundered columns. The main entrance is a sixth-century, bronze-paneled Byzantine

St. Mark's...Cathedral, Church, or Basilica?

All three are correct. The church is also a cathedral, because it's the home church of the local bishop. It's a basilica, because the Roman Catholic Church gives that special designation to certain churches of religious importance. Coincidentally, it's also a basilica in the architectural sense. Its floor plan (if you ignore the transepts) has a central nave with flanking side aisles, a layout patterned after the ancient Roman public buildings called "basilicas." The transepts turn the basilica plan into a cross—in this case, a Greek cross, as it has four equal arms.

door that likely swung in Constantinople's Hagia Sophia church. Their prize booty was the four bronze horses that adorn the balcony, stolen from Constantinople during the Fourth Crusade. (These are copies; the originals are inside the church museum.) The atrium you're about to enter was added to serve as their pedestal. No wonder the architectural style of St. Mark's has been called "Early Ransack."

INTERIOR

• *Enter the atrium of the basilica. Immediately after being admitted by the dress-code guard, find a place in the atrium to view its ceiling mosaics. Don't be bullied by the crowd. Step aside and find an eddy to enjoy the amazing space at your tempo. Start by finding a golden arch overhead with scenes of Noah's Ark.*

❷ Atrium Mosaic of Noah's Ark and the Great Flood

Of all the famous mosaics of St. Mark's, this Flood scene is one of the oldest (13th century) and finest. The mosaics, with their picture symbols, were easily understood in medieval times, even by illiterate masses.

The scenes show Noah and his sons sawing logs to build the Ark. Venetians—who were great ship builders—could relate. At

ST. MARK'S BASILICA

its peak, Venice's Arsenale warship-building plant employed several thousand workers.

Below that are scenes of Noah putting all species of animals into the Ark, two by two. (Who's at the head of the line? Lions.) Then the Flood hits in full force, drowning the wicked. Noah sends out a dove twice to see whether there's any dry land where he can dock. He finds it, leaves the Ark with a gorgeous rainbow overhead, and offers a sacrifice of thanks to God. Easy, huh?

A few steps from Noah's arch is a dome full of mosaics telling the story of Genesis. Ringing the base of the dome, there's Adam lonely in the Garden of Eden, the creation of Eve, the happy couple, and then trouble: from succumbing to temptation, to fig leaf, to banishment.

• *Now that our medieval literacy rate has risen, rejoin the slow flow of people. You'll climb a few steps, and into the church. Just inside the door, step out of the flow and survey the church.*

❸ The Nave: Mosaics Above and Below

As your eyes adjust to the dark, notice that the entire upper part of the church is decorated in mosaic—nearly 5,000 square yards (imagine paving a football field with contact lenses). These golden mosaics are in the Byzantine style, though many were designed by artists from the Italian Renaissance and later. The often-overlooked lower walls are covered with green-, yellow-, purple-, and rose-colored marble slabs, cut to expose the grain, and laid out in geometric patterns. Even the floor

is mosaic, with mostly geometrical designs. It rolls like the sea. Venice is sinking and shifting, creating these cresting waves of stone.

Those familiar with Eastern Orthodox churches will find familiar elements in St. Mark's: a central floor plan, domes, mosaics, and iconic images of Mary and Christ as Pantocrator—ruler of all things. As your eyes adjust, the mosaics start to give off a mystical, golden luminosity, the atmosphere of the Byzantine heaven. The air itself seems almost visible, like a cloud of incense. It's a subtle effect, one that grows as the filtered light changes. There are more

Christ as Pantocrator

Most Eastern Orthodox churches—whose roots lay in the Greek Byzantine world—have at least one mosaic or painting of Christ in a standard pose: as "Pantocrator," a Greek word meaning "Ruler of All." St. Mark's features several images of Christ as Pantocrator (for example, over the altar, in the central dome, and over the entrance door). The image, so familiar to Orthodox Christians, may be a bit foreign to Protestants, Catholics, and secularists.

As King of the Universe, Christ sits (usually on a throne) facing directly out, with penetrating eyes. He wears a halo divided with a cross. In his left hand is a Bible, while his right hand blesses, with the fingers forming the Greek letters *chi* and *rho,* the first two letters of "Christos." The thumb touches the fingers, symbolizing how Christ unites both his divinity and his humanity. On either side of Christ's head are the Greek letters "IC XC," short for "IesuC XristoC."

beautiful, bigger, more overwhelming, and even holier churches, but none is as stately.

• *Find the chandelier in the nave (in the shape of a cathedral space station), and run your eyes up the support chain to the dome above. This has one of the church's greatest mosaics.*

❹ Pentecost Mosaic

In a golden heaven, the dove of the Holy Spirit shoots out a pinwheel of spiritual lasers, igniting tongues of fire on the heads of the 12 apostles below, giving them the ability to speak other languages without a Rick Steves phrase book. You'd think they'd be amazed, but their expressions are as solemn as...icons. One of the oldest mosaics in the church (c. 1125), it has distinct "Byzantine" features: a gold background and apostles with halos, solemn faces, almond eyes, delicate blessing hands, and rumpled robes, all facing forward.

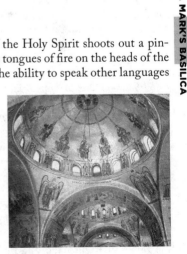

Mosaics

St. Mark's mosaics are pictures made by pressing small tiles of colored stone or glass (called *tesserae*) into wet plaster. Ancient Romans paved floors, walls, and ceilings with them. When Rome "fell," the art form died out in the West but was carried on by Byzantine craftsmen. They perfected the gold background effect by sandwiching pieces of gold leaf between glass. The surfaces of the tiles are purposely cut unevenly to capture light and give off a shimmering effect. The reflecting gold mosaics helped to light thick-walled, small-windowed, lantern-lit Byzantine churches, creating a golden glow that symbolized the divine light of heaven.

St. Mark's mosaics tell the entire Christian history from end to beginning. Entering the church, you're greeted with scenes from the end of the world (Apocalypse) and the Pentecost. As you approach the altar, you walk backward in time to the source, experiencing Jesus' Passion and Crucifixion, his miraculous life, and continuing back to his birth and Old Testament predecessors. Over the altar at the far end of the church (and over the entrance door at the near end) are images of Christ—the beginning and the end, the Alpha and Omega of the Christian universe.

This is art from a society still touchy about the Bible's commandment against making "graven images" of holy things. Byzantium suffered two centuries of iconoclasm, in which statues and paintings were broken and burned as sinful "false gods." So the Pentecost Mosaic emphasizes otherworldliness rather than literal human detail.

• *Shuffle along with the crowds up to the center of the church.*

❺ Central Dome Ascension Mosaic

Here at the center of the church, notice the layout: the church has four equal arms, each topped with a dome, radiating out to form a Greek cross (+). The symmetrical floor plan symbolizes perfection, rather than the more common Latin cross of the Crucifixion (emphasizing man's sinfulness).

Now gape upward into the central dome, the very heart of the church. Christ—having lived his miraculous life and having been crucified for man's sins—ascends into the starry sky on a rainbow. He raises his right hand and blesses the universe. This isn't the

ST. MARK'S BASILICA

dead, crucified, mortal Jesus featured in most churches, but a powerful, resurrected God, the ruler of all.

Christ's blessing radiates, rippling down to the ring of white-robed apostles below. They stand amid the trees of the Mount of Olives, waving goodbye as Christ ascends. Mary is with them, wearing blue with golden Greek crosses on each shoulder and looking ready to play patty-cake. From these saints, goodness descends, creating the Virtues and Beatitudes that ring the base of the dome between the windows. In Byzantine churches, the window-lit dome represented heaven, while the dark church below represented earth—a microcosm of the hierarchical universe.

Beneath the dome at the four corners, the four Gospel writers ("Matev," "Marc," "Luca," and "Ioh") thoughtfully scribble down the heavenly events. This wisdom flows down as water pouring from jugs, symbolizing the four great rivers below them, spreading through the church's four equal arms (the "four corners" of the world), and baptizing the congregation with God's love. The church building is a series of perfect circles within perfect squares—the cosmic order—with Christ in the center solemnly blessing us. God's in his heaven, saints are on earth, and all's right with the world.

The Church as Theater

Look around at the church's furnishings and imagine a service here. The ❻ **rood screen** (like the iconostasis in a Greek church), topped

with 14 saints, separates the congregation from the high altar, heightening the "mystery" of the Mass. The ❼ **pulpit** (the purple one on the right) was reserved for the doge, who led prayers and made important announcements.

Even today, the Venetian church service is a theatrical multimedia spectacle. It combines words (prayers, Bible readings in Latin and Greek), music (chants, choir, organ, musicians), set design (the mosaics, rood screen), costumes and props (robes, reliquaries, candles, incense), and even stage direction (processionals through the crowd). Coincidentally or not, the first modern opera—also a multimedia theatrical experience—was written here in Venice by St. Mark's *maestro di cappella*, Claudio Monteverdi (1567-1643).

• *In the north transept (left of the altar) is an area usually reserved for prayer. The worshippers are facing a big stone canopy, which houses a small painting of the Virgin Mary.*

ST. MARK'S BASILICA

❸ Nicopeia (North Transept)

Venetians then and now pray to a painted wooden icon of Mary and Baby Jesus known as Nicopeia, or Our Lady of Victory. Supposedly painted by the evangelist Luke, it was once enameled with bright paint and precious stones, and Mary was adorned with a crown and necklace of gold and jewels (now on display in the Treasury). For centuries, Nicopeia was venerated by the Byzantines, who asked Mary to protect them in battle. When Venetian Crusaders captured it, the icon came to protect Venice. This Madonna has helped the city persevere through plagues, wars, and crucial soccer games.

ST. MARK'S MUSEUMS

Inside the church are three sights, each requiring a separate admission. These let you experience the richness of Byzantium up close and learn about the mosaics. They also provide great views over the inside of the church, as well as to St. Mark's Square outside.

❾ Treasury (Tesoro)

• *Locate the tiny, two-room Treasury in the south transept.*

If you're not into metalworking or religious objects, you may find the Treasury's cramped collection somewhat underwhelming, but the objects become more interesting when you consider that some are nearly 2,000 years old. It's a beautiful collection of chalices, reliquaries, and jewels, most of them stolen from Constantinople. As Venice thought of itself as the granddaughter of Rome and the daughter of Byzantium, Venetians consider these treasures not stolen, but inherited. Less sophisticated thieves would have smelted these pieces, but the Venetians safely stored them here for posterity. Some pieces represent the fruits of labor by different civilizations over a thousand-year period. For example, an ancient rock-crystal chalice made by the Romans might have been augmented later with Byzantine enamels then finished with gold filigree by Venetian goldsmiths. This is marvelous handiwork, but all the more marvelous for having been done when Western Europe was still mired in the Dark Ages.

• *Entering, you'll be directed into the small room of the reliquaries in glass cases.*

Relics Room: The first display cases (to the left) contain a glass reliquary with the bones of Doge Orseolo (r. 976-978), who built the church that preceded the current structure, and the bones of St. George, the legendary dragon slayer.

Straight ahead, the glass case over the glowing alabaster altar contains elaborate gold-and-glass reliquaries holding relics of Jesus' Passion—his torture and execution. The central reliquary showing Christ tied to a column and being whipped (from 1125) holds a stone from that very column he was tied to. You may scoff, but of

Europe's many "Crown of Thorns" relics, these have at least some claim of authenticity. Legend has it that Christ's possessions were gathered up in the fourth century by Constantine's mother and taken to Constantinople. During the Crusade heist of 1204, Venetians brought them here. They've been paraded through the city every Good Friday for 800 years.

• *Now enter the...*

Main Room: *Start with the large glass case in the center of the room. It holds the most precious Byzantine objects (mostly war booty brought here during the Fourth Crusade in 1204). Work your way around the case, taking your time with these beautiful and precious treasures.*

The first piece you encounter is a hanging lamp (with protruding seashells and fish) made from a fourth-century Roman rock crystal framed in 11th-century Byzantine metalwork. Just behind the lamp, a black bucket, carved in the fourth century with scenes of satyrs chasing nymphs, epitomizes the pagan world that was fading as Christianity triumphed.

Circling to the right, you'll come across a couple of rectangular golden icons with (extremely precious) blue lapis lazuli scenes of the Crucifixion. Next, browse the array of chalices (cups used for bread and wine during Mass) made of amber-colored sardonyx, agate, and rock crystal, all trimmed in gold filigree.

Around back, see a display of a Byzantine specialty: enamel work (which we'll see at the Golden Altarpiece). The "Grotto of the Virgin" is made from a Roman-era piece of rock crystal sitting on a Byzantine-enamel pedestal, with a gilded Venetian Virgin.

Nearby is an incense burner shaped like a domed church. And finally, find the jewel-encrusted icon of Archangel Michael—standing like an action hero, ready to conquer evil in the name of Christ.

• *Along the walls, find the following displays (working counterclockwise around the room).*

The first three glass cases have more bowls and urns. Note a Venetian specialty: elaborately laced filigree (twisted wires of precious metal). You'll also see an old dagger, a huge topaz, and a turquoise-blue bowl from Persia. These blend elements from the three medieval cultures that cross-pollinated in the Eastern Mediterranean: Venetian, Byzantine, and Islamic.

Next, on a wooden pedestal, comes the Urn of Artaxerxes I (next to window in right wall). This Egyptian-made object was fashioned from extremely hard diorite. It once held the ashes of the great Persian king who ruled 2,500 years ago and is mentioned in the Bible as a friend to the Israelites.

The next cases hold religious paraphernalia used for High Mass—chalices, reliquaries, candlesticks, and a 600-year-old

ST. MARK'S BASILICA

Byzantium, the Fourth Crusade, and Venice

The Byzantine Empire was the eastern half of the ancient Roman Empire that *didn't* "fall" in AD 476. It remained Christian, Greek-speaking, and enlightened for another thousand years.

In AD 330, Constantine, the first Christian emperor, moved the Roman Empire's capital to the newly expanded city of Byzantium, which he humbly renamed Constantinople. With him went Rome's best and brightest. When the city of Rome decayed and fell, plunging Western Europe into its "Dark Ages," Constantinople lived on. Western Europeans considered it to be the leading city in Christendom, and the Byzantine emperor was thought of as the civilized world's supreme ruler.

From its earliest days, Venice had strong ties with Byzantium. In the sixth century, Byzantine Emperor Justinian invaded northern Italy, briefly reuniting East and West, and making Ravenna his regional capital. In 810, Venetians asked the emperor in Constantinople to protect them from Charlemagne's marauding Franks.

Soon Venetian merchants were granted trading rights to Byzantine ports in the Adriatic and eastern Mediterranean. They traded raw materials from Western Europe for luxury goods from the East. By the 10th century, about 10,000 Venetian merchants lived and worked in Constan- tinople. Meanwhile, relations between Byzantine Christians and Roman Catholics were souring across Europe over religious grounds—and because Constantinople's local merchants felt crowded out by the powerful Venetians, the corporate titans of the day. In 1171, the Byzantine emperor expelled the Venetian merchants from Constantinople; after another decade of conflict, the entire Roman Catholic population—about 60,000 people—was either slaughtered or expelled from the city in what historians call the Massacre of the Latins.

Powerful, rich Venice wasn't about to stand for it—the Venetians had virtually no economy without trade. Two decades later, they saw their chance: The pope was organizing the Fourth Crusade to "save" the Holy Land from Muslim influence. Venice offered her ships to transport more than 30,000 Crusaders. They set out bound for Jerusalem—but the ships, led by the Venetian doge, diverted to Constantinople. The Crusaders sacked the Byzantine capital and occupied it from 1204 to 1261, turning the city into a quarry—one wide open for plunder. During that period, any ship traveling from Constantinople to Venice was required to bring with it a souvenir for the Venetian Republic. Eventually the

Byzantine Empire

Venice
Genoa
Pisa
Rome
Ravenna
Constantinople
Nicaea
Athens
Antioch
Jerusalem

■ = Empire in 1025

riches of Constantinople ended up in Venice—much of it here, in St. Mark's Basilica.

You can still see much of what the Venetians carried home: the bronze horses, bronze doors of Hagia Sophia, Golden Altarpiece enamels, the Treasury's treasures, the Nicopeia icon, and much of the marble that now covers the (brick) church. A good portion of the artistic riches adorning the church and filling its treasury was 700 years old when it was brought here...800 years ago.

The Venetians were clearly thieves, albeit thieves with good taste. While you could argue that much of the treasure belongs in Turkey today, a good Venetian would argue that had they not "rescued" it, much of it (especially anything made from precious metal) never would have survived the centuries.

After the Fourth Crusade, Venice rose while the Byzantine Empire faded. Then both civilizations nose-dived when Constantinople finally fell to the Ottomans in 1453, severely damaging Venice's trading empire and ending Byzantium entirely. Constantinople, however, soon began to thrive again—once a bustling Christian city of a thousand churches, it flourished again as the newly Islamic city of Istanbul. Meanwhile, Christian scholars and artists fled to the West, fueling the Renaissance.

Today, we find hints of Byzantium in the Eastern Orthodox Church, in mosaics and icons, and in the churches of Venice and Ravenna.

ceremonial crosier (reminiscent of a shepherd's staff) still used today by the chief priest on holy days.

Next is the Ciborio di Anastasia (far left corner), a small marble canopy that once arched over the blessed communion wafer during Mass. The object may be a gift from "Anastasia," the name carved on it in Greek. She was a lady-in-waiting in the court of the emperor Justinian (483-565). Christian legend has it that she was so beautiful that Justinian (a married man) pursued her amorously, so she had to dress like a monk and flee to a desert monastery.

Moving to the next wall, you'll see two large golden panels that once fronted an altar. The bottom one shows 14 scenes from the life of St. Mark. Flanking the panels are two golden candlesticks. Study the one on the left from top to bottom. What detail! Find the smiling angels at the top, the literary lion, the man with the weight on his shoulders, the two queens flanking the Crucifixion...all the way down to the roots. Nearby, see a photo of a Madonna adorned with the jewels, gold, and enamel that are used to grace the Nicopeia.

Finally, next to the Madonna, notice the granite column that extends below current floor level—you can see how the floor has risen as the basilica has settled in the last 1,000 years.

• *Return to the nave and follow the crowds through the turnstile and behind the main altar to the ...*

⑩ Golden Altarpiece (Pala d'Oro)

Under the green marble canopy, supported by four intricately carved, seventh-century alabaster columns (plundered from far away), sits the **high altar.** Inside the altar is an urn (not visible) with the mortal remains of Mark, the Gospel writer. (Look through the grate of the altar to read *Corpus Divi Marci Evangelistae,* or "Body of the Evangelist Mark.") He rests in peace, as an angel had promised him. Shh.

As you shuffle along, notice the marble canopy's **support columns** carved with New Testament scenes.

The **Golden Altarpiece** itself is a stunning golden wall made of 250 blue-backed enamels with religious scenes, all set in a gold frame and studded with 15 hefty rubies, 300 emeralds, 1,500 pearls, and assorted sapphires, amethysts, and topaz. The Byzantine-made enamels were part of the Venetians' plunder of 1204, subsequently pieced together by Byzantine craftsmen specifically for St. Mark's high altar. It's a bit much

The Legend (Mixed with a Little Truth) of Mark and Venice

Mark (died c. AD 68) was a Jewish-born Christian, and he might have actually met Jesus. He traveled with fellow con-

vert Paul, eventually settling in Alexandria as the city's first Christian bishop. On a trip to Rome, Peter—Jesus' right-hand man—asked him to write down the events of Jesus' life. This became the Gospel of Mark.

During his travels, Mark stopped in the lagoon (in Aquileia on the north coast of the Adriatic), where he dreamed of a Latin-speaking angel who said, *"Pax tibi Marce, evangelista meus"* ("Peace to you, Mark, my evangelist"), promising him rest after death. Back in Alexandria, Mark was attacked by an anti-Christian mob. They tied him with ropes and dragged his body through the streets until he died.

Eight centuries later, his body lay in an Alexandrian church that was about to be vandalized by Muslim fanatics. Two Venetian traders on a business trip saved the relics from desecration by hiding them in a basket of pork—a meat considered unclean by Muslims—and quickly setting sail. The doge received the body, and in 832 they built the first church of St. Mark's to house it. After construction of the current church started in 1063, Mark's relics were temporarily lost, and it took another miracle to find them, hidden inside a column. Today, Venetians celebrate Mark on the traditional date of his martyrdom, April 25.

ST. MARK'S BASILICA

to take in all at once, but get up close and find several details you might recognize:

In the center, Jesus as Ruler of the Cosmos sits on a golden throne, with a halo of jewels and pearls. Like a good Byzantine Pantocrator, he dutifully faces forward and gives his blessing while stealing a glance offstage at Mark ("Marcus") and the other saints.

Along the bottom row, Old Testament prophets show off the books of the Bible they've written. With halos, solemn faces, and elaborately creased robes, they epitomize the Byzantine icon style.

Mark's story is told in the vertical panels on each side. In the bottom left panel, Mark meets Peter (seated) at the gates of Rome. Peter gives Mark the eyewitness account of Jesus' life that Mark would write down in his Gospel. Mark's story ends in the bottom right panels with the two Venetian merchants returning by ship, carrying his coffin here in 829 to be laid to rest.

Cloisonné enameling like this was a Byzantine specialty. A piece of gold leaf is stamped with a design, then filled in with pools of enamel paste, and then fired. Look at a single saint to see the detail work: The gold background around the saint is the gold-leaf medallion that gets stamped. The golden folds in the robe are the raised edges of the impression; in the recessed areas, each different color of the robe was baked on in a separate firing. Some saints even have pearl crowns or jewel collars pinned on. This kind of craftsmanship—and the social infrastructure that could afford it—made Byzantium seem like an enchanted world during Europe's dim Middle Ages.

After you've looked at some individual scenes, back up as far as this small room will allow and let yourself be dazzled by the whole picture—this "mosaic" of Byzantine greatness—and marvel at the fact that it's still here. The altarpiece contains 30 pounds of gold, but Napoleon's plundering soldiers thought it was just gold leaf, so they didn't bother melting it down. And during World War II, the altarpiece almost certainly would have been snatched by the Nazis, had it not been hidden away in an Umbrian villa.

This magnificent altarpiece sits on a swivel (notice the mechanism at its base) and is swung around on festival Sundays so the entire congregation can enjoy it, as Venetians have for so many centuries.

⑪ San Marco Museum (Museo di San Marco)

• *The steep staircase up to the museum is in the atrium near the main entrance. Follow signs to* Museo e Loggia, *or* Loggia dei Cavalli, Museo. *In the first room, take a moment to view the models and drawings of the church at various stages of its history. In the big cutaway model, notice how the original domes, once squat, were made taller in the 13th century, leaving today's church with a dome-within-a-dome structure.*

Next are the museum's three highlights: view of the interior (right), view of the square (out the door to the left), and bronze horses (directly ahead). Belly up to the stone balustrade (on the right) to survey the interior.

View of Church Interior

Scan the church, with its thousands of square yards of mosaics, then take a closer look at the Pentecost Mosaic (first dome above you). The unique design at the very top signifies the Trinity: throne (God), Gospels (Christ), and dove (Holy Spirit). The couples below the ring of apostles are the people of the world (I can find Judaea, Cappadocia, and Asia), who, despite their different languages, still understood the Spirit's message.

If you were a woman in medieval Venice, you'd enjoy this same close-up view, because in the Middle Ages, women climbed the same stairs you just did and found a spot along the balconies at your feet. The balcony was for women, the nave for men, and the altar for the priests. Back then the rood screen (the fence with the 14 figures on it) separated the priest from the public. The doge was also allowed to address his public from the pulpit, thereby amplifying the power of his political speeches with the force of God.

Looking down at the nave, appreciate the patterns of the mosaic floor—one of the finest in Italy—that unfurl like a Persian carpet.

• *From here, the museum loops you along the left gallery to the far (altar) end of the church, then back to the bronze horses. Along the way, you'll see...*

Mosaic Fragments

These mosaics once hung in the church, but when they became damaged or aesthetically old-fashioned, they were replaced by new and more fashionable mosaics. These few fragments avoided the garbage can. You'll see mosaics from the church's earliest days (and most "Byzantine" style, c. 1070) to more recent times (1700s, more realistic and detailed). Many are accompanied by small photos that show where the fragment used to fit into a larger scene.

The mosaics—made from small tiles of stone or colored glass pressed into wet clay—were assembled on the ground, then cemented onto the walls. Artists drew the pattern on paper, laid it on the wet clay, and slowly cut the paper away as they replaced it with tiles. The first mosaic on your left as you enter shows a reproduction of a paper "cast" of a mosaic.

Continuing on, down a set of stairs, you'll see other artwork and catch glimpses of the interior of the church from the north transept. Here you get a close-up view of the **Tree of Jesse mosaic,** showing Jesus' distant ancestor at the root and his mom at the top. This mosaic is from 1540, during the High Renaissance—it's much more modern than those decorating the domes, which date mostly from the 1200s.

• *Continue on to the Sala dei Banchetti (WCs near the room's entrance).*

Sala dei Banchetti

This large, ornate room—once the doge's banquet hall—is filled with religious objects, tapestries, and carpets that once adorned the church, Burano-made lace vestments, illuminated music manuscripts, a doge's throne, and much more.

Try reading some music. The manuscripts date from the 16th century—before the age of treble and bass clefs. You'll see a C clef along the left margin of each staff. Notice that it is a "sliding clef" and could mark a different line of the staff. This established which line was middle C. From this, you could chant notes in proper relationship to each other, following the rhythm indicated.

In the center of the hall stands the most prestigious artwork here, the **Pala Feriale**, by Paolo Veneziano (1345). These 14 scenes painted on wood formed a cover for the basilica's Golden Altarpiece. The top row shows seven saints, including crucified Christ. Below are seven episodes in Mark's life, told with impressive realism. In the first panel, Mark kneels before a red-robed Saint Peter and receives his calling. Next, he arrives in Alexandria and makes his first convert. Then Jesus appears to Mark. Mark is beaten to death and dragged through the streets.

Pay special attention to the dramatic panel with the sailboat that recounts the Venetian merchants' trip home with Mark's relics. A storm billows the ship's sails, ripples the flag, churns the waves, and scares the crew as the ship heads toward the rocks. But then Mark himself appears miraculously at the stern and calms the storm, bringing the ship (and his own body) safely to Venice. Paolo proudly signed his name along the bottom of this most impressive panel. In the next panel, Mark's long-lost body is rediscovered hidden in a column. Finally, worshippers gather at Mark's tomb by the altar of the basilica.

• *Now the route doubles back toward the museum entrance, through displays of stone fragments from the church, finally arriving at the...*

Bronze Horses (La Quadriga)

Stepping lively in pairs and with smiles on their faces, these four bronze horses exude a spirited exuberance. They long stood in the most prominent spot in Venice—above the main door of St. Mark's Basilica, overlooking St. Mark's Square. Originally they were part of a larger ensemble shown pulling a chariot, *Ben-Hur* style.

The realism is remarkable: the halters around their necks, the bulging veins in their faces, their chest muscles, and the creases in their necks as they rear back. With flashing eyes, flaring nostrils, erect ears, and open mouths, they're the picture of equestrian energy.

They are clearly teammates. Each raises its hoof at the same time and same height. They cock their heads to the side, seemingly communicating with their brothers with equine ESP.

These bronze statues are rare survivors of that remarkable ancient technology known as the lost-wax method. They were not hammered into shape by metalsmiths, but cast—made by pouring molten bronze into clay molds. Each horse weighs nearly a ton.

During the Dark Ages, barbarians melted most metal masterpieces down for reuse, but these survived. Originally gilded, they still have some streaks of gold leaf. Long gone are the ruby pupils that made their fiery eyes glisten in the sun.

Their expressive faces seem to say, "Oh boy, Wilbur, have we done some travelin'." That's because megalomaniacs through the ages have coveted these horses not only for their artistic value, but because they symbolize Apollo, the god of the sun...and symbol of power.

The horses are old—much older even than Venice. Legend says they were made in Greece during the time of Alexander the Great (fourth century BC). They were then taken by Nero to Rome. Constantine brought them to his new capital in Constantinople to adorn the chariot racecourse. In 1204, during the Fourth Crusade, the Venetians stole them. They placed them on the balcony of St. Mark's from where the doge would speak to his people—the horses providing a powerful backdrop. Six centuries later, Napoleon conquered Venice and took the horses. They stood atop a triumphal arch in Paris until Napoleon fell and they were returned to their "rightful" home in Venice.

In the 1970s, the horses made their shortest and final journey. With the threat of oxidation from polluted air, they were replaced by modern copies. The originals galloped for cover inside the basilica, where they are displayed today.

For all their travel, this fearsome foursome still seems fresh. They're more than just art. They stand as a testament to how each civilization conquers the previous one, assimilates the best elements from it, and builds upon it.

• *The visit ends outside on the balcony overlooking St. Mark's Square.*

Loggia and View of St. Mark's Square

You'll be drawn repeatedly to the viewpoint of the square, but remember to look at the facade also to see how cleverly all the looted architectural elements blend together. Ramble among the stat-

ues of water-bearing slaves that serve as drain spouts. The horses are modern copies (note the 1978 date on the hoof of the horse to the right).

Be a doge, and stand aside the bronze horses overlooking St. Mark's Square. Under the gilded lion of St.

Mark, and flanked—like Apollo—by the four glorious horses, he inspired the Venetians in the square below to great things.

Admire the mesmerizing, commanding view of the center of this city, which so long ago was Europe's great superpower. Today it's just a small town with a big history and a one-of-a-kind basilica that attracts visitors from across the globe.

DOGE'S PALACE TOUR

Palazzo Ducale

Venice is a city of beautiful facades—palaces, churches, carnival masks—that cover darker interiors of intrigue and decay. The Doge's Palace, with its frilly pink exterior, hides the fact that the "Most Serene Republic" (as Venice called itself—"serene" meaning stable) was far from serene in its heyday.

The Doge's Palace housed the fascinating government of this rich and powerful empire. It also served as the home for the Venetian ruler known as the doge (pronounced "dohzh"), or duke. For four centuries (about 1150 to 1550), this was the most powerful half-acre in Europe. The rest of Europe marveled at the way Venice could govern itself without a dominant king, bishop, or tyrant. The doges wanted their palace to reflect the wealth and secular values of the Republic, impressing visitors and serving as a reminder that the Venetians were Number One in Europe.

Today, you'll walk through majestic rooms where doges lived and where the Venetian government met to administer the empire. Many rooms are decorated with large and colorful paintings by Venice's greatest artists. You'll end your visit by crossing the famed Bridge of Sighs into the dank bowels of the notorious prisons.

Orientation

Cost: €25 combo-ticket includes the Correr Museum, €13 for kids ages 6-14 and students 15-25, family ticket available; also covered by Museum Pass.

Hours: Sun-Thu 8:30-21:00, Fri-Sat until 23:00, Nov-March daily until 19:00.

Information: Tel. 041-271-5911, http://palazzoducale.visitmuve. it.

Doge's Palace

1. Doge's Apartments (1st floor)
2. Executive & Legislative Rooms (3rd floor)
3. Judicial Rooms & Armory Museum (3rd floor)
4. Hall of the Grand Council & Sala dello Scrutinio (3rd floor)
5. Café (courtyard level)

DOGE'S PALACE

Avoiding Lines: You have several options for skipping long ticket-buying lines (the first is best):

• Buy your combo-ticket at the never-crowded Correr Museum. Or if you're purchasing a Museum Pass (which covers the Doge's Palace—see the beginning of the Sights in Venice chapter) get it at one of the less-crowded museums covered by the pass. With ticket or pass in hand, enter at the "prepaid tickets" entrance.

• Buy your ticket online (http://palazzoducale.visitmuve.it; must be done at least 48 hours in advance; ticket good for 3 months from date of purchase; €1 surcharge).

• Visit the palace after about 16:00, when the line diminishes.

• Book a guided Secret Itineraries Tour (see next page).

Getting There: The palace is next to St. Mark's Basilica, on the lagoon waterfront, and just off St. Mark's Square. Vaporetto stop: San Marco or San Zaccaria.

Tours: The fine **Secret Itineraries Tour** follows the doge's footsteps through rooms not included in the general admission ticket. Though the tour skips the palace's main hall, you're welcome to visit the hall afterward on your own. Three 75-minute English-language tours run each morning. Reserve ahead, as tours can fill up several weeks in advance—although you can try just showing up at the information desk (€28, includes Doge's Palace admission but not Correr Museum, €15 with combo-ticket; reserve over the phone or online: tel. 041-4273-0892, http://palazzoducale.visitmuve.it, €1 online surcharge). Don't confuse this with the Doge's Hidden Treasures Tour, which isn't worth its fee.

The **audioguide** is dry but informative (€5, 1.5 hours, need ID for deposit). Guidebooks are available in the bookshop.

Length of This Tour: Allow 1.5 hours. If you need to shave some time off your visit, head straight to the third floor (the Square Room) and follow my tour from there to the Hall of the Grand Council. Skip the prisons.

Services: Some WCs are in the courtyard; more are halfway up the stairs to the balcony level. An elevator is available off the courtyard. Any bag bigger than a large purse must be checked (free) in the courtyard.

Eating: A café is off the palace courtyard (it's tucked in the gallery behind the Stairway of Giants, and the tour route also deposits you there). I'd head instead for the good sandwich bars on Calle de le Rasse (two blocks behind the palace—see page 268).

Starring: Big rooms bare of furnishings but crammed with history, Tintoretto and Veronese masterpieces, and the doges.

The Tour Begins

Exterior

"The Wedding Cake," "The Tablecloth," or "The Pink House" is also sometimes known as the Doge's Palace. The style is called Venetian Gothic—a fusion of Italian Gothic with a delicate Islamic flair. The columns originally had bases on the bottoms, but these were covered over as the col-

DOGE'S PALACE

umns sank, and the square was built up over the centuries. If you compare this lacy, top-heavy structure with the massive fortress-palaces of Florence, you realize the wisdom of building a city in the middle of the sea—you have no natural enemies except gravity. This unfortified palace in a city with no city wall was the doge's way of saying, "I am an elected and loved ruler. I do not fear my own people."

The palace was originally built in the 800s, but most of what we see came after 1300, as it was expanded to meet the needs of the empire. Each doge wanted to leave his mark on history with a new wing, but so much of the city's money was spent on the palace that finally a law was passed levying an enormous fine on anyone who even mentioned any new building. That worked for a while, until one brave (and wealthy) doge proposed a new wing, paid his fine... and started building again.

• *Enter the Doge's Palace from along the waterfront. After you pass through the turnstile, ignore the* Recommended Itinerary *signs for a moment, and enter the courtyard.*

Courtyard and Stairway of Giants (Scala dei Giganti)

Here in this vast space, you're surrounded by the buildings that housed Venice's ruling class. The courtyard is a hodgepodge of ar-chitectural styles, reflecting how the palace was refurbished re-peatedly over the centuries: bare brick walls, round Renaissance arches, Baroque flourishes, and Gothic spires. Notice the two fine wellheads, as the courtyard once functioned as a cistern.

At one end of the court-yard, the palace is attached to the basilica, symbolically weld-ing church and state. Both buildings have ugly brick behind a painted-lady veneer of marble. In this tour, we'll see the similarly harsh inner workings of an outwardly serene, polished republic.

• *Head to the far end of the courtyard (near the basilica), and stand at the foot of the grand staircase topped by two statues.*

Imagine yourself as a foreign dignitary on business to meet the doge. You'd enter the palace up these stairs topped with two nearly nude statues of, I think, Moses and Paul Newman (more likely, Neptune and Mars, representing Venice's prowess at sea and at war). The doge and his aides would be waiting for you at the top, between the two statues and beneath the winged lion. No matter

Paintings by Titian, Veronese, and Tintoretto

Only the top Venetian painters decorated the Doge's Palace. It was once rich in Titians, but fires in the late 1500s destroyed nearly all the work by the greatest Venetian master. As the palace was hastily reconstructed, the empty spaces left by the Titians were quickly patched in with works by Veronese and Tintoretto.

Veronese used the best pigments available—made from minerals and precious stones—and his colors have survived vividly. These Veronese paintings are by the artist's hand and are fine examples of his genius. Tintoretto, on the other hand, didn't really have his heart in these commissions, and the pieces here were done by his workshop.

The paintings of the Doge's Palace are a study of long-ago Venice, with fine views of the old city and its inhabitants. The extravagant women's gowns in the paintings by Veronese show off a major local industry—textiles. While the paintings are not generally of masterpiece quality, they're historically interesting. They prove that in the old days, Venice had no pigeons.

who you were—king, pope, or emperor—you'd have to hoof it up. The powerful doge would descend the stairs for no one.

Many doges were crowned right here, between the two statues. The doge was something like an elected king—which makes sense only in the dictatorial republic that was Venice. Technically, he was just a noble selected by other nobles to carry out their laws and decisions. Many doges tried to extend their powers and rule more as divine-right kings. Many others just put on their funny hats and accepted their role as figureheads and ceremonial ribbon-cutters. Because doges served a lifelong term, most were geezers, elected in their 70s and committed to preserving Venetian traditions.

• *Let's go inside. Cross back to the entrance and follow the signs up the tourists' staircase to the first-floor balcony (loggia). From this point on, it's hard to get lost. It's a one-way system, so just follow the arrows. Admire the views from the balcony, then join the flow. Midway along the balcony, you'll find a face in the wall, the...*

Mouth of Truth

This fierce-looking androgyne opens his/her mouth, ready to swallow a piece of paper, hungry for gossip. Letterboxes like this (some with lions' heads) were scattered throughout the palace. Originally, anyone who had a complaint or suspicion about anyone else could accuse him anonymously *(denontie secrete)* by simply dropping a slip of paper in the mouth. This set the blades of justice turning inside the palace.

• *A few steps toward Paul Newman is the entrance to the...*

Golden Staircase (Scala d'Oro)

The palace was architectural propaganda, designed to impress visitors. As ambassadors arrived to meet the doge, they were routed up this ceremonial staircase. With its 24-karat gilded ceiling, it was something for them to write home about.

• *Start up the first few steps of the Golden Staircase. Midway up, at the first landing, turn right, which loops you through a dozen rooms. These rooms are often closed or used for temporary exhibitions, but if they happen to be open for you, enter and enjoy the...*

Doge's Apartments (Appartamento del Doge)

The dozen or so rooms on the first floor are where the doge actually lived. The blue-and-gold-hued Sala dei Scarlatti (Room 5) is typical of the palace's interior decoration: gold-coffered ceiling, big stone fireplace, silky walls with paintings, and a speckled floor. There's very little original furniture, as doges were expected to bring their own. Despite his high office, the doge had to obey several rules that bound him to the city. He couldn't leave the palace unescorted, he couldn't open official mail in private, and he and his family had to leave their own home and live in the Doge's Palace.

The large Room 6, the Sala dello Scudo (Shield Hall), is full of maps and globes. The main map illustrates the reach of Venice's maritime realm, which stretched across most of the eastern Mediterranean. The Venetian Republic was a mighty trading empire, built not on vast land holdings but upon a network of ports and a mastery of the sea. With the maps in this room you can trace the eye-opening trip across Asia—from Italy to Greece to Palestine, Arabia, and "Irac"—of local boy Marco Polo (c. 1254-1325). Finally, he arrived at the other side of the world. This last map (at the far end of the room) is shown "upside-down," with south on top, giving a glimpse of the Venetian worldview circa 1550. It depicts China, Taiwan (Formosa), and Japan (Giapan), while America is a nearby island made up of California and lots of Terre Incognite with *antropofagi* (cannibals).

In Room 7, the Sala Grimani, are several paintings of the lion of St. Mark, including the famous one by Vittore Carpaccio of a smiling lion (on the long wall). The lion holds open a book with these words, *"Pax Tibi Marce..."* ("Peace to you, Mark"), which, according to legend, were spoken by an angel welcoming St. Mark to Venice. In the background are the Doge's Palace and the Campanile.

Find Room 10, the Sala dei Filosofi (Philosophers' Hall), look for the first doorway on the right, pop up the humble stairway, and look back at a Titian quickie, painted in just three days. This fresco of St. Christopher carrying the Christ Child across the lagoon was made for a doge who believed that if you looked at St. Christopher, you wouldn't die that day.

• *The visitors route through the Doge's Apartments returns you to the Golden Staircase. So, whether you visited the apartments or not, continue up the Golden Staircase to the third floor, which was the "public" part of the palace. As you ascend the stairs, look back at the floor below and marvel at its 3-D pattern. The room right at the top of the stairs is the...*

Square Room (Atrio Quadrato)

In this room, visitors would catch their breath and prepare to be admitted into the heart of the palace. The ceiling painting, *Justice Presenting the Sword and Scales to Doge Girolamo Priuli,* is by Jacopo Tintoretto. (Stand

Executive & Legislative Rooms

ROOM 11 — COLLEGIO HALL

ROOM 12 — SENATE HALL

Courtyard

Not to Scale

ROOM OF THE 4 DOORS

SQUARE ROOM

GOLDEN STAIRCASE

HALL OF THE COUNCIL OF 10

1. TINTORETTO – Justice Presenting the Sword and Scales
2. TITIAN – Doge Kneeling
3. TIEPOLO – Venice Receiving Neptune
4. VERONESE – The Rape of Europa
5. TINTORETTO – Bacchus and Ariadne
6. VERONESE – Discussion
7. VERONESE – Mars and Neptune with Campanile and Lion
8. TINTORETTO – Triumph of Venice
9. Clocks

at the top of the painting for the full 3-D effect.) It's a late-Renaissance masterpiece, worthy of any museum in the world. So what? As you'll soon see, this palace is wallpapered with Titians, Tintorettos, and Veroneses. Many have the same theme you see here: a doge, in his ermine cape, gold-brocaded robe, and funny one-horned hat with earflaps, kneeling in the presence of saints, gods, or mythological figures.

• *Enter the next room.*

Room of the Four Doors (Sala delle Quattro Porte)

This was the central clearinghouse for all the goings-on in the palace. Visitors presented themselves here and were directed to their destination—the courts, councils, or the doge himself.

The room was designed by Andrea Palladio, the architect who did the impressive Church of San Giorgio Maggiore, across the Grand Canal from St. Mark's Square. On the intricate stucco ceiling, notice the feet of the women dangling down below the edge (above the windows), extending the illusion.

On the wall to the right of the door you entered from is a **painting by Titian** (ho-hum), showing a woman embodying Faith holding the Cross of Jesus, while a doge kneels with great piety. Notice old Venice in the misty distance under the cross. This is one of many paintings you'll see of doges in uncharacteristically humble poses—paid for, of course, by the doges themselves.

At the end of the room, find G. B. Tiepolo's well-known *Venice Receiving Neptune* high up on the wall above the windows.

(This is a copy, but the original is often displayed on an easel nearby.) The painting shows Venice as a woman—Venice is always a woman to artists—reclining in luxury. She's dressed in the ermine cape and pearl necklace of a doge's wife (dogaressa). Crude Neptune, enthralled by the First Lady's beauty, arrives bearing a seashell bulging with gold ducats. A bored Venice points and says, "Put it over there with the other stuff."

• *Enter the small room with the big fireplace and several paintings.*

Ante-Collegio Hall (Sala dell'Anticollegio)

If the doge agreed to see you, you'd wait in this room—combing your hair, adjusting your robe, popping a breath mint, and preparing the gifts you'd brought. While you cooled your heels and warmed your hands at the elaborate fireplace, you might look at some of the paintings—among the finest in the palace and the world of art.

The Rape of Europa (on the wall opposite the fireplace), by Paolo Veronese, most likely shocked many small-town visitors with its risqué subject matter. Here Zeus, the king of the Greek gods, appears in the form of a bull with a foot fetish, seducing a beautiful bare-breasted earthling, while cupids spin playfully overhead. The Venetian Renaissance looked back to pagan Greek and Roman art, a big change from the saints and crucifixions of the Middle Ages. This painting is no medieval condemnation of sex and violence, but rather a celebration in cheery pastel colors of the earthy, optimistic spirit of the Renaissance.

Tintoretto's *Bacchus and Ariadne* (to the right of the fireplace) is another colorful display of Venice's sensual tastes. The God of Wine seeks a threesome, offering a ring to the mortal Ariadne, who's being crowned with stars by Venus, who turns slowly in zero gravity. The ring is

DOGE'S PALACE

the center of a spinning wheel of flesh, with the three arms like spokes.

But wait, the doge is ready for us. Let's go in.
• *Enter the next room and approach your imaginary doge.*

Collegio Hall (Sala del Collegio)

Flanked by his cabinet of six advisers—one for each Venetian neighborhood—the doge would sit on the wood-paneled platform at the far end to receive ambassadors, who laid their gifts at his feet and pleaded their countries' cases. All official ceremonies, such as the ratification of treaties, were held here.

At other times, it was the "Oval Office" where the doge and his cabinet (the executive branch) would meet in private, pull files from the cabinets (along the right wall) regarding business with Byzantium, or rehearse a meeting with the pope. The wooden benches around the sides (where they sat) are original. The clock on the wall is a backward-running 24-hour clock with Roman numerals and a sword for its single hand.

The **ceiling** is gilded, with paintings by Veronese. These are not frescoes (painting on wet plaster), like those in the Sistine Chapel, but actual canvases painted in Veronese's studio and then placed on the ceiling. A couple are worth pointing out.

The T-shaped painting of the woman admiring the spider web (on the ceiling, opposite the big window) represents the Venetian symbol of ***Discussion***. You can imagine the webs of truth and lies woven in this room by the doge's scheming advisers.

In ***Mars and Neptune with Campanile and Lion*** (the ceiling painting near the entrance), Veronese presents four symbols of the Republic's strength—military, sea trade, city, and government (plus a cherub about to be circumcised by the Campanile).

In the big paintings on the walls (not by Veronese), note that nearly each one features a different doge identified by his oval family crest.
• *Enter the large Senate Hall.*

Senate Hall (Sala del Senato)

As the name implies, this huge hall is where some 120 senators met to pass legislation. While the doge presided from the stage, senators mounted the podium (middle of the wall with windows) to address their colleagues.

Venice prided itself on its self-rule (independent of popes, kings, and tyrants), with most power placed in the hands of these annually elected noble men. Which branch of government really ruled? All of them. It was an elaborate system of checks and balances to make sure no one rocked the gondola, no one got too powerful, and the ship of state sailed smoothly ahead.

Tintoretto's large *Triumph of Venice* on the ceiling (central painting, best viewed from the top) is an allegory of the city in all her glory. Lady Venice is up in heaven with the Greek gods, while barbaric lesser nations swirl up to give her gifts and tribute. Do you get the feeling the Venetians were proud of their city?

On the wall are two large **clocks,** one of which has the signs of the zodiac and phases of the moon. And there's one final oddity in this room, in case you hadn't noticed it yet. In one of the wall paintings (above the entry door), there's actually a doge... not kneeling.

• *Exiting the Senate Hall, pass again through the Room of the Four Doors, then around the corner into a hall with a semicircular carved-wood platform.*

Hall of the Council of Ten (Sala del Consiglio dei Dieci)

The dreaded Council of Ten—10 judges, plus the doge and his six advisers—met here to dole out punishment to traitors, murderers, and "morals" violators.

Venice developed a worldwide reputation for swift, harsh, and secret justice. The Council of Ten had their own force of police officers, guards, spies, informers, and even assassins. They had their own budget and were in practice accountable to no one, at times making them the de facto ruling body of the "Republic." It seemed no one was safe from the spying eye of the "Terrible Ten." You could be accused of crimes anonymously (by a letter dropped into a Mouth of Truth), swept off the streets, tried, judged, and thrown into the dark dungeons in the palace for the rest of your life without so much as a Miranda warning.

It was in this room that the Council decided who lived or died, and who was decapitated, tortured, or merely thrown in jail. The small, hard-to-find **door** leading off the platform (the fifth panel to the right of center) leads directly through secret passages to the prisons and torture chambers.

Overhead, the large central ceiling painting by Veronese (a copy of the original stolen by Napoleon and still in the Louvre)

Judicial Rooms

➊ Secret Door to Prisons
➋ VERONESE – Copy of Jupiter Descending
➌ Stairs up to Armory Museum
➍ Armory Museum (on Mezzanine)
➎ Stairs down to Hall of the Grand Council

(Not to Scale)

ROOM OF THE 4 DOORS
GOLDEN STAIRCASE
HALL OF THE COUNCIL OF 10
SALA DELLA BUSSOLA
BARRIER
Courtyard
ARMORY MUSEUM

shows *Jupiter Descending from Heaven to Strike Down the Vices,* redundantly informing the accused that justice in Venice was swift and harsh. To the left of that, Veronese painted the happy result: Juno showering Lady Venice with coins, crowns, and peace.

Though the dreaded Council of Ten was eventually disbanded, today their descendants enforce the dress code at St. Mark's Basilica.

• *Pass through the next room, turn right, and head up the stairs to the Armory Museum.*

Armory Museum (L'Armeria)

The aesthetic of killing is beyond me, but I must admit I've never seen a better collection of halberds, falchions, ranseurs, targes, morions, and brigandines in my life. The weapons in these three rooms make you realize the important role the military played in keeping the East-West trade lines open.

Room 1: In the glass case on the right, you'll see the suit of armor worn by the great Venetian mercenary general Gattamelata (far right, on horseback), as well as "baby's first armor" (how soon they grow up!). A full suit of armor could weigh 66 pounds. Before gunpowder, crossbows (look up) were made still more lethal by turning a crank on the end to draw the bow with extra force.

Room 2: In the thick of battle, even horses needed helmets. The hefty broadswords were brandished two-handed by the strongest and bravest soldiers who waded into enemy lines. Opposite the window stands the fine armor of

Henry IV, a 16th-century king of France. Behind him is a cell for VIP prisoners.

Room 3: At the far (left) end of the room is a very, very early (17th-century) attempt at a 20-barrel machine gun. On the walls and weapons, the "C-X" insignia means that this was the private stash of the "Council of Ten."

Room 4: In this room, rifles and pistols enter the picture. Don't miss the glass case in the corner, with a tiny crossbow, some torture devices (including an effective-looking thumbscrew), the wooden "devil's box" (a clever item that could fire in four directions at once), and a nasty, two-holed chastity belt. These disheartening "iron breeches" were worn by the devoted wife of the Lord of Padua. Out the windows are fine views of San Giorgio Maggiore. And the window around the corner, to the left, comes with fine views of the Riva.

• *Exit the Armory Museum (after enjoying a closer look at that early machine gun). Go downstairs, turn left, and traverse the long hall with a wood-beam ceiling (and often-interesting exhibits in the side rooms). Now turn right and open your eyes as wide as you can to see the...*

Hall of the Grand Council (Sala del Maggiore Consiglio)

It took a room this size to contain the grandeur of the Most Serene Republic. This huge room (175 by 80 feet) could accommodate up to 2,600 people at one time. The engineering is remarkable. The ceiling is like the deck of a ship—its hull is the rooftop, creating a huge attic above that.

The doge presided from the raised **dais,** while the nobles—the backbone of the empire—filled the center and lined the long walls. Nobles were generally wealthy men over 25, but the title had less to do with money than with long bloodlines. In theory, the doge, the Senate, and the Council of Ten were all subordinate to the Grand Council of nobles who met here to elect them.

On the wall over the doge's throne is Tintoretto's monster-piece, *Paradise,* the largest oil painting in the world. At 570 square feet, it could be sliced up to wallpaper an apartment with enough left over for placemats.

Christ and Mary are at the top of heaven, surrounded by 500 people. It's rush hour in heaven, and all the good Venetians made it. The painting leaves you feeling that you get to heaven not by being a good Christian, but by being a good Venetian. Tintoretto worked

Hall of the Grand Council

Piazzetta

SALA DELLO SCRUTINIO

HALL OF THE GRAND COUNCIL

Courtyard

❶ JACOPO TINTORETTO – Paradise
❷ VERONESE – Apotheosis of Venice
❸ Doge Falier (blacked out)
❹ DOMENICO TINTORETTO – Siege of Constantinople
❺ Battle of Lepanto

From Armory Museum

To Prisons & Bridge of Sighs

Not to Scale

on this in the last years of his long life. On the day it was finished, his daughter died. He got his brush out again and painted her as saint number 501. She's dead center with the blue skirt, hands clasped, getting sucked up to heaven. (At least, that's what an Italian tour guide told me.)

Veronese's *Apotheosis of Venice* (on the ceiling at the Tintoretto end—view it from the top) is a typically unsubtle work showing Lady Venice being crowned a goddess by an angel.

Ringing the top of the hall are portraits, in chronological order, of the first 76 doges. The one at the far end that's blacked out (in the left corner) is the notorious **Doge Marin Falier,** who opposed the will of the Grand Council in 1355. He was tried for treason, beheaded, and airbrushed from history.

Along the entire wall to the right of *Paradise,* a series of paintings called the **Siege of Constantinople** (by Tintoretto's son, Domenico) chronicles Venice's greatest military (if not moral) victory: the conquest of the fellow Christian city of Constantinople during the Fourth Crusade (1204, see sidebar on page 88). Focus on the fifth painting from the left, showing the dramatic climax of the siege. In the background are the mighty walls of Constantinople, which had repelled every attack for nearly a thousand years. But the sneaky Venetians circled around back and attacked where the walls rose straight up from the water's edge. Skillful Venetian oarsmen cozied their galleys right up to the dock, allowing soldiers to scoot along crossbeams attached to the masts and on to the top of the city walls. In the foreground, an archer cranks up his crossbow. The gates are opened, the Byzantine emperor parades out to surrender, and tiny Doge Dandolo (dressed in gold with his fancy doge's hat) says, "Let's go in and steal some bronze horses."

Step into the adjoining **Sala dello Scrutinio.** If the windows are open, there's a fine view of the domes of the basilica, the palace courtyard below, and Paul Newman. Another window overlooks the Piazzetta; from its balcony, a newly elected doge was presented to the people of Venice. A noble would announce, "Here is your doge, if it pleases you." That was fine, until one time when the people weren't pleased. From then on they just said, "Here is your doge."

The room's huge paintings burst with action. The enormous *Battle of Lepanto* depicts the great Venetian empire's last hurrah. The Venetians' sleek ships with skilled oarsmen plowed through the Ottoman navy to victory in 1571.

But Venice had already begun its long slide into historical oblivion. With the rise of new sea-trading powers like Spain and Portugal, Venice's East-West trade monopoly was broken. One by one, the Ottomans gobbled up Venice's trading outposts. Venice remained a glorious city to visit, but not the world power she once was. Finally, in 1797, the French general Napoleon marched into town shouting *"Liberté, égalité, fraternité,"* the Most Serene Republic was conquered, and the last doge was forced to abdicate.

• *Our final stop is the prisons. Consider reading about them here in the Grand Council Hall, where there are more benches and fewer rats.*

To reach the prisons, exit the Hall of the Grand Council by squeezing through the door to the left of Tintoretto's monsterpiece. Follow signs for Prigioni/Ponte dei Sospiri, *passing through several rooms. You'll reach a narrow staircase going down, following signs to the prisons. (It's near Room 31; if you miss it, you'll pass the prisons altogether and end up at the bookshop near the exit.) Then cross the covered Bridge of Sighs over the canal to the prisons.*

Prisons

Musty, humid, and clammy, with heavy stone walls and thick iron bars—these are rooms that wouldn't rate a single star in a Rick Steves book. These were the palace's special dungeons. In the privacy of his own home, a doge could oversee the sentencing, torturing, and jailing of political opponents.

Circle the cells, walking down narrow corridors and glancing into the various cells. Justice here was harsh. The cells consisted of cold stone with heavily barred windows, a wooden plank for a bed, a shelf, and a bucket. (My question: What did they put on the shelf?) You can feel the cold and damp.

In the far corner of the complex, look closely at the window-sills of the cells. There are carvings scratched by prisoners, dating from olden days up until the 1930s.

Surprisingly, these cells were considered the modern "new" prisons. The originals were in the basement of the Doge's Palace, called "the wells" because they were so deep, wet, and cramped. By the 1500s, the notorious wells were so full of political prisoners that these new prisons were built across the canal from the palace and connected with a covered bridge—the Bridge of Sighs.

While a small taste of the prisons is enough for most visitors, if you have more time and interest, explore the cellblocks one and two floors down (following signs for *Complete Tour*). Or stay on this floor, where there's a room of displays, including ceramic shards found in archaeological digs. Adjoining that are more cells, includ-ing one (the farthest) where you can see the bored prisoners' com-pelling and sometimes artistic sketches on the walls. The singing gondoliers outside are a reminder of how tantalizingly close these pitiful prisoners were to one of the world's finest cities.

• *Wherever you roam, you'll end up where you entered. Head back over the bridge that once carried prisoners to their grim fate, and stand in the middle.*

Bridge of Sighs

Gaze through the stonework win-dows at the view of Venice. Ac-cording to romantic legend, crimi-nals were tried and sentenced in the palace, then marched across the canal to the dark prisons. On this bridge, they got one last look at Venice. They gazed out at the sky, the water, and the beautiful buildings, and...sighed.

• *Take one last look at all the tour-ists and the heavenly Church of San Giorgio Maggiore, heave one last sigh, and leave the palace.*

DOGE'S PALACE

CORRER MUSEUM TOUR

Museo Correr

A doge's hat, an empress' bathroom, gleaming statues by Canova, and paintings by the illustrious Bellini family—for some people, that's a major museum, for others a musty bore. But the Correr Museum has one more thing to offer, and that's a quiet refuge—an elegant Neoclassical space—in which to rise above St. Mark's Square when the piazza is too hot, too rainy, or too overrun with tourists. Besides, the museum is included if you've bought a ticket to the Doge's Palace...whether you want it or not. Those who enter are rewarded with an easy-to-manage overview of Venice's art and history.

Because the Correr is more a museum for browsing, use this tour to get you started, then let the collection surprise you.

Orientation

Cost: €25 combo-ticket includes the Doge's Palace, €13 for kids ages 6-14 and students 15-25, family ticket available; also covered by Museum Pass.

Tickets to tour the Clock Tower (see page 36) include admission to the Correr but not the Doge's Palace.

Hours: Daily 10:00-19:00, Nov-March 10:30-17:00.

Getting There: The entrance is on St. Mark's Square in the building at the far end of the square, opposite the basilica. Climb the staircase to the first-floor ticket office and bookstore.

Information: Tel. 041-240-5211, http://correr.visitmuve.it.

Renovation: Like many museums in Venice, the Correr is often under renovation or reorganized for special exhibits, occasionally causing room numbers and locations of pieces to change.

Length of This Tour: Allow one to two hours. With less time, stick to the first floor and skip the second-floor paintings.

Correr Museum—First Floor

To St. Mark's Basilica

To Marciana Nat'l Library

CAMPANILE

NATIONAL ARCHAEO-LOGICAL MUSEUM

Piazza

TOURISTS

San

ARMORY →

Marco

ARSENALE →
THE SEA →
COINS →

GOVERNMENT OFFICES

PIGEONS

CANOVA

ENTRY UP STAIRS FROM PIAZZA SAN MARCO

CAFÉ

LOGGIA 3   NAPOLEONICA 3

ROOM 1

TICKETS

BALLROOM 2

18 | 19
17 | 20
16 | 21
15 | 22

STAIRS TO SECOND FLOOR

14
13 WC
12
11
10
9
8
7
6
5
4
3

IX | VIII
VII
SISI ROOMS   VI
V
IV

I | II | III

Not to Scale

Baggage Check: Free and mandatory for bags bigger than a large purse.

Cuisine Art: The classy museum café offers a peaceful retreat. It has good sandwiches, pastas, and salads, and a few tables have outstanding views of St. Mark's Square (same hours as museum, no museum entry required).

Starring: Canova statues, a royal suite, Venetian historical artifacts, the Bellini family, and a Carpaccio.

The Tour Begins

The Correr Museum is housed in the Napoleonic Wing of the grand edifice that rings St. Mark's Square. The building was started in 1809 by Napoleon, who wanted a private ballroom and reception hall overlooking the square. (On the facade, a line of Roman emperors reminded everyone of his authority.) Napoleon never danced in the ballroom, which was only completed five years after his Waterloo. After Napoleon fell and the Austrian Habsburgs annexed Venice, this palatial wing was their imperial residence. It eventually became a museum, named for the Venetian art collector who donated the collection to the city.

This tour covers the two long, skinny floors that parallel St. Mark's Square: The first floor contains imperial rooms, Canova statues, and Venetian history; the second floor displays Venetian paintings. The collection is often in flux, and delightful temporary exhibitions often take the place of the permanent displays. Be flexible and enjoy things in a general way.

FIRST FLOOR

• *You'll enter the museum through the grand ballroom—Room 2, used for gala events. (If routed a different way, don't worry.) Make your way to a group of nine rooms in the corner.*

Imperial Rooms for Empress Sisi

In 1856, 18-year-old Empress Elizabeth of Austria (fondly nicknamed "Sisi") arrived in Venice with her husband Emperor Franz Josef. The two spent a few weeks in these chandeliered rooms. The famously beautiful-yet-reclusive Sisi was the Princess Diana of the age. Though the Venetians loathed their Austrian overlords, Sisi's charm won many over, and she returned to Venice later for a longer stay. Years later, estranged from her husband and court life, she was murdered by an Italian anarchist while vacationing in Switzerland.

The nine opulent rooms reflect the eclectic tastes of 19th-century aristocrats. You'll stroll through the dining room, with its squiggly-lined "grotesque" decor, and the red-walled throne room, where (in 1838) the Habsburg Emperor Ferdinand was presented with his Italian holdings. Sisi's study has a nice Murano chandelier, and her dressing room (Room VI) has a ceiling painting of the Goddess of Art that's actually Sisi herself. In Sisi's bedroom (VII), the bed (not Sisi's) belonged to Napoleon's stepson, who was declared "Prince of Venice." Finally, you reach the Oval Room, where Sisi and close friends enjoyed their private meals together.

• *The Imperial Rooms lead into a handful of rooms with statues by Canova. Browse here (to the left and right, if crowd flow permits) to see what's currently on display.*

Canova Rooms

Rooms 2-6 are dedicated to the famed Neoclassical sculptor Antonio Canova (1757-1822). Son of a Venetian stonemason, Canova grew up with a chisel in his hand in a studio along the Grand Canal, precociously mastering the sentimental, elegant Rococo style of the late 1700s. At 23, he went to Rome and beyond, studying ancient statues at the recently discovered ruins of Pompeii. These archaeological finds inspired a revival of classical style. Canova's pure, understated "neo"-classical style soon became the rage all over Europe.

Called to Paris, Canova became Napoleon's court sculptor and carved perhaps his best-known work: Napoleon's sister as a semi-nude Venus, reclining on a couch (now in the Borghese Gallery in Rome). Canova combined Rococo sentiment with the cool, minimal lines of classicism.

Look for these major Canova works:

Orpheus and Eurydice (*Orfeo e Euridice*, 1776) shows Orpheus leading his beloved back from hell, when she is suddenly tugged from behind by the cloudy darkness. She calls for help. Orpheus

looks back and smacks his forehead in horror...but he can do nothing to help, and he has to hurry on.

In this youthful work, Canova already shows elements of his later style: high-polished, slender, beautiful figures; an ensemble arrangement, with more than one figure; open space between the figures that's almost as compelling as the figures themselves; and a statue group that's interesting from many angles.

Carved by a teenage Canova, this piece captures the Rococo spirit of Venice in the late 1700s—it's beautiful, but tinged with bittersweet loss. Even Canova's later works—which were more sober, minimalist, and emotionally restrained—retained the grace and romantic sentiment of the last days of the Venetian Republic.

In ***Daedalus and Icarus*** (*Dedalo e Icaro*, 1778-1779), serious Daedalus straps wax-and-feather wings, which he's just crafted, onto his son's shoulders. The boy is thrilled with the new toy, not knowing what we know—that the wax in the wings will soon melt in the sun and plunge him to his death. Daedalus' middle-aged, slightly saggy skin contrasts with Icarus' supple form. Canova displays the tools of his family's stonemason trade on the base.

Canova was only 20 when Venice's procurator commissioned this work from the hometown prodigy. It was so realistic that it caused a stir—skeptics accused Canova of not really sculpting it, but making it from plaster casts of live humans.

The statue of **Paris** (*Paride,* 1807)—looking like a guy with black measles—is not a marble statue of Paris; it's a plaster of Paris, a life-size model that Canova used in carving the real one in stone. The dots are sculptor's "points," which tell the sculptor how far into the block he should chisel to establish the figure's rough outline.

• *Now, enter the world of Venice's doges (Rooms 7-10).*

Government Offices

Some of the rich furnishings are reminders that these rooms once housed the administrative offices of a wealthy, sophisticated, trade-oriented republic. Among the displays (which can change often), you might see pictures of doges and other bigwigs, a doge's cap, rare books in walnut bookcases, and a Murano chandelier under a wood-beamed ceiling.

• *Move to Room 11 to view Venetian coins. The collection runs chronologically, clockwise around the room (starting on the far side of the room in the year 814).*

Coins and the Treasury

The Venetian ducat weighed only a bit more than a US penny, but was mostly gold (by decree, 99 percent pure gold, weighing 3.5 grams). First minted around 1280 (find Giovanni Dandolo's *zecchino,* or "sequin," in the first glass case to the right of the door that leads into the next room), it became the strongest currency in all Europe for nearly 700 years, eventually replacing the Florentine florin. In Renaissance times, 100 ducats would be an excellent salary for a year. The most common design on the ducat coin showed Christ on the "heads" side, standing in an oval of stars. "Tails" featured the current doge kneeling before St. Mark and the inscription "sacred money of Venice" *(SM Veneti).*

Hanging above the newest coins, find **Tintoretto's** *St. Justina and the Treasurers* (1580), showing three red-robed treasury officials who handled ducats in these offices. The richness of their fur-lined robes suggests the almost religious devotion that officials were expected to have as caretakers of the "sacred money" of Venice.

To the left is a painting of a doge: He's throwing his personal money to the crowds, as was expected after a doge's election. With this tradition, Venetians clamored for a wealthy ruler.

• *Advance into Room 12.*

Venice and the Sea

Venice's wealth came from its sea trade. Raw materials from Europe were exchanged for luxury goods from eastern lands controlled by Muslim Ottomans and Byzantine Christians.

Among the displays, you may see various **models of galleys.** These fast oar- and wind-powered warships rode shotgun for Venice's commercial fleets plying the Mediterranean. With up to 150 men (four per oar, some prisoners, most proud professionals) and three horizontal sails, they could cruise from Venice to Constantinople in about a month. In battle, they specialized in turning on a dime to aim cannons, or in quickly building up speed to ram other ships with their formidable prows. Also displayed are large lanterns from a galley's stern.

To see these galleys in action, find two paintings of the ***Battle of Lepanto*** (*Battaglia di Lepanto,* c. 1571). These capture the con-

fusion of a famous battle fought off the coast of Greece in 1571 between the Venetians (part of a coalition of Christians) and the Muslim Ottomans. Sort it out by their flags. The turbaned Ottomans fought under the crescent moon. On the Christian side, Venetians had the winged lion, the pope's troops flew the cross, and Spain was marked with the Habsburg eagle.

The fighting was fierce and hand-to-hand as the combatants boarded each other's ships and cannons blasted away point-blank. Miguel de Cervantes fought in this battle; he lost his hand and had to pen *Don Quixote* one-handed.

Thanks largely to Venice, the Christians won, sinking 113 enemy ships and killing up to 30,000. It was a major psychological victory, as it was a turning point in the Ottoman threat to Europe.

But for Venice, it coincided with the end of an era. Despite the victory, the city—already in decline—lost 4,000 men and many ships, and never fully recovered its trading empire in Ottoman lands. Moreover, Spain's cannon-laden sailing ships proved to be masters of the waves, making Spain the next true naval power.

Venice's shallow-hulled galleys, so swift in the placid Mediterranean, were no match on the high seas.

• *Next up: Room 13.*

The Arsenale

Find the various sketches that depict the city's famed shipbuilding center—the Arsenale, located near the tail of Venice. This rect-

angular, artificial harbor was surrounded by work-shops where ships could be mass-produced as though on a modern assembly line (but it was the workers who moved). If needed, they could crank out a galley a day. The Arsenale's entrance was and still is guarded by two stone lions.

• *Browse the next couple of rooms (14-15), with displays that change often, showing off larger-scale exhibits. Continuing on (Rooms 16-18) you pass through the fascinating **Armory**, filled with everything from swords and pikes to early guns.*

Next, you enter two sections technically considered separate museums but included as if part of the Correr. Walk through six rooms filled with ancient statues (Archaeological Museum) until you reach the corner room and enter the so-called Monumental Rooms of the...

Marciana National Library

This "library" has two rooms: a reading room and a classroom, meant for the sons of the elites and therefore the future rulers of Venice. While the rooms are now empty of furniture, they are still rich in paintings—mostly on the ceilings. These constantly reminded the boys of the importance and value of education and good character.

First you enter the library reading room. There were once rows of desks in the center (the most valuable codices would have been chained to them) and low shelves around the sides where other books were kept. In Renaissance times, Venice was a major center of printing and secular knowledge, and you may see some early manuscripts on display.

On the ceiling are 21 tondi (round paintings). The three tondi in the second row (from the entrance) are by Paolo Veronese. Many of the ceiling paintings illustrate the virtues needed to overcome obstacles on the road to learning: Look for the bare-breasted figure of Lust being driven away by Madam Diligence, who tells the young student to get back to his books. The walls are richly decorated with portraits of famous scholars and ancient philosophers who twist and turn in their niches in a typical Mannerist style.

Study the central painting, *Ecstasy*, where the figure on the right rises above her base desires and contemplates the radiant divine light. Education in Renaissance Venice was quite philosophical. Knowledge freed the individual from being sidetracked by simple and material goals, and revealed loftier truths through intellect. This also brought fame and glory (the trumpet and laurel branch). The high thinking of the philosophers portrayed in this room all applaud that enlightened approach to life.

Classes and lectures were once held in the smaller room beyond the large hall. On the ceiling, a trompe l'oeil effect makes the room appear even higher than it is. The painting in the center, by Titian, shows Lady Wisdom seated in the clouds and holding a scroll as she contemplates her reality in a mirror. Check out the antique globes and a huge, pre-Columbian map of the world. Surveying this room, you really get a sense of how high-minded Venetian culture was in its day.

• *That's it for the first floor. For some, that may be enough. But to round out the museum, there's a fine collection of Venetian paintings upstairs. To get to them, backtrack to Room 14 (WCs nearby) and climb the stairs, following signs to* La Quadreria—Picture Gallery. *Enter Room 25.*

SECOND FLOOR: VENETIAN PAINTING

The collection is laid out chronologically, with thoughtful English descriptions throughout, letting you trace the development of Venetian painting from golden Byzantine icons to Florentine-inspired 3-D to the natural beauty of Bellini and Carpaccio. I've highlighted just a few to look for.

Medieval to Renaissance

Sweep quickly through the first rooms (25-31). Start with the grandfather of Venetian art, Paolo Veneziano. His **Six Saints** (Room 25) dates from about 1350 and has the Venetian focus on decoration and

Correr Museum—Second Floor

BELLINI PAINTINGS → 36 | 34 → MESSINA'S PIETÀ
33 ← BRUEGHEL
— 32
31 → PORTRAIT OF A YOUNG MAN
CARPACCIO → 38
29
Piazza 27 ↑ 28
San 26
Marco 25 → PAOLO VENEZIANO

STAIRS FROM FIRST FLOOR

Not to Scale

warm colors, combining the gold-backed style of Byzantine icons with budding realism and individualized faces. Skipping ahead to Room 29, find two long panels by the **Master of the Jarves Cassoni** (early 15th century) depicting the joyous exploits—feasting, hunting, and sailing—of Europe's aristocrats, dressed in their gold-brocade finery.

In Room 31, Antonio Leonelli da Crevalcore's *Portrait of a Young Man* (c. 1475) shows the subject dressed in red. He is not a saint, king, or pope, but an ordinary citizen painted, literally, wart and all. Behind the young man, the curtain opens to reveal a new world—a spacious 3-D vista courtesy of the Tuscan Renaissance.

• *The large Room 32 often has interesting large-scale exhibits. Now, seek out a few paintings of special interest, starting in Room 33.*

Influences from North and South

The detailed, everyday landscapes of Northern masters strongly influenced Venetian artists. In Pieter Brueghel II's *Adoration of the Magi* (Room 33), Baby Jesus is lost in a snowy scene of the secular working world, in a stable (lower left) worshipped by the Magi. Venetians learned that landscape creates its own mood, and humans don't have to be the center of every painting.

The Sicilian painter Messina wowed Venice with his *Pietà* (Room 34) when he visited in 1475, bringing a Renaissance style and Flemish painting techniques. After a thousand years of standing rigidly on medieval crucifixes, the body of Christ finally softens into a natural human posture. The scene is set in a realistic, distant landscape.

The Bellini Family

One family single-handedly brought Venetian painting into the Renaissance—the Bellinis (Room 36). You may see a *Crucifixion* (c. 1450) by **Jacopo Bellini** (c. 1400-1470), the patriarch of the clan. Jacopo had studied in Florence when Donatello and Brunelleschi were pioneering 3-D naturalism. His daughter **Nicolosia** (though not a painter) married the pioneering artist Mantegna, whose precise lines and statuesque figures influenced his brothers-in-law.

Elder son **Gentile** (c. 1429-1507) took over the family business and established a reputation for documenting Venice's rulers and official ceremonies. With his straightforward style and attention to detail he captured the ordinary essence of a regal man in his *Portrait of Doge Mocenigo.*

Younger son **Giovanni** (c. 1430-1516) became the most famous Bellini, the man who pioneered new techniques and subject matter, trained Titian and Giorgione, and almost single-handedly invented the Venetian High Renaissance. In his *Crucifixion,* he weeds out all the crowded, medieval mourners, leaving only Mary and John. Behind, he paints a spacious (Mantegnesque) landscape, with a lake and mountains in the distance. Our eyes follow the winding road from Christ to the airy horizon, ascending like a soul to heaven.

In his *Dead Christ Supported by Two Angels,* Giovanni explores human anatomy, with exaggerated veins, a heaving diaphragm, and even a hint of pubic hair.

It was Giovanni who would help reinvent the art of painting with the new invention of oil-based paint. Armed with this more transparent paint, artists could add subtler shades of color and rely less on sharply outlined forms.

• *Finish the tour with a stop in Room 38, where you'll find a distinctive Venetian masterpiece by...*

Vittore Carpaccio

In *Two Venetian Gentlewomen* (*Due Dame Veneziane,* c. 1490), the great narrative Venetian painter Carpaccio depicts two well-dressed Venetians looking totally bored, despite being surrounded by a wealth of exotic pets and amusements. One lady absentmindedly plays with a dog, while the other stares into space. Romantics imagined them to be kept ladies awaiting lovers, but the recent

discovery of the once-missing companion painting tells us they're waiting for their menfolk to return from
hunting. If you like Carpaccio, the
Scuola Dalmata di San Giorgio (between St. Mark's Square and Arsenale) has the world's best collection;
see page 47.

The colorful details and love of
luxury are elements that would dominate the Venetian High Renaissance.
Fascinating stuff, but my eyes—like
theirs—are starting to glaze over...

ACCADEMIA TOUR

Galleria dell'Accademia

The Accademia (ack-ah-DAY-mee-ah) is the greatest museum anywhere for Venetian Renaissance art and a good overview of painters whose works you'll see all over town. Venetian art is underrated and, I think, misunderstood. It's nowhere near as famous today as the work of the florescent Florentines, but—with historical slices of Venice, ravishing nudes, and very human Madonnas—it's livelier, more colorful, and simply more fun.

Orientation

Cost: €15, sometimes more during special exhibitions; passes that cover Venice's city-run museums are not valid here.

Hours: Tue-Sun 8:15-19:15, Mon until 14:00, last entry one hour before closing.

Information: Tel. 041-522-2247, www.gallerieaccademia.it.

Avoiding Lines: Just 400 people are allowed into the gallery at one time, so you may have to wait. It's most crowded on Tue mornings and whenever it rains; it's least crowded Wed, Thu, and Sun mornings (before 10:00) and late afternoons (after 17:00). While it's possible to book tickets in advance (€2/ticket surcharge; either book online or call 041-520-0345), it's generally not necessary if you avoid the busiest times.

Renovation: The museum is nearing the end of a major, multiyear expansion and renovation. As a result, rooms close, paintings come and go, and the actual locations of the pieces are hard to pin down. Still, the museum contains sumptuous art—the best in Venice. Be flexible. Use this book's photos to find the art. If you don't see a particular piece, check Room 23 (near the end of our tour), which seems to be a catchall holding pen for displaced art (see page 135).

Getting There: The museum faces the Grand Canal, just over the Accademia Bridge (vaporetto stop: Accademia). It's a 15-minute walk from St. Mark's Square—just follow the signs.

Visitor Information: Some of the Accademia's rooms have information in English. The bookshop sells guidebooks for €14.

Tours: The dull audioguide costs €6.

Length of This Tour: Allow one hour.

Baggage Check: You must use a pay locker for large bags.

Eating: For forgettable food at inflated prices but priceless Grand Canal views, **Bar Foscarini** is right next door (at the base of the Accademia Bridge); for a less expensive, far more characteristic Venetian experience, walk less than five minutes to the delightful **Enoteca Cantine del Vino Già Schiavi** *cicchetti* bar (both described on page 270, along with other options nearby). A cheap café is at the opposite end of the embankment from Bar Foscarini, and a handful of cafés line Calle Nuova Sant'Agnese, which connects this area to the Peggy Guggenheim Collection.

Nearby: While you're in the Accademia neighborhood, consider visiting the Ca' Rezzonico, Peggy Guggenheim Collection, historic La Salute Church, and Punta della Dogana contemporary art museum (see page 40).

Starring: Titian, Veronese, Giorgione, Bellini, and Tintoretto.

The Tour Begins

VENICE: SWIMMING IN LUXURY

The Venetian love of luxury shines through in Venetian painting. We'll see grand canvases of colorful, spacious settings peopled with happy locals in extravagant clothes having a great time. The museum proceeds chronologically from the Middle Ages to the 1700s. But before we start at the medieval beginning, let's sneak a peek at a typically colorful work by the greatest Venetian Renaissance master, Titian.

• *Buy your ticket, check your bag, and head upstairs to a large hall filled with gold-leaf altarpieces. At the top of the stairs, turn left and enter the small Room 24.*

❶ Titian, *Presentation of the Virgin (Presentazione della Vergine),* 1534-1538

A colorful crowd gathers at the foot of a stone staircase. A dog eats a bagel, a mother handles a squirming baby, an old lady sells eggs, and onlookers lean out the windows. Suddenly the crowd turns and points at something. Your eye follows up the stairs to a larger-than-life high priest in a jeweled robe.

But wait! What's that along the way? In a pale blue dress that

ACCADEMIA

Accademia

- HIGH RENAISSANCE
- ROOM 11
- ⑩
- ROOM 10
- ⑨
- ⑧
- To Zattere
- To Eateries & Zattere
- Camp. Calbo
- RIO TERÀ ANTONIO FOSCARINI
- Not to Scale
- Courtyard
- ROOM 12
- ROOM 13
- ROOM 9
- ROOM 6
- ROOM 8
- ROOM 7
- ROOM 5 ⑦
- ROOM 2
- ROOM 14
- ELEGANT DECAY
- ROOM 4
- EARLY REN.
- ROOM 3
- ⑥ ⑤
- ④
- RIO TERÀ DE LA CARITÀ
- ROOM 16
- ROOM 15
- ROOM 17
- ⑪
- ROOM 20
- ⑫
- ROOM 19
- ROOM 21 "CARPACCIO ROOM"
- Courtyard
- ③
- MEDIEVAL ROOM 1
- To Cafés, Peggy Guggenheim Collection & La Salute
- WC
- ROOM 18
- ROOM 22
- ROOM 24
- ① ②
- STAIRS
- ROOM 23 "DISPLAYED HIGHLIGHTS"
- ⑬
- ENTRANCE (BELOW)
- CAFE
- To Frari & Ca' Rezzonico
- PIZZA
- WC
- Campo de la Carità
- To San Marco & Rialto
- ACCADEMIA BRIDGE
- Accademia
- Grand Canal

① TITIAN – Presentation of the Virgin

② VENEZIANO – Madonna and Child with Two Donors

③ JACOBELLO – Coronation of the Virgin in Paradise

④ GIOVANNI BELLINI – Enthroned Madonna with Child

⑤ MANTEGNA – St. George

⑥ GIO. BELLINI – Madonna and Child between St. Catherine and Mary Magdalene

⑦ GIORGIONE – The Tempest

⑧ VERONESE – Feast in the House of Levi

⑨ TITIAN – Pietà

⑩ TINTORETTO – The Removal of St. Mark's Body

⑪ GENTILE BELLINI – Procession in St. Mark's Square

⑫ CARPACCIO – The Legend of Saint Ursula

⑬ Displaced Highlights & Temporary Exhibitions

ACCADEMIA

sets her apart from all the other colored robes, dwarfed by the enormous staircase and columns, the tiny, shiny figure of the child Mary almost floats up to the astonished priest. She's unnaturally small, easily overlooked at first glance. When we finally notice her, we realize all the more how delicate she is amid the bustling crowd, hard stone, and epic grandeur. Venetians love this painting and call it, appropriately enough, the "Little Mary."

The painting is a parade of colors. Titian leads your eyes from the massive buildings to the deep blue sky and mountains in the background to the bright red robe of the man in the crowd to glowing Little Mary. Titian painted the work especially for this room, fitting it neatly around the door on the right. The door on the left was added later, cutting into Titian's masterpiece.

This work is typical of Venetian Renaissance art. Here and throughout this museum, you will find: 1) bright, rich color; 2) big canvases; 3) Renaissance architectural backgrounds; 4) slice-of-life scenes of Venice; and 5) 3-D realism. It's a religious scene, yes, but it's really just an excuse to display secular splendor—Renaissance architecture, colorful robes, and human details.

Now that we've gotten a taste of Renaissance Venice at its peak, let's backtrack and see art by some of Titian's predecessors.

• *Return to Room 1, stopping at a painting (near the stairs) of Mary and Baby Jesus.*

MEDIEVAL ART
❷ Paolo Veneziano, *Madonna and Child with Two Donors (Madonna col Bambino e Due Committenti)*, c. 1325

Mary sits in heaven. The child Jesus is a baby in a bubble, a symbol of his "aura" of holiness.

Notice how two-dimensional and unrealistic this painting is. The sizes of the figures reflect their religious importance—Mary is huge, being the mother of Christ as well as the "Holy Mother Church." Jesus is next in size, then the two angels who crown Mary. Finally, in the corner, are two mere mortals kneeling

ACCADEMIA

in devotion. The golden halos let us know who's holy and who's not. Medieval Venetian artists, with their close ties to the East, borrowed techniques such as gold-leafing, frontal poses, and "iconic" faces from the religious icons of Constantinople (modern-day Istanbul).

Most of the paintings in Room 1 are altarpieces like this one, intended to sit in a church for the faithful to meditate on during services. Many feature the Virgin Mary being crowned in triumph. Very impressive. But it took Renaissance artists to remove Mary from her golden never-never land, clothe her in human flesh, and bring her down to the real world we inhabit.

• *Farther along in Room 1 (perhaps in the far left corner), you'll find...*

❸ Jacobello del Fiore, *Coronation of the Virgin in Paradise (Incoronazione della Vergine in Paradiso),* 1438

This swarming beehive of saints and angels is an attempt to cram as much religious information as possible into one space. The architectural setting is a clumsy try at three-dimensionality (the railings of the wedding-cake structure are literally glued on). The color-coordinated saints are simply stacked one on top of the other, rather than receding into the distance as they would in real life.

• *Enter Room 2 at the far end of this hall.*

EARLY RENAISSANCE (1450-1500)

Only a few decades later, artists rediscovered the natural world and ways to capture it on canvas. With this Renaissance, or "rebirth," of the arts and attitudes of ancient Greece and Rome, painters took a giant leap forward. They weeded out the jumble of symbols, fleshed out cardboard characters into real people, and placed them in spacious 3-D settings.

❹ Giovanni Bellini, *Enthroned Madonna with Child, Sacra Conversazione,* a.k.a. *San Giobbe Altarpiece,* c. 1480

Mary and the Baby Jesus meet with saints beneath an arched half-dome, engaging in a sacred conversation *(Sacra Conversazione).* A trio of musician angels jams at her feet. In its original church setting, the painting's pillars and arches matched the real ones around it, as though Bellini had blown a hole in the wall and built another chapel, allowing us mortals to mingle with the saints.

Giovanni Bellini (bell-EE-nee) takes only a few figures, places them in this spacious architectural setting, and balances them, half on one side of Mary and half on the other. Left to right, you'll find St. Francis (medieval founder of an order of friars), John the Baptist, Job, St. Dominic (founder of another order of monks), St. Sebastian, and St. Louis.

The painting has a series of descending arches. At the top is a Roman arch. Hanging below that is a triangular canopy. Then comes a pyramid-shaped "arch" formed by the figures themselves, with Mary's head at the peak, echoed below by the pose of the three musicians. Subconsciously, this creates a mood of serenity, order, and balance, not the hubbub of the *Coronation.* Look at St. Sebastian—even arrows can't disturb his serenity.

In Bellini's long career, he painted many altarpieces in the *Sacra Conversazione* formula: The Virgin and Child surrounded by saints "conversing" informally about holy matters while listening to some tunes. The formula, developed in the 1430s and 1440s by Fra Angelico (1400-1455) and other Florentine artists, became a common Renaissance theme. Compare this painting with other *sacras* by Bellini in the Frari Church (see page 141) and the Church of San Zaccaria (see page 234).

• *Climb the small staircase, pass through Room 3 into the small Room 4, and find a small painting...*

❺ Andrea Mantegna, *St. George (San Giorgio)*, c. 1460

This Christian dragon slayer is essentially a Greek nude sculpture with armor painted on. He rests his weight on one leg in the same asymmetrical pose *(contrapposto)* as a classical sculpture, Michelangelo's *David,* or an Italian guy on the street corner. The doorway he stands in resembles a niche designed for a classical statue.

Mantegna (mahn-TAYN-yah) was trained in the Tuscan tradition, in which painters were like sculptors, "carving" out figures (like this) with sharp outlines, filling them in with color, and setting them in distant backdrops like the winding road behind George. When Mantegna married Giovanni Bellini's sister, he brought Florentine realism and draftsmanship to his in-laws.

St. George radiates Renaissance optimism—he's alert but relaxed, at rest but ready to spring into action, humble but confident. With the broken lance in his hand and the dragon at his feet, George is the strong Renaissance Man slaying the medieval dragon of superstition and oppression.

• *Nearby, find three women and a baby on a black background.*

❻ Giovanni Bellini, *Madonna and Child between St. Catherine and Mary Magdalene (Madonna col Bambino tra Sta. Caterina e Maria Maddalena),* c. 1490

In contrast to Mantegna's sharp-focus 3-D, this painting features three female heads on a flat plane with a black-velvet backdrop.

Their features are soft, hazy, and atmospheric, glowing out of the darkness as though lit by soft candlelight. It's not the sculptural line that's important here, but color—warm, golden, glowing flesh tones. The faces emerge from the canvas like cameos.

Bellini painted dozens of Madonna and Childs in his day. (Others are nearby.) This Virgin Mary is pretty, but she's upstaged by the sheer idealized beauty of Mary Magdalene (on the right). Mary Magdalene's hair is down, like the prostitute that legend says she was, yet she has a childlike face, thoughtful and repentant. This is the perfect image of the innocent woman who sinned by loving too much.

Bellini was the teacher of two more Venetian greats, Titian and Giorgione, schooling them in the new medium of oil painting. Mantegna painted *St. George* using tempera paint (pigments dissolved in egg yolk), while Bellini pioneered oils (pigments in vegetable oil)—a more versatile medium. Applying layer upon transparent layer, Bellini painted creamy complexions with soft outlines, bathed in an even light. His gift to the Venetian Renaissance was the "haze" he put over his scenes, giving them an idealized, glowing, serene, and much-copied atmosphere. (You can see more of Bellini's work at the Correr Museum, Frari Church, and the Church of San Zaccaria.)

• *In Room 5, find a well-known work...*

❼ Giorgione, *The Tempest (La Tempesta),* c. 1505

It's the calm before the storm. The atmosphere is heavy—luminous but ominous. There's a sense of mystery. Why is the woman nursing her baby in the middle of the countryside? And the soldier—is he ogling her or protecting her? Will lightning strike? Do they know that the serenity of this beautiful landscape is about to be shattered by an approaching storm?

The mystery is heightened by contrasting elements. The armed soldier contrasts with the naked mother and her baby. The austere, ruined columns contrast with the lusciousness of Nature. And, most important, the stillness of the foreground scene is in direct opposition to the threatening storm in the background. The landscape itself is the main subject, creating a mood, regardless of what the painting is "about."

Giorgione (jor-JONE-ay) was as mysterious as his few paintings, yet he left a lasting impression. A student of Bellini, he learned to use haziness to create a melancholy mood of beauty. But nothing beautiful lasts—flowers fade, Mary Magdalenes grow old, and Giorgione died at 33. In *The Tempest*, the fleeting stillness is about to be shattered by the slash of lightning, the true center of the composition.

• *Browse through several rooms, eventually climbing five steps into the large Room 10 to see three epic Venetian Renaissance canvases.*

VENETIAN HIGH RENAISSANCE (1500-1600)
❽ Paolo Veronese, *Feast in the House of Levi* (*Convito in Casa di Levi*), 1573

Parrrrty!! Stand about 10 yards away from this enormous canvas, to where it just fills your field of vision...and hey, you're invited. Venice loves the good life, and the celebration is in full swing. You're in a huge room with a great view of Venice. Everyone's dressed to kill in colorful silk and velvet robes. Conversation roars, and the servants bring on the food and drink.

This captures the Venetian attitude (more love, less attitude) as well as the style of Venetian Renaissance painting. Remember:

1) bright colors, 2) big canvases, 3) Renaissance architectural settings, 4) scenes of Venetian life, and 5) 3-D realism. Painters had mastered realism and now gloried in it.

The *Feast in the House of Levi* is, believe it or not, a religious work painted for a convent. The original title was *The Last Supper*. In the center of all the wild goings-on, there's Jesus, flanked by his disciples, sharing a final meal before his Crucifixion.

This festive feast captures the optimistic spirit of Renaissance Venice. Life was a good thing and beauty was to be enjoyed. Renaissance men and women saw the divine in the beauties of Nature and glorified God by glorifying man.

Uh-uh, said the Church. In its eyes, the new humanism was the same as the old hedonism. The false spring of the Renaissance froze quickly after the Reformation, when half of Europe left the Catholic Church and became Protestant, and the Catholic Church countered with the Counter-Reformation.

Veronese (vayr-oh-NAY-zay) was hauled before the Inquisition, the Church tribunal that punished heretics. What did he mean by painting such a bawdy Last Supper? With dwarf jesters? And apostles picking their teeth (between the columns, left of center)? And dogs and cats? And a black man, God forbid? And worst of all, some German soldiers—maybe even Protestants!—at the far right?

Veronese argued that it was just artistic license, so they asked to see his—it had expired. But the solution was simple. Rather than change the painting, just fine-tune the title. *Sì, no problema.* Veronese got out his brush, and *The Last Supper* became the *Feast in the House of Levi*, written in Latin on the railing to the left: *"FECIT D. COVI. MAGNV. LEVI"*.

❾ Titian, *Pietà,* c. 1573

Jesus has just been executed, and his followers grieve over his body before burying it. Titian painted this to hang over his own tomb.

Titian was the most famous painter of his day—perhaps even more famous than Michelangelo. He excelled in every subject: portraits of dukes, kings, and popes; racy nudes for their bedrooms; solemn altarpieces for churches; and pagan scenes from Greek mythology. He was cultured and witty, a fine musician and businessman—an all-around Renaissance kind of guy.

Titian was old when he painted this. He had seen the rise and decline of the Renaissance and had experienced much sadness in his own life. Unlike Titian's colorful and exuberant "Little

Mary," done at the height of the Renaissance, this canvas is dark, the mood more somber.

The dead Christ is framed by a Renaissance arch like the one in Bellini's *Enthroned Madonna*, but here the massive stones overpower the figures, making them look puny and helpless. The lion statues are downright scary. Instead of the clear realism of Renaissance paintings, Titian uses rough, messy brushstrokes, a technique that would be picked up by the Impressionists three centuries later. Titian adds a dramatic compositional element—starting with the lion at lower right, a line of motion sweeps up diagonally along the figures, culminating in the grief-stricken Mary Magdalene, who turns away, flinging her arm and howling out loud.

The kneeling figure of an old, bald man is a self-portrait of the aging Titian, tending to the corpse of Jesus, who symbolizes the once powerful, now dead Renaissance Man. In the lower right, a painting-within-the-painting shows Titian and his son kneeling, asking the Virgin to spare them from the plague of 1576. Unfortunately, Titian's son eventually died of the plague.

❿ Tintoretto, *The Removal of St. Mark's Body* *(Trafugamento del Corpo di San Marco)*, 1562-1566

The event that put Venice on the map is frozen at its most dramatic moment. Muslim fundamentalists in Alexandria are about

to burn St. Mark's body (there's the smoke from the fire in the center), when suddenly a hurricane appears miraculously, sending them running for cover. (See the wisps of baby-angel faces in the storm, blowing on the infidels? Look hard, on the left-hand side.) Meanwhile, Venetian merchants whisk away the body.

Tintoretto makes us part of the action. The square tiles in the courtyard run straight away from us, an extension of our reality, as though we could step right into the scene—or the merchants could carry Mark into ours.

Tintoretto would have made a great black-velvet painter. His colors burn with a metallic sheen, and he does everything possible to make his subject popular with common people.

In fact, Tintoretto was a common man himself, self-taught, who apprenticed only briefly with Titian before striking out on his own. He sold paintings in the marketplace in his youth and insisted on living in the poor part of town, even after he became famous.

Tintorettos abound here, in the next room, and throughout Venice. Look for these characteristics, some of which became stan-

ACCADEMIA

dard features of the Mannerist and Baroque art that followed the Renaissance: 1) heightened drama, violent scenes, strong emotions; 2) elongated bodies in twisting poses; 3) strong contrasts between dark and light; 4) bright colors; and 5) diagonal compositions.

(Tintoretto fans will want to see his "Sistine Chapel"; 📖 see the Scuola San Rocco Tour chapter.)

• *Spend some time in this room, the peak of the Venetian Renaissance and the climax of the museum. From here on, there are three must-visit spots: Room 20 (Gentile Bellini), Room 21 (Vittore Carpaccio), and Room 23 (displaced highlights). Find each room with the help of your map. Start in Room 20, with...*

⓫ Gentile Bellini, *Procession in St. Mark's Square (Processione in Piazza San Marco)*, 1496

Here's a chance to look back at Venice in its heyday. Painted by Giovanni's big brother, this wide-angle view—more than any human eye could take in at once—reminds us how little Venice has changed over the centuries. There is St. Mark's: gleaming gold with mosaics, the four bronze horses, the three flagpoles out front, the old Campanile on the right, and the Doge's Palace. There's the guy selling 10 postcards for a euro. (But there's no Clock Tower with the two bronze Moors yet, the pavement's different, the church is covered with gold, and there are no café orchestras playing "New York, New York.") Every detail is in perfect focus, regardless of its distance from us, and presented for our inspection.

Take some time to linger over this and the other views of old Venice in this room. Opposite the big procession is a painting by Carpaccio showing a slice of Venetian life circa 1500: the old wooden drawbridge version of the Rialto, nobles in private gondolas with their fancy-pants gondoliers, elegant faces of city folk, pent-up promiscuity awaiting carnival. Notice it's a man's world. (According to an old Venetian rhyme, "A woman is to be silent, good looking, and stay at home with children.")

• *From here, walk left through Room 19 and into Room 21.*

⓬ Vittore Carpaccio, *The Legend of Saint Ursula*, c. 1490

This ensemble of nine paintings tells the story of Ursula, patron saint of girls needing to get married (and needing a dowry). Working clockwise around the room you follow her odyssey.

The first scene sets things up: She wants to escape marriage to a non-Christian. Her father, the king, sends her and her suitor from Brittany to Rome to see the pope in hopes that the young man will convert. (Notice how the artist had no idea what Brittany looked like.) Then the story ramps up: Somehow she meets Attila and his Huns, she and her 11,000 ladies in waiting are massacred, and it all ends with her funeral and ascension. While the scenes are hard to follow, they nicely show off Venice's architecture, ships, and textiles. Carpaccio gives us a trip back in time—a fantasy chance to visit Venice 500 years ago.

• *Finally, visit the largest room in the museum, Room 23.*

⓭ Displaced Highlights and Temporary Exhibitions (Room 23)

This giant hall is the upper half of an old Gothic church. The nave was divided under Napoleon's rule, and this became the fine arts academy—the Accademia. It's now home to fine temporary exhibitions, and where art displaced by the gallery's ongoing renovation often ends up. If you missed any of the works described up until now, you may be able to track them down here.

• *You've seen the highlights of the Accademia, which means you've seen the highlights of the Venetian Renaissance. Now you're free to get back out into the amazing city that inspired all this beauty.*

FRARI CHURCH TOUR

Basilica di Santa Maria Gloriosa dei Frari

For me, this church offers the best art-appreciation experience in Venice, because so much of its great art is in situ—right where it was designed to be seen, rather than hanging in museums. Because Venice's spongy ground could never support a real stone Gothic church (such as those you'd find in France), the Frari is made of light and flexible brick. As with Venetian architecture in general, the white limestone foundation insulates the building from the wet soil.

The church was built by the Franciscan order, which arrived in Venice around 1230 (the present building was consecrated in 1492).

Franciscan men and women were inspired by St. Francis of Assisi (c. 1182-1226), who dedicated himself to a nonmaterialistic lifestyle—part of a reform movement that spread across Europe in the early 1200s. The Roman Church felt distant and corrupt, and there was a hunger for religious teaching that connected with everyday people. While some of these movements were dubbed heretical (like that of the Cathars in southern France), the Franciscans (and Dominicans) eventually earned the Church's blessing.

Many great Venetians chose to be buried in this church, and we'll see their impressive tombs. Its high-quality altarpieces make the church a kind of mini museum of sacred art.

The spirit of St. Francis of Assisi warms both the church of his "brothers" *(frari)* and the art that decorates it. The Franciscan love of all of creation—Nature and Man—later inspired Renaissance painters to capture the beauty of the physical world and human emotions, showing worshippers the glory of God in human terms.

Orientation

Cost: €3.

Hours: Mon-Sat 9:00-18:00, Sun from 13:00.

Information: Tel. 041-272-8611, www.basilicadeifrari.it.

Dress Code: Modest dress is recommended.

Getting There: It's on Campo dei Frari, near the San Tomà vaporetto and *traghetto* stops. From the dock, follow signs to *Scuola Grande di San Rocco.* For a pleasant stroll from the Rialto Bridge, take the 📖 Rialto to Frari Church Walk.

Tours: You can rent an **audioguide** for €2.

🎧 Download my free Frari Church **audio tour.**

Length of This Tour: Allow one hour. Don't miss Titian's *Assumption,* Donatello's statue, or Bellini's altarpiece.

Eating: The church square is ringed with small, simple, reasonably priced cafés. The Bottega del Caffè Dersut (around to the left, facing the side of the church, inside seating only) serves salads and fresh sandwiches.

Nearby: For efficient sightseeing, combine your visit with the Scuola San Rocco, located behind the Frari Church. The Ca' Rezzonico is a seven-minute walk away, following signs to *Accademia.*

Starring: Titian, Giovanni Bellini, Paolo Veneziano, and Donatello.

The Tour Begins

• *Enter the church, let your eyes adjust, and stand just inside the door with a good view down the long nave toward the altar.*

❶ Church Interior and Choir, 1250-1443

The simple, spacious (110-yard-long), well-lit Gothic church—with rough wood crossbeams and a red-and-white color scheme—is truly a remarkable sight in a city otherwise crammed with exotic froufrou. Traditionally, churches in Venice were cross-shaped, but because the Franciscans were an international order, they weren't limited to Venetian tastes. This new T-shaped footprint featured a long, lofty nave—flooded with light and suited to large gatherings—where common people heard sermons. The T, or tau, is the symbol of the Franciscan order. St. Francis chose the tau as his personal symbol, wearing it on his clothes and using it in place of his signature.

The carved-marble choir area in the center of the nave allowed

Frari Church

To Scuola
San Rocco

Not to Scale

To
Accademia

Campo
San Rocco

② ALTAR

③ **④**

⑥

S
A
C
R
I
S
T
Y

TRANSEPT

⑤ CHAPTER
HOUSE

CHOIR

⑦

⑧

N
A
V
E

⑨

⑩

Campo
dei
Frari

To
Rialto

①

! TOUR BEGINS TICKETS

ENTRY

① View of Church Interior
& Choir

② TITIAN – Assumption
of the Virgin

③ Tomb of Doge Foscari

④ DONATELLO – Statue of
John the Baptist

⑤ VENEZIANO – Madonna
and Child with Doge
Francesco Dandolo

⑥ GIO. BELLINI – Madonna
and Child with Saints
and Angels

⑦ TITIAN – Madonna of
Ca' Pesaro

⑧ Longhena's Tomb of Pesaro

⑨ Canova Monument

⑩ Tomb of Titian

FRARI CHURCH

friars to hold smaller, more intimate services. As worshippers entered the church and looked down the long nave to the altar, they were greeted by Titian's glorious painted altarpiece—then, as now, framed by the arch of the choir entrance. When Titian was chosen to paint the altarpiece, he surely had this perspective in mind.

• *Note that Titian is buried here (to the right)—we'll return to his tomb later. For now, walk prayerfully toward Titian's heavenly Virgin, passing through the gorgeously carved wooden stalls of the 1480s* **choir.** *Notice the fine inlay above the chairs, showing the Renaissance enthusiasm for Florentine-style depth and perspective. Surviving choirs such as this are rare. (In response to Luther's challenge, Counter-Reformation churches did away with choirs and altar screens in order to get priests closer to their flocks.)*

❷ Titian, *Assumption of the Virgin,* 1516-1518

Glowing red and gold like a stained-glass window, this altarpiece sets the tone of exuberant beauty found in this church. At the end of her life (though looking 17 here), Mary was miraculously "assumed" into heaven. As cherubs lift her up to meet a Jupiter-like

God, the stunned apostles on earth reach up to touch the floating bubble of light.

Look around. The church is littered with chapels and tombs "made possible by the generous financial support" of rich people who donated to the Franciscans for the good of their souls (and usually for tomb-topping statues of themselves, as well). But the Franciscans didn't sell their main altar; instead they hired the new whiz artist, Titian, to create a dramatic altar painting.

Unveiled in 1518, the work scandalized a Venice accustomed to simpler, more contemplative church art. The rich colors, twisting poses, and mix of saccharine angels with blue-collar apostles were unheard of. Most striking, this Virgin is fully human—a real woman in the golden glow of heaven, not a stiff icon on a throne. The Franciscans thought this woman aroused excitement rather than spirituality. They agreed to pay Titian only after the Holy Roman Emperor offered to buy the altar if they refused.

In a burst of youthful innovation, Titian (c. 1490-1576) had rewritten the formula for church art, hinting at changes to come with the Mannerist and Baroque styles. He energized the scene with a complex composition, overlapping a circle (Mary's bubble) and a triangle (draw a line from the apostle reaching up to Mary's face and down the other side) on three horizontal levels (God in heaven, Man on earth, Mary in between). Together, these elements draw our eyes from the swirl of arms and legs to the painting's focus—the radiant face of a triumphant Mary, "assumed body and soul into heaven."

• *Flanking the painting are marble tombs lining the walls. On the wall to the right of the altar is the...*

❸ Tomb of Doge Foscari, 15th Century

This heavy, ornate tomb honors the great Venetian who ruled Venice at the peak of its power. Doge Francesco Foscari (1373-1457) assumed control of the city's powerful seafaring empire and then tried to expand it onto the mainland. Unfortunately, he ended up battling Milan in a 31-year war of attrition that swept through northern Italy. Meanwhile, on the unprotected eastern front, the Ottomans took Constantinople (1453) and scuttled Venice's trade. Venice's long slide into historical oblivion had begun. Financially drained city fathers forced Foscari to resign, turn in his funny hat, and hand over the keys to the Doge's Palace.

• *In the first chapel to the right of the altar, you'll find...*

❹ Donatello, *Statue of John the Baptist,* 1438

In the center of the altarpiece, the cockeyed prophet of the desert—emaciated from his breakfast of bugs 'n' honey and dressed in animal skins—freezes midrant when he spies something in the distance. His jaw goes slack, he twists his face and raises his hand to announce the coming of...the Renaissance.

Florentine expatriates in Venice considered the Frari their home church. They commissioned the Florentine Donatello to make this wooden statue in a style reminiscent of home. The Renaissance began in Florence, where Donatello (1386-1466) created realistic statues with a full range of human emotions. This warts-and-all John the Baptist contrasts greatly with, say, Titian's sweet Mary. Florentine art (including painting) was sculptural, strongly outlined, and harshly realistic, with muted colors. Venetian art was painterly, soft focus, and beautiful, with bright colors. Notice how the statues flanking John (sculpted at about the same time but by lesser artists) are clearly behind Donatello's work in realism.

• *Enter the sacristy through the door at the far end of the right transept. You'll bump into an elaborate altar crammed with* **reliquaries.** *The most treasured relic is in the center—a vial supposedly containing a drop of Christ's blood. With that religious mindset, let's see some great Venetian altarpieces, starting with one that helped start it all. Facing the relic, enter the room to the right.*

❺ Paolo Veneziano, *Madonna and Child with Doge Francesco Dandolo,* c. 1339

Paolo Veneziano (literally, "Paul the Venetian") was the first "name" artist in Venice, the man who helped shape the distinctive painting style of his city. In turn, Veneziano was inspired by Byzantine artists who had come to Venice in search of greater freedom of expression. They had chafed under strict societies (Byzantine and, in some locales, Islamic) that frowned on painting figurative images. In Venice, these expats found an eager community of rich patrons who indulged their love of deeper color, sentiment, movement, and decoration. (Venice clung to this style for so long that its art eventually lagged behind the rest of Western Europe.)

In this altarpiece, Veneziano paints Byzantine icons and sets them in motion. Baby Jesus turns to greet a kneeling Doge Dandolo, while rosy-cheeked Mary turns to acknowledge the doge's wife. None other than St. Francis presents "Francis" (Francesco) Dandolo to the Madonna. Both he and St. Elizabeth (on the right) bend at the waist and gesture as naturally as 14th-century icons can.

Notice the color. Venetians were enthusiastic about color. With the thriving glass industry, Venetian painters had access to more and better pigments than their rivals from other towns. Veneziano's painting, like others we'll see, has the city's emblematic colors—blue, gold, and red.

• *This room also has a* **clock** *intricately carved from a single piece of wood. Now return to the relics room and the glowing altarpiece at the end of the room.*

⊙ Giovanni Bellini, *Madonna and Child with Saints and Angels,* 1488

This masterpiece, by Giovanni Bellini, and the delightful chapel it stands in were funded by the Pesaro family, who negotiated an acceptable price for their family tomb. (More on them as we go.)

Mary sits on a throne under a half-dome, propping up Baby Jesus (who's just learning to stand), flanked by saints and serenaded by musician angels. Bellini (c. 1430-1516), the father of the Venetian Renaissance, had learned the budding realism of Veneziano, but he took it to another level. He painted fake columns and a dome to match the real ones in the gold frame, making the painting seem to be an extension of the room. He completes the illusion with glimpses of open sky in the background. Next, he fills the artificial niches with symmetrically posed, thoughtful saints—left to right, find Saints Nicholas, Peter, Mark, and Sean Connery (Benedict).

Bellini combined the meditative poses of the Venetian Byzantine tradition with Renaissance improvements in modern art. He helped pioneer the transition from painting with medieval tempera (egg yolk-based) to painting in oil (pigments dissolved in vegetable oil). Oils allowed a subtler treatment of colors because artists could apply them in successive layers. And because darker colors aren't so muddy when painted in oil, they "pop"—effectively giving the artist a brighter palette.

Bellini virtually invented the formula (later to be broken by his precocious pupil, Titian) for Venetian altarpieces. Instead of just standing around, his saints seem to interact in a holy conversation *(Sacra Conversazione).*

Renaissance humanism demanded Madonnas and saints that were accessible and human. Bellini delivers, but places them in a physical setting so beautiful that it creates its own mood of serene holiness. The scene is lit from the left, but nothing casts a harsh shadow—Mary and the babe are enveloped in a glowing aura of reflected light from the golden dome. The beauty is in the details— the writing in the dome, the red brocade backdrop, the swirls in the marble steps, and the angels' dimpled legs.

• *To see the next great altarpiece, return to the nave and head left, toward the door you entered through. Just past the choir, look right and find Titian's colorful painting on the wall.*

❼ Titian, *Madonna of Ca' Pesaro,* 1519-1526

Titian's second altarpiece for the Frari Church displays all that he'd learned from his forebears. Like his teacher Bellini, he puts Mary (seated) and baby (standing) on a throne, sur-rounded by saints having a holy conversation. Also like Bellini, he paints fake columns that echo the church's real ones.

But wait. Mary is off-center, Titian's ide-alized saints mingle with Venetians sporting five o'clock shadows, and the stairs run diago-nally away from us. Mary sits not on a throne but on a pedestal. Baby Jesus is restless. The precious keys of St. Peter seem to dangle un-noticed. These things upset traditional Renais-sance symmetry, but they turn a group of figures into a true scene. St. Peter (center, in blue and gold, with book) looks down at Jacopo Pesaro, who kneels to thank the Virgin for his recent naval victory over the Ottomans (1502). A flag-carrying lieutenant drags in a turbaned captive. Meanwhile, St. Francis talks to Baby Jesus while gesturing down to more members of the Pesaro family. The little guy looking out at us (lower right) is the Pesaro descendant who administered the trust fund to keep prayers coming for his dead uncle.

Titian combines opposites: a soft-focus Madonna with photo-realistic portraits, chubby winged angels with a Muslim prisoner, and a Christian cross with a battle flag. In keeping with the spirit of St. Francis' humanism, Titian lets mere mortals mingle with saints. And we're right there with them.

• *Let's see some tombs, starting with one made for another Pesaro ancestor. It's the hard-to-miss monument with black statues wearing ragged white clothes.*

❽ Longhena's Tomb of Pesaro

This eye-catching wall of stone was built for the next generation of wealthy Pesaro family members, and honors the only one to become a doge. It's the work of Baldassare Longhena, the same man who designed the over-the-top La Salute church. As the Renaissance world moved into the Baroque, the style became more busy, exuberant, and awe-inspiring. Longhena's (politically incorrect) black statues represent African prisoners who seem to support the upper story on their brawny shoulders (cushioned by pillows), where Doge Pesaro oversees it all.

• *Contrast Longhena's emotional Baroque tomb from the 1600s with the calmer Neoclassical lines of the 1700s in the next tomb over, the pyramid-shaped...*

❾ Canova Monument, 1827

Antonio Canova (1757-1822, see his portrait above the door) was Venice's greatest sculptor. He created gleaming white, highly polished statues of beautiful Greek gods and goddesses in the Neoclassical style. (See several of his works at the Correr Museum.)

The pyramid shape is timeless, suggesting pharaohs' tombs and the Christian Trinity. Mourners, bent over with grief, shuffle up to pay homage to the master artist. Even the winged lion is choked up.

Follow me here. Canova himself designed this pyramid-shaped tomb, not for his own use but as the tomb of an artist he greatly admired: Titian. But the Frari picked another design for Titian's tomb, so Canova used the pyramid for an Austrian princess...in Vienna. After his death, Canova's pupils copied the design here to honor their master. In fact, Canova isn't buried here. But inside the tomb's open door, you can (barely) see an urn, which contains his heart.

• *We'll finish with a tomb directly across the nave from the Canova Monument—the tomb of Venice's greatest artist.*

❿ Tomb of Titian, 1852

The enormous carved marble monument is labeled "Titiano Ferdinandus MDCCCLII." The tomb celebrates both the man (the center statue shows Titian with a beard and crown of laurels) and his famous paintings (depicted in the background reliefs).

FRARI CHURCH

Titian was the greatest Venetian painter, excelling equally in inspirational altarpieces, realistic portraits, joyous mythological scenes, and erotic female nudes.

He moved to Venice as a child, studying first as a mosaic-maker and then under Giovanni Bellini and Giorgione before establishing his own bold style, which featured teenage Madonnas (see a relief of *The Assumption of the Virgin* behind Titian). He became wealthy and famous, traveling Europe to paint stately portraits of kings and nobles, and colorful, sexy works for their bedrooms. Titian resisted the temptation of big money that drew so many of his contemporary Venetian artists to Rome. Instead he always returned to his beloved Venice (see winged lion on top)...and favorite Frari Church.

In his old age, Titian painted dark, tragic masterpieces, including the *Pietà* (see relief in upper left) that was intended for his tomb but ended up in the Accademia (see page 132). Nearing 90, he labored to finish the *Pietà* as the plague enveloped Venice. Over a quarter of the population died, including Titian's son and assistant, Orazio. Heartbroken, Titian died soon afterward. His tomb was built three centuries later to remember and honor this great Venetian. The inscription reads: "To Titian from Ferdinand I, the Habsburg Emperor who paid for this."

Thanks to Titian's genius, the beauty of the heavenly world could be brought down to earth, to be enjoyed by everyday people.

• *While this church is a great example of art in situ, in a sense, all of Venice is art in situ. At the Frari, you're away from the touristy center. Before returning to the mobs, why not explore some back lanes and lonely canals from here and enjoy a softer, more meditative side of town?*

SCUOLA SAN ROCCO TOUR

Scuola Grande di San Rocco

The 50-plus paintings in the Scuola Grande di San Rocco—often called "Tintoretto's Sistine Chapel"—present one man's very personal vision of Christian history. Tintoretto spent the last 20 years of his life working practically for free, driven by the spirit of charity that the Scuola, a Christian organization, promoted. For Tintoretto fans, this is the ultimate. Even for the art-weary, his large, dramatic canvases, framed in gold on the walls and ceilings of a grand upper hall, are an impressive sight.

Orientation

Cost: €10, free for kids under 18.

Hours: Daily 9:30-17:30.

Information: Tel. 041-523-4864, www.scuolagrandesanrocco.org.

Getting There: It's next to the Frari Church (vaporetto: San Tomà). For an easy route on foot from the Rialto Bridge, take the 📖 Rialto to Frari Church Walk, following signs to *Scuola Grande di San Rocco*.

Tours: The €5 audioguide provides only sketchy descriptions.

Mirrors: Use the mirrors scattered about the museum's Great Upper Hall. Much of this art is on the ceiling and, therefore, a pain in the neck.

Length of This Tour: Allow one hour.

Nearby: Right next door is the Church of San Rocco, featuring still more Tintorettos (free, same hours as the Scuola).

Starring: Tintoretto, Tintoretto, and Tintoretto.

Scuola San Rocco

To Frari
To Accademia

Campo
San Rocco

❶ TOUR BEGINS

TICKETS &
AUDIOGUIDE
KIOSK

ENTRY →

**GROUND
FLOOR**

To
San Rocco
Church

SHOP

WC

STAIRS UP TO
GREAT HALL

Not to Scale

❶❷ ❶❸ ❶❹ ❶❺

CEILING

❾ ❿ ⓫

PAINTINGS

**GREAT
UPPER
HALL**
(UPSTAIRS)

❺
❻   ❹
ALBERGO ❸
❼   ❽

❷

STAIRS FROM/TO
GROUND FLOOR

❶ The Annunciation
❷ View of the Great Upper Hall
❸ St. Roch in Glory
❹ Christ Before Pilate
❺ Christ Crowned with Thorns
❻ The Way to Calvary
❼ The Crucifixion
❽ Three Apples

❾ Moses Strikes Water from
the Rocks
❿ The Miracle of the Bronze Serpent
⓫ The Fall of Manna in the Desert
❶❷ The Adoration of the Shepherds
❶❸ The Resurrection
❶❹ Tintoretto's Carved Face
❶❺ The Last Supper

The Tour Begins

The art of the Scuola is contained in three rooms—the Ground Floor Hall (where you enter) and two rooms upstairs, including the Great Upper Hall, with the biggest canvases. Your ticket also admits you to the Scuola's small and skippable treasury (one more flight up).

• *Enter on the ground floor, which is lined with big, colorful Tintoretto canvases. Begin with the first canvas on the left—a great introduction to Tintoretto's distinctive style.*

GROUND FLOOR HALL
❶ *The Annunciation*

An angel swoops through the doorway, dragging a trail of naked baby angels with him, to tell a startled Mary that she'll give birth to Jesus. This canvas has many of Tintoretto's typical characteristics:

- **The miraculous and the everyday mingle side by side.** Glorious angels are in a broken-down house with stacks of lumber and a frayed chair.
- **Bright light and dark shadows.** A bright light strikes the brick column, highlighting Mary's face and the angel's shoulder, but casting dark shadows across the room.
- **Strong 3-D sucks you into the scene.** Tintoretto literally tears down Mary's wall to let us in. The floor tiles recede sharply into the distance, making Mary's room an extension of our real space.
- **Colors that are bright, almost harsh,** with a metallic "black-velvet" sheen, especially when contrasted with the soft-focus haze of Bellini, Giorgione, Veronese, and (sometimes) Titian.
- **Twisting, muscular poses.** The angel turns one way, Mary turns the other, and the baby angels turn every which way.
- **Diagonal composition.** Shadows run diagonally on the floor as Mary leans back diagonally.
- **Rough brushwork.** The sketchy pattern on Mary's ceiling contrasts with the precise photo-realism of the brick column.

And finally, *The Annunciation* exemplifies the general theme of the San Rocco paintings—God intervenes miraculously in our everyday lives in order to save us.

• *Let's get right to the highlights. Climb the staircase, taking time to*

Jacopo Tintoretto (1518-1594)

The son of a silk dyer ("Tintoretto" is a nickname meaning "little dyer"), Tintoretto applied a blue-collar work ethic to painting, becoming one of the most prolific artists ever. He trained briefly under Titian, but their egos clashed. He was influenced more by Michelangelo's recently completed *Last Judgment*, with its muscular, twisting, hovering nudes and epic scale.

By age 30, Tintoretto was famous, astounding Venice with the innovative *St. Mark Freeing the Slave* (now in the Accademia). He married, had eight children (three of whom became his assistants), and dedicated himself to work and family, shunning publicity and living his whole life in his old Venice neighborhood.

Twenty years of his life were spent decorating the Scuola Grande di San Rocco. It was a labor of love, showing his religious faith, his compassion for the poor, and his artistic passion.

admire the plague scenes (that are not by Tintoretto), which hint at the mission of the Scuola. Admire the impressive...

❷ View of the Great Upper Hall

Wow! This enormous hall—lined with wood paneling, lit by lanterns, and topped with a golden coffered ceiling crusted with Tintoretto paintings—is where members of the Scuola convened. The Scuola Grande di San Rocco was a kind of Venetian "Elks Club" whose favorite charity was poor plague victims. Tintoretto was himself a member. His paintings here explore themes dear to this charitable fraternity, like the suffering of the victimized, and the joy that comes from helping them out.

• *Before we tackle the big canvases in this huge room, let's start where Tintoretto did, with his very first painting for the Scuola. It's in the Albergo Hall (Sala d'Albergo)—the small room in the left corner of the Great Upper Hall. On the ceiling of the Albergo Hall is an oval painting of St. Roch, best viewed from the doorway.*

ALBERGO HALL: CHRIST'S PASSION
❸ *St. Roch in Glory,* 1564

Start at the feet of St. Roch (San Rocco), a French medical student in the 1300s who dedicated his short life to treating plague victims. His work inspired the Scuola, established in his name.

This is the first of Tintoretto's 50-plus paintings in the Scuo-

la. It's also the one that
got him the job, beating
entries by Veronese and
others.

Tintoretto amazed
the judges by showing the
saint from directly be-
neath, as though he hov-
ered above in a circle of

glory. This Venetian taste for dramatic angles and illusion would
later become standard in Baroque ceilings. Tintoretto trained by
dangling wax models from the ceiling and lighting them from odd
angles.

• *On the walls are scenes of Christ's trial, torture, and execution. Christ's
troubles mirrored those of the sick and poor that the Scuola vowed to help.
Start with the painting to the right of the door (as you face it), then work
counterclockwise around the room.*

❹ Christ Before Pilate (Ecce Homo)

Jesus has been arrested and brought
before the Roman authorities in a
cavernous hall. Although he says
nothing in his own defense, he stands
head and shoulders above the crowd,
literally "rising above" the slanders.
Tintoretto shines a bright light on his
white robe, making Christ radiate in-
nocence.

At Christ's feet, an old, bearded
man in white stoops over to record
the events on paper—it's Tintoretto
himself.

❺ Christ Crowned with Thorns

Jesus was beaten, whipped, then mocked by the soldiers, who
dressed him as a king "crowned" with thorns. Seeing the blood-
stains on the cloth must have touched the hearts of Scuola members, generating compassion for those who suffer.

❻ The Way to Calvary

Silhouetted against a stormy sky, Jesus and two other prisoners
trudge up a steep hill, carrying their own crosses to the execution
site. The cycle culminates with...

❼ The Crucifixion

The crucified Christ is the calm center of this huge and chaotic
scene that fills the wall. Workers struggle to hoist crosses, mourn-

ers swoon, riffraff gamble for Christ's clothes, and soldiers mill about aimlessly. Scarcely anyone pays any attention to the Son of God...except us, because Tintoretto directs our eye there.

All the lines of sight point to Christ at the center: the ladder on the ground, the cross being raised, the cross still on the ground, the horses on the right, and the hillsides that slope in. In a trick of

multiple perspectives, the cross being raised seems to suck us in toward the center, while the cross still on the ground seems to cause the figures to be sucked toward us.

Above the chaos stands Christ, high above the horizon, higher than everyone, glowing against the dark sky. Tintoretto lets us appreciate the quiet irony lost on the frenetic participants—that this minor criminal suffering such apparent degradation is, in fact, triumphant.

• *Displayed on an easel to the left of and beneath* The Crucifixion *is a small fragment of...*

❽ *Three Apples*

This fragment, from the frieze around the upper reaches of the Albergo Hall, was discovered folded under the frieze in 1905. Because it was never exposed to light, it still retains Tintoretto's original bright colors. All of his paintings are darker today, despite cleaning, due to the irreversible chemical alteration of the pigments. Imagine the original brightness of these rooms.

• *Now step back out into the Great Upper Hall.*

GREAT UPPER HALL

Thirty-four enormous oil canvases, set into gold frames on the ceiling and along the walls of this impressive room, tell biblical history from Adam and Eve to the Ascension of Christ. Tintoretto's storytelling style is straightforward, and anyone with knowledge of the Bible can quickly get the gist. Tintoretto's success in the Albergo Hall won him the job of the enormous Great Upper Hall.

The ceiling displays Old Testament scenes; the walls show events from the New Testament. Beyond that, the layout is not chronological but symbolic, linked by common themes. Tintoretto shows how God leads mankind to salvation. Evil enters the world

*(vertical sidebar text)* SCUOLA SAN ROCCO

with the Original Sin of *Adam and Eve* (at the Albergo end of room, on the ceiling). From there, man must go through many trials, as the ceiling shows—the struggles of Moses and the Israelites, Jonah, and Abraham. But God is always there to help—bringing water in the desert, healing the sick, feeding the hungry. The New Testament scenes on the walls show how God helps man spiritually, from sin to salvation. This art captures the charitable spirit of the school—just as God helps those who suffer, so should we.

• *Let's look at a few pieces in depth. Start with the big rectangular painting on the ceiling at the Albergo end of the hall.*

❾ Moses Strikes Water from the Rocks

Moses (in pink, in the center) hits a rock in the desert with his staff, and it miraculously spouts water, which the thirsty Israelites catch

in jars. The water spurts like a ray of light. Moses is a strong, calm center to a spinning wheel of activity.

Tintoretto worked fast, and, if nothing else, his art is exuberant. He trained in fresco painting, which must be finished before the plaster dries. With these paintings, he sketched an outline right onto the canvas, then improvised details as he went.

The sheer magnitude of the San Rocco project is staggering. This canvas alone is 300 square

feet—like painting a bathroom with an artist's tiny brush. The whole project, counting the Albergo Hall, Great Upper Hall, and the Ground Floor Hall together, totals some 8,500 square feet—more than enough to cover a typical house, inside and out. (The Sistine Chapel ceiling, by comparison, is 5,700 square feet.)

• *Now continue up the hall to the center of the room for the biggest painting of all. For the best perspective, view it from the top (the Albergo end), not directly underneath.*

❿ The Miracle of the Bronze Serpent

The tangle of half-naked bodies (at the bottom of the painting) represents the children of Israel, wrestling with poisonous snakes and writhing in pain. At the top of the pile, a young woman gestures toward Moses (in pink), who points to a pole carrying a bronze serpent. Those who looked at the statue were miraculously healed. His work all done, God (above in the clouds) high-fives an angel.

This was the first of the Great Hall panels Tintoretto painted in response to a terrible plague that hit Venice in 1575. About one in three died. Four hundred a day were buried. Like today's Red Cross, the Scuola sprang into action, raising funds, sending doctors, and giving beds to the sick—and aid to their families. Tintoretto saw the dead and dying firsthand. While capturing their suffering, he gave a ray of hope that help was on the way: Turn to the cross, and be saved by your faith.

There are dozens of figures in the painting, shown from every conceivable angle. Tintoretto was well aware of where it would hang and how it would be viewed. Walk around beneath it and see the different angles come alive. The painting becomes a movie, and the children of Israel writhe like snakes.

• *The rectangular panel at the altar end of the hall is...*

⓫ The Fall of Manna in the Desert

It's snowing bread, as God feeds the hungry Israelites with a miraculous storm. They stretch a blanket to catch it and gather it up in baskets. Up in the center of the dark cloud is a radiant, almost transparent God, painted with sketchy brushstrokes to suggest he's an unseen presence.

Tintoretto tells these Bible stories with a literalness that was very popular with the poor, uneducated sick people who sought help from the Scuola. He was the Spielberg of his day, with the technical know-how to bring imagination to life, to make the miraculous tangible.

• *You could grow old studying all the art here, so we'll select just a couple of the New Testament paintings on the walls. Start at the Albergo end. As you face the altar, it's the first painting on the left.*

⓬ The Adoration of the Shepherds

Christ's glorious life begins in a straw-filled stable with cows, chickens, and peasants who pass plates of food up to the new parents. It's night, with just a few details lit by moonlight: the kneeling shepherd's forehead and leggings, the serving girl's shoulders, the faces of Mary and Joseph...and little Baby Jesus, a smudge of light.

Notice the different points of view. Tintoretto clearly has placed us on the lower floor, about eye level with the cow, looking up through the roof beams at the night sky. But we also see Mary and Joseph in the loft above as though they were at eye level. By using multiple perspectives (and ignoring the laws of physics), Tintoretto could portray every detail at its perfect angle and create an otherworldly atmosphere. • *In the middle of the long wall, on the same side, find...*

SCUOLA SAN ROCCO

⓫ The Resurrection

Angels lift the sepulchre lid, and Jesus springs forth in a blaze of light. The contrast between dark and light is extreme, with great dramatic effect.

• *Head for* The Last Supper, *in the corner to the left of the altar. On the way there, look on the wall for a* ⓮ *woodcarving of Tintoretto (third statue from altar, directly opposite entry staircase). The artist holds the tools of his trade. His craggy, wrinkled face peers out from under a black cap and behind a scraggly beard.*

⓯ The Last Supper

A dog, a beggar, and a serving girl dominate the foreground of Christ's final Passover meal with his followers. More servants work in the background. The disciples themselves are dining in the dark, some with their backs to us, with only a few stray highlights to

show us what's going on. Tintoretto emphasizes the human, everyday element of that gathering, in contrast to, say, Leonardo da Vinci's more stately version. And he sets the scene at a diagonal for dramatic effect. The angle connects this holy scene with Mass as it's being performed.

The table stretches across a tiled floor, a commonly used device to create 3-D space. But Tintoretto makes the more distant tiles unnaturally small to exaggerate the distance. Similarly, the table and the people get proportionally smaller and lower until, at the far end of the table, tiny Jesus (with glowing head) is only half the size of the disciple at the near end.

Theatrically, Tintoretto leaves it to us to piece together the familiar narrative. The disciples are asking each other, "Is it I who will betray the Lord?" Jesus, meanwhile, unconcerned, hands out Communion bread.

Though Tintoretto garnered plenty of fame and well-paying jobs throughout his long and prolific career, he asked for almost no money for his work at the Scuola. It stands as one man's very personal contribution to the poor, to the Christian faith, and to art.

CA' REZZONICO TOUR

Museum of 18th-Century Venice (Museo del Settecento Veneziano)

Endowed by nature with a pleasing physical appearance, a confirmed gambler, a great talker, far from modest, always running after pretty women...I was certain to be disliked. But, as I was always willing to take responsibility for my actions, I decided I had a right to do anything I pleased.

—The Memoirs of Giacomo Casanova

Venice in the 1700s was the playground for Europe's aristocrats, including the wealthy Rezzonico (ret-ZON-ee-koh) family, who owned this palace. Today, the Ca' Rezzonico (a.k.a. the Museo del Settecento Veneziano) contains furniture, decoration, and artwork from the period. This grand home on the Grand Canal is the best place in town to experience the luxurious, decadent spirit of Venice in the Settecento (the 1700s).

Orientation

Cost: €10.

Hours: Wed-Mon 10:00-18:00, Nov-March until 17:00, closed Tue year-round, ticket office closes one hour before museum.

Getting There: The museum is located in Dorsoduro, on the west bank of the Grand Canal at the Ca' Rezzonico vaporetto stop. It's a 10-minute walk from the Accademia Bridge and 20 minutes from the Rialto.

Information: Tel. 041-241-0100, http://carezzonico.visitmuve.it.

Tours: The **audioguide** costs €5 (€6/2 people) and lasts 1.5 hours.

Length of This Tour: Allow one hour (more if you want to explore the third floor on your own). If you have less than an hour, focus on Rooms 1-7 on the first floor, with their Tiepolo ceilings and ambience.

Baggage Check: Free and required for large items.

Cuisine Art: The museum's café has simple fare (*panini* and pasta, no museum entry required). The delightful Campo San Barnaba is just a three-minute walk away; for eateries on and near that square, see page 271.

Starring: A beautiful palace with 18th-century furnishings and paintings by G. B. Tiepolo, Canaletto, and Guardi.

OVERVIEW

Our Ca' Rezzonico tour covers two floors. The first floor has palatial rooms decorated with period furniture and ceiling frescoes by G. B. Tiepolo. The second floor displays paintings that bring the era to life, by Canaletto, Guardi, G. D. Tiepolo, Longhi, and others. (The third-floor painting gallery—which is skippable—shows lots of flesh in lots of rooms.)

The Tour Begins

CA' REZZONICO

• *If you're arriving by vaporetto, admire Ca' Rezzonico's heavy stone facade facing the Grand Canal. The dock was, of course, the main entrance back in the 1700s. Then, as you enter the palazzo courtyard, admire the 1700s-era gondola on display. Picture this arriving at the Ca's dock for a party during Carnevale. A charcoal heater inside kept the masked and caped passengers warm, as they sipped prosecco and chatted in French, enjoying their winter holiday away from home.*

Buy tickets on the ground floor, then ascend the grand staircase to the first floor (where you show your ticket).

FIRST FLOOR

• *You'll start in the ballroom. From here, simply follow the one-way route through the numbered rooms.*

Room 1: Ballroom

This would be a great place for a wedding reception. At 5,600 square feet, it could be the biggest private venue in the city. Stand in the center, and the room gets even bigger, with a ceiling painting that opens up to the heavens and trompe l'oeil (optical illusion) columns and arches that open onto fake alcoves.

Imagine a party here in the 1700s when the Rezzonicos reigned supreme. Guests dance under candlelit chandeliers to Vivaldi's *Four Seasons*. Servants glide by with drinks and finger foods.

Ca' Rezzonico—First Floor

(Not to Scale)

STAIRS UP TO
SECOND FLOOR

G r a n d

STAIRS
FROM
GROUND
FLOOR

TOUR
BEGINS

B A L L R O O M

ROOM 1

BRUSTOLON

11   10   9

8

TIEPOLO
7

12

SEDAN CHAIR

(ON CEILING)
TIEPOLO
2

CARRIERA
4   5

TIEPOLO
6

3

C a n a l

The gentlemen wear powdered wigs, linen shirts with lacy sleeves, tight velvet coats and breeches, striped stockings, and shoes with big buckles. They carry snuffboxes with dirty pictures inside the lids. The ladies powder their hair, pile it high, and weave in stuff—pictures of their children or locks of a lover's hair. And everyone carries a mask on a stick to change identity in a second.

The chandeliers of gold-covered wood are original. But while most of the furniture we'll see is from the 1700s, it's not from the Rezzonico family collection.

• *Promenade across the floor, bearing right into the next room.*

Room 2: Nuptial Allegory Salon

In fact, there *was* a wedding here—see the happy couple on the ceiling, arriving in a chariot pulled by four white horses and serenaded by angels, cupids, and Virtues. It was in this room, in 1758, that Ludovico Rezzonico exchanged vows with Faustina Savorgnan, under the bellies of the horses painted for the occasion by Giovanni Battista ("John the Baptist") Tiepolo. G. B. Tiepolo (1696-1770), the best-known decorator of Europe's palaces, was at the height of his fame and technique. He knocked

CA' REZZONICO

Famous 18th-Century Venetians

Canaletto (Giovanni Antonio Canal): Painter of Venice views

Antonio Canova: Neoclassical sculptor

Giacomo Casanova: Gambler, womanizer, revolutionary

Carlo Goldoni: Playwright of realistic comedies

Francesco Guardi: Painter of romantic Enlightened ideas

Giovanni Battista (G. B.) Tiepolo: Painter of Rococo ceilings

Giovanni Domenico (G. D.) Tiepolo: Painter son of the more famous Tiepolo

this out in 12 days. His bright colors, mastery of painting figures from every possible angle, wide knowledge of classical literary subjects, and sheer, unbridled imagination made his frescoes blend seamlessly with ornate Baroque and Rococo furniture.

The *Portrait of Clement XIII,* pink-cheeked and well-fed, shows the most famous Rezzonico, who presided over the family's greatest era. This portrait shows him as a military man, with his billowing cape and commander's baton. Elected pope in 1758, Clement spent his reign defending the Jesuit society from anti-Catholic European nobles.

The Rezzonico were a family of *nouveaux riches* who bought their way into the exclusive club of Venetian patrician families. The state, which needed money for its military adventures, actually sold noble status to parvenu families like the Rezzonico. These upwardly mobile families then followed a strategy to be accepted by the old nobility. Over the course of several generations, the Rezzonico bought and decorated this fancy palace, married into high society, managed to secure a prestigious Venetian office, and even put one of their relatives on the papal throne. In early times, art was about scoring religious points to gain entry to heaven. In the 18th century, wealthy people commissioned art like the works in this palace simply to gain respect. They also threw great parties.

A **prayer kneeler** (in the tiny adjoining chapel, Room 3) looks heavily used, dating from the sin-and-repent era of Settecento Venice.

Room 4: Pastel Room
Several portraits grace this room, showing aristocratic ladies and gentlemen of the era. Several are by Europe's most celebrated painter of portraits in pastels—the

Venetian artist Rosalba Carriera (1673-1757). Wealthy French and English tourists on holiday wanted a souvenir of Venice, and Carriera obliged, with miniature portraits on ivory rather than the traditional vellum (soft animal skin). These were products of narcissism—the Instagram photos of the 18th century that proclaimed, "Look how charming/interesting I am."

She progressed to portraits in pastel, a medium that caught the luminous, pale-skin, white-haired, heavy-makeup look that was considered so desirable. Still, her *Portrait (Ritratto) of Sister Maria Caterina* has a warts-and-all realism that doesn't hide the nun's heavy eyebrows, long nose, and forehead vein, which only intensifies the spirituality she radiates.

At age 47, Carriera was invited to Paris, where she became the toast of the town. Returning triumphantly to Venice, she settled into her home on the Grand Canal and painted until her eyesight failed.

Also in the room is a portrait (not by Carriera) of **Cecilia Guardi Tiepolo.** She was the wife of G. B. Tiepolo, sister of famous painter Francesco Guardi, and mother of not-very-famous painter Lorenzo Tiepolo, who painted this when he was 21.

Room 5: Tapestry Room

This room's decor gives a sense of the Rococo luxury of the wealth of Venice in the 1700s. There are tapestries, furniture, a mirror, and a door with Asian themes that shows an opium smoker on his own little island paradise (lower panel). In a century dominated by the French court at Versailles, Venice was one of the few cities that could hold its own. The furniture ensemble of gilded wood chairs, tables, and chests hints

Giacomo Casanova (1725-1798)

I began to lead a life of complete freedom, caring for nothing except what pleased me.
   —The Memoirs of Giacomo Casanova

Casanova, a real person who wrote an exaggerated autobiography, typifies the Venice that so entranced the rest of Europe. In his life, he adopted many personae, worked in a number of professions, and always took the adventurous path.

Casanova was born just across the Grand Canal from the Ca' Rezzonico. The son of an actor, Casanova trained to be a priest, but was expelled for seducing nuns. To Venetians he was first known as a fiery violinist at fancy parties in palaces such as the Ca' Rezzonico. He would later serve time in the Doge's Palace prison, accused of being a magician.

As a professional gambler and charmer, he roamed Europe's capitals seducing noblewomen, dueling with fellow men of honor, and impressing nobles with his knowledge of Greek literature, religion, politics, and the female sex. His memoirs, published after his death, cemented his reputation as a genial but cunning rake, rogue, and rapscallion.

at the Louis XIV (claw-foot) style, but the pieces were made in a Venetian workshop.

Despite Venice's mask of gaiety, in the 1700s it was a poor, politically bankrupt, dirty city. Garbage floated in the canals, the streets were either unpaved or slippery with slime, and tourists could hardly stand visiting St. Mark's Basilica or the Doge's Palace because of the stench of mildew. But its reputation for decay and sleaze was actually romanticized into a metaphor for adventures into shady morality. With licensed casinos and thousands of courtesans (prostitutes), it was a fun city for foreigners freed from hometown blinders.

Room 6: Throne Room

"Nowhere in Europe are there so many and such splendid fêtes, ceremonies, and public entertainments of all kinds as there are in Venice," wrote a visitor from France. As you check out the view of the Grand Canal, imagine once again that you're attending a party here. You could watch the *Forze d'Ercole* (Force of Hercules) acrobats, who stood in boats and kept building a human pyramid—of up to 50 bodies—until they tumbled, laughing, into the Grand

Canal. At midnight the hosts would dim the mirrored candleholders on the walls, so you could look out on a fireworks display over the water.

Carnevale, Venice's prime party time, stretched from the day after Christmas to Lent. Everyone wore masks. Frenchmen, dressed as turbaned Ottoman Turks, mingled with Turkish traders dressed as harlequins. Fake Barbary pirates fought playfully with skin-blackened "Moors." And long-nosed Pulcinella clowns were everywhere, reveling in the time when all social classes partied as one because "the mask levels all distinctions."

The **ceiling fresco,** again by Giovanni Battista Tiepolo, certainly trompes my oeil. (It's best viewed from the center.) Tiepolo

opens the room's sunroof, allowing angels to descend to earth to pick up the Rezzonico clan's patriarch. The old, bald, bearded fellow is crowned with laurels and begins to rise on a cloud up to the translucent temple of glory. The angels hold Venice's Golden Book, where the names of the city's nobles were listed. In 1687, the Rezzonico family bought their way into the exclusive club. Tiepolo captures the moment just as the gang is exiting through the "hole" in the ceiling. The leg of the

lady in white seems to dangle over the "edge" of the fake oval. Tiepolo creates a zero-gravity universe that must have astounded visitors. Walk in circles under the fresco, and watch the bugling angel spin.

• *Pass through the large next room and into...*

Room 7: Tiepolo

This was the game room, and you can see a card table in the center. The big walnut cabinet along the wall is one of the few original pieces of furniture from the Rezzonico collection.

The ceiling painting by G. B. Tiepolo depicts Nobility and Virtue as a kind of bare-breasted, Thelma-and-Louise duo defeating Treachery, who tumbles down. The painting—which is on canvas, not a fresco like the others—was moved here from another palazzo.

Portraits around the room are by Tiepolo and his sons, Lorenzo and Giovanni Domenico. The paintings are sober and down-to-earth, demonstrating the artistic range of this exceptional

family. G. B. was known for his flamboyance, but he passed to his sons his penchant for painting wrinkled, wizened old men in the Rembrandt style. In later years, G. B. had the pleasure of traveling with his sons to distant capitals, meeting royalty, and working on palace ceilings. Giovanni Domenico (G. D.) contributed some of the minor figures in the Ca' Rezzonico ceilings and went on to a successful artistic career of his own—as we'll see upstairs.

Room 9: Library
In the 1800s, the English poet Robert Browning (1812-1889) spent his later years here. Imagine him in this study, in a melancholy mood after a long winter, reading a book and thinking of words from a poem of his: "Oh to be in England, now that April's there...."

Room 10: Lazzarini
The big, colorful paintings are by Gregorio Lazzarini (1655-1730), Tiepolo's teacher. Tiepolo took Lazzarini's color, motion, and twisted poses and suspended them overhead.

Room 11: Brustolon
Andrea Brustolon (1662-1732) carved Baroque fantasies into the custom-made tables, chairs, and vase stands that he crafted in his Venice workshop. In black ebony, reddish boxwood, and brown walnut, they overwhelm with the sheer number of figures, yet each carving is a gem worth admiring. The big vase stand is a harmony of different colors: a white vase supported by ebony slaves in chains and a brown boxwood Hercules. The slaves' chains are carved from a single piece of wood—a racist motif, but an impressive artistic feat.

The room's flowery Murano glass chandelier—of pastel pinks, blues, and turquoise—is original.

• *Backtrack to Room 10, then turn right into the large, sparsely decorated reception space (the* portego*).*

Room 12: Portico *(Portego)*

That funny little cabin in the room is a **sedan chair,** a servant-powered taxi for Venice's nobles. Four strong-shouldered men ran poles through the iron brackets on either side, then carried it on their shoulders, while the rich rode in red-velvet luxury above the slimy streets.

• *The staircase to the second floor is in Room 12, in the middle of the long wall.*

SECOND FLOOR

The first floor showed the rooms and furniture of the 1700s. The second-floor paintings depict the people who sat in those chairs.

• *Begin in Room 13, lined with paintings. Of special interest are two works by Venice's great painter of urban landscapes, Canaletto, found on the opposite wall.*

Room 13: Painting *Portego* (Canaletto)

Rich tourists wanting to remember their stay in Venice sought out Giovanni Antonio Canal, a.k.a., Canaletto (1697-1768), for a "postcard" view. The ***View of Rio dei Mendicante*** chronicles every chimney, every open shutter, every pair of underwear hanging out to dry.

Canaletto was a young theater-set painter working on Scarlatti operas in Rome when he decided his true calling was painting reality, not Baroque fantasy. He moved home to Venice, set up his easel outside, and painted scenes directly from nature. It was considered a very odd thing to do in his day.

The ***Grand Canal from Palazzo Balbi*** to Rialto captures the view you'd see from the palazzo two doors down. With photographic clarity, Canaletto depicts buildings, boats, and shadows on the water, leading the eye to the tiny, half-hidden Rialto Bridge on the distant horizon.

Despite the seeming photo-realism and crystal clarity, these wide-angle views are more than any human eye could take in without turning side to side. Canaletto,

CA' REZZONICO

Ca' Rezzonico—Second Floor

who meticulously studied the mathematics of perspective, was not above tweaking those rules to compress more of Venice into the frame.

In the *Grand Canal from Palazzo Balbi to Rialto,* notice there are shadows along both sides of the canal—physically impossible, but more picturesque. His paintings still have a theater-set look to them, but here, the Venice backdrop is the star.

To meet the demand for postcard scenes of Venice, Canaletto resorted in later years to painting from engravings or following formulas. But these two early works reflect his pure vision to accurately paint the city he loved.

Grand Tour visitors routinely reported that Venice pleased the eye but not the heart or mind. Just as they experienced the city without feeling any real passion, these paintings let you see it, marvel, and move on.

• *From here, we'll move roughly clockwise around the second floor. Head for the door behind your right shoulder. Room 14 is actually a maze of several rooms.*

Room 14: G. D. Tiepolo's Frescoes from the Villa Zianigo

The son of G. B. Tiepolo decorated the family villa with frescoes for his own enjoyment. They're far more down-to-earth than G. B.'s high-flying fantasies. *New World* features butts, as ordinary folk crowd around a building with a peep-show window. The only faces we see are the two men in profile—Giovanni Domenico Tiepolo (far right, with eyeglass) and his father, G. B. (arms folded)—and baby brother Lorenzo (center). The **Pulcinella Room** (far right corner) has several scenes (including one overhead) of the hook-nosed, white-clothed, hunchbacked clown who, at Carnevale time, represented the lovable country bumpkin. But here, he and his similarly

dressed companions seem tired, lecherous, and stupid. The decadent gaiety of Settecento Venice was at odds with the *Liberté, Egalité,* and *Fraternité* erupting in France.

The 18th century was a time of great change. The fresh ideas and innovations of the Enlightenment swept more adaptable societies upward into a thriving new modern age. Meanwhile, a Venice in denial declined.

Venetians bought into their own propaganda. The modern ideas coming out of France threatened the very foundation of what La Serenissima was all about. Over time Venetians stopped trading, stopped traveling, and became stuck in the mud. Like Marie Antoinette retreating into her little hamlet at Versailles, the aristocracy of Venice withdrew into their palaces. Insisting their city remained exceptional, Venetian society chose to dance rather than to adapt. As Venice fell, its appetite for decadence grew. Through the 18th century, the Venetians partied and partied, as if drunk on the wealth accumulated through earlier centuries as a trading power.

• *Backtrack a bit and explore more of the maze of Room 14, winding your way into a room with a harpsichord.*

Room 15: Harpsichord Room

The 1700s saw the development of new keyboard instruments that would culminate by century's end in the modern piano. This particular specimen has strings that are not hammered (like a piano) but plucked. At this point, a pluck was just a pluck—always the same volume. When hammers were introduced shortly after this, the novelty of being able to play both soft and loud sounds prompted Italians to name the instrument the *pianoforte* (the soft-loud).

Room 17: Parlor

Francesco Guardi (1712-1793), like Canaletto, supplied foreigners with scenes of Venice. But Guardi uses rougher brushwork that casts a romantic haze over the decaying city.

The Parlor (Il Parlatorio delle Monache di S. Zaccaria) is an interior landscape featuring visiting day at a convent school. The girls, secluded with their servant girls behind grills, chat and have tea with family members, friends, ladies with their pets, and potential suitors. Convents were like finishing schools for aristocratic girls, where they got an education and learned manners before re-entering the world. Note the puppet show (starring spouse-abusing Pulcinella).

Guardi's *Il Ridotto di Palazzo Dandolo* shows partygoers in masks at a Venetian palace licensed for gambling. Casanova and others claimed that these casino houses had back rooms for the private use of patrons and courtesans. The men wear the traditional *bautta*—a three-piece outfit consisting of a face mask, three-cornered hat, and cowl. This getup was actually required by law in certain seedy establishments to ensure that every sinner was equally anonymous. The women wear Lone Ranger masks, and parade a hint of cleavage to potential customers.

• *Continuing along, you'll pass back through the Painting Portico and into...*

Room 18: Longhi

There is no better look at 1700s Venice than these genre scenes by Pietro Longhi (1701-1785), depicting everyday life among the upper classes. See ladies and gentlemen going to the hairdresser or to the dentist, dressed in the finery that was standard in every public situation. These small easel works provide a psychoanalytic insight into society. They come with an overwhelming sense of boredom.

There's no dynamism. There aren't even any windows. It's a society closed to the world, without initiative, and—it seems—with no shortage of leisure time.

Contrast these straightforward scenes with one final work by G. B. Tiepolo—a sumptuous ceiling painting of nude gods and goddesses. The Rococo fantasy world of aristocrats was slipping increasingly into the more prosaic era of the bourgeoisie.

• *Pass through several rooms to the far corner.*

Room 21: Alcove

Casanova daydreamed of fancy boudoirs like this one, complete with a large bed (topped with a Madonna by Rosalba Carriera), a walnut dresser, Neoclassical wallpaper, and silver toiletries. Even the presence of the baby cradle would not have dimmed his ardor.

• *The final and most skippable part of the museum is the **top floor**, containing a large collection of Venetian paintings amassed by a local scholar named Egidio Martini. Most are by lesser-known artists from the 1600s and 1700s, but there's one room of 19th- and early-20th-century works, including a few Impressionists.*

CA' REZZONICO

PEGGY GUGGENHEIM COLLECTION TOUR

Peggy Guggenheim (1898-1979)—an American-born heiress to the Guggenheim mining fortune and niece of Solomon Guggenheim (who built New York's modern-art museum of the same name)—made her mark as a friend, lover, and patron of modern artists.

As a gallery owner, she introduced Europe's avant-garde to a skeptical America. As a collector, she gave instant status to modern art that was too radical for serious museums. As a patron, she fed starving artists such as Jackson Pollock. And as a person, she lived larger than life, unconventional and original, with a succession of lovers that enhanced her reputation as a female Casanova.

In 1948, Peggy "retired" to Venice, renovating a small, unfinished palazzo on the Grand Canal. Today it's a fun museum, decorated much as it was during her lifetime, with one of the best collections anywhere of 20th-century art. It's the only museum I can think of where the owner is buried in the garden.

Orientation

Cost: €15, €10.50 for ages 10-18 and students under 26, free for kids under 10. While it's possible to book tickets online, it's generally unnecessary.

Hours: Wed-Mon 10:00-18:00, closed Tue.

Information: Tel. 041-240-5411, www.guggenheim-venice.it.

Getting There: The museum overlooks the Grand Canal, a five-minute walk from the Accademia Bridge (vaporetto: Accademia) or from La Salute Church (vaporetto: Salute). A cool way to cross the Grand Canal is via the Santa Maria del Giglio *traghetto* (see page 24 for more on riding the *traghetto*).

Tours: An **audioguide** costs €7. You can also call ahead to book a 1.5-hour **guided tour** (€85 for up to 18 people).

Visitor Information: Art interns guarding the works are happy to tell you about particular pieces if you ask. The ticket desk and museum shop sell an excellent €5 guidebook.

Length of This Tour: Allow one hour.

Baggage Check: Free and required for anything bigger than a small purse.

Cuisine Art: There's a $$ café on site, but you have plenty of better options in the Dorsoduro neighborhood, especially in the area around the Accademia.

Nearby: If you like contemporary art, this is your neighborhood. Browse the art galleries, and visit the Punta della Dogana museum (next to La Salute, see page 40).

Starring: Picasso, Kandinsky, Mondrian, Dalí, Pollock...and Peggy herself.

The Tour Begins

You'll enter a garden courtyard sprinkled with statues. There's a wing to the left (with the café) and a wing to the right (with the main collection, where you start), plus a modern annex. The collection is (very) roughly chronological, starting with Cubism and ending with post-World War II artists.

The collection's strength is its Abstract, Surrealist, and Abstract-Surrealist art. The placement of the paintings may change, so use this chapter as an overview, not a painting-by-painting tour. What makes this collection unique is that it hangs here in Peggy's home, much as it did in her lifetime. Another plus is that it's staffed by fresh young art students, not the tired civil servants that you meet at Venice's publicly run museums.

• *For a unique introduction to this unique woman, start your tour in her sculpture garden. Pay your respects to the woman who changed the art world. In the far corner of the garden (along a brick wall), find...*

PEGGY'S GRAVE (AND THAT OF HER DOGS)

"Here Lie My Beloved Babies" marks the grave of Peggy's many dogs, her steady companions as she grew old. Note the names of some of these small, long-haired Lhasa Apsos. Along with "Cappuccino" and "Baby," you'll see "Pegeen," after her daughter,

Peggy Guggenheim Collection

Grand Canal

TERRACE

LIVING ROOM ABSTRACT

LIBRARY ABSTRACT

MARINI SCULPTURE

GUEST BEDROOM SURREALISM

PEGGY'S BED-ROOM

PEGEEN

WC

CHAGALL "RAIN"

DINING ROOM CUBISM

ENTRANCE HALL

EAST WING POLLOCK

KITCHEN KANDINSKY

SCHULHOF COLLECTION

To Salute

SCULPTURE GARDEN

DOGS' GRAVE

PEGGY'S GRAVE

← ! TOUR BEGINS

MUSEUM CAFÉ

EXIT

WC

TICKET CHECK

MUSEUM SHOP

CALLE SAN CRISTOFOLO

TEMPORARY EXHIBITIONS

WC

To ← Accademia

FONDAMENTA VENIER DEI LEONI

ENTRY

Rio de le Toresele

Not to Scale

and "Sir Herbert," for Herbert Read, the art critic who helped Peggy select her collection.

Peggy's ashes are buried alongside, marked with a simple plaque: "Here Rests Peggy Guggenheim 1898-1979." Over your right shoulder, the flourishing olive tree is a gift from one of Peggy's old traveling buddies—Yoko Ono.

In the nonconformist 1960s, Peggy's once shocking art and unconventional lifestyle became more acceptable, even commonplace. By the 1970s, she was universally recognized as a major force in early modern art and was finally even honored by the Venetians with the nickname, *L'Ultima Dogaressa*—The Last Dogaressa.

• *Now walk through Peggy's collection and her life. From the sculpture garden, head up the stairs and through the black wrought-iron doors, into the...*

ENTRANCE HALL: MEET PEGGY GUGGENHEIM

Picture Peggy Guggenheim greeting guests here—standing before the **trembling-leaf mobile by Alexander Calder,** flanked by Picasso and Magritte paintings, surrounded by her yapping dogs and meowing cats, and wearing her Calder-designed earrings, Mondrian-print dress, and Catwoman sunglasses.

During the 1950s and 1960s, this old palazzo on the Grand Canal was a mecca for "Moderns," from composer Igor Stravinsky to actor Marlon Brando, from painter Mark Rothko to writer Truman Capote, from choreographer George Balanchine to Beatle John Lennon and performance artist Yoko Ono. They came to sip cocktails, tour the great art, talk about ideas, and meet the woman who had become a living legend.

Pablo Picasso, *On the Beach,* 1937

Curious, balloon-animal women play with a sailboat while their friend across the water looks on. Of all of Peggy's many paintings, this was her favorite.

By the time Peggy Guggenheim first became serious about modern art (about the time this was painted), Pablo Picasso—the most famous and versatile 20th-century artist—had already been through his Blue, Rose, Fauve, Cubist, Synthetic Cubist, Classical, Abstract, and Surrealist phases, finally arriving at a synthesis of these styles. Peggy had some catching up to do.

René Magritte, *Empire of Light,* 1953-1954

Magritte found that, even under a sunny blue sky, suburbia has its dark side. The improbable combination of daylight sky and nighttime street in one scene is the kind of bizarre paradox that Surrealists loved.

• *Enter the first room to the left, and you'll see a skinny dining-room table in the center.*

CUBISTS IN THE DINING ROOM

Peggy's **dining-room table** reminds us that this museum was, indeed, her home for the last 30 years of her life. Most of the furniture is now gone, but the walls are decorated much as they were when she lived here, with paintings and statues by her friends, colleagues, and mentors. Here, she entertained countless artists and celebrities (more name-dropping), from actor Paul Newman to poet Allen Ginsberg, from sculptor Henry Moore to playwright Tennessee Williams, from James Bond creator Ian Fleming to glass sculptor Dale Chihuly.

Most of the art in the dining room dates from Peggy's childhood, when she was raised in the lap of luxury in New York, oblivious to the artistic upheavals going on in Europe. Her grandfather, Meyer Guggenheim, had emigrated from Switzerland to America and then had the good fortune to invest in the silver mines at Leadville, Colorado.

In 1912, the *Titanic* went down, taking Peggy's playboy tycoon father with it...and leaving his 14-year-old daughter with a small but comfortable trust fund and a man-sized hole in her life.

Approaching adulthood, Peggy rejected her traditional American upbringing. She started hanging out at a radical bookstore, got a nose job (a botched operation, leaving her with a rather bulbous schnozz)...and began planning a trip to Europe.

In 1920, 21-year-old Peggy arrived in Paris, where a revolution in art was taking place.

• *Find the following art (or similar pieces) in the Dining Room. (These and other items sometimes move around—if you don't see them where I mention them, keep looking.)*

Pablo Picasso, *The Poet,* 1911

The young Picasso, a Spaniard living in Paris, shattered the Old World into brown shards ("cubes") and reassembled it in Cubist style. It's a vaguely recognizable portrait of a man from the waist up—tapering to a head at the top, smoking a pipe(?), and cradling the traditional lyre of a poet. While the newfangled motion-picture camera could capture a moving image, Picasso suggests motion with a collage of stills.

Marcel Duchamp, *Nude (Study), Sad Young Man on a Train,* 1911-1912

In a self-portrait, Duchamp poses gracefully with a cane, but the moving train jiggles the image into a blur of brown. Duchamp is best known not for paintings like this, but for his outrageous conceptual pieces: his urinal-as-statue *(Fountain)* and his moustache on the *Mona Lisa* (titled *L.H.O.O.Q.,* which—when spoken aloud in French—is a pun that translates loosely as "she has a hot ass"). In a 2004 poll of British artists, Duchamp's urinal was named the most influential modern artwork of all time.

Constantin Brancusi, *Maiastra,* c. 1912

For the generation born before air travel, flying was magical. This high-polished bird is the first of many by Brancusi, who dreamed of flight. But this bronze bird just sits there. For centuries, a good sculptor was one who could capture movement in stone. Brancusi reverts to the essential forms of "primitive" African art, in which even the simplest statues radiate mojo.

• *Head next door, into the mainly Kandinsky Kitchen.*

ABSTRACTION AND VARIOUS "-ISMS"

In the Roaring Twenties, Peggy spent *her* twenties right in the center of avant-garde craziness: Paris. For the rest of her life, Europe—not America—would be her permanent address.

In Paris, trust-funded Peggy lived the bohemian life. Post-WWI Paris was cheap and, after the bitter war years, ready to party. Days were spent drinking coffee in cafés, talking ideas with the likes of activist Emma Goldman, writer Djuna *(Nightwood)* Barnes, and photographer Man Ray. Nights were spent abusing the drug forbidden in America (alcohol), dancing to jazz music into the wee hours, and talking about Freud and s-e-x.

One night, at the top of the Eiffel Tower, a dashing artist and intellectual nicknamed "The King of Bohemia" popped the question. Peggy and Laurence Vail soon married and had two children, but the partying only slowed somewhat. This thoroughly modern couple dug the wild life and the wild art it produced.

Vassily Kandinsky, *White Cross,* 1922

I see white, I see crosses, but where's the white cross? Oh, there it is on the right, camouflaged among black squares.

Like a jazz musician improvising from a set scale, Kandinsky plays with new patterns of related colors and lines, creating something that's simply beautiful, even if it doesn't "mean" anything. As Kandinsky himself would say, his art was like "visual music—just open your eyes and look."
• *Wander briefly through the hall to find...*

Marc Chagall, *Rain,* 1911

The rain clouds gather over a farmhouse, the wind blows the trees and people, and everyone prepares for the storm. Quick, put the horse in the barn, grab an umbrella, take a leak, and round up the goats in the clouds.

Marc Chagall, a Russian living in France, reinvented scenes from his homeland with a romantic, weightless, childlike joy in topsy-turvy Paris.
• *Step from the hall into the Living Room.*

Piet Mondrian, *Composition with Red,* 1938-1939

Like a blueprint for Modernism, Mondrian's T-square style boils painting down to its basic building blocks—black lines, white canvas, and the three primary colors (red, yellow, and blue) arranged in orderly patterns. This stripped-down canvas even omits yellow and blue.

Mondrian started out painting realistic landscapes of the orderly fields in his native Holland. Increasingly, he simplified things into horizontal and vertical grids, creating rectangles of different proportions. This one has horizontal lines to the left, vertical ones to the right. The horizontals appear to dominate, until we see that they're balanced by the tiny patch of red.

For Mondrian, who was heavily into Eastern mysticism, up vs. down and left vs. right were metaphors for life's ever-shifting dualities: good vs. evil, man vs. woman, fascism vs. communism. The canvas is a bird's-eye view of Mondrian's personal landscape.

• *Continue into the Library next door, for more abstraction. Then pass through the hall and out the wrought-iron doors onto the terrace.*

EXHIBITIONISTS ON THE TERRACE

You fall in love with the city itself. There is nothing left over in your heart for anyone else.

—Peggy Guggenheim

The obviously exuberant figure in Marino Marini's equestrian statue, *The Angel of the City* (1948), faces the Grand Canal, spreads his arms wide, and tosses his head back in sheer joy, with an eternal hard-on for the city of Venice. Every morning, Peggy must have felt a similar exhilaration as she sipped coffee while taking in this unbelievable view.

Marini originally designed his bronze rider with a screw-off penis (which sounds dirtier than it is) that could be removed for prudish guests or by curious ones. Someone stole it for some unknown purpose, so the current organ is permanently welded on.

The palazzo—formally Palazzo Venier dei Leoni—looks modern but is old. Construction began in 1748, but only the ground floor was completed. Legend has it that members of a rival family across the canal squelched plans for the upper stories so their home wouldn't be upstaged. The palazzo remained unfinished until Peggy bought it in 1948 and spruced it up. She added the annex in 1958. The **lions** *(leoni)* of the original palace still guard the waterfront entrance.

Peggy's outlandish and rather foreign presence in Venice—drinking, dressing up outrageously, and sunbathing on her rooftop for all to see—was not immediately embraced by the Venetians. But for artists in the 1950s and 1960s, Peggy's palazzo was *the* place to be, especially when the Biennale brought the jet set. Everyone from actor Alec Guinness, to political satirist Art Buchwald, to gossip columnist Hedda Hopper signed her guest book. Picture Peggy and guests, decked out in evening clothes, hopping into her custom-built gondola (nicknamed *La Barchessa,* after the doge's private boat) to ride slowly down the canal for a martini or a Bellini at Harry's Bar.

• *Now enter the Guest Bedroom for a hefty dose of Surrealism.*

ABSTRACT SURREALISTS

In 1928, Peggy's marriage to Laurence Vail ended, and she entered into a series of romantic attachments. Though not stunningly attractive, she was easy to be with, and she truly admired artistic men.

In 1937, she began an on-again, off-again relationship with playwright Samuel *(Waiting for Godot)* Beckett. Beckett steered her toward modern painting and sculpture—things she'd never paid much attention to.

She started hanging out with the French Surrealists, from artist Marcel Duchamp to writer André Breton to filmmaker/artist Jean *(Beauty and the Beast)* Cocteau. Duchamp, in particular, mentored her in modern art, encouraging her to use her money to collect and promote it. Nearing 40, she moved to London and launched a new career.

Paul Delvaux, *The Break of Day,* 1937

Full-breasted ladies with roots cast long shadows and awaken to a mysterious dawn. If you're counting boobs, don't forget the one reflected in the nightstand mirror.

Yves Tanguy, *The Sun in Its Jewel Case,* 1937

In May 1938, this painting was featured at Guggenheim Jeune, the art gallery Peggy opened in London. Tanguy's painting sums up the turbulent art that shocked a sleepy London during that first season.

Weird, phallic, tissue-and-bone protuberances cast long shadows across a moody, dreamlike landscape—the landscape of the mind. (Peggy said the picture "frightened" her, but added, "I got over my fear...and now I own it.") The

Abstract Art

Abstract art simplifies. A man becomes a stick figure. A squiggle is a wave. A streak of red expresses anger. Arches make

you want a cheeseburger. These are universal symbols that everyone from a caveman to a banker understands. Abstract artists capture the essence of reality in a few lines and colors, even things a camera can't—emotions, theoretical concepts, musical rhythms, and spiritual states of mind.

Most 20th- and 21st-century paintings are a mix of the real world ("representation") and the colorful patterns of "abstract" art. An abstract artist purposely "abstracts" only some elements of camera-eye reality to make the resulting canvas more provocative, expressive, or challenging.

figures are abstract (unrecognizable), and the mood is surreal, producing the style cleverly dubbed Abstract Surrealism.

Peggy was drawn to Yves Tanguy and had a short but intense affair with the married man. Tanguy, like his art, was wacky and spontaneous, occasionally shocking friends by suddenly catching and gobbling up a spider and washing it down with white wine. The Surrealists saw themselves as spokesmen for Freud's "id," the untamed part of the personality that thinks dirty thoughts when the "ego" goes to sleep.

The Guggenheim Jeune gallery exhibited many of the artists we see in this museum, including Kandinsky, Mondrian, and Calder. Guggenheim Jeune closed as a financial flop after just two years, but its shocking paintings certainly created a buzz in the art world, and as the years passed the gallery's failure gained a rosy glow of success.

Salvador Dalí, *The Birth of Liquid Desires,* 1931-1932

Salvador Dalí could draw exceptionally well. He painted "unreal" scenes with photographic realism, making us believe they could truly happen. This air of mystery—the feeling that anything is possible—is both exciting and unsettling. His men explore the caves of the dream world and morph into something else before our eyes.

Personally, Peggy didn't like Dalí or his work, but she dutifully bought this canvas (through his wife, Gala) to complete her collection.

Max Ernst, *The Antipope,* c. 1942

The horse-headed nude in red is a portrait of Peggy—at least, that's what she thought when she saw it. She loved the painting and insisted that Ernst, whom she would later marry, give it to her as a wedding present, renamed *The Mystic Marriage.*

Others read more into it. Is the horse-headed warrior (at right) Ernst himself? Is he being wooed by one of his art students? Is that Peggy's daughter, Pegeen (center), watching the scene, sadly, from a distance? And is Peggy turning toward her beloved Max, subconsciously suspicious of the young student...who would (in fact) end up stealing Max from her? Ernst uses his considerable painting skill to bring to light a tangle of secret urges, desires, and fears—hidden like the grotesque animal faces in the reef they stand on.

PARIS AND NEW YORK

Peggy moved back to Paris in 1939 and rented an apartment on the Ile St. Louis. In September, Nazi Germany invaded Poland, sparking World War II. All of France waited...and waited...and waited for the inevitable Nazi attack on Paris.

Meanwhile, Peggy spent her days shopping for masterpieces. Using a list compiled by Duchamp and others, she personally visited artists in their studios—from Brancusi to Dalí to Giacometti—often negotiating directly with them. (Picasso initially turned Peggy down, thinking of her as a gauche, bargain-hunting housewife. When she entered his studio he said, "Madame, you'll find the lingerie department on the second floor.") In a few short months, she bought 37 of the paintings now in the collection, perhaps saving them from a Nazi regime that labeled such art "decadent."

In 1941, with the Nazis occupying Paris and most of Europe, Peggy fled her adopted homeland. With her stash of paintings and her new companion, Max Ernst, she sailed from Lisbon to safety in New York.

Peggy spent the war years, 1941-1945, in America. She married Ernst, and their house in New York City became a gathering place for exiled French Surrealists and young American artists. In 1942, she opened a gallery/museum in New York called Art of This Century that featured, well, essentially the collection we see here in Venice. But patriotic, gung-ho America was not quite ready for the nonconformist, intellectual art of Europe.

• *Now head into the East Wing.*

THE POSTWAR YEARS

Certain young American painters—from Mark Rothko to Robert Motherwell to Robert De Niro Sr. (the actor's father)—were strongly influenced by Peggy's collection. Adopting the abstract style of Kandinsky, they practiced surrealist spontaneity to "express" themselves in the physical act of putting paint on canvas. The resulting style (duh): Abstract Expressionism.

Jackson Pollock, *Enchanted Forest*, 1947

"Jack the Dripper" attacked America's postwar conformity with a can of paint, dripping and splashing a dense web onto the canvas. Picture Pollock in his studio, jiving to the hi-fi, bouncing off the walls, throwing paint in a moment of alcohol-fueled enlightenment.

Peggy helped make Pollock a celebrity. She bought his earliest works (which show Abstract-Surrealist roots), exhibited his work at her gallery, and even paid him a monthly stipend to keep experimenting.

By the way, if you haven't yet tried the Venetian specialty *spaghetti al nero di seppia* (spaghetti with squid in its own ink), it looks something like this.

In 1946, Peggy published her memoirs, titled *Out of This Century: The Informal Memoirs of Peggy Guggenheim*. The front cover was designed by Max Ernst, the back by Pollock. Peggy herself was now a celebrity.

• *Step into the boudoir.*

PEGGY IN THE BEDROOM

As America's 1950s postwar factories turned swords into kitchen appliances, Peggy longed to return "home" to Europe. The one place that kept calling to her was Venice, ever since she visited here with Laurence Vail in the 1920s. "I decided Venice would be my future home," she wrote. "I felt I would be happy alone there."

In 1947, after a grand finale exhibition by Pollock, she closed the Art of This Century gallery, crated up her collection, and moved to Venice. In 1948, she bought this palazzo and moved in.

This was Peggy's bedroom. She painted it turquoise. She commissioned the **silver headboard by Alexander Calder** for her canopy bed, using its silver frame to hang her collection of earrings, handmade by the likes of Calder and Tanguy. Venetian mirrors hung on the walls, along with a sentimental portrait of herself and her sister as children. Ex-husband Laurence Vail's collage-decorated bottles sat on the nightstand.

The same year she moved in, Peggy showed her collection in its own pavilion at the Biennale, Venice's world's fair of art, and it was the hit of the show. Europeans were astounded and a bit dumbfounded, finally seeing the kind of "degenerate" art forbidden during the fascist years, plus the radical new stuff coming out of New York City.

In 1951, Peggy met the last great love of her life, an easygoing, blue-collar Italian with absolutely no interest in art. She was 53, Raoul was 30. When Raoul died in 1954 in a car accident, Peggy comforted herself with her pets.

• *The tiny corner room adjoining the bedroom displays paintings by...*

PEGEEN

Peggy's daughter, Pegeen, inherited some of Laurence Vail's artistic talent, painting childlike scenes of Venice, populated by skinny Barbie dolls with antennae. She married twice, had four children, suffered badly from depression, and died of a barbiturate overdose in 1967.

The Guest Bedroom (where the Surrealists are) was a busy place. Pegeen and her brother, Sinbad, visited their mother in Venice, as did Peggy's ex-husbands and their new loves. Other overnight guests ranged from sculptor Alberto Giacometti (who honeymooned here), to author and cultural explorer Paul Bowles, to artist Jean Arp.

REST OF THE MUSEUM

• *We've seen the core of Peggy's collection (and home). But the museum complex also houses other pieces donated by Peggy's fellow art lovers, as well as a fine garden.*

Schulhof Collection

The recently acquired Schulhof Collection brings the museum into the late 20th century. It's exhibited in the small wing perpendicular to the main house (which you can enter from near Peggy's bedroom).

In the 1950s and '60s, the trend was toward bigger canvases, abstract designs, and experimentation with new materials and techniques. Enjoy the simple lines and colors of big, empty canvases by Americans Ellsworth Kelly, Barnett Newman, and Mark

Rothko. They were following in the footsteps of abstract artists such as Mondrian and Kandinsky (whose work they must have considered busy). Calder's mobile is like a hanging Kandinsky, brought to life by a gust of wind. The geometrical forms here reflect the same search for order, but these artists painted to the 5/4 asymmetry of Dave Brubeck's jazz classic, "Take Five."

Other painters explored a new dimension: texture. Some works (such as those by de Kooning) have very thick paint piled on. Some (by Dubuffet or Tàpies) applied material such as real dirt and organic waste to the canvas. Fontana punctured the canvas so that the fabric itself (and the hole) becomes the subject. The canvas is a tray, serving up a delightful array of substances with interesting colors, patterns, shapes, and textures.

In the psychedelic '60s, Pop Art (Warhol) raised pop-ular cultural icons to the level of high art, and Op Art (Riley) featured optical illusions that mess with your mind when you stare at them. Cy Twombly added crayon-scribbled doodles to the canvas, suggesting handwritten messages with mysterious meanings. By the way, many of the Schulhof artists—Calder, Fontana, Chillida, Riley, and Twombly—were first introduced to the world at the Venice Biennale.

Sculpture Garden

Peggy opened her impressive collection of sculpture to the Venetian public for free. It features first-rate works by all the greats, from Brancusi to Giacometti (some pieces are on loan from private collectors). After so much art already, you might find the trees—so rare in urban Venice—more interesting.

Other Exhibits

The long building facing the main palazzo from across the garden houses temporary exhibits, along with a café and shop.

Here you'll find a selection of paintings and sculptures by the postwar generation of Italians artists who were strongly influenced by Peggy's collection.

You'll see a lone canvas by Modigliani, pieces by the Futurists, and some fine sculptural works by the father of Futurism, **Umberto Boccioni.** His *Dynamism of a Speeding Horse + Houses* (1915), assembled from wood, cardboard, and metal, captures the blurred motion of a modern world—accelerated by technology, then shattered by World War I, which would leave nine million Europeans dead and everyone's moral compass spinning. (In fact, this statue was shattered by the destructive force of Boccioni's own kids, who scattered the cardboard "houses" while using it as a rocking horse.)

Boccioni's bronze *Unique Forms of Continuity in Space* (1913) seems inspired by the flowing works by Picasso and Duchamp we saw earlier. The energetic cyborg speeds forward, rippled by the winds of history, as it strides purposefully into the future. This work may look familiar—check your pocket for one of Italy's €0.20 coins and compare.

Peggy sponsored young artists, including **Tancredi**—just one name, back when that was odd—who was given a studio in the palazzo's basement. Tancredi had a relationship with daughter Pegeen, with her mother's blessing.

Step into the **café** just to peruse the fascinating black-and-white photos of Peggy standing alongside her art, taken in the very same rooms in which the paintings now hang. If, after your visit here, you still don't like modern art, think of what Peggy used to tell puzzled visitors: "Come back again in 50 years."

LA SALUTE CHURCH TOUR

Santa Maria della Salute

Where the Grand Canal opens up into the lagoon stands one of Venice's most distinctive landmarks, the church dedicated to Santa Maria della Salute (Our Lady of Health). The architect, Baldassare Longhena—who also did St. Mark's Square's "new" wing and the Ca' Rezzonico—remade Venice in the Baroque style. Crown-shaped La Salute was his crowning achievement, and the last grand Venetian structure built before Venice's decline began.

Orientation

Cost: Free entry to church; €4 to visit the Sacristy.

Hours: Daily 9:30-12:00 & 15:00-17:30.

Information: Tel. 041-274-3928, www.seminariovenezia.it.

Getting There: The church is on the Grand Canal, near the point where the canal spills into the lagoon. It's a 10-minute walk from the Accademia Bridge (past the Peggy Guggenheim Collection). By boat, vaporetto #1 delivers you to its doorstep. The *traghetto* from S.M. del Giglio is nearby.

Musical Services: Vespers service with organ music Mon-Thu at 15:30, followed by Mass at 16:00. Mass also on Sun at 11:00, followed by organ music at 11:45.

Length of This Tour: Allow 30 minutes.

Starring: Baldassare Longhena's church, minor works by Titian and Giordano, and the Sacristy, with major works by Tintoretto and Titian.

The Tour Begins

EXTERIOR

The white stone church has a steep dome that rises above the octagonal structure. It's encrusted with Baroque scrolls, leafy Corinthian columns, and 125 statues, including the lovely ladies lounging over the central doorway. The architect conceived of the church in the shape of a crown.

During the bitter plague of 1630, the Virgin Mary took pity on the city of Venice, miraculously allowing only one in three Venetians (46,000 souls) to die. During this terrible time, Venetians built this church in honor of Our Lady of Health. Her statue tops the lantern, and she's dressed as an admiral, hand on a rudder, welcoming ships to the Grand Canal.

Even today, Mary's intercession is celebrated every November 21, when a floating bridge is erected across the Grand Canal so Venetians can walk from San Marco across the water and right up the seaweed-covered steps to the front door.

At age 32, architect Baldassare Longhena (1598-1682) supported the city's heaviest dome by sinking thousands of pilings into the sandy soil to provide an adequate foundation. The 12 Baroque scrolls at the dome's base function as buttresses to help support the mammoth structure.

INTERIOR
❶ View from the Entrance

The church has a bright, healthy glow, with white stone (turned gray because of a fungus) illuminated by light filtering through the dome's windows. The nave is circular, surrounded by chapels. In contrast to the ornate Baroque exterior, the inside is simple, with only Corinthian columns and two useless balcony railings up in the dome. The red, white, and yellow marble of the floor adds a cheerful note.

Longhena focuses our immediate attention on the main altar. Every other view is blocked by heavy pillars. A master of "theatrical architecture," Longhena reveals the side chapels only one by one, as we walk around and explore. Viewed from the center of the church, the altar and side chapels are framed by arches.

Some of the "marble" is actually brick covered with marble

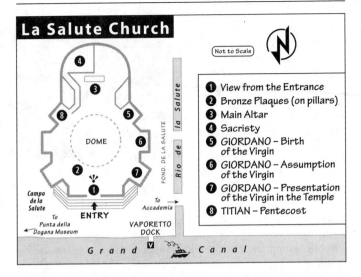

La Salute Church

Not to Scale

DOME

Campo de la Salute

To Punta della Dogana Museum

ENTRY

FOND. DE LA SALUTE

Rio de la Salute

To Accademia

VAPORETTO DOCK

G r a n d   C a n a l

❶ View from the Entrance
❷ Bronze Plaques (on pillars)
❸ Main Altar
❹ Sacristy
❺ GIORDANO – Birth of the Virgin
❻ GIORDANO – Assumption of the Virgin
❼ GIORDANO – Presentation of the Virgin in the Temple
❽ TITIAN – Pentecost

dust. The windows, with clear glass in a honeycomb pattern, bring in maximum light.

• *Look at the pillars near the entrance, opposite the altar, to find the...*

❷ Bronze Plaques

The church is dedicated not just to physical health but to spiritual health as well. The plaques relate that on September 16, 1972, Albino Luciani, the future Pope John Paul I, visited here and paid homage to the Virgin of Health (six years later, he fell sick and died after only 30 days in office).

❸ Main Altar

The marble statues on the top of the main altar tell the church's story: The Virgin and Child (center) are approached for help by a kneeling, humble Lady Venice (left). Mary shows compassion and sends an angel baby (right) to drive away Old Lady Plague.

The icon of a black, sad-eyed Madonna with a black baby (12th-century Byzantine) is not meant to be ethnically accurate. Here, a "black" Madonna means an otherworldly one.

• *Find the entrance to the Sacristy, if it's open (entry location varies). There's a fee to get in, but those who don't want to pay can get a glimpse of the paintings for free by standing outside the entry.*

❹ Sacristy

Along the right wall is Tintoretto's big and colorful *Marriage at Cana* (1551). The receding dinner table leads the eye to Jesus, who is surrounded by the bustle of the wedding feast. On the right, the host (in gray) orders the servant to bring more wine. The apostles at

LA SALUTE CHURCH

the table portray leading Venetian artists of the day. (The man
in front with an orange robe and
big white beard may be Titian.)

On the ceiling are three
ultra-dramatic paintings by Titian, with gruesome subjects
(pick up a mirror for easier
viewing): *Cain Clubbing Abel*,
Abraham Sacrificing His Son,
and *David Slaying Goliath* (c. 1543-1544). The panels—featuring stormy clouds, windblown hair, flat tones, and overwrought
poses—date from Titian's "Mannerist crisis." After visiting Rome
and seeing the work of Michelangelo in the Sistine Chapel, Titian
abandoned his standard, sweet, and tested style to paint epic, statuesque, and dramatic works in the Mannerist style. To appreciate his
range of styles, contrast the ceiling panels with the painting over
the altar, Titian's stately *St. Mark Enthroned with Saints* (c. 1511).

• *Back in the circular nave, there are six side chapels—three to the left,
three to the right. Start near the main altar, on the right side (to your
right as you face the altar).*

Side Chapel Paintings

Luca Giordano (1632-1705) celebrates the Virgin in three paintings with similar compositions—heaven and angels above, dark
earth below. Giordano, a prolific artist from Naples, was known as
"Luca fa presto" (Fast Luke) for the speed (some would say sloppi-
ness) with which he dashed off his paintings.

• *In the chapel to the right of the altar is...*

❺ **Giordano, *Birth of the Virgin*** (1674): Little baby Mary in
her mom's arms seems like nothing special. But God the Father
looks down from above and sends the dove of the Holy Spirit.

• *In the middle chapel (on the right side), look for...*

❻ **Giordano, *Assumption of the Virgin*** (1667): Mary, at the
end of her life, is being taken gloriously, by winged babies, up from
the dark earth to the golden light of heaven. The apostles cringe in
amazement. A later artist thought his statue was better and planted
it right in our way.

• *In the chapel closest to the entrance, see...*

❼ **Giordano, *Presentation of the Virgin in the Temple*** (early
1670s): Notice how the painting fits the surrounding architecture.
It's great to enjoy art in situ. The child Mary (in blue, with wispy
halo) ascends a staircase that goes diagonally "into" the canvas.
Giordano places us viewers at the foot of the stairs. The lady in the
lower left asks her kids, "Why can't you be more like her?!"

• *From here, look directly across to the other side of the nave at Titian's*

Pentecost, *in the chapel closest to the main altar. The painting looks its best from this distance and angle.*

   ❽ **Titian,** *Pentecost* (1546): The dove of the Holy Spirit sends spiritual rays that fan out to the apostles below, giving them

tongues of fire above their heads. They gyrate in amazement, each one in a different direction. Using floor tiles and ceiling panels, Titian has created the 3-D illusion of a barrel-arched chapel, with the dove coming right into the church through a fake window. But the painting was not designed for this location and, up close, the whole fake niche looks...fake.

SAN GIORGIO MAGGIORE TOUR

If you look out over the canal from St. Mark's Square, you can't miss the classical facade, dome, and tower of San Giorgio Maggiore. This iconic church is only a five-minute vaporetto ride away. Even if you're not interested in Palladio's influential architecture, Tintoretto's famous *Last Supper*, or the stunning bell-tower views of Venice and the lagoon, it's worth a trip just to escape tourist-mobbed St. Mark's Square. And from San Giorgio Maggiore, you view the Doge's Palace, and Venice, as if you're aboard an approaching ship.

Orientation

Cost: Admission to the church is free. It costs €6 to go up the bell tower.

Hours: Church open daily 9:00-19:00, Nov-March 8:30-18:00. The last ascent in the tower elevator is 20 minutes before closing time. The elevator is closed during Sunday Mass.

Information: Tel. 041-522-7827.

Avoiding Crowds: The church is never crowded, but the bell tower and elevator can be. Come early or late to have it to yourself.

Getting There: Getting to San Giorgio Maggiore (alone on its own island) requires a vaporetto ride. The one-hop, five-minute ride on #2 from the San Zaccaria docks is €5 (pier is just past the Bridge of Sighs, dock B, direction: Piazza Roma). A regular €7.50 vaporetto ticket gives you 75 minutes—which could cover your return trip if you do a quick visit. To get back to St. Mark's Square, take the #2 headed the opposite way (direction: San Zaccaria). Boats come every 12 minutes in each direction.

Church Services: Mass is held on Sundays at 11:00; during that time, the church is open to worshippers, but not sightseers. In the winter, when it's too cold inside the church, Mass is held in the adjacent chapel (enter to the right of the high altar).

Monastery Tours: Escorted audioguide tours of the Benedictine monastery depart on the hour (€16/1 hour). They include the monastery and an ensemble of modern art and architecture within it.

Length of This Tour: Allow one hour.

Eating: The fine little harborside **$ San Giorgio Café,** rarely used by tourists, is about 150 yards around the left of the church. Its terrace is peaceful—except at lunchtime, when it's mobbed by librarians (daily 10:00-20:00, off-season 11:00-15:00).

The Rest of the Island: You can walk along the left side of the church to the San Giorgio Café and view the pleasure boats in the marina. Inside the pink building just beyond the café is **Le Stanze del Vetro,** a super-modern space with rotating exhibits relating to glass. Typically their spring exhibition features contemporary glass art, while their fall show highlights a historic Venetian master (free entry, Thu-Tue 10:00-19:00, closed Wed, tel. 041-522-9138, www.lestanzedelvetro.org).

Starring: Palladio, Tintoretto, and views of Venice.

The Tour Begins

EXTERIOR

The facade looks like a Greek temple, a style well-known today because of its architect, Andrea Palladio (1508-1580). Palladio's hugely influential treatise on architecture inspired centuries of architects in England and America with its expert application of Greco-Roman styles. Countless villas, palaces, and churches look like this. They are "Palladian."

Palladio's ingenious facade overlaps two temple fronts. Four tall columns, topped by a triangular pediment resembling a Greek porch, mark the entryway to the tall, central nave. This is superimposed over the facade of the lower side aisles. Behind the facade rises a dome topped with a statue

San Giorgio Maggiore

1. View down the Nave
2. Main Altar
3. TINTORETTO – Last Supper
4. TINTORETTO – Manna from Heaven
5. Choir
6. BASSANO – Nativity and Adoration of the Shepherds
7. Crucifix
8. DOMENICO TINTORETTO – St. Benedict and Other Saints
9. DOMENICO TINTORETTO – The Stoning of St. Stephen
10. Statue of an Angel
11. To View from the Bell Tower
12. To Le Stanze del Vetro Glass Exhibit

of St. George (the Christian slayer of medieval dragons) holding a flag. The whole complex is completed by the bell tower, which echoes the Campanile in St. Mark's Square across the water.

This church feels so striking because it just doesn't fit with old-school Venice. Palladio makes no concession to the Byzantine legacy of Venice that you see across the water at the Doge's Palace.

• *Walk into the interior of the church.*

INTERIOR
❶ View down the Nave, then up the Nave

The interior matches the outer facade, with a high nave flanked by lower side aisles. The walls are white (Palladio's favorite color); the

windows have clear, rather than stained, glass; and the well-lit church has the clarity, orderliness, and mathematical perfection of the classical world. In keeping with Palladio's classical sensitivity, all decor is in harmony (compared to the relative chaos of, say, the Frari Church). Oh, the stout, stony symmetry and mathematical purity—with light spilling in from the canal—it's enough to give a Renaissance architect a...never mind.

• *Head down the nave to the...*

❷ Main Altar

The altar, made after the voyages of Columbus and company, is topped with a bronze globe of the world. When this place was being built, Church doctrine was being challenged by the discovery of the New World, the founding of secular societies, and the groundbreaking scientific advancements of the Enlightenment. With this altar, the globe is embraced as if to declare the universality of the Christian message. God, overhead, is wearing a triangular halo, reminding us he's part of the Trinity.

• *On the wall to the right of the altar is a masterpiece by Tintoretto (you can walk around to get a closer look).*

❸ Tintoretto, *Last Supper,* 1592-1594

This is the last of several versions of the Last Supper by Tintoretto (1518-1594) that decorate Venice, each one different and inventive

(compare it with the Scuola San Rocco version, pictured on page 153). Here, the table stretches diagonally away from us on a tiled floor. The convincing perspective effect is theatrical, engaging the viewer. The scene is crowded— servants and cats mingle with wispy angels. A blazing lamp, radiating supernatural light, illuminates the otherwise dark interior. At the far left, a beggar is fed, illustrating Christ's concern for the poor. The devilish guy on the right rejects a basket of communion wafers while eyeing a more hedonistic banquet. Your eyes go straight to a well-lit Christ, serving his faithful with both hands—wholeheartedly. While most Last Suppers capture the moment Jesus says, "One of you will betray me," this one depicts Jesus sharing the first Eucharist (in keeping with the Counter-Reformation notion that only proper Roman Catholic Christians can be saved).

San Giorgio was the church for a Benedictine monastery, an order that stressed a simple lifestyle and concern for the poor. They hired Tintoretto (a common-man's painter) and worked closely with him to hone the message that all are welcome—saints, servants, beggars, sinners—into the Christian faith. The monks appreciated Tintoretto's jumble of the spiritual with the mundane, proclaiming that God works miraculously with us on an everyday level.

This canvas works together theologically with the other canvas flanking the altar.

• *On the wall to the left of the altar is...*

❹ Tintoretto, *Manna from Heaven*, 1591-1592

This painting illustrates the Benedictine motto: Work and pray. Here we see the sunny morning after the storm, when God rained bread down on the hungry Israelites. Many are working, others relax prayerfully, and others gather the heavenly meal in baskets, basking in the glow of the miracle. The message: Work and pray, and God will take care of you.

• *Behind the altar is the...*

❺ Choir

This beautiful space features 82 stalls elaborately carved in walnut. Here, monks stood and sang, carrying on the prayers, chants, and traditions of the Benedictine order, whose relationship with the island stretched back to AD 982 (the monastery closed in 1807, but was revived on a smaller scale in the 20th century). The choir was designed with acoustics in mind, and the barrel-vault ceiling is backed up with a woofer-shaped apse—ideal for amplifying Gregorian chant. (Suddenly I feel a cough coming on...my, the echoes.)

MORE ART INSIDE THE CHURCH

As long as you're here, check out a few more works. They're minor pieces in art-drenched Venice, but they'd be stars in any American museum.

Back near the entrance, in the first chapel on the right as you face the altar, is Jacopo Bassano's ❻ *Nativity and Adoration of the Shepherds,* where a radiant Baby Jesus lights the dim canvas. In the next chapel is a carved ❼ **Crucifix** once attributed to Florentine dome builder Filippo Brunelleschi.

In the transepts are two works by Jacopo Tintoretto's son, Domenico. In the right transept, the

static ❽ *St. Benedict and Other Saints* shows the early monk (to left, in black, bald and bearded) along with Pope Gregory (who wrote about him) having a heavenly vision. ❾ *The Stoning of St. Stephen* (left transept) shows that Domenico had his father's raw talent, but not his flair for dramatic compositions that recede into the distance.

On your way to the bell tower, you'll pass the original ❿ **statue of an angel** that once stood atop the tower (a copy stands there today). Made in the 18th century of laminated wood covered in lead, it was destroyed by lightning in 1993. Restorers have pieced it back together.

• *You'll find the elevator to the top of the bell tower in the far left corner.*

BELL TOWER
⓫ View from the Bell Tower

The bell tower here is less crowded than the Campanile at St. Mark's and has an unobstructed view in all directions (St. Mark's has a lattice grill to keep suicidal people from jumping).

Start by looking at the city (to the north), and go clockwise:

Facing North (toward the city): This is the famous view of Venice's skyline, dominated by St. Mark's Campanile. The big, long, brick church farther inland is Santi Giovanni e Paolo. Farther to the right (east) is the barely visible basin of the Arsenale, the former shipyard, which in its medieval heyday bragged that it was capable of producing a ship a day. Farther still is the green parkland where the Venice Biennale international exhibition is held annually (alternating each year between art and architecture). North of Venice, in the hazy distance (just to the right of Santi Giovanni e Paolo), you can glimpse several islands. Tiny San Michele (with cypress trees) is the city's cemetery—from here, the island looks connected to Venice. Murano, the next closest, appears to be an extension of the forested cemetery. Burano is to the distant right, with its leaning bell tower. And Torcello (trust me) is just beyond Burano.

Facing East and South: Look out at the lagoon, which leads to the open Adriatic. This tower was once used to spot approaching enemy boats. The lagoon is too shallow for serious shipping; posts mark the channels dredged to let boats pass through. There's a strict speed limit: 5 knots per hour (kph) on the small canals, 7 kph on the Grand Canal, and 11 kph around the perimeter of the island city.

The long, narrow sandbar island of Lido in the distance is six miles long and only a half-mile wide (with cars and ferry service to the mainland). The green dome on the island marks the Lido's town center, home to modern hotels and beaches. The Lido serves as a natural breakwater against the wind and waves of the Adriatic Sea, helping create the placid waters of the Venetian lagoon. At the right end of the Lido (visible from here, but not obvious) is the narrow opening to the Adriatic, where the long-delayed underwater flood barriers are being built. Designed to block the *acqua alta* flooding, the multibillion-dollar project involves the construction of a series of hinged barriers that will rise up to block high tides threatening the lagoon.

Once a year, the mayor of Venice sails to the opening of the Adriatic to celebrate the ritual marriage of Venice and the sea—the same ritual performed centuries ago by the doges in their gold-leaf boat.

Between the Lido and San Giorgio are several smaller islands, which have been home over the centuries to monasteries and hospitals. The plain, rectangular white building on San Servolo, the

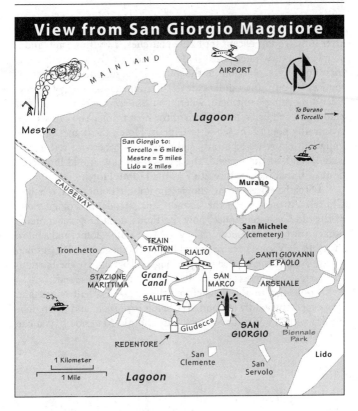

View from San Giorgio Maggiore

MAINLAND

AIRPORT

N

Lagoon

To Burano & Torcello

Mestre

San Giorgio to:
Torcello = 6 miles
Mestre = 5 miles
Lido = 2 miles

CAUSEWAY

Murano

San Michele
(cemetery)

TRAIN STATION

Tronchetto

RIALTO

SANTI GIOVANNI E PAOLO

STAZIONE MARITTIMA

Grand Canal

SAN MARCO

ARSENALE

SALUTE

Giudecca

REDENTORE

SAN GIORGIO

Biennale Park

San Clemente

San Servolo

Lido

1 Kilometer

1 Mile

Lagoon

little island just before the Lido, was a hospital for the insane in the 18th century and now houses a university.

At your feet are the green gardens and the cloisters of the former abbey of San Giorgio.

Facing West: Below is the church, with its dome topped by a green St. George carrying a flag (or is his arm still missing?).

You can see the back sides of the white statues atop Palladio's facade. Arcing gracefully to the left is the island of Giudecca, which is oh-so-close to the island you're on, but must be reached by a short swim or vaporetto #2. The Giudecca, which has al-

ways been isolated from the rest of the city, was a popular place to build villas in Venice's heyday. The island's separation also made it a perfect place for exiles such as Michelangelo, who found refuge and peace here between commissions—there's even a street named after him. Today, except for a few churches, a youth hostel, and a couple of luxury hotels, the Giudecca is home to locals going about their quiet lives, oblivious to the tourism that dominates the rest of Venice. If you want a quiet café away from the tourist mobs, consider a morning jaunt here, where you can see the city sprawl out before you and listen to the hum of the boat traffic. You can see the swimming pool of the jet-setty Ciprani Hotel, the domes of other Palladian churches (the only sights on this otherwise residential island), and, at the far end, the Molino Stucky, an old industrial flour mill that reopened in 2007 as the Hilton Hotel.

Directly across from you is the grand dome of La Salute Church. At the head of the Grand Canal stands the golden globe of the old Customs House, now the Punta della Dogana contemporary art museum. Looming beyond La Salute's dome, and a bit to the right, is Venice's cruise port. How many megaships are in town today? And in the far distance, through the smog, are the burning smokestacks and cranes of lovely Mestre, on the mainland.

Looking Up: The bells chime the hours and half-hours, and ring especially loudly at noon. Try being here then, and when people ask you, "How did you enjoy San Giorgio Maggiore?" you can say, "What?"

SAN GIORGIO MAGGIORE

VENICE'S LAGOON TOUR

San Michele • Murano • Burano • Torcello

Fascinating islands hide out in Venice's lagoon, a calm section of the Adriatic protected from wind and waves by the natural breakwater of the Lido. The brackish marsh—a mix of fresh water and silt from the mainland's rivers, plus the tide-driven saltwater of the Adriatic—is dotted with a maze of sandbars. The lagoon is big (212 square miles) and so shallow that you could walk across most of it without getting your hair wet. Centuries ago, the shallow water and treacherous sandbars made the isle of Venice safe from attack by land or sea. Venice is the only great medieval city that never needed a wall.

Cradled by the lagoon, north of the city, are four islands easily laced together in a pleasant day trip, a nice escape from the hubbub of Venice. Though they're all basically satellites of Venice, each one has its own personality and claims to fame: Murano is known for glass; Burano for lace and photogenic, exuberantly colorful houses; and tranquil Torcello for its antique church's fine mosaics. San Michele is the cemetery island, the last stop for its residents, but the first stop for the vaporetto from Venice. The lagoon is home to many more islands, but these four are the most worthwhile for visitors.

We'll sail first from Venice to Murano (stopping at San Michele on the way), and then to Burano, from where we'll make a side-trip to Torcello before returning to Venice.

Orientation

Getting There: This tour assumes you're traveling by **vaporetto,** but there are other options (see next page). Since single vaporetto tickets (€7.50) are only valid for 75 minutes, getting a vaporetto pass for this lagoon excursion makes more sense

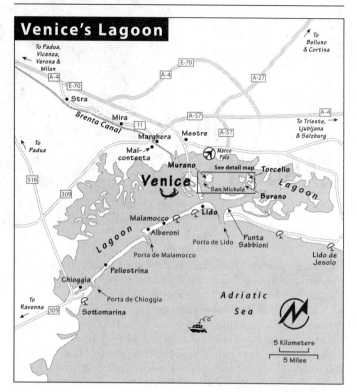

Venice's Lagoon

To Padua, Vicenza, Verona & Milan

To Belluno & Cortina

E-70

A-4

A-4

A-27

A-4

E-70

Stra

Mira

Brenta Canal

11

Marghera

Mestre

A-57

A-57

To Trieste, Ljubljana & Salzburg

To Padua

Mal-contenta

Marco Polo

Murano

See detail map

Torcello

516

309

Venice

San Michele

Lagoon

Burano

Lagoon

Malamocco

Lido

Alberoni

Porta de Lido

Punta Sabbioni

Porta de Malamocco

Lido de Jesolo

Pellestrina

Chioggia

Adriatic

To Ravenna

309

Porta de Chioggia

Sea

Sottomarina

5 Kilometers

5 Miles

(for details on tickets and passes, see page 19). Make sure to confirm vaporetto times by downloading the latest schedule from www.actv.it.

CitySightseeing also runs **hop-on, hop-off boats** (€20/24 hours) to Murano, Burano, and Torcello (but not San Michele). You can take their Line A boat from St. Mark's Square to Murano, then switch to the Line B boat in Murano, which runs to Torcello and Burano and then back to Murano. Boats generally depart every half-hour 9:00-18:30 (less frequently in winter; confirm schedule at www.city-sightseeing.it).

For guided tours of the islands, see the sidebar in this chapter.

Avoiding Crowds: You aren't the only tourist in Venice spending your day seeing these sights, in this same order. Vaporetti can be very crowded; if you want a seat for the longer rides, consider showing up at the boat dock a bit early to get in line. CitySightseeing boats are often less crowded than vaporetti.

Planning Your Time: Since it takes a minimum of three hours round-trip from St. Mark's to Torcello, allow at least six hours to blitz all four islands. Eight hours (or more) lets you slow down, browse, and enjoy. For an hour-by-hour itinerary, see page 13. If you only have a few hours to spare, stick to visiting either Murano or Burano/Torcello. Murano is much quicker to reach and a must for glass enthusiasts, but Burano and Torcello have more compelling sights overall. Keep in mind that Burano's good Lace Museum and Torcello's dull church museum are closed Mondays.

Cemetery (San Michele): Daily 7:30-18:00, Oct-March until 16:30; reception to the left as you enter, free WC to the right, no picnicking.

Glass Museum (Murano): €14, daily 10:30-18:30, Nov-March until 16:30, Fondamenta Giustinian 8, tel. 041-739-586, http://museovetro.visitmuve.it.

Lace Museum (Burano): €5, Tue-Sun 10:30-17:00, Nov-March until 16:30, closed Mon year-round, some English descriptions, tel. 041-730-034, http://museomerletto.visitmuve.it.

Santa Maria Assunta Church (Torcello): €5, €12 combo-ticket covers museum, church, and bell tower and includes audioguide; daily 10:30-18:00, Nov-Feb 10:00-17:00; museum and bell tower close 30 minutes earlier, museum closed Mon year-round; museum tel. 041-730-761.

Visitor Information: Pick up a free map of the lagoon and its islands from any TI. Two words you'll see all day: *vetri* (glass, Murano's specialty) and *merletti* (lace, Burano's specialty).

Starring: World-famous Venetian glass and lace, the mosaics of the oldest Venetian church, outrageously colorful fishermen's villages, and the quieter side of Venice.

STARTING YOUR JOURNEY

Our tour starts at the Fondamente Nove vaporetto stop, on Venice's north shore (the "back" of the fish).

Fondamente Nove is a pleasant 15-minute walk from Rialto or St. Mark's. Start by making your way to Campo Santa Maria Formosa. Then navigate north, following signs to the Church of SS. Giovanni e Paolo. Continue north, walking alongside the long straight canal, on Fondamenta dei Mendicanti. When you reach the lagoon, turn left and walk a few blocks to Fondamente Nove.

Alternatively, you could reach Fondamente Nove by vaporetto: From San Zaccaria (near St. Mark's), take the #4.1 (35 minutes). From the train or bus station, take #4.2 (30 minutes).

Note that during summer, there are (slightly faster) express vaporetti that go directly to Murano-Colonna (if you're OK with skipping the first stop on our tour, the cemetery on San Michele): From San Zaccaria, catch the #7, or from the train/bus stations catch the #3.

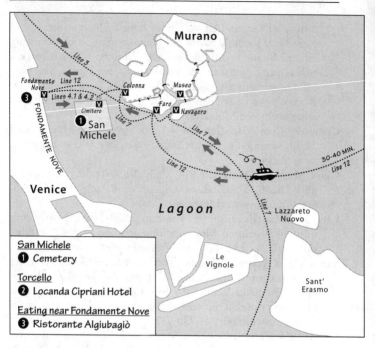

THE ROUTE

From Fondamente Nove, take the #4.1 or #4.2 vaporetto for Murano (about every 10 minutes). On the way, get off at the Cimitero stop on the island of San Michele to see the cemetery (6-minute ride). Continue on to Murano, arriving at the Murano-Colonna stop (3-minute ride). Sightsee Murano, as you make your way to the Murano-Faro stop, where you board vaporetto #12 for the trip to Burano (30-40 minutes). From Burano, you can side-trip to Torcello (on the #12, 5-minute trip each way). To return to Venice from Burano, take vaporetto #12 all the way back to Fondamente Nove (45 minutes). For a longer, more scenic return past even more lagoon islands, you could take the #14 from Burano to the San Zaccaria dock near St. Mark's Square (70 minutes).

The Tour Begins

• *After leaving Fondamente Nove, the next stop of the #4.1 and #4.2 vaporetto lines is Cimitero. On the way you may see a sculpture in the water of two people in a boat heading toward the cemetery. It's* The Barque of Dante, *ferrying Dante and Virgil to the afterlife. At the dock, hop off for a short visit to...*

Lagoon Tour

1 Kilometer

1 Mile

Lagoon

10-MIN. WALK

SANTA MARIA ASSUNTA

Laghi

Madonna del Monte

Mazzorbo

Torcello ②

Line 12

San Giacomo

Burano

~ Bridges

San Francesco del Deserto

Lines 12 & 14

Crevan

To Treporti, Punta Sabbioni & (#14) Lido & San Zaccaria

Sant' Erasmo

SAN MICHELE

The cemetery island's location—directly across the water from the emergency room of Venice's Santi Giovanni e Paolo hospital—is just a coincidence. The stopover is easy, since boats come every 10 minutes. If you even half-enjoy wandering through old cemeteries, you'll dig this one—it's full of flowers, trees, scurrying lizards, and birdsong, and has an intriguing chapel.

The island, which is dedicated to St. Michael and holds a Renaissance church, became Venice's cemetery in 1806 when Napoleon decreed that it was unhygienic to bury bodies within a city. As a result, Venice's coffins were shipped out to San Michele, and since then, Venetians have been buried here. You'll find the dearly departed (many with their photos) sorted into sections *(campi)* of priests *(preti)*, nuns *(suore)*, monks *(frati)*, children *(bambini)*, civilian victims of war, soldiers, military sailors *(marinai)*, and so on. The cemetery is divided into numbered zones called *recinti*.

Foreign Romantics and artists who made Venice their adopted hometown have also chosen this spot as their final resting place. Because many came from other cultures and weren't Catholic, you'll find them in the Evangelico (Protestant) section, Recinto XV; and the Greco (Orthodox) section, Recinto XIV. To find these sections—with the graves of the most famous foreigners—go basically straight ahead from the entrance to the far end, following the maps and signs.

In Recinto XV lies Idaho-born poet **Ezra Pound.** While his works are less familiar than his contemporaries', he was a huge in-fluence on his fellow Modern-

ists, most notably James Joyce and T. S. Eliot. A fan of Mus-solini, he made anti-American broadcasts during World War II. Instead of being tried for treason after the war, he spent 12 years in a hospital for the "criminally insane." Eliot, Rob-ert Frost, Ernest Hemingway, and others eventually lobbied for his release, which came in 1958. From the Evangelico gate, he's in the near-left quarter of the section—look for a small stone in a large plot, with three large bushes.

Nearby is the grave of Nobel Laureate and onetime US Poet Laureate **Joseph Brodsky** (1940-1996), who was expelled from So-viet Russia, lived the rest of his life in America, and asked to be buried here in Venice. It's in the far-left quarter, facing the gravel path and Ezra Pound.

Recinto XIV (the "Greco" section) is nearby: Exit the Evan-gelico gate and turn left, following the wall until you reach the gate marked *Rec. Greco.* Inside, find Russian-

born Modernist composer **Igor Stravin-sky** (far right corner, alongside his wife) and the Russian dancer/choreographer **Diaghilev** (the canopied tomb along the far wall, piled with ballet slippers left in homage by his admirers).

• *Return to the dock and catch any #4.1 or #4.2 vaporetto heading toward the right (boats leave every 10 minutes). While you're waiting, look for the blue funeral boat with a rack on wheels for the coffin. It's usually moored next to the vaporetto.*

It's just a three-minute crossing to the Murano-Colonna stop. (If the vaporetto's too crowded, you could just swim it.) As you approach the island of Murano, you'll see its ghostly lighthouse *(faro)* off to the right. In centuries past, the *faro* guided boats from the open sea into town. Near the lighthouse is the stop where you'll leave Murano for the island of Burano.

▲MURANO

Murano is famous for its glass factories. A 1292 Venetian law re-

stricted glass production (and its dangerous furnaces) to Murano to prevent fires on the main island... and to protect the secrets of Venetian glassmaking. Originally, glassmakers made mosaic tiles, later branching out to produce the ornate vases, beaded necklaces, glass sculptures, and wine decanters you'll see here today.

Murano may seem dominated by glassworks and the glass shops that line its main canal, but there's much more to the island. If you take time to wander, you'll find impressive churches, scenically situated restaurants, and untouristed residential areas.

❶ Fondamenta dei Vetrai: From the Colonna vaporetto

stop, skip the glass shops in front of you, walk to the right, and wander up the street along the canal, Fondamenta dei Vetrai (Glassmakers' Embankment). The Faro district of Murano, on the other side of the canal, is packed with factories *(fabriche)* and their furnaces *(fornaci).* The brick buildings give Murano a 19th-century, Industrial Age look and feel. At #14 is the entry to the island's small indoor **shopping mall,** with a Despar supermarket on the upper floor (closed Sun).

You'll pass dozens more **glass shops** along the canal. Window-shopping here can be as much fun as buying—the personality, style, and prices of wares vary wildly from place to place. Early

Murano

SANTA MARIA DEGLI ANGELI

F. E SEBASTIANO VENIER

Serenella **V**

RAMO DA MULA

Venier **V**

Da Mula **V**

LA MURRINA GLASS SHOP

GLASS MUSEUM

F. SE NOVE

SAN PIETRO MARTIRE

MALL & SUPER-MARKET

VENINI GLASS SHOP

RIVA LONGA

SANTA MARIA E SAN DONATO

Line 3

Colonna **V**

Lines 4.1 & 4.2

To San Michele & Venice

1 FONDAMENTA DEI VETRAI

F. DAN. MANIN

FIRE TOWER

6

FARO

F. ANDREA NAVAGERO

Museo

Lagoon

Line 7

7 Faro **V**

LIGHT-HOUSE

Navagero **V**

200 Meters

200 Yards

To Venice

Line 12

Line 7

To Burano

To Venice

1 Fondamenta dei Vetrai
2 Church of San Pietro Martire
3 Residential Murano: Ramo da Mula
4 Glass Museum
5 Santa Maria e San Donato Church
6 Mosaici Donà Murano
7 Ai Dogi

along this promenade, at #47, is the high-class **Venini** shop, with glass that's a cut above much of what else is on offer here, and with an interior showing off the ultimate in modern Venetian glass design (closed Sun). The storefronts along here display everything from knickknacks to vases to, well, glasses. If a window display grabs your attention, step inside; you may even see a glass maestro working on small-scale works in one corner of a showroom. Note that the really cheap places likely aren't selling authentic Murano glass; if that matters to you, ask before you buy. (Several shops sport signs pointedly reminding potential customers that their glass may be a bit more expensive...because it's not made in China.) If your browsing starts turning to buying, be sure to read my tips on page 291. And remember, if you see something you like, get it...you may not find it elsewhere.

Continue up Fondamenta dei Vetrai until you see a **tower** (built as a fire lookout in this city of furnaces) on your right and a church on your left.

2 **Church of San Pietro Martire:** The church (free but donations appreciated) features Giovanni Bellini's solid-color *Virgin Enthroned with Mark and a Kneeling Doge* (right wall of the nave

in the center). This vo-
tive painting—showing
a doge being introduced
to the Virgin Mary by St.
Mark—was the doge's way
of asking for divine pro-
tection and favor during
his reign. The doge wears
a luxurious ermine cloak
(a symbol of royalty) and a
ducal crown hat.

The **sacristy/museum** (€2, closed Sat-Sun) has ornately
carved caryatids (human pillars, c. 1660) with expressive faces and
arms posed every which way. The lower carved panels between the
caryatids depict scenes from the life of John the Baptist, culminating in his beheading in the far corner. In the next rooms, see
ceremonial religious objects and statues, then check out the photos
(at the landing midway up the steps) of these objects being used in
modern-day Venetian parades. Upstairs are piles of relics in glass
cases, along with the corresponding certificates of authenticity issued by the Vatican.

❸ **Residential Murano:** For a slice of local life, continue past
the church along the canal, bending left and passing the big, green
metal bridge. Keep going as the promenade bears left and feeds
you down the street called Ramo da Mula, and wander this very
tidy "subdivision." In this old shell there's a new vibrancy, as tour-
ist-swamped Venice's high rents and real-estate prices have driven
locals to the outlying islands. Behind the glass shops, Murano is
a workaday community of 6,000 residents. It has real neighborhoods, with moms shopping at markets, schools filled with noisy
children, bikes in the front yards, and benches warmed by Venetian
old-timers.

Backtrack to the embankment, and use the green bridge to
cross the Grand Canal of Murano. Once across, turn right. Just
after the first real side street, you'll pass another unique shop,
La Murrina, with elegant and modern home-decor items, such
as striking chandeliers (closed Tue, Riva Longa 17, tel. 041-527-
4605).

Continue past the shop, then pass a smaller Co-op supermarket and the Murano-Museo vaporetto stop. Where the canal bends
left, look for a large white building.

❹ **Glass Museum:** Inside the building is Murano's Glass
Museum *(Museo del Vetro)*, which gives a very modern look at the
history of glassmaking. Worth visiting only if you're a die-hard
glass fan, the museum begins with an introductory video on techniques, then displays historical examples of the past 500 years

of Venetian glassmaking. Videos in several rooms show masters practicing their craft, and the last exhibit displays fine modern pieces. Of note is the room about the production of miniatures (namely portraits and landscape scenes), which were all the rage in the late 1800s.

❺ **Santa Maria e San Donato Church:** One hundred yards farther along the canal is Santa Maria e San Donato Church, the

architectural highlight of Murano. Note the fine Byzantine Romanesque exterior—especially the stonework of its apse, facing the canal. At the base of the towering campanile is an elaborate memorial to residents of the Veneto (the region surrounding Venice) who have been lost fighting in all wars. Now head inside the church (free). The interior takes you back to the 12th century. Built when St. Mark's Basilica was under construction, the highlights are its inlaid stone floor and the gorgeous mosaic above the altar. It features Mary as God's mother, gliding in from heaven on her carpet, blessing the faithful with two open hands.

From the church, backtrack to the green bridge and cross back toward San Pietro Martire. Near the church, cross the narrow canal and turn right onto Fondamenta Daniele Manin.

❻ **Mosaici Donà Murano:** This fourth-generation shop, at #86, makes glass pieces for mosaics. Many of the beautiful panels you've seen in churches here or in Venice had their origin on Murano. Glass plates in different textures and colors come out like pizzas, then are cut into smaller pieces for easy placement. Small bags of mixed glass pieces make an affordable, fun, and lightweight souvenir (closed Sun, www.mosaicidonamurano.com).

Continue down Fondamenta Daniele Manin, then turn left on the street called Bressagio, which takes you toward the white-stone lighthouse *(faro)*. To your right are some of Murano's actual glass factories and their showrooms, including...

❼ **Ai Dogi:** At #25, the Ai Dogi factory's showroom has an open kiln area where you can watch a glassblower at work. While most such demos on Murano come with a pushy sales pitch, Ai Dogi just lets you watch a maestro work his magic (roughly 9:30-15:30—often with a lunch break, no activity Sat-Sun or on particularly hot days).

• *To continue our tour, walk over to the Murano-Faro vaporetto stop and catch the #12 vaporetto to* **Burano** *(2-3/hour, 30-40 minutes, boat destination may say* Treporti *or* Punta Sabbioni*). If you'd prefer to*

Guided Tours to Murano
(and Elsewhere)

I recommend the self-guided tour in this chapter. But if you'd like to test your ability to resist a smooth-talking Italian glass salesman, or if you'd like to join a group for your trip out to Murano (and the others), consider these two other ways to get there.

By Speedboat Tour to Murano, Burano, and Torcello

The easiest—and priciest—way to see Murano, Burano, and Torcello is to pay €20 for a rushed and touristy four-hour speedboat tour, run by Alilaguna (the same outfit that runs the airport boats; this trip is called the "green line"). They leave three times a day in summer from the San Marco-Giardinetti dock; look and listen for guides calling out for potential passengers (generally every half-hour 9:00-16:00, fewer cruises Nov-March, tel. 041-240-1711, www.alilaguna.it). The tours are speedy indeed—live guides race through the commentary in up to five languages—and boats stop for roughly 40 minutes at each island. The stops are for glassblowing and lacemaking demonstrations followed by sales spiels, leaving no time to explore on your own.

A Free Ride to Murano—with a Sales Pitch

You can also get to Murano for free on a speedboat. Tourists are practically kidnapped from St. Mark's Square by the aggressive sales reps who then ferry them out to the island (35-minute ride). Your only obligation is to sit through a fairly interesting 20-minute glassmaking demonstration and sales pitch. After that, you're on your own. (In fact, they don't promise you a trip back to Venice.)

During the demonstration, the glassblower typically sticks a rod with raw glass on the end into a furnace, melts the glass, and expands it by blowing through the hollow rod. Then he shapes it with tongs into a vase, a glass, or a piece of art. This is followed by an almost comically high-pressure sales pitch in the showroom. (The spiel is brief, and there really is no obligation to buy anything.) If you do buy something, see page 291 for tips on having a purchase shipped home.

If you just want to see a glassblower in action, you don't need to go out to Murano—visit **Vetri d'Arte** in Palazzo Rota, near St. Mark's Square (see the Shopping in Venice chapter for details). But if you do visit Murano, you'll likely be approached by a local salesman trying to lure you into his shop for a free demo. If you'd rather see a similar demo in a lower-pressure environment, drop into the Ai Dogi shop near the Murano-Faro vaporetto stop (listed in this chapter).

head straight back to Venice, take either the #3 vaporetto (for the train station and bus station), the #4.2, #12, or #13 (for Fondamente Nove), or the #7 (for St. Mark's Square). The #4.1 is a much slower way back, as it loops around Murano before heading back to Fondamente Nove.

▲▲BURANO

Famous for its lace and outlandishly colorful houses, Burano is a sleepy island with a sleepy community (pop. 2,700)—village Venice without the glitz. Its vibrantly painted homes look like Venice before the plaster peeled off. Each adjoining townhouse is painted its own color. When Venice was a showy city of merchants, Burano was a humble town of fishermen. Though tourists clog the island's main drag by day, at night it's quiet. Laundry hangs over alleyways, and sunshades (typical of the area) cover the doors of residents' homes. The church's bell tower leans at a five-degree angle...the same as Pisa's. Beyond the touristy core, Burano holds many back lanes and Technicolor-tranquil canals.

This town's history is ancient, dating back to when the island was, like Torcello, a haven for mainlanders fleeing from barbarian invasions. "Burano" likely comes from "Porta Boreana"—the city gate from the settlers' hometown that faced the bracing Bora wind. It's that same wind that meant survival on the lagoon. It kept away the malaria-carrying mosquitoes that made other places (like Torcello) less habitable, and whisked sailing fishermen away from the stagnant waters nearby. (Nevertheless, Burano is often engulfed in the fog that's so common on the lagoon—the island's vividly painted facades helped those fishermen find their way home in the mist.)

Burano can be covered in a 15-minute stroll. From the vaporetto dock, follow the crowds into the center. The tight **main drag** is packed with tourists and lined with shops, some of which sell Burano's locally produced white wine. Soon you'll hit the first of many picture-perfect Burano canals; turn left and follow it straight ahead to a bridge, which deposits you on the main square, **Piazza Galuppi**—jammed with lace shops, restaurants, and happy shutterbugs.

Lace Shops: Most tourists visit Burano for its lace, and they're not disappointed. Lace is cheaper in Burano than in Venice, and serious shoppers should comparison-shop in Venice before visit-

Burano

Torcello

Lagoon

❶ Merletti d'Arte dalla
Lidia Lace Shop
❷ Lace Museum
❸ Bell Tower
❹ Trattoria al Gatto
Nero da Ruggero

ing Burano. Of the many lace shops, I like **Merletti d'Arte dalla Lidia** for its fine private museum (in the rear of the shop and upstairs). Paola, who speaks English, gives visitors a warm welcome as she shows off masterpieces of lace from all over Europe. Use a magnifying glass to marvel at the intricate knots, and be sure to go

upstairs (just off the big square opposite the leaning tower at Via Baldassarre Galuppi 215, tel. 041-730-052, www.dallalidia.com).

Lace Museum: Lace fans enjoy the Lace Museum (Museo del Merletto di Burano), with a small but modern and well-presented exhibit about Burano's favorite product. The visit begins on the ground floor, with a 20-minute film telling the history of Burano and the significance of lace during Venice's golden age. You'll learn how the intricate patterns of lace were inspired by the ornate

Boating in Venice

Italian law stipulates that a luxury tax is levied on all boats—except in Venice, where they're considered a necessity. Venetians go everywhere by boat. Calling a taxi? A boat comes. Going to the hospital to have a baby? Just hop on the vaporetto. Garbage day? You put your bag on the canal edge, and a garbage boat mashes it and takes it away.

Many residents own a boat, though it's not always practical for everyday activities. If you want to cruise to the grocery store, you first have to check the tide table to make sure your boat can fit beneath certain bridges. And parking is always a huge problem everywhere—either you know a friend nearby with a grandfathered parking space, or your partner has to "circle the block" while you shop.

Locals rely more on the public vaporetti and *traghetti*. While tourists pay plenty for these boats, Venetians ride cheap and easy. An all-year pass costs less than €1 a day.

Gondolas are strictly for tourists these days, but in earlier times, these flat-bottomed boats were the only way to negotiate the tricky, shallow lagoon. The oarsman had to stand up in the back of the boat to see oncoming sandbars. Today, boats ply confidently between the shifting sandbanks of the lagoon, thanks to thoroughfares defined by modern pilings.

While many Venetians own a car for driving on the isle of Lido or the mainland, they admit they're "not very much beloved on the road."

Gothic facades of Venice, the city where they claim the craft was invented, or at least perfected. Then you'll head upstairs to see lots of actual antique lace (slide the drawers to see more samples) as well as some actual, antique lacemakers, squinting at the windows while they work.

San Martino Vescovo Church and Leaning Bell Tower: Enter the church from the corner of the square (free entry but donations appreciated, typically closed 12:00-15:00). It has a fine, restored Tiepolo painting of the Crucifixion (along the left wall of the nave, near the back).

Now circle around the back of the church to appreciate the bell tower's angle of repose (from the main street, it actually looks straight). Here at the far end of the island, the mood shifts. A grassy area, with benches and a waterside promenade, makes for a pretty picnic spot. Continuing all the way around the church brings you into a peaceful yet intensely colorful small-town world and, eventually, back to the main street or the vaporetto dock. The park next to the dock is also good for a picnic.

Eating on Burano: You'll find plenty of touristy eateries on Burano, all enthusiastic about their fish. While you have plenty of options for a quick bite, if you want to dine, consider family-run **$$$ Trattoria al Gatto Nero da Ruggero.** For three generations, they've been serving good, traditional dishes outside overlooking the peaceful canal or in the dressy interior (Tue-Sat 12:30-15:00 & 18:00-21:00, Sun 12:30-15:00, closed Mon, reservations smart, crisp service, 5-minute walk from the ferry dock and from the thriving main tourist drag at Fondamenta de la Giudecca 88, tel. 041-730-120, www.gattonero.com).

• *To reach our tour's next stop,* **Torcello,** *reboard vaporetto #12, making sure it's stopping at Torcello (likely at :12 and :32 past each hour; 5-minute trip). If you want to skip Torcello and return to Venice. See the end of the chapter for your options.*

▲TORCELLO

This is the birthplace of Venice, where some of the first mainland refugees settled, escaping the barbarian hordes. Yet today, it's the least-developed island (pop. 20) in the most natural state, marshy and shrub-covered. There's little for tourists to see except the church, the oldest in Venice, which still sports some impressive mosaics. It's a 10-minute walk, with full sun, from the vaporetto dock to the church.

As you stroll from the dock through a salty canalside landscape, think of the original inhabitants. Romanized farmers came here, escaping the Germanic barbarians who started streaming through the mainland in the fifth century. By the 11th century, the teeny island had 11 churches. But one look around makes it easy to understand why this place was inhospitable—the farming was poor, there was no fresh water, and mosquitoes and malaria were big problems. Even though residents diverted the flow of mainland rivers, the lagoon silted up around them anyway, and the island was slowly abandoned.

Approaching the church, you'll pass by the remote yet fancy **Locanda Cipriani Hotel** next door. With just five rooms, it's hosted Thomas Mann, Queen Elizabeth II, and Princess Diana. Its restaurant is the most expensive of the five or so that vie to feed the lunch crowd on Torcello. Of these, the best pick is probably the **$$$ Villa 600,** with its shaded garden terrace (Thu-Tue 12:00-15:30, bar open 11:00-18:30, closed Wed, tel. 041-527-2254, www. villa600.it).

Santa Maria Assunta Church: This complex consists of four sights—the church itself, the bell tower (behind the church, climb a ramped stairway for great la-

goon views), a small museum (facing the church, in two separate buildings, but with little to see—mainly just sparsely described old artifacts, including a few sixth-century mosaic fragments), and the smaller, free church of Santa Fosca (by the Sacrum sign). The main church is the only one of these really worth paying to visit, but various combo-tickets let you get into the other sights as you like. There's a pay WC in a corner behind the museum.

The circular ruins in front of the church are what's left of a baptistery from the ninth century; in those days, you couldn't enter a church until you were baptized.

Inside the church, the brick walls and wood beams of the ceiling are classically Venetian building materials—that is, flexible, to accommodate the ever-shifting sands underneath.

The **altar** has the relics of St. Heliodorus (d. 390), a local-born bishop who was the travel partner of the famed St. Jerome on a trip to the Holy Land. The columns of the rood screen (separating the altar area from the congregation) were obviously scavenged from elsewhere—note the variety of capitals.

The **apse mosaic** (over the altar) shows Mary and Baby Jesus above and the 12 apostles below. Her three stars symbolize her virginity: before, during, and after giving birth to Jesus.

In the **right apse,** with its sumptuous vault, find Christ Pantocrator, ruler of all, flanked by archangels Michael and Gabriel. On the ceiling, Christ is represented by the sacrificial lamb.

The mosaic on the **back wall** is justifiably famous and worth examining. Six horizontal bands depict the Last Judgment (and other scenes). From top to bottom, see:

1. The Crucifixion.

2. A striding Christ pulling an elderly, bearded Adam (with Eve behind him) out from Limbo while stepping on a devil.

3. Christ, in an almond-shaped bubble, as the Creator, flanked by John the Baptist, Mary, and other holy souls in Paradise. From

the bottom of the bubble pours a river of fire, which runs down the wall to hell.

4. Angels preparing the Throne of Judgment—empty except for a book (whose seven seals, it was predicted, will be broken during Judgment Day). Note Adam and Eve kneeling below.

5. and 6. Archangel Michael (over the door) weighing souls on a scale, while mischievous devils try to tip the scales in their favor.

On the right are the fires of hell, where sinners—many of them turbaned Muslims—are tormented by black-skinned demons. A crude display of the seven deadly sins appears at the lower right: pride (crowned heads in flames), lust (bodies in flames), gluttony (guys eating even their fingers), envy (skulls with worms eating out their coveting eyes), anger (men waist-deep in cold water to cool down), greed (fancy earrings), and laziness (useless hands and cut-off feet).

• *Avoid the eighth deadly sin—missing your vaporetto—by allowing at least 10 minutes to get from the church back to the boat dock.*

From Torcello, return to Burano on the #12 vaporetto (generally 3/ hour, at :17, :37, and :51). The first two depart Burano for Fondamente Nove, where we started this tour (45 minutes). Most travelers will want to avoid the third departure, which goes from Burano to Treporti and Punta Sabbioni, ports on the northern arm of the mainland, on the peninsula of Cavallino. (From Torcello, you may have to switch boats at Burano.)

For a longer cruise back to Venice that ends near St. Mark's Square, you can take the #14 from Burano, which stops at Treporti and Punta Sabbioni, then the Lido, and finally the San Zaccaria dock near St. Mark's Square (hourly, 70-minute trip).

ST. MARK'S TO RIALTO LOOP WALK

Just a few right and left turns (simple!) can get you from St. Mark's Square to the Rialto Bridge via a completely different route from the one most tourists take. Along the way, take in some lesser sights in the area west of St. Mark's Square. Then we'll return to St. Mark's along the tourists' main drag, the Mercerie.

Orientation

Length of This Walk: Allow one hour for a leisurely walk.
San Moisè Church: Free, Mon-Sat 9:30-12:30 & 15:30-18:30.
La Fenice Opera House: €10 for dry 45-minute audioguide tour, generally open daily 9:30-18:00, theater box office open daily 10:00-17:00.
Rialto Market: The souvenir stalls are open daily, the produce market is closed on Sunday, and the fish market is closed on Sunday and Monday. The market is lively only in the morning.

The Walk Begins

St. Mark's Square
• *From the square, walk to the waterfront and stop between the two columns. You're walking on recently raised Venice—in 2006, the stones were taken up and six inches of extra sand put down to minimize flooding.*

You're at the front porch of Venice. Survey this grand scene with your back to the water. It reflects the Renaissance ideal of an urban layout: A proper city needs a formal entry. These pillars say "welcome to an aristocratic republic." The library (on your left) represents wisdom. The palace (right), with Lady Justice (never blindfolded in Venice) on top, represents righteousness. Medieval towns

St. Mark's to Rialto Loop Walk

1. Harry's American Bar
2. San Moisè Church
3. La Fenice Opera House
4. Ponte de la Verona
5. Campo Manin & Daniele Manin Statue
6. Scala Contarini del Bovolo
7. Teatro Goldoni
8. Rialto Bridge
9. Campo San Bartolomeo
10. Casino

were cluttered. A grand Renaissance city has grand vistas. At the far end, the Clock Tower lets all know how much daylight is left ("XXIIII" is not set at midnight but changes with sunset). This monumentality wasn't always here. Before the 16th century there was no library. That's where you'd find the baker, butcher, and cheese shops.

• *Now, turn left to walk past the library, heading for a white pavilion.*

Beyond the library stands the old mint—looking pretty Fort Knox-y. In the 16th century the Venetian ducat—the dollar of Europe—was minted here.

Along the busy waterfront, you'll see the various boats that ply Venice's waters. Classic wooden motorboats operating as water taxis. Hotel shuttle boats bringing guests here from distant, $700-a-night hotels.

Run the gauntlet of souvenir stands to the entrance to the **Giardinetti Reali** (Royal Gardens, once the site of a huge grain-storage depot that was destroyed by Napoleon). The grounds (with ample benches) offer some precious greenery in a city built of stone on mud.

After the park entrance, the walkway takes you to a cute 18th-century former coffeehouse pavilion. Go around the left side of the pavilion and—from atop the bridge—look across the mouth of the Grand Canal to view the big dome of La Salute Church. The guy balancing a bronze ball on one foot is on top of the old Customs House, which now houses the Punta della Dogana contemporary art museum.

• *Twelve steps down and 20 yards ahead on the right is...*

❶ Harry's American Bar

Hemingway put this bar on the map by making it his hangout in the late 1940s. Today, you'll see plenty of dressed-up Americans looking around for celebrities. The discreet (and overpriced) restaurant upstairs is where the glitterati hang out. The street-level bar is for gawkers. If you wear something a bit fancy (or artsy bohemian), you can pull up a stool at the tiny bar by the entrance and pay too much for a Bellini (prosecco and peach puree), which was invented right here.

• *Head inland down Calle Vallaresso, one of Venice's most exclusive streets, past fancy boutiques such as Tiffany, Brunello Cucinelli, and Roberto Cavalli. At the T intersection, turn left and head west on Salizada San Moisè (which becomes Calle Larga XXII Marzo)—the Fifth Avenue of Venice with Gucci, Prada, Versace, and company. (A left turn down Calle del Ridotto leads to the fine, recommended canalfront bar, L'Ombra del Leone.) Continue to the first bridge and a square dominated by the fancy facade of a church. Climb the bridge and, against a soundtrack of tourists negotiating with hustling gondoliers, look back at the ornate...*

❷ San Moisè Church

This is the parish church for St Mark's; because of tourist crowds at the basilica, this is where the community worships. While it's

one of Venice's oldest churches, dating from the 10th century (note the old tower on the right), its busy facade is 17th-century Baroque. This was an age when big shots who funded such projects expected to see their faces featured (see the bust of Mr. Fini in the center—flanked by tombs of his brother and nephew all actually buried into the facade). Moses (Moisè) caps the facade.

Inside, the altarpiece depicts Mount Sinai, with Moses (kneeling) receiving the two tablets with the Ten Commandments. The alcove to the left of the altar has Tintoretto's 16th-century *Christ Washing the Disciples' Feet.*

• *Continue over the bridge, down Calle Larga XXII Marzo, a big street that seems too wide and large for Venice. It was created during the 19th century by filling in a canal. You can make out the outline of the sidewalks that once flanked the now-gone canal. Pass by the Vivaldi lookalikes selling concert tickets and (mostly Senegalese) immigrants illegally selling knockoffs of Prada bags.*

Halfway down the street, after passing the grand Borsa (the former stock exchange), turn right on tiny Calle del Sartor da Veste. Go straight, crossing a bridge. At the next square, you'll find...

❸ La Fenice Opera House (Gran Teatro alla Fenice)

Venice's famed opera house, completed in 1792 (read the "MDC-CXCII" on the facade), was started as a business venture by a group of nobles who recognized that Venice was short on entertainment opportunities for the well-heeled set. (In the 18th century, aristocrats strolled around several months out of the year with little to do.)

La Fenice was reduced to a hollowed-out shell by a disastrous fire in 1996. After a vigorous restoration campaign, "The Phoenix"—true to its name—has risen again from the ashes. La Fenice resumed opera productions in 2004, opening with *La Traviata*. The theater is usually open daily to the public (for information, see page 37).

Venice is one of the cradles of the art form known as opera. An opera is a sung play and a multimedia event, blending music, words, story, costume, and set design. Some of the great operas were first performed here in this luxurious setting. Verdi's *Rigoletto* (1851) and *La Traviata* (1853) were actually commissioned by La Fenice. The man who put words to some of Mozart's opera tunes was a Venetian, Lorenzo da Ponte, who drew inspiration from the city's libertine ways and joie de vivre. In recent years, La Fenice's musical standing was overshadowed by its reputation as a place for the wealthy to parade in furs and jewels.

• *Passing La Fenice, continue north along the same street (though its name is now Calle de la Verona), to a small bridge over a quiet canal.*

❹ Ponte de la Verona

Pause atop this bridge, where reflections can make you wonder which end is up. Looking above you, see bridges of stone propping up leaning buildings.

People actually live in Venice. Notice their rooftop gardens, their laundry, their plumbing, the electricity lines snaking into their apartments, and the rusted iron bars and bolts that hold their crumbling homes together. On one building, find centuries-old relief carvings—a bearded face and a panel of an eagle with its prey. Below you is an old water gate indicating that this was once a merchant's house.

While many Venetians own (and love) their own boats, parking watercraft is a huge problem. Getting a spot is tough, and when you finally find one, it's very expensive and rarely near your apartment. (For more on boating in Venice, see page 210.)

People once swam freely in the canals. Find the sign that reads *Divieto di Nuoto* ("swimming not allowed").

• *Continue north. At the T intersection, turn right on Calle de la Mandola. You'll cross over a bridge into a spacious square dominated by a statue and an out-of-place modern building.*

❺ Campo Manin

The centerpiece of the square is **a statue of Daniele Manin** (1804-1857), one of a group of patriotic visionaries who foresaw the unification of Italy (the Risorgimento) 20 years before it happened. The statue faces the red house Manin lived in. Chafing under Austrian rule, the Venetians rose up in 1848. The Austrians laid siege to the city (1849) and bombarded it into surrender. The fiery leader Manin was banished and spent his final years in Paris, still proudly drumming up support for modern Italy. In a rare honor, he's buried at St. Mark's Basilica.

• *Scala Contarini del Bovolo is a block south of here, with yellow signs pointing the way. Facing the Manin statue, turn right and exit the square down an alley. Turn left with the street, then immediately follow yellow signs to the right, into a courtyard with one of Venice's hidden treasures.*

❻ Scala Contarini del Bovolo

The Scala is a cylindrical brick tower with five floors of spiral staircases faced with white limestone banisters.

Built in 1499, it was the external staircase of a palace (external stairs saved interior space for rooms). Architecture buffs admire the successful blend of a Gothic building with a Renaissance staircase. The garden is a graveyard of old cistern wellheads.

If the tower is open, you can pay €5 to wind your way up the "snail shell" (*bovolo* in the local dialect). It's 113 steps to the top, where you're rewarded with views of the Venetian skyline.

• *Unwind and return to the Manin statue. Continue east, circling around the right side of the big Cassa di Risparmio bank, marveling at its Modernist ugliness. At Campo San Luca, walk halfway through the square, then turn left (north) on Calle del Forno. Heading north, glance 20 yards down the street to the right at the flag-bedecked...*

❼ Teatro Goldoni

Though this theater dates from the 1930s, there's been a theater here since the 1500s, when Venice was at the forefront of secular entertainment. Many of Carlo Goldoni's (1707-1793) groundbreaking comedies were first performed here. Before Goldoni's time, most Italian theater was formulaic and somewhat contrived, but Goldoni portrayed real-life situations of the new middle class—and with a refreshing sense of humor and honesty. Thanks in part to his ample use of the Venetian dialect, he remains especially popular in his native city, and the theater was renamed in his honor. Today, Teatro Goldoni is still a working theater of mainly Italian productions.

• *Continue north on Calle del Forno. You're very close to the Grand Canal. Keep going north. At the small square, jog left and then right onto a lane that leads past a big modern Co-op supermarket to the Grand Canal. Walk right out to the end of the small wooden pier for a grand view. On your right is the Rialto Bridge. The two palaces a few steps behind you are Venice's City Hall—blue posts with golden lions mark city government buildings. Notice the speedboats with shiny varnish parked and awaiting their VIPs. Now look down the Grand Canal (opposite the Rialto Bridge). Obelisks atop the palace across the canal mark the former home of a five-star admiral—a rank only bestowed in wartime—and the family gets obelisk bragging rights for centuries. (Today those twin obelisks mark the ritzy hotel where George Clooney got hitched.)*

Continue to the...

❽ Rialto Bridge

Of Venice's more than 400 bridges, only four cross the Grand Canal. Rialto was the first among these four.

The original Rialto Bridge, dating from 1180, was a platform supported by boats tied together. It linked the political side (Palazzo Ducale) of Venice with the economic center (Rialto). Rialto, which takes its name from *rivo alto* (high bank), was one of the earliest Venetian settlements. When Venice was Europe's economic superpower, this was where bankers, brokers, and merchants conducted their daily business.

Rialto Bridge II was a 13th-century wooden drawbridge. It was replaced in 1588 by the current structure, with its bold single arch (spanning 160 feet) and arcades on top designed to strengthen the stone span. Its immense foundations stretch 650 feet on either side. Heavy buildings were then built atop the foundations to hold everything in place. The Rialto remained the only bridge crossing the Grand Canal until 1854.

Marking the geographical center of Venice (midway down the Grand Canal), the Rialto is the most sensible location for retail shops. The government built it with the (accurate) expectation that it'd soon pay for itself with rent from the shops built into it. Like the (older) Ponte Vecchio in Florence, the Rialto was originally lined with luxury gold and jewelry shops. The bridge is cleverly designed to generate maximum rent: three lanes, two rows of 12 shops each, with a warehouse area above each shop under the lead-and-timber roof.

Reliefs of the Venetian Republic's main mascots, St. Mark and St. Theodore, crown the arch. Barges and vaporetti run the busy waterways below, and merchants vie for tourists' attention on top.

The Rialto has long been a symbol of Venice. Aristocratic inhabitants built magnificent palaces just to be near it. The poetic Lord Byron swam to it all the way from Lido Island. And thousands of marriage proposals have been sealed right here, with a kiss, as the moon floated over La Serenissima.

• *From here, you can continue this walk and return to St. Mark's Square or pick up my Rialto to Frari Church Walk (next chapter). Either way, you might want to take a break to check out the fish and produce market that lies just over the bridge. To continue this walk, follow me along the Mercerie, the most direct (and tourist-clogged) route back to St. Mark's. From the base of the Rialto Bridge (on the San Marco side), go 100 yards directly to...*

❾ Campo San Bartolomeo

This square is one of the city's main crossroads. Locals routinely meet at the statue of Carlo Goldoni, the beloved and innovative 18th-century playwright for whom Teatro Goldoni, which we saw earlier, was named. The pharmacy on this square (marked by a green cross) keeps an electronic counter in its window, ticking down the population of Venice as it shrinks (52,981 on my last visit).

• *Head to the right 100 yards, down Via 2 Aprile, setting your sights on the green and red umbrellas on the corner. They mark a stretch of town once famous for selling umbrellas and handbags. From there, turn left and follow the crowds 100 yards more along Marzaria San Salvador, a.k.a. the...*

Mercerie

You're in the city's high-rent district. The Mercerie (or "Marzarie," in Venetian dialect) is a string of connecting streets lined mostly with tacky tourist shops. Much of the glass displayed here is Chinese, not Venetian. (If you're shopping for glass that's actually made in Venice, look for the Murano seal.)

• *When you get to the yellow two-way arrow "directing" you to San Marco, head right and then follow the flow left another 100 yards until you reach a bridge that makes for a fun gondola-viewing perch. At the top of the bridge, belly up to the railing on the left. Above the arcade on your left is the little iron balcony of the city's best-preserved...*

⑩ Casino

While humble from the outside, the interior is a great example of a classic Venetian space. If the windows are open, spy the lacy pastel and stucco ceilings inside. Though only a few of Venice's casinos still exist, the city once had over a hundred of these "little houses"—city-center retreats for the palazzo-dwelling set. For many patricians, they served as 18th-century man caves, used for entertaining, gambling, and/or intimate encounters. For well-to-do women, casinos provided a different kind of escape: Inspired by Madame de Pompadour (Louis XV's mistress), ladies would hold court with writers, artists, and avant-garde types.

• *Cross the bridge and continue straight for 100 yards along Marzaria San Zulian. On the way, notice the metal, two-foot-high flood barrier braces at shop doors—and how merchandise is elevated in anticipation of high water (local insurance doesn't cover floods).*

When you hit the next schizophrenic Per S. Marco arrow (in front of the church), go right a few steps, then left onto Marzaria dell'Orologio, a street named for where you're heading: the Clock Tower. You're approaching St. Mark's Square (back where you started this walk) and the city's front door.

RIALTO TO FRARI CHURCH WALK

Cross the Rialto Bridge, and dive headlong into Venice's thriving market area. The area west of the Grand Canal feels less touristy—a place where more "real" Venetians live. This chapter is less a collection of sights than it is an easy-to-follow route from the Rialto Bridge to the Frari Church and Scuola San Rocco. We'll start by exploring a few down-home places near the Rialto, especially the lively produce and stinky fish markets. Then we'll pick up the pace and walk a direct route through the San Polo area. Along the way, you'll see everyday shops, pubs, and quiet squares that are at least a bit off the tourist path. We'll end at the Frari Church and nearby Scuola San Rocco—a delightful artistic dessert.

Orientation

Length of This Walk: To walk directly from the Rialto Bridge to the Frari Church only takes 20 minutes. But allow a leisurely hour to see the markets and explore along the way.

When to Go: The markets are lively only in the morning. The produce market is closed on Sunday, and the fish market is closed on Sunday and Monday.

Church of San Polo: €3, Mon-Sat 10:30-17:00, closed Sun.

Tragicomica Mask Shop: Daily 10:00-19:00, on Calle dei Nomboli at #2800, tel. 041-721-102, www.tragicomica.it. The owners are generally happy to show their workshop on weekdays to customers who buy a mask, though it's best to make a reservation.

Rialto to Frari Church Walk

The Walk Begins

Start atop the Rialto Bridge. Gaze down the bridge (away from the St. Mark's side) at the long street lined with a gauntlet of merchants' stands. This area around Rialto is where Venice got its start centuries ago as a global commercial power. The neighborhood still houses the city's main market. And behind all those tourist-trinket stands are still real jewelry shops with a long tradition. In fact, it's been called "Street of Jewelers" for more than 500 years.

• *Let's walk into the heart of Venice's historic commercial center. Head down the bridge and start up the street. About 50 yards onward, you'll see an old square on your right. Go to its fountain.*

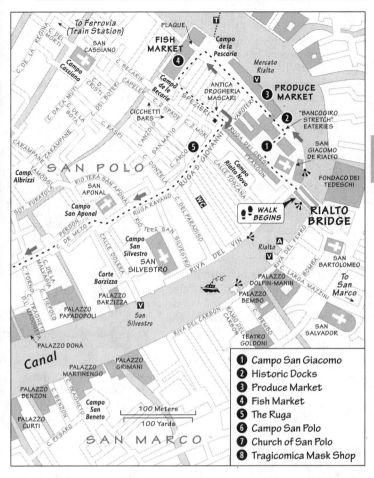

1. Campo San Giacomo
2. Historic Docks
3. Produce Market
4. Fish Market
5. The Ruga
6. Campo San Polo
7. Church of San Polo
8. Tragicomica Mask Shop

❶ Campo San Giacomo

This square, named for the church that faces it, was ground zero for Venice's lively global trade in the 1500s. As ships docked near Rialto Bridge and un-loaded their goods, this courtyard became the center of trade and banking. It was decked out in High Renaissance style in the year 1520 (see the date "MDXX" on the arcade directly opposite the church). The square was designed to collect rainwater and store it in a cistern that once fed this fountain (for more on this ingenious system, see page 22).

Traders needed bankers, so this square also became Venice's "Wall Street." The line of buildings on the long side of the courtyard (now restaurants) was once a strip of banks. It's still called Bancogiro, which means the place where merchants banked. In the days when carrying cash meant carrying gold and silver—heavy and dangerous—paper transfers between bank accounts were a godsend. Today, these popular eateries are worth checking out (described on page 265).

Opposite the church, find the granite statue of a hunchback supporting steps leading to a column. Back when this neighborhood was the Wall Street of medieval Europe, this column was the closest thing they had to a *Wall Street Journal*. Someone climbed the stair each noon and stood on the column to read aloud the daily news from the doge: which ships had docked, which foreign ambassadors were in town, the price of pepper, and so on. Behind the hunchback is Calle de la Sicurtà, named for the maritime insurance companies that once did business here.

The church facade is one of the oldest in town. Back before clocks had minute hands, its porch was a shelter for the poor.

The spirit of St. James the Minor, for whom the church is named, watched over the business community, encouraging honesty in a time when banking regulations were nonexistent.

Today the church's tranquil interior hosts an exhibition of historical musical instruments. Step inside (it's free) to see a collection of old stringed instruments (mandolins, violins) that Venice helped popularize.

• *Let's explore deeper. Facing the church, turn left and walk between the Bancogiro buildings to the edge of the Grand Canal.*

❷ Historic Docks

Back when the Rialto Bridge was still a drawbridge (until the 1590s), big ships docked right here. Imagine the commotion as ships tied up to load and unload their spices, oil, wine, and jewels. They'd exchange money and goods at the Bancogiro banks—notice that the buildings face this way, too. The large white building nearby was and still is the city's fiscal administration building. Notice how it tilts out (probably because the bridge's huge foundation is compressing the mud beneath it).

Now walk toward the Rialto Bridge along the canal to a little canalside dead-end. Take in the great view of the bridge. The big building directly across the Grand Canal was originally the German merchants' hall (see the "Germanicus" seal). It's been reincarnated as a shopping center popular for its roof terrace with a magnificent view.

You're standing under a former prison. Study the iron grills over the windows. Notice the interlocking pipes with alternating joints—you couldn't cut just one to escape.

• *Now let's see where goods are still unloaded today—at Venice's market. From the prison, walk back along the canal and proceed through the triple archway. You'll reach the stands (in the square named Casaria) of Venice's...*

❸ Produce Market *(Erberia)*

Colorful stalls offer fresh fruit and vegetables, some quite exotic. Nothing is grown on the island of Venice, so everything is shipped in daily from the mainland or distant points on the lagoon. The Mercato Rialto vaporetto stop is a convenient place for boats to unload their wares, here in the heart of fish-shaped Venice. With the city's narrow streets, everything must be hand-hauled on dollies by hardworking stevedores and deliverymen. At #203 (halfway down the first set of stalls, on the left), the shop called Macelleria Equina sells horse *(cavallo)* and donkey *(asino)* meat. Continue along the canal, exploring the produce stalls.

• *Follow your nose straight ahead until you enter the brick open-air arcade that houses the fish market. Turn left and explore your way through the other arcade, as well.*

❹ Fish Market *(Pescaria)*

This market is especially vibrant and colorful in the morning. The open-air stalls have the catch of the day—Venice's culinary specialty. Find eels, scallops, crustaceans with five-inch antennae, and squid destined for tonight's risotto soaking in their own ink. This is the Venice that has existed for centuries: Workers toss boxes of fish from delivery boats while shoppers step from the *traghetto* (gondola shuttle) into the action. It's a good peek at workaday Venice. Shoppers are exacting and expect to know if the fish is fresh or frozen, farmed or wild, Atlantic or Mediterranean (look for labels at some stands). Local fish are small and considered particularly tasty because of the high concentration of salt at this end of the Adriatic. Any salmon you see are farmed, mostly from northern Europe. It's not unusual to pay €30 per kilo (about 2.2 pounds) for the best fish.

In the courtyard between the two market buildings, find the plaque on the wall that lists the minimum length a fish must be for it to be sold. Sardines must be seven centimeters; *peocio* (mussels) must be three centimeters. (Below that, someone has added a penis joke.)

• *Continue exploring the market while walking away from the water. You emerge on* **Campo de la Becarie** *("Butchers Square"). Turn left and follow Ruga dei Spezieri ("Spicers Road") for about 100 yards. Along the way, pop into Antica Drogheria Mascari (on the right at #380), a small storefront that hides a vast enoteca inside holding 600 different Italian wines arranged by region, plus spices and lots of gifty edibles. Thirty yards past the drogheria, turn right. You're at the head of a major street, called Ruga Vechia San Giovanni.*

❺ The Ruga

This busy street is lined with shops that Venetians actually patronize for their basic goods. It gets progressively less touristy and more practical the farther you go. There are fewer trinkets and more clothes, bread, shoes, blenders, shampoo, and underwear.

Note that the second street you pass on the right, Sotoportego dei Do Mori, leads to several *cicchetti* bars I recommend. These local bars (clustered around Calle de le Do Spade) serve the Venetian version of tapas. If it's lunchtime, consider dropping by one or more for a progressive feast. (See these options listed on page 264.)

• *At this point, you can pretty much put this book down and walk for a while checking out the scene. Walk up the Ruga, which changes names as you go. Just keep heading basically straight (little jogs are OK). When in doubt, follow signs pointing to* Ferrovia *(train station). Our next stop is just a few minutes away—the vast, hard-to-miss square called...*

❻ Campo San Polo

One of the largest squares in Venice, Campo San Polo is shaped like an amphitheater, with its church tucked away in the corner (just ahead of you). Antica Birraria la Corte, a fine and family-friendly pizzeria/*ristorante,* is located at the far side (see listing on page 268). The square's amphitheater shape was determined by a curved canal at the base of the buildings on the right. Today, the former canal is now a *rio terà*—a street made of land-fill. A few rare trees grace the square, as do rare benches occupied by grateful locals. In the summer, bleachers and a screen are erected for open-air movies.

• *On the square is the...*

❼ Church of San Polo (S. Paolo Apostolo)

This church, one of the oldest in Venice, dates from the ninth century (English description at ticket desk). The wooden, boat-shaped ceiling recalls the earliest basilicas built after Rome's fall. While the church is skippable for many, art enthusiasts visit to see Tintoretto's *Last Supper* (near the entrance) and Giovanni Battista Tiepolo's *Virgin Appearing to St. John of Nepomuk* (middle of the long wall).

The highlight here is a series of dramatic paintings by Tiepolo's son Domenico—*The Stations of the Cross.* Spend some time following the stops Jesus made from the moment he was condemned to death, to carrying his own cross, to crucifixion, to his bloody burial in the tomb. Find Domenico's happy ending on the ceiling—the Resurrection, with Jesus springing from the tomb.

• *From the Church of San Polo, continue about 200 yards (following* Ferrovia *signs). Along the narrow alley called Calle dei Nomboli, on the right at #2800 and directly across the alley from the Casa Goldoni museum, you'll see the...*

❽ Tragicomica Mask Shop

One of Venice's best mask stores, Tragicomica is also a workshop that offers a glimpse into the process of mask making. Venice's masks have always been a central feature of the celebration of Carnevale—the local pre-Lent, Mardi Gras-like blow-out. (The translation of Carnevale is "goodbye to meat," referring to the lean days of Lent. For more on Carnevale, see the sidebar on page 6.) You'll see Walter, Alessandra, and Giuliana hard at work.

Many masks are patterned after standard characters of the theater style known as commedia dell'arte: the famous trickster Harlequin, the beautiful and cunning Columbina, the country bumpkin Pulcinella (who later evolved into the wife-beating Punch of marionette shows), and the solemn, long-nosed Doctor *(dottore)*. For more on masks, see the "Mask Making" sidebar in the Shopping in Venice chapter.

• *Continuing along, cross the bridge and veer right. You'll soon see purple signs directing you to* Scuola Grande di San Rocco. *Follow these until you bump into the back end of the Frari Church, with Scuola San Rocco next door. (Each sight is good enough to merit its own chapter in this book.) If you're looking for perhaps the best Venetian art in situ, you've found it.*

ST. MARK'S TO SAN ZACCARIA WALK

San Zaccaria, one of the oldest churches in Venice, is just a few minutes on foot from St. Mark's Square. The church features a Bellini altarpiece and a mysterious submerged crypt that might be the oldest place in Venice. This short, easy-to-follow walk gets you away from the bustle of St. Mark's, includes a stroll along the waterfront, and brings you right back to where you started.

Orientation

Length of This Walk: Allow about an hour for a leisurely walk and stop inside the church (though the actual distance is short).

Church of San Zaccaria: Free, €1.50 to enter crypt, €0.50 coin to illuminate Bellini's altarpiece, Mon-Sat 10:00-12:00 & 16:00-18:00, Sun 16:00-18:00 only. Mass is held daily at 18:30 and Sun also at 10:00 and 12:00.

The Walk Begins

❶ Piazzetta dei Leoni

Facing St. Mark's Basilica, start in the small square to the left of the church (Piazzetta dei Leoni), with the 18th-century stone lions that kids love to play on. See the well and those drains in the pavement (behind the lions)? The felines are sitting on a cistern, fed by four drains.

Notice the nicely restored north side of the basilica, with fine 14th-century reliefs. Notice also the prayer entrance below the exquisite Porta dei Fiori. To the left, behind a black metal fence, is the tomb of Daniele Manin, the great 19th-century Italian and Venetian patriot.

The big white building at the far end of the square houses the

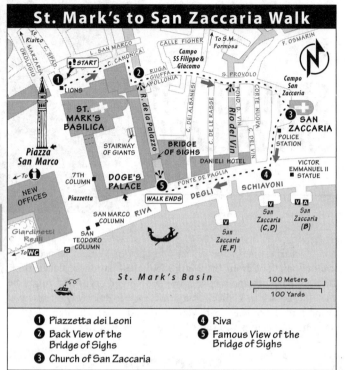

St. Mark's to San Zaccaria Walk

1 Piazzetta dei Leoni
2 Back View of the Bridge of Sighs
3 Church of San Zaccaria
4 Riva
5 Famous View of the Bridge of Sighs

offices of Venice's "patriarch," the special title given to St. Mark's bishop. Venice's most famous patriarch went on to be Pope John XXIII, the popular "Sixties Pope," who oversaw major reforms in the Catholic Church (Vatican II). Locals still refer to him as "Il Papa Buono" (the good pope). A plaque on the building calls him "Beato Giovanni XXIII," and in 2013, Pope Francis made him a saint.

• *Head east along Calle de la Canonica, past a fine English-language bookstore, then turn right and circle behind the basilica. Passing some of the sexiest gondoliers in town, you'll reach a bridge (Ponte Selfie Stick) with a...*

❷ Back View of the Bridge of Sighs

This lesser-known view of the Bridge of Sighs also lets you see the tourists who are ogling it, with cameras cocked. You can just see the Lady Justice relief (centered above the windows), with her sword and scales—a reminder that the courts were to the right and the prison to the left.

On the basilica side of the bridge is a common sight in neighborhood Venice: a streetside altarpiece and donation box. As the street signs tell you, the bridge you're on marks the boundary between two traditional neighborhoods, the *sestiere* (district) of San Marco and that of Castello.

• *Continue east, passing through a lively, small square. Notice the two archaic relics of bygone days—an old well and a newspaper stand. You'll cross another bridge with a view of a "Modern Bridge of Sighs," which connects two wings of the exclusive Danieli Hotel. Continue east another 50 yards, through the Gothic gate of what was once a cloistered Benedictine convent, and into a square where you see the...*

❸ Church of San Zaccaria

Back in the ninth century—when Venice was just a collection of wooden houses and before there was a St. Mark's Basilica—a stone church and monastery stood here. Today's structure dates mostly from the 15th century.

The tall facade by Mauro Codussi (who also did the Clock Tower in St. Mark's Square) and others is early Renaissance. The "vertical" effect produced by the four support pillars that rise up to an arched crown is tempered by the horizontal, many-layered stories and curved shoulders.

In the northwest corner of Campo San Zaccaria (near where you entered) is a weathered plaque from 1620 listing all the things that were prohibited "in this square" *(in questo campo),* including games, obscenities, dishonesty, and robbery, all "under grave penalty" *(sotto gravis pene).*

• *Enter the church. The second chapel on the right holds the...*

Body of Zechariah (S. Zaccaria)

Of the two bodies in the chapel, the lower one in the glass case is the reputed body of the church's namesake—Zechariah, the father of John the Baptist. Back when mortal remains were venerated and thought to bring miracles to the faithful, Venice was proud to own the bones of St. Zechariah ("San Zaccaria," also known as Zacharias).

• *The church is blessed with fine art. On the opposite side of the nave (second chapel on the left), you'll find...*

Giovanni Bellini, *Madonna and Child with Saints (Sacra Conversazione)*, 1505

Mary and the baby, under a pavilion, are surrounded by various saints interacting in a so-called *sacra conversazione* (holy conversation), which in this painting is more like a quiet meditation. The saints' mood is melancholy, portrayed with lidded eyes and downturned faces. A violinist angel plays a sad solo at Mary's feet.

This is one of the last of Bellini's paintings in the *sacra conversazione* formula, the newer type of altarpiece that liberated the Virgin, Child, and saints from the separate cells of the older triptych style. Compare this to his other variations on this theme in the Accademia (see Accademia Tour chapter) and Frari Church (see Frari Church Tour chapter). The life-size saints stand in an imaginary niche in the church wall—the pavilion's painted col-

umns match those of the real church. We see a glimpse of trees and a cloudy sky beyond. Bellini establishes a 3-D effect using floor tiles. The four saints pose symmetrically, and there's a harmony in the big blocks of richly colored robes—blue, green, red, white, and yellow. A cool white light envelops the whole scene, creating a holy ambience. (To add even more light, drop a €0.50 coin in the box in front of the altar.)

The ever-innovative Bellini was productive until the end of his long life—he painted this masterpiece at age 75. The German artist Albrecht Dürer said of him: "He is very old, and still he is the best painter of them all."

• *On the right-hand side of the nave is the entrance to the...*

Crypt

Before you descend into the crypt, the first room (Chapel of Sant'Atanasio) contains **Tintoretto's *Birth of John the Baptist*** (c. 1560s, on the altar), which tells the back story of Zechariah. In the background, old Zechariah's wife, Elizabeth, props herself up in bed while nurses hold and coo over her newborn son, little John the Baptist. The birth was a miracle, as she was past childbearing age. On the far right, old bearded Zechariah—the star of this church—witnesses the heavens opening up, bringing this miracle to earth.

The five **gold thrones** (displayed in this room or one of the next rooms) were once seats for doges. Every Easter, the current doge would walk from St. Mark's Square to this religious center and thank the nuns of San Zaccaria for giving the land for the square.

The small next room contains religious objects as well as an engraving of the doge parading into Campo San Zaccaria.

Next comes the **Chapel of San Tarasio,** dominated by an impressive 15th-century prickly gold altarpiece by Antonio Vivarini. The predella (seven small scenes beneath the altarpiece) may be by Paolo Veneziano, the 14th-century grandfather of Venetian painting. Look down through glass in the floor to see the 12th-century mosaic floor from the original church. In fact, these rooms were parts of the earlier churches.

Finally, go down the nearby staircase to the **crypt**—the foundation of a church built in the 10th century. The crypt is low and the water table high, so the room is often flooded, submerging the bases of the columns. An old stone altar topped with a Virgin statue heightens the mystery...calling up echoes of the Dark Ages.

• *Emerge from the Church of San Zaccaria back into the small campo. Before leaving the campo, check out the small (free) art gallery tucked behind the trees, the thirst-quenching water fountain, and the pink Carabinieri police station (a former monastery), marked by the Italian flag. Then exit the square at the far end, and head south until you pop out at the waterfront, right on the...*

❹ Riva

The waterfront promenade known as the "Riva" was built not for tourists but as part of the port of San Marco. Until recently, big ships tied up here. Today it's home to some of the town's finest and most famous hotels—and provides a great view of the Church of San Giorgio Maggiore (one stop away on vaporetto #2).

Before turning right, look left. The big equestrian monument depicts **Victor Emmanuel II,** who helped lead Italy to unification and became the country's first king in 1861. Beyond that (over the bridge) is the four-columned **La Pietà Church,** where Antonio Vivaldi once directed the music. Five bridges farther along (not visible from here) are the Arsenale and Naval Museum (described in the Sights in Venice chapter).

For a peek at the *most* famous and luxurious hotel, turn right, cross over one bridge, and nip into the **Danieli Hotel.** Tuck in your shirt, stand tall and aristocratic, and (with all the confidence of a paying guest) be swept by the revolving door into the sumptuous interior of what was once the Gothic Palazzo Dandolo. As was the design of Venetian *palazzi,* the ground floor was originally a warehouse with the offices and living quarters upstairs. While you check out the Danieli's restaurant menu (that's why you're there, isn't it?), admire the lobby, the old-style chandeliers, the water-taxi drive-up entrance, and the occasional celebrity. Since 1820, the Neo-Gothic Danieli has been Venice's most exclusive hotel. Exquisite as all this is, it still gets flooded routinely in the winter.

• *Facing the water, turn right and head west toward St. Mark's Square. The commotion atop a little bridge marks the...*

❺ Famous View of the Bridge of Sighs

The Bridge of Sighs connects the Doge's Palace (left) with the doge's prison (right). The bridge let justice be very swift indeed, as

convicted criminals could, upon sentencing, be escorted directly from the palace's secretive courtroom to prison without being seen in public.

Notice the beefy bars on the prison. There were no windows, so throughout the year it would alternate between very hot and very cold. The top floor, below the lead roof, was nicknamed "The Oven." While designed for 300 people, the prison routinely held 500.

From this historic bridge (according to romantic legend), prisoners took one last look at Venice before entering the dark and unpleasant prison. And sighed. Lord Byron picked up on the legend in the early 1800s and gave the bridge its famous nickname, making this sad little span a big stop on the Grand Tour. Look high up on your left—although that rogue Casanova wrote of the bridge in his memoirs, he was actually imprisoned here in the Doge's Palace. Check out the carved relief on the palace corner, to your left, showing the biblical scene of drunken Noah spilling his wine.

Nowadays, while the bridge is a human traffic jam of gawking tourists during the day, it remains breathtakingly romantic in the lonely late-night hours.

• *Your tour's over, and the place where you started is just around the corner. (By the way, if you need some quick cash, this is a great place to pick a pocket. There's lots of bumping, and everyone's distracted...)*

SLEEPING IN VENICE

I've listed rooms in five areas: St. Mark's bustle, the Rialto action, the quiet Dorsoduro area behind the Accademia art museum, near the train station, and on the mainland in Mestre (handy for drivers and train travelers, but far from the action). In general, the closer to St. Mark's you are, the less value and more touristy atmosphere you'll get.

Hotels in Venice can be tricky to locate. If necessary, ask locals for help when you get close. Hotel websites are particularly valuable for Venice because they often include detailed directions and printable maps. Also keep your eyes peeled for green or white oval signs with drawings of keys by the door; these often mark accommodation entrances. The website Venicexplorer.net allows you to search using a hotel's address number and district, which I've included in my listings (click "Venice Civic Number" on the website to open the search window); it's better than Google Maps, which can choke on Venetian addresses. Remember that Venice has six districts: San Marco, Castello, Cannaregio, San Polo, Santa Croce, and Dorsoduro.

As many hotels in central Venice are in historic buildings, rooms tend to be small and stairs are often plentiful. Unless noted, these listings do not have an elevator.

I rank accommodations from **$** budget to **$$$$** splurge. To get the best deal, contact my family-run accommodations directly by phone or email. When you book direct, the owner avoids a roughly 20 percent commission and may be able to offer you a discount. Book your accommodations well in advance if you'll be traveling during peak season (April-June and Sept-Oct) or if your trip coincides with a major holiday or festival (see the appendix).

For romantic splurges, consider Hotel al Ponte Antico, Hotel Flora, Pensione Accademia, or Locanda la Corte—in that order of price and experience. Big institutional places cost about the same as a modest hotel but come with a lack of stress that some visitors prefer. The best ones, well-located and a good value, are Don Orione Religious Guest House, Domus Ciliota, Foresteria della Chiesa Valdese, and Foresteria Levi. All of these accommodations are described in this chapter. For those on a tight budget, Venice's little, relatively dumpy hotels and the Generator youth hostel are cheapest.

Over the past decade, Venice's hotel capacity has nearly doubled. Several big new hotels and countless little boutique hotels have opened, and many private homes have been converted to short-term rentals. Now the city is overbuilt for guest accommodations. Demand is soft, and so are the prices. Rates can spike during festivals. Almost all places drop prices in July and August, and again from November through March (except during Christmas and Carnevale). Hoteliers are eager to fill their rooms in the off-season. Consider prices negotiable. A €180 double can cost €80-90 in winter.

For some travelers, short-term, Airbnb-type rentals can be a good alternative; search for places in my recommended hotel neighborhoods. Several of my recommended hotels also rent apartments (these are noted in my listings).

For more information and tips, see the "Sleeping" section in the Practicalities chapter.

NEAR ST. MARK'S SQUARE

To get here from the train station or Piazzale Roma bus station, ride the slow vaporetto #1 to San Zaccaria or the fast #2 (which also leaves from Tronchetto parking lot) to San Marco. Consider using your ride to follow my tour of the Grand Canal (□ see Grand Canal Cruise chapter); to make sure you arrive via the Grand Canal, confirm that your boat goes *"via Rialto."* If the following places are full, or you're looking for more formal accommodations, see the listings under "Other Accommodations in Venice," later.

Flexible Floors

All over town, from palaces to cheap, old hotels, you'll find speckled floors (*pavimento alla Veneziana*). While they might look like basic linoleum, these are historic—protected by the government and a pain for Venetian landlords to maintain. As Venice was built, it needed flexible flooring to absorb the inevitable settling of the buildings. Through an expensive and laborious process, several layers of material were built up and finished with a broken marble top that was shaved and polished to what you see today. While patterns were sometimes designed into the flooring, it's often just a speckled hodgepodge. Keep an eye open for this. Once a year, the floor is rubbed with natural oil to maintain its flexibility, and craftspeople still give landlords fits when repairs are needed.

Laundry: For full service, look for **Lavanderia Gabriella,** a few streets north of St. Mark's Square. **Effe Erre** is a modern self-service *lavanderia* near the recommended Hotel al Piave. For details see page 17.

East of St. Mark's Square

Located near the Bridge of Sighs, just off the Riva degli Schiavoni waterfront promenade, these places rub drainpipes with Venice's most palatial five-star hotels.

$$$$ Hotel Campiello, lacy and bright, was once part of a 19th-century convent. Ideally located 50 yards off the waterfront on a tiny square, its 16 rooms offer a tranquil, friendly refuge for travelers who appreciate comfort and professional service (RS%, air-con, elevator, just steps from the San Zaccaria vaporetto stop, Castello 4647; tel. 041-520-5764, www.hcampiello.it, campiello@hcampiello.it; family-run for four generations, currently by Thomas, Nicoletta, and Monica). They also rent three modern, upscale, and quiet family apartments for up to six people, under rustic timbers just steps away from the hotel.

$$$$ Hotel Fontana, two bridges behind St. Mark's Square, is a pleasant family-run place with 15 sparse but classic-feeling rooms overlooking a lively square (RS%, several rooms with terraces, family rooms, air-con, elevator, closed Jan, on Campo San

Provolo at Castello 4701, tel. 041-522-0533, www.hotelfontana.it, info@hotelfontana.it, cousins Diego and Gabriele).

$$$$ Hotel la Residenza is a grand old palace facing a peaceful square. It has 16 rooms on three levels (with no elevator) and a huge, luxurious lounge. This is a good value for romantics—you'll feel like you're in the Doge's Palace after hours (air-con; from the Riva, go down Calle del Dose to Campo Bandiera e Moro at Castello 3608, tel. 041-528-5315, www.venicelaresidenza.com, info@ venicelaresidenza.com, Giovanni).

$$$ Locanda al Leon, which feels a little like a medieval tower house, is conscientiously run and rents 12 rooms just off Campo Santi Filippo e Giacomo (RS%, some view rooms, family rooms, air-con, one- and two-bedroom apartments, Campo Santi Filippo e Giacomo, Castello 4270, tel. 041-277-0393, www. hotelalleon.com, leon@hotelalleon.com, Giuliano and Marcella). Their annex down the street, **B&B Ca' Marcella,** has three newer, classy, and spacious rooms for the same rates (check in at main hotel).

$$ Albergo Doni, situated along a quiet canal, is dark and quiet. This time-warp—with creaky floors and 13 well-worn, once-classy rooms—is run by friendly Tessa and her two brothers, Barnaba and (now "retired") Italian stallion Nikos (RS%, cheaper rooms with shared bath, family rooms, ceiling fans, a few rooms have air-con, Wi-Fi in common areas, on Fondamenta del Vin at Castello 4656, tel. 041-522-4267, www.albergodoni.it, albergodoni@ hotmail.it). The hotel also has three nice overflow apartments at the same prices (but without breakfast).

North of St. Mark's Square
$$$$ Hotel Orion rents 21 simple, welcoming, pricey rooms in the center of the action (you're paying a premium for the location). Steep stairs (there's no elevator) take you from the touristy street into a peaceful world high above (RS%—use code RSTEVES, air-con, 2 minutes inland from St. Mark's Square, 10 steps toward St. Mark's from San Zulian Church at Calle Spadaria 700a, tel. 041-522-3053, www.hotelorion.it, info@hotelorion.it).

$$$ Hotel al Piave, with 25 rooms above a bright, tight lobby and breakfast room, is comfortable and cheery, and you'll enjoy the neighborhood (RS%, family rooms, lots of narrow stairs, air-con, on Ruga Giuffa at Castello 4838, tel. 041-528-5174, www. hotelalpiave.com, info@hotelalpiave.com; Mirella, Paolo, Ilaria, and Federico).

$$$ Locanda Casa Querini rents six bright, high-ceilinged rooms on a quiet square tucked away behind St. Mark's. You can enjoy your breakfast or a sunny happy-hour picnic sitting at their

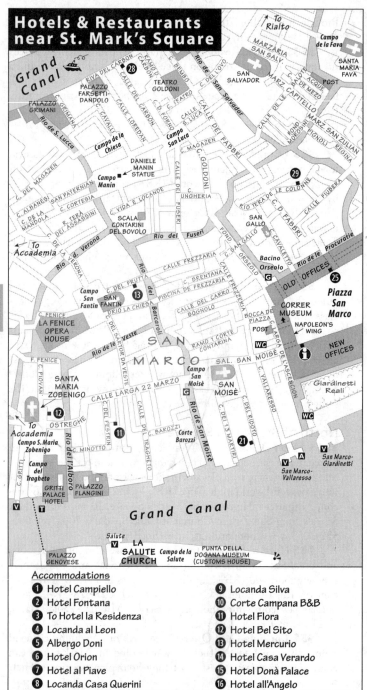

Hotels & Restaurants near St. Mark's Square

Accommodations

1 Hotel Campiello
2 Hotel Fontana
3 To Hotel la Residenza
4 Locanda al Leon
5 Albergo Doni
6 Hotel Orion
7 Hotel al Piave
8 Locanda Casa Querini
9 Locanda Silva
10 Corte Campana B&B
11 Hotel Flora
12 Hotel Bel Sito
13 Hotel Mercurio
14 Hotel Casa Verardo
15 Hotel Donà Palace
16 Hotel all'Angelo

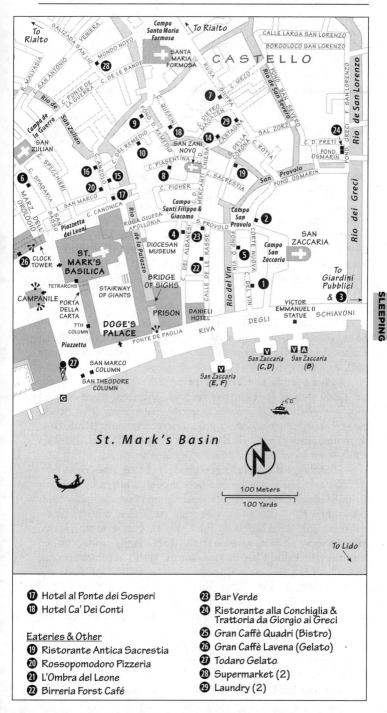

SLEEPING

17 Hotel al Ponte dei Sosperi
18 Hotel Ca' Dei Conti

Eateries & Other
19 Ristorante Antica Sacrestia
20 Rossopomodoro Pizzeria
21 L'Ombra del Leone
22 Birreria Forst Café

23 Bar Verde
24 Ristorante alla Conchiglia & Trattoria da Giorgio ai Greci
25 Gran Caffè Quadri (Bistro)
26 Gran Caffè Lavena (Gelato)
27 Todaro Gelato
28 Supermarket (2)
29 Laundry (2)

tables right on the sleepy little square (RS%, family rooms, in-room fridges, air-con, halfway between San Zaccaria vaporetto stop and Campo Santa Maria Formosa at Castello 4388 on Campo San Zaninovo/Giovanni Novo, tel. 041-241-1294, www.locandaquerini. com, info@locandaquerini.com; Patrizia and Caterina).

$$$ Locanda Silva is a well-located hotel with a functional 1960s feel and a small terrace. It rents 23 simple rooms with small bathrooms (RS%, a few cheaper rooms with shared bathrooms, closed Dec-Jan, family rooms, air-con, lots of stairs, on Fondamenta del Remedio at Castello 4423, tel. 041-522-7643, www. locandasilva.it, info@locandasilva.it; Sandra and Katia).

$$ Corte Campana B&B, run by enthusiastic and helpful Riccardo and his Californian wife Grace, rents three quiet, spacious, characteristic rooms in a homey flat just behind St. Mark's Square. For one room, the private bath is down the hall (cash only, 2-night minimum, family rooms, air-con, elevator, on Calle del Remedio at Castello 4410, tel. 041-523-3603, mobile 389-272-6500, www.cortecampana.com, info@cortecampana.com).

Near Campo Santa Maria Formosa

A bit farther north of the options listed above, these are in the quiet, somewhat less touristy Castello area, beyond the inviting Campo Santa Maria Formosa (for locations, see the map on page 261).

$$$ Locanda la Corte is perfumed with elegance without being snooty. Its 14 attractive, high-ceilinged, wood-beamed rooms—Venetian-style, done in earthy pastels—circle a small, sun-drenched courtyard and a ground-level restaurant (RS%, family rooms, air-con, on Calle Bressana at Castello 6317, tel. 041-241-1300, www.locandalacorte.it, info@locandalacorte.it).

$$ Alloggi Barbaria, a good budget choice, rents eight simple, characterless rooms on one floor around a bright but institutional-feeling common area. Beyond Campo San Zanipolo/Santi Giovanni e Paolo, it's a fair walk from the action, but in a pleasant residential neighborhood. The Ospedale vaporetto stop is two minutes away on foot, with no steps (RS%, family rooms, limited continental breakfast, air-con in summer, Wi-Fi in common areas, on Calle de le Capucine at Castello 6573, tel. 041-522-2750, www. alloggibarbaria.it, info@alloggibarbaria.it, friendly Fausto). You can reach the Ospedale stop on vaporetto #5.2 from the train or bus stations, or via the Alilaguna blue line from the airport.

West of St. Mark's Square

These more expensive hotels are solid choices in a more elegant neighborhood.

$$$$ Hotel Flora sits buried in a sea of fancy designer boutiques and elegant hotels almost on the Grand Canal. It's formal, with uniformed staff and grand public spaces, yet the 40 rooms have a homey warmth and the garden oasis is a sanctuary for well-heeled, foot-weary guests (RS%, air-con, elevator, great family-size apartment, on Calle Bergamaschi at San Marco 2283a, tel. 041-520-5844, www.hotelflora.it, info@hotelflora.it).

$$$$ Hotel Bel Sito offers pleasing Old World character, 34 smallish rooms, generous public spaces, a peaceful courtyard, and a picturesque location—facing a church on a small square between St. Mark's Square and the Accademia (RS%, some view rooms, air-con, elevator; near Santa Maria del Giglio vaporetto stop—line #1, on Campo Santa Maria Zobenigo/del Giglio at San Marco 2517, tel. 041-522-3365, www.hotelbelsitovenezia.it, info@hotelbelsitovenezia.it, graceful Rossella).

$$$$ Hotel Mercurio, a lesser value a block in front of La Fenice Opera House, offers 29 peaceful, comfortable rooms (some view rooms, family rooms, air-con, lots of stairs, on Calle del Fruttariol at San Marco 1848, tel. 041-522-0947, www.hotelmercurio.com, info@hotelmercurio.com).

NEAR THE RIALTO BRIDGE

These places are on opposite sides of the Grand Canal, within a short walk of the Rialto Bridge. Express vaporetto #2 brings you to the Rialto quickly from the train station, the Piazzale Roma bus station, and the parking-lot island of Tronchetto, but you'll need to take the "local" vaporetto #1 to reach the minor stops closer to the last two listings. To locate the following hotels, see the map on page 260.

$$$$ Hotel al Ponte Antico is exquisite, professional, and small. With nine plush rooms, a velvety royal living/breakfast room, and its own dock for water taxi arrivals, it's perfect for a romantic anniversary. Because its wonderful terrace overlooks the Grand Canal, Rialto Bridge, and market action, its rooms without a canal view may be a better value (air-con, 100 yards from Rialto Bridge at Cannaregio 5768, use Rialto vaporetto stop, tel. 041-241-1944, www.alponteantico.com, info@alponteantico.com, Matteo makes you feel like royalty).

$$$ Pensione Guerrato, right above the colorful Rialto produce market and just two minutes from the Rialto Bridge, is run by friendly, creative, and hardworking Roberto, Piero, Monica, and Matilde. Their 800-year-old building—with 22 spacious, charming rooms—is simple, airy, and wonderfully characteristic. It's a great value considering the location and charm (RS%, cheaper rooms with shared bath, family rooms, air-con, on Calle drio la Scimia at San Polo 240a, take vaporetto #1 to Rialto Mercato stop to save walk over bridge, tel. 041-528-5927, www.hotelguerrato.

com, info@hotelguerrato.com). My tour groups book this place for 60 nights each year. Sorry. The Guerrato also rents family apartments in the old center (great for groups of 4-8).

$$$ Hotel al Ponte Mocenigo is off the beaten path—a 10-minute walk northwest of the Rialto Bridge—but it's a great value. This 16th-century Venetian palazzo has a garden terrace and 15 comfy, beautifully appointed, and tranquil rooms (RS%, air-con, take vaporetto #1 to San Stae stop, head inland along right side of church and find Santa Croce 1985, tel. 041-524-4797, www. alpontemocenigo.com, info@alpontemocenigo.com, Sandro and Valter).

NEAR THE ACCADEMIA BRIDGE

As you step over the Accademia Bridge, the commotion of touristy Venice is replaced by a sleepy village laced with canals. This quiet area, next to the best painting gallery in town, is a 15-minute walk from the Rialto or St. Mark's Square. The fast vaporetto #2 to the Accademia stop is the typical way to get here from the train station, Piazzale Roma bus station, Tronchetto parking lot, or St. Mark's Square (early and late, #2 terminates at the Rialto stop, where you change to #1). For hotels near the Zattere stop, vaporetto #5.1 (or the Alilaguna speedboat from the airport) are good options.

South of the Accademia Bridge, in Dorsoduro

$$$$ Pensione Accademia fills the 17th-century Villa Maravege like a Bellini painting. Its 27 comfortable, elegant rooms gild the lily. You'll feel aristocratic gliding through its grand public spaces and lounging in its wistful, breezy gardens (family rooms, air-con, no elevator but most rooms on ground floor or one floor up, on Fondamenta Bollani at Dorsoduro 1058, tel. 041-521-0188, www. pensioneaccademia.it, info@pensioneaccademia.it).

$$$$ Hotel la Calcina, the home of English writer John Ruskin in 1876, maintains a 19th-century formality. It comes with three-star comforts in a professional yet intimate package. Its 25 nautical-feeling rooms are squeaky clean, with nice wood furniture, hardwood floors, and a peaceful waterside setting facing Giudecca Island (some view rooms, air-con, no elevator and lots of stairs, rooftop terrace, buffet breakfast outdoors in good weather on platform over lagoon, near Zattere vaporetto stop at south end of Rio de San Vio at Dorsoduro 780, tel. 041-520-6466, www. lacalcina.com, info@lacalcina.com).

$$$$ Casa Rezzonico, a tranquil getaway far from the crowds, rents seven inviting, nicely appointed rooms with a grassy private garden terrace. All the rooms overlook either the canal or the garden (RS%, family rooms, air-con, near Ca' Rezzonico vaporetto stop—line #1, a few blocks past Campo San Barnaba on

Fondamenta Gherardini at Dorsoduro 2813, tel. 041-277-0653, www.casarezzonico.it, info@casarezzonico.it, brothers Matteo and Mattia).

$$$$ Hotel Galleria has nine old-fashioned and velvety rooms, half with views of the Grand Canal. Some rooms are quite narrow, but you can open your window to watch boats pass by at any time. It's run with a family feel by Luciano (one cheaper room with detached private bath, breakfast in room, ceiling fans, 30 yards from Accademia art museum, next to recommended Foscarini pizzeria at Dorsoduro 878a, tel. 041-523-2489, www.hotelgalleria.it, info@hotelgalleria.it).

$$$$ Hotel Belle Arti, with a stiff, serious staff, lacks personality but has a grand entry, an inviting garden terrace, and 67 heavily decorated rooms (air-con, elevator, 100 yards behind Accademia art museum on Rio Terà A. Foscarini at Dorsoduro 912a, tel. 041-522-6230, www.hotelbellearti.com, info@hotelbellearti.com).

$$$$ Don Orione Religious Guest House is a big cultural center dedicated to the work of a local man who became a saint in modern times. With 80 rooms filling an old monastery, it feels cookie-cutter-institutional (like a modern retreat center), but is also classy, clean, peaceful, and strictly run. It's beautifully located, comfortable, and supports a fine cause: Profits go to mission work in the developing world (family rooms, groups welcome, air-con, elevator, on Rio Terà A. Foscarini, Dorsoduro 909a, tel. 041-522-4077, www.donorione-venezia.it, info@donorione-venezia.it).

$$$ Ca' San Trovaso rents six pleasant rooms in a little three-floor, formerly residential building. The location is peaceful, on a small, out-of-the-way canal (RS%, some view rooms, breakfast in your room, tiny roof terrace, apartments available with 3-night minimum, near Zattere vaporetto stop, off Fondamenta de le Romite at Dorsoduro 1350, tel. 041-241-2215, mobile 349-125-3890, www.casantrovaso.com, info@casantrovaso.com, Anna and Alessandra).

$$$ Casa di Sara, a colorfully decorated B&B, is hidden in a leafy courtyard in a humble back-street area overlooking a canal. Their four quiet rooms and tiny roof terrace offer the maximum in privacy (air-con, along Fondamenta de le Romite at Dorsoduro 1330, mobile 342-596-3563, www.casadisara.com, info@casadisara.com, Emanuele).

North of the Accademia Bridge

These places are between the Accademia Bridge and St. Mark's Square.

$$$$ Novecento Hotel rents nine plush rooms on three floors, complemented by a big, welcoming lounge, an elegant living

SLEEPING

Map labels:

Campo S. Pantalon
To Frari & Rialto
PALAZZO GIUSTINIANI
V San Tomà
T
SANTA MARGARITA
Rio de
Ca' Foscari
PALAZZO BALBI
PALAZZO MOCENIGO
PALAZZO VECCHIA
C. CORNER
C. FORNO
CA' FOSCARI
PALAZZO CONTARINI DELLE FIGURE
C. MOCENIGO
S. SAN SAMUELE
25
Campo Santa Margarita
Campiello Squelini
PALAZZO GIUSTINIAN
PALAZZO MORO LIN
12
27
CA' REZZONICO
CALLE BERNARDO
San Samuele
PALAZZO GRASSI
Campo San Samuele
C. DEL ORBI
11
SAN BARNABA
V Ca' Rezzonico
V
PALAZZO MALIPIERO CAPPELLO
Campo S. Barnaba
21
Rio del Malpaga
3
24
Rio Toletta
PALAZZO LOREDAN
SAN VIDAL
23
Campo Squero
22
1
PALAZZO CONTARINI DEGLI SCRIGNI
10
Campo San Vidal
29
16
15
Accademia
8
SACA D. LA TOLETTA
PALAZZO QUERINI
V
ACCADEMIA BRIDGE
OGNISSANTI
7
SAN TROVASO
14
WC
ACCADEMIA GALLERY
13
4
To 28
Rio del Ognisanti
Campo San Trovaso
GONDOLA WORKSHOP
D O R S O
20 32
19
SANTA MARIA DELLA VISITAZIONE
5
SANTA AGNESE
18
6
V Zattere
A
Campo Santa Agnese
2
SANTA MARIA GESUATI
17
V

Giudecca Canal

Accommodations

1. Pensione Accademia
2. Hotel la Calcina
3. Casa Rezzonico
4. Hotel Galleria
5. Hotel Belle Arti
6. Don Orione Religious Guest House
7. Ca' San Trovaso
8. Casa di Sara
9. Novecento Hotel
10. Foresteria Levi
11. Domus Ciliota
12. Hotel San Samuele

Eateries

13. Bar Foscarini
14. Enoteca Cantine del Vino Già Schiavi
15. Bar al Maraveje & Bar Toletta
16. Al Vecio Marangon Ristorante

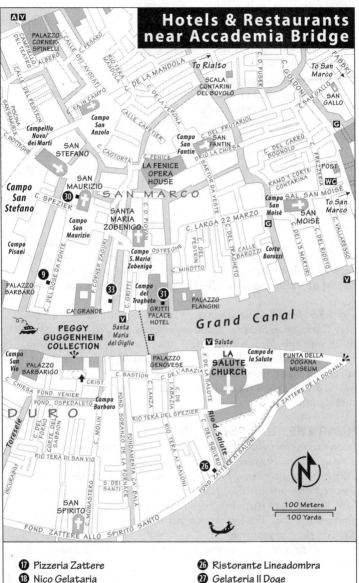

Hotels & Restaurants near Accademia Bridge

SLEEPING

17 Pizzeria Zattere
18 Nico Gelataria
19 Terrazza dei Nobili
20 Pizzeria Oke
21 Ristoteca Oniga
22 Osteria Enoteca Ai Artisti
23 Pizzeria al Profeta
24 Enoteca e Trattoria la Bitta
25 Campo Santa Margarita Eateries & Nightlife

26 Ristorante Lineadombra
27 Gelateria Il Doge
28 To Supermarket

Nightlife
29 Interpreti Veneziani Concerts
30 Music Museum
31 Musica a Palazzo
32 El Chioschetto alle Zattere
33 Venice Jazz Club

room, and a small breakfast garden. This boutique hotel is nicely located and has a tasteful sense of style, mingling Art Deco with North African and Turkish decor (air-con, lots of stairs, on Calle del Dose, off Campo San Maurizio at San Marco 2684, tel. 041-241-3765, www.novecento.biz, info@novecento.biz).

$$$$ Foresteria Levi, run by a foundation that promotes research on Venetian music, offers 32 quiet, institutional yet comfortable and spacious rooms—some are loft quads, a good deal for families (RS%, air-con, elevator, on Calle Giustinian at San Marco 2893, tel. 041-277-0542, www.foresterialevi.it, info@foresterialevi.it). From the base of the Accademia Bridge, it's just over the tiny Ponte Giustinian.

$$$ Domus Ciliota is a big, efficient, and sparkling-clean place—well-run, well-located, church-owned, and plainly furnished—with 30 dorm-like rooms and a peaceful courtyard. If you want industrial-strength comfort with no stress and little character, this is a fine value. During the school year, half the rooms are used by students (air-con, elevator; just off Campo San Stefano at San Marco 2976; tel. 041-520-4888, www.ciliota.it, info@ciliota.it).

$$$ Hotel San Samuele rents 10 tidy rooms in an old *palazzo* near Campo San Stefano. Antique furniture and restored original floors give this place a homey feel. It's in a great locale, and the rooms with shared bath can be a good deal (RS%, no breakfast, fans, some stairs, on Salizada San Samuele at San Marco 3358, tel. 041-520-5165, www.hotelsansamuele.com, info@hotelsansamuele.com, Judith).

NEAR THE TRAIN STATION

I don't recommend the train station area. It's crawling with noisy, disoriented tourists with too much baggage and people whose life's calling is to scam visitors out of their money. It's so easy just to hop on a vaporetto upon arrival and sleep in the Venice of your dreams. Still, some like to park their bags near the station, and if so, these places stand out. The farther you get from the station, the more pleasant the surroundings.

Laundry: A self-service launderette is across the Grand Canal from the station (see page 17).

Close to the Station

These hotels are very close to the station, but each is down a side street, away from the throngs along the main drag.

$$$$ Hotel Abbazia fills a former abbey with both history and class. The refectory makes a grand living room for guests, a garden fills the old courtyard, and the halls leading to 50 rooms are monkishly wide (RS%, air-con, no elevator, some ground-floor

SLEEPING

rooms, fun-loving staff, 2 blocks from the station on the very quiet Calle Priuli dei Cavaletti, Cannaregio 68, tel. 041-717-333, www. abbaziahotel.com, info@abbaziahotel.com).

$$ Hotel S. Lucia, 150 yards from the train station, is oddly modern and sterile, with bright and spacious rooms and tight showers. Its 13 rooms are simple and clean. Guests enjoy their sunny garden area out front (cheaper rooms with shared bath, air-con, closed Nov-Feb, on Calle de la Misericordia at Cannaregio 358, tel. 041-715-180, www.hotelslucia.com, info@hotelslucia.com, Gianni, Alessandra, and their son, Lorenzo).

$ Hotel Rossi, sitting quietly at the end of a dead-end street off the main Lista di Spagna, rents 14 tired, well-worn rooms that are cheap in every sense—the budget-minded will find it tolerable for a night or two, but consider yourself forewarned (cheaper rooms with shared bath, air-con, lots of stairs, on Calle de le Procuratie, Cannaregio 262, tel. 041-715-164, hotelrossi.venezia@gmail.com).

Across the Bridge from the Train Station

These two places are in a quieter area on the other side of the Grand Canal from the train station—you'll have to haul your bags across a big bridge. Both are also convenient to the bus station at Piazzale Roma.

$$$ Albergo Marin is loosely run, with 19 nice but sloppily kept rooms. It's close enough to the station to be convenient, but far enough to be quiet, sane, and residential (air-con, on Ramo de le Chioverete at Santa Croce 670b, tel. 041-718-022, www. albergomarin.it, info@albergomarin.it, Giacomo).

$$ Hotel Ai Tolentini is a pleasant couple-hundred yards from the Piazzale Roma bus station—just far enough to make you feel like you're actually in Venice. The seven rooms are on two floors, up narrow stairs above a restaurant that can be noisy (no breakfast, air-con, on Calle Amai at Santa Croce 197g, tel. 041-275-9140, www.albergoaitolentini.it, info@albergoaitolentini.it).

Farther from the Station, Toward the Jewish Ghetto and Rialto

While still walkable from the station, these listings are just outside the chaotic station neighborhood, in a far more pleasant residential zone close to the former Jewish Ghetto. The nearest Grand Canal vaporetto stop is San Marcuola.

$$$ Locanda Ca' San Marcuola is a peaceful, characteristic, good-value oldie-but-goodie renting 14 fine rooms a few steps from the Grand Canal (family rooms, air-con, elevator, next to San Marcuola vaporetto stop on Campo San Marcuola, Cannaregio 1763, tel. 041-716-048, www.casanmarcuola.com, info@casanmarcuola. com).

Hotels & Restaurants near the Train Station

Accommodations
1. Hotel Abbazia
2. Hotel S. Lucia
3. Hotel Rossi
4. Albergo Marin
5. Hotel Ai Tolentini
6. Locanda Ca' San Marcuola
7. Locanda Herion

Eateries
8. To Osteria L'Orto dei Mori
9. To Osteria Ai 40 Ladroni

10. Osteria Enoteca Timon
11. To Trattoria Al Mariner
12. Gam Gam Kosher
13. Pizzeria Vesuvio
14. Enoteca Cicchetteria Do Colonne
15. Antica Birraria la Corte
16. Gelateria Il Doge

Other
17. Supermarket
18. Launderette

SLEEPING

Road to Mestre & Mainland

To Tronchetto

SANTA LUCIA TRAIN STATION (FERROVIA)

SCALZI

Ferrovia W

Ferrovia Scalzi

SCALZI BRIDGE

SAN SIMEONE PICCOLO

CAMP. DE LE CHIOVERETE

100 Meters
100 Yards

WC

Ferrovia

Canale de Santa Chiara

To Stazione Marittima & Tronchetto

RAMPA SAN BASILIO

PONTE DELLA LIBERTA

Canale de la Liberta

PEOPLE MOVER

GROCERY

Piazzale Roma

CALATRAVA BRIDGE

Giardino Papadopoli

PUBLIC PARKING GARAGE

Piazzale Roma

BUS STATION

SAN MARCO GARAGE

RIO TERA SAN ANDREA

Campiello de Lana

SAN NICOLO DA TOLENTINO

PHARMACY

SANTA   CROCE

Canale de Santa Maria Maggiore

Rio de la Cazziola

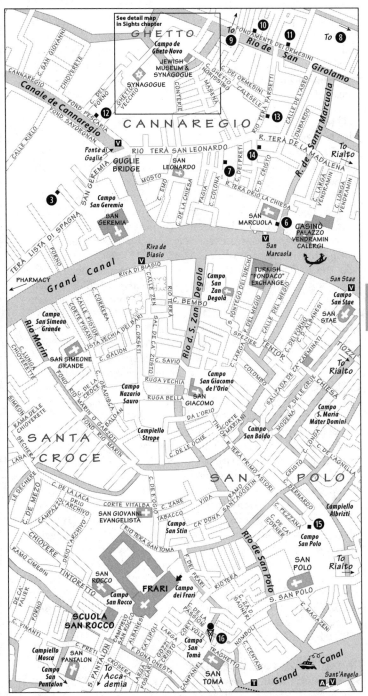

SLEEPING

$$ **Locanda Herion,** tucked down a sleepy lane just off a busy shopping street, rents 13 beige-tiled, homey rooms (RS%—use code STEVES, a few shared terraces, one room is wheelchair accessible, air-con, on Campiello Augusto Picutti, Cannaregio 1697a, tel. 041-275-9426, www.locandaherion.com, info@locandaherion.com).

OTHER ACCOMMODATIONS IN VENICE
More Venice Hotels

Big, Fancy Hotels that Discount Shamelessly: Several big, plush, $$$$ places with greedy, sky-high rack rates frequently have steep discounts if you book through their websites. Unless otherwise noted, all of these are on the "Hotels & Restaurants near St. Mark's Square" map (earlier in this chapter). If you want sliding-glass-door, uniformed-receptionist kind of comfort and formality in the old center, these are worth considering: **Hotel Giorgione** (big, garish, shiny, near Rialto Bridge—see the "Hotels & Restaurants near the Rialto Bridge" map on page 261; www.hotelgiorgione.com); **Hotel Casa Verardo** (elegant and quietly parked on a canal behind St. Mark's, more stately, 22 rooms, www.casaverardo.it); **Hotel Donà Palace, Hotel all'Angelo,** and **Hotel al Ponte dei Sospiri** (three sister hotels sitting Las Vegas-like in the touristy zone a few blocks behind St. Mark's Basilica, with formal service and 100 overpriced rooms that are getting a bit long in the tooth, all on Calle Larga San Marco, www.carrainhotelsgroup.com); and **Hotel Ca' Dei Conti** (5 minutes northeast of St. Mark's Square, palatial and perfectly located but its high-priced rooms are worth it only when deeply discounted, www.cadeiconti.com).

Other Options: If all my other listings are full, try one of the following $$$ hotels. Rates for these places vary widely with the season and demand: **Hotel Violino d'Oro** is a beautiful boutique hotel (Via XXII Marzo, San Marco 2091, tel. 041-277-0841, www.violinodoro.com). Its sister hotel, **Hotel Anastasia,** is more modest, with limited reception staff (San Marco 2141, tel. 041-277-0776, www.hotelanastasia.com). **Hotel American Dinesen** offers 30 plush rooms with all the comforts (near Peggy Guggenheim Collection at Fondamenta Bragadin, Dorsoduro 628, tel. 041-520-4733, www.hotelamerican.com). **Hotel La Fenice et des Artistes** has 68 classy but unpretentious rooms on a sleepy square (near opera house at Campiello della Fenice, San Marco 1936, tel. 041-523-2333, www.fenicehotels.com). **Hotel dei Dragomanni** is modern, stylish, and pricey (facing Grand Canal at San Marco 2711, tel. 041-277-1300, www.hoteldragomanni.com).

Cheap Dormitory Accommodations

$$ **Foresteria della Chiesa Valdese** is ramshackle, chilly, run-

down, yet charming. It rents 75 beds—mostly in tight (6- to 10-bed) dorms, but with nine fine doubles and some larger private rooms sleeping up to six. It comes with generous public spaces and classic paintings on the walls and ceilings. Its profits support the charity work of the Waldesian and Methodist Church. Reservations for the dorms are accepted only four days in advance (some view rooms; must check in and out when office is open— 8:30-20:00; free concerts on site Wed and Sat, no air-con, elevator, near Campo Santa Maria Formosa on Fondamenta Cavagnis at Castello 5170, see the "Hotels & Restaurants near the Rialto Bridge" map, tel. 041-528-6797, www.foresteriavenezia.it, info@ foresteriavenezia.it).

¢ **Generator Venice,** on Giudecca Island with 243 beds and grand views across the Bay of San Marco, is a godsend for backpackers shell-shocked by Venetian prices. Though the facility has many 21st-century touches, at heart it's still a classic hostel—big rooms stacked with bunk beds (rates vary wildly, private and family rooms available, office open 24 hours, Fondamenta Zitelle 86, tel. 041-877-8288, www.staygenerator.com/venice, venice@ staygenerator.com). From the bus or train stations, take vaporetto #4.1 (faster) or #2 (more frequent) to the Zitelle stop, then walk right along the embankment to #86. (From the Tronchetto parking lot, take vaporetto #2.)

STAYING ON THE MAINLAND, IN MESTRE

Drivers wanting to do a one-day blitz of Venice can sleep in Mestre for two nights and park right at their hotel. Mestre (MEH-streh) is a gloomy, industrial, concrete burg where Venice's causeway meets the mainland. The streets surrounding the Mestre station are a stark contrast to Venice: big, dingy buildings, rough corners, and modern roads buzzing with traffic. These places are cheaper than hotels of a similar standard in Venice proper, but unless you have a car, it's hard to justify sleeping here when the magic of Venice is so close. Bunking here does have a few other advantages, though: Your money buys more comfort and amenities; it's extra handy for side-tripping by rail to other towns (such as Padua, Vicenza, and Verona); and it's more likely to have affordable rooms when Venice proper is chockablock with festivals.

It's easy to get between Mestre and Venice. From the big Mestre station, trains depart about every 10 minutes, zipping to Venezia Santa Lucia Station (right on the Grand Canal) in about 10 minutes for €1.35 (buy tickets at machines; validate before boarding). Alternatively, you can catch bus #2, right in front of Mestre's train station, and ride it to Venice's Piazzale Roma (also right on the Grand Canal, across from the train station) in 15 minutes (€1.50, covered by Venice's transit passes).

These hotels all charge around €100-150 for a double in peak season, but rates are extremely soft. In slow times, you can get a much better deal. All of these are quite modern when compared to the typically musty, Old World options in Venice. My Mestre recommendations all have parking—mostly pay on-site or discounted at the big Parcheggio Stazione garage across from the station (figure €10-16/day; request when you reserve), but a few offer free parking.

Right in Front of the Station

$$$ **Hotel Tritone,** a high-rise Best Western hotel with 60 rooms varying in decor from business to mod, has the most convenient location, facing Mestre's train station (air-con, elevator, pay parking; leaving the station, cross the street, turn right, and walk to the end of the block to find Viale Stazione 16, tel. 041-538-3125, www.hoteltritonevenice.com, info@hoteltritonevenice.com).

$$ **Hotel Paris** is a few doors down from the station and worth considering if you can get a deal. It has 18 small, modern, modestly stylish rooms (air-con, on-site parking, Via Venezia 11, tel. 041-926-037, www.hotelparis.it, info@hotelparis.it). It's hiding in a drab sea of apartment blocks: Leaving the station, cross the street, turn left along Viale Stazione, and turn right after one block up Via Venezia.

A Bit Farther, but Still Walkable

While slightly less handy to the station (about a 10-minute walk), these options are a better value and have more of a neighborhood feel. To reach them from the station, cross the street and go up Via Piave. After about four blocks, turn left for Hotel Villa Costanza or Hotel Cris, or (soon after) right for Hotel Aaron. For these hotels, the bus (which stops along Via Piave) can be a faster and easier way to reach Venice than the train (and lets you skip the station-area chaos).

$$ **Hotel Villa Costanza** is the nicest place I could find in Mestre. This stylish, professional-feeling boutique hotel fills an old villa on a sleepy residential street with 26 classy rooms, an inviting modern lounge, and a covered terrace (RS%, air-con, elevator, on-site pay parking, Via Monte Nero 25, tel. 041-932-624, www.hotelvillacostanza.com, info@hotelvillacostanza.com, Monica).

$$ **Hotel Cris,** a simpler option with a quiet courtyard up the street from Hotel Villa Costanza, has 18 nondescript rooms (air-con, free on-site parking, Via Monte Nero 3a, tel. 041-926-773, www.hotelcris.it, info@hotelcris.it).

$$ **Hotel Aaron** oozes modern artistic style, with 20 sleek, good-value, spacious rooms on a pleasant street just off Viale Piave. Frequent online discounts can make this a great value (air-con,

elevator, on-site pay parking, Via Felisati 187, tel. 041-538-5868, www.hotelaaron.com, info@hotelaaron.com).

Behind Mestre Station, in Marghera

If you leave the station through its back door (follow the underground tunnel connecting platforms to the end beyond tracks 12/13), you'll pop out into Marghera, a much more pleasant, residential-feeling area, with freestanding homes, gardens, and trees. Exiting the station, turn left down the first street, then right onto Via Rizzardi. This main drag is lined with lots of big tour hotels (where cut-rate tour companies shoehorn their groups at Venice's doorstep), as well as this smaller, charming option.

$$ Casa Villa Gardenia, just before the roundabout on the right (about a 10-minute walk from the station's tracks), is sweetly run by Lorenza, who rents six rooms in a pleasant old villa (family rooms, air-con, free on-site parking, Via Rizzardi 36c, Marghera, tel. 041-930-207, www.casavillagardenia.it, info@casavillagardenia.com).

Beyond Mestre

This place, beyond the urban core of Mestre, combines fine prices with easy bus links into Venice.

$ Villa Mocenigo Agriturismo, about 20 miles from Marco Polo Airport, is a working, family-run farm with 10 simple rooms in a peaceful rural location between Venice and Padua (dinner about €20/person, air-con, free parking, Via Viasana 59 in Mirano-Venezia, tel. 041-433-246, mobile 338-362-9268, www.villamocenigo.com, info@villamocenigo.com). Email for directions. Buses to Venice stop a 10-minute walk away (2/hour, 45 minutes).

EATING IN VENICE

Looking for an "untouristy restaurant" in Venice is like looking for the same thing at Disneyland. A restaurateur once confided in me that no restaurant in Venice can be truly untouristy: They all want and need the tourist euro. Simply put, Venice's restaurants exist to feed tourists. But while some cater to groups and sloppy big spenders, others respect their clientele—both locals and travelers. My recommended places, even though they're touristy, are popular with actual Venetians, who still eat out and have their favorites.

EATING TIPS

I rank eateries from **$** budget to **$$$$** splurge. For even more advice on eating in Venice, including details on ordering, dining, and tipping in restaurants, the type of eateries you'll encounter, where to find budget meals, picnicking help, and Italian cuisine and beverages (including wine), see the "Eating" section of the Practicalities chapter.

Restaurant Hours: Most restaurants close their kitchens between lunch and dinner, typically reopening around 19:00 or later. Even if a restaurant is fully booked for later that evening, it may accommodate walk-in diners who are willing to eat early and quickly.

Eating Well: While touristy restaurants are the norm in Venice, you can still make the most of your meal by dining at one of my recommended listings and following these tips. First trick: Walk away from triple-language menus or laminated pictures of food. Second trick: For freshness, eat fish. Many seafood dishes are the catch of the day. Third trick: Eat later. A place may feel touristy at 19:00, but if you come back at 21:00, it can be filled with locals...or, at least, Italian visitors. Tourists eat barbarically early, which is fine with the restaurants because they turn tables that would otherwise be used only once in an evening.

Budget Eating: The keys to eating affordably in Venice are pizza, bars/cafés (see below), self-service cafeterias, and picnics. For a colorful picnic experience, gather your ingredients in the morning at a produce market (most fun at and around the big Rialto Market).

Bars/Cafés: Venetians often eat a snack—*cicchetti* or *panini*—while standing at a bar. (You'll usually pay more if you sit.) You can get a filling plate of typically Venetian appetizers at nearly any bar.

I like small, fun, stand-up mini meals at **cicchetti bars** best. Unique to Venice, *cicchetti* bars specialize in finger foods and appetizers that combine to make a speedy and tasty meal. *Cicchetti* (the Venetian version of tapas) was designed as a quick meal for working people. The selection and ambience are best on workdays—Monday through Saturday for lunch or early dinner (see "The Stand-Up Progressive Venetian Pub-Crawl Dinner" sidebar in this chapter). I list a couple of stretches in Venice where you can go from bar to bar sampling *cicchetti*.

Sandwiches are sold fast and cheaply at bars everywhere (order a *panini, piadini,* or *tramezzini*). A great "sandwich row" of cheap cafés is near St. Mark's Square. You can eat your sandwich at the bar or take it with you.

Aperitivo: A favorite Italian tradition is the *aperitivo* (predinner drink). The dominant *aperitivo* among Venetians is the *spritz*. This refreshing cocktail mixes white wine, soda, and ice with a liquor of your choice and is garnished with an olive or skewer of fruit. When you order, you'll be asked if you'd like your *spritz con Campari* (bitter) or *con Aperol* (sweeter). Between 18:00 and 20:00, this happy pink drink dominates Venice's watering holes.

NEAR THE RIALTO BRIDGE
North of the Bridge

These restaurants and wine bars are located near or beyond Campo Santi Apostoli, on or near the Strada Nova, the main drag going from Rialto toward the train station.

$$$ Trattoria da Bepi, bright and alpine-paneled, feels like a classic, where Loris carries on his mother's passion for good, traditional Venetian cuisine. Ask for the seasonal specialties: The

EATING

Hotels & Restaurants near the Rialto Bridge

Accommodations
1. Locanda la Corte
2. To Alloggi Barbaria
3. Hotel al Ponte Antico
4. Pensione Guerrato
5. Hotel al Ponte Mocenigo
6. Hotel Giorgione
7. Foresteria della Chiesa Valdese

100 Meters
100 Yards

CANNAREGIO

CASTELLO

SAN MARCO

EATING

18. Osteria al Ponte Storto
19. Trattoria Antiche Carampane
20. To Antica Birraria la Corte
21. Osteria alle Testiere
22. Osteria al Mascaron
23. Peter Pan Kebabs & Pizza
24. La Boutique del Gelato
25. Gelatoteca Suso
26. Supermarket (3)
27. Devil's Forest Pub
28. Inishark Pub

seafood appetizer plate and crab dishes are excellent. There's good seating inside and out. If you trust Loris, you'll walk away with a wonderful dining memory (Fri-Wed 12:00-14:30 & 19:00-22:00, closed Thu, reservations recommended, half a block off Campo Santi Apostoli on Salizada Pistor, Cannaregio 4550, tel. 041-528-5031, www.dabepi.it).

$$$ La Cantina is a rustic yet sophisticated *enoteca*—you won't find a menu here. Rather than cook (there's no kitchen), they serve *cicchetti* and gourmet cold plates of meat, cheese, and fish. Though short on smiles and expensive (meat-and-cheese plates—€18/person, seafood plates—€35/person), you'll enjoy good ingredients paired with fine wines. You can sit inside and watch the preparation scene or enjoy the parade of passersby from great seats right on the Strada Nova (Mon-Sat 11:00-22:00, closed Sun, facing Campo San Felice on Strada Nova near Ca' d'Oro, Cannaregio 3689, tel. 041-522-8258).

$$$$ Vini da Gigio, a more expensive option, has a traditional Venetian menu and a classy but unsnooty setting that's a pleasant mix of traditional and contemporary (Wed-Sun 12:00-14:30 & 19:00-22:30, closed Mon-Tue, 4 blocks from Ca' d'Oro vaporetto stop on Fondamenta San Felice, behind the church on Campo San Felice, Cannaregio 3628a, tel. 041-528-5140, www.vinidagigio.com).

East of the Rialto Bridge

The next few places hide away in the twisty lanes between the Rialto Bridge and Campo Santa Maria Formosa. Osteria da Alberto is a tad farther north of the others.

$ Bacarando Bar has a youthful feel, with clearly marked and priced little dishes at the counter and table seating (daily 11:00-24:00, tel. 342-800-3823). It's behind Campo San Bartolomeo (if the statue turned around, walked to the far right-hand corner, and explored the back lanes there, he'd find Bacarando in Corte dell'Orso).

$$ Osteria al Portego is a small and popular neighborhood eatery near Campo San Lio. Carlo serves good meals, bargain-priced house wine, and excellent €1-3 *cicchetti*—best enjoyed around 18:00 (picked over by 21:00). The *cicchetti* here can make a great meal, but consider sitting down for a dinner from their menu. From 12:00-14:30 & 17:30-21:30, their six tables are reserved for those ordering from the menu; reserve ahead if you want a table (daily 11:30-15:00 & 17:30-22:00, on Calle de la Malvasia, Castello 6015, tel. 041-522-9038, Federica). From Campo San Bartolomeo, continue over a bridge to Campo San Lio, turn left, and follow Calle Carminati straight 50 yards over another bridge.

$$ Osteria da Alberto, up near Campo Santa Maria Novo,

Pizza in Venice

While not the home of pizza, Venice is enthusiastic about it. For tourists, a great way to enjoy a delightful Venetian setting at a painless price is to have a €10 pizza with a beer or carafe of house wine at a canalside restaurant. Consider one of these places (all described in more detail in this chapter):

Several fun-loving, youthful pizzerias feature inexpensive and good pizzas, big pizza parlor-type interiors, and relaxing outdoor seating, such as **Pizzeria al Profeta** (with a leafy gar-

den, near Campo San Barnaba), **Pizzeria Oke** (with casual tables overlooking the Giudecca Canal), **Antica Birraria la Corte** (on a big, breezy neighborhood square), **Pizzeria Vesuvio** (with streetside tables, near the Jewish Ghetto), and **Rossopomodoro** (a big and thriving pizzeria near San Marco). For basic pizza with one of the city's most picturesque settings— on the Grand Canal under the Accademia Bridge—check out **Bar Foscarini.** And for top-shelf pizza served in a more formal restaurant setting, consider **Terrazza dei Nobili** (with elegant seating overlooking the Giudecca Canal).

For takeout, you'll find hole-in-the-wall shops in every neighborhood baking round, family-size pizzas (about 20 inches across) for €8-15, or "normal" ones (12 inches) for €4-8. Some sell *pizza al taglio* (by the slice, usually reheated). Take-out prices increase dramatically as you near the Rialto and St. Mark's Square. For instance, at the base of the Rialto Bridge, family-size pizzas are cut into eight slices for about €4.50 each, but around Campo Santa Maria Formosa or Campo San Barnaba, they're cut into six larger slices (€2 each). For more tips on pizza, see the "Eating" section of the Practicalities chapter.

EATING

is one of my standbys, with locals at lunch and tourists at dinner. They offer up excellent daily specials: seafood dishes, pastas, and a good house wine in a woody and characteristic interior. It's smart to reserve at night—I'd request a table in front (daily 12:00-15:00 & 18:30-22:00; on Calle Larga Giacinto Gallina, midway between Campo Santi Apostoli and Campo San Zanipolo/Santi Giovanni e Paolo, and next to Ponte de la Panada bridge, Cannaregio 5401; tel. 041-523-8153, www.osteriadaalberto.it, run by Graziano and Giovanni).

Rialto Market Area

The north end of the Rialto Bridge is a great area for menu brows-ing, bar-hopping, drinks, and snacks; it also has fine sit-down res-taurants. As with market neighborhoods anywhere, you'll find lots of hard-working holes-in-the-wall with a line on the freshest of ingredients and catering to local shoppers needing a quick, afford-able, and tasty bite. This area is very crowded by day, nearly empty early in the evening, and packed with young, trendy Venetians later.

My listings include a stretch of dark and rustic pubs serving *cicchetti* (Venetian tapas), a strip of trendy places fronting the Grand Canal, a few little places on the market, and a couple of "normal" restaurants serving solid pasta, pizza, and *secondi*.

The *Cicchetti* Strip: Four Venetian Tapas Bars

The 100-yard-long stretch starting two blocks inland from the Rialto Market (along Sotoportego dei Do Mori and Calle de le Do Spade) is beloved among Venetian *cicchetti* enthusiasts for its delightful bar munchies, good wine by the glass, and fun stand-up conviviality. These **$** places serve food all day, but the spread is best at around noon (unless otherwise noted, generally open daily 12:00-15:00 & 18:00-20:00 or 21:00). Each place offers a fine bar-and-stools scene, and a couple can be treated like a restaurant—order from their rustic menu and grab a table. Scout these places in advance (listed in the order you'll reach them, if coming from the Rialto Bridge) to help decide which ambience is right for the experience you have in mind. Then pick one, dig in, and drink up.

At each place, look for the list of snacks and wine by the glass at the bar or on the wall. When you're ready for dessert, try dip-ping a Burano biscuit in a glass of strawberry-flavored *fragolino* or another sweet dessert wine. Most bars offer glasses of house wine for €1, better wine for around €3, and *cicchetti* for €1.50-2.

Bar all'Arco, a bustling one-room joint, is particularly enjoy-able for its *cicchetti* (Mon-Sat 10:00-17:00, closed Sun, San Polo 436; Francesco, Anna, Matteo).

Cantina Do Mori has been famous with locals (since 1462) and savvy travelers (since 1982) as a convivial place for wine. They serve a forest of little edibles on toothpicks and *francobolli* (a spicy selection of 20 tiny, mayo-soaked sandwiches nicknamed "stamps"). Go here to be abused in a fine atmosphere—the frowns are part of the shtick—and be aware that prices can add up quickly (closed Sun, can be shoulder-to-shoulder, San Polo 430).

Osteria ai Storti, with a cool photo of the market in 1909, is more of a sit-down place (tables inside and on street). It's run by Alessandro, who speaks English and enjoys helping educate travel-ers (around corner from Cantina Do Mori on Calle San Matio, San Polo 819).

Cantina Do Spade is run by Francesco, who clearly lists the *cicchetti* (mostly deep fried) and wines of the day. It's also good for sit-down restaurant-style meals (30 yards down Calle de le Do Spade from Osteria ai Storti at San Polo 860, tel. 041-521-0583).

The Bancogiro Stretch: Five Places Overlooking the Grand Canal

Just past the Rialto Bridge, between Campo San Giacomo and the Grand Canal, this strip of popular places in a recently renovated old building has some of the best canalside seating in Venice. I call this the "Bancogiro Stretch" (the restaurants front a former banking building called Bancogiro).

Each place has a unique character and formula. Unless otherwise noted, all are open daily and serve drinks, *cicchetti,* and somewhat pricey sit-down meals. While you can get a drink anytime, dinner is typically served only after 19:00 or 19:30. During meals, they charge more and limit table seating to those ordering full lunches or dinners; but between mealtimes you can enjoy a drink or a snack at fine prices. After dinner hours, the Bancogiro Stretch—especially in the surrounding alleys that house low-rent bars—becomes a youthful and trendy nightspot. Before or after dinner, this strip is one of the best places in town for a *spritz.*

Here's the rundown (in the order you'll reach them from the Rialto Bridge): **$$$ Bar Naranzaria** serves Italian dishes with a few Japanese options. **$$ Caffè Vergnano** is your cheapest option—especially during mealtimes (vegetarian dishes and a busy microwave oven). **$$$ Osteria al Pesador** has a friendly staff and serves local specialties. **$$$ Osteria Bancogiro** has the best reputation for dinner, a passion for the best cheese, and good *cicchetti* options at the bar (nice cheese plate, closed Mon, tel. 041-523-2061, www.osteriabancogiro.it). The more modern **$$ Bar Ancòra** seems to be most popular with the local bar crowd, with a live piano player crooning lounge music during busy times (*cicchetti* at the bar).

Other Good Eateries near the Rialto Market

$ Al Mercà Bar ("At the Market"), a few steps away and off the canal, is a lively little nook with a happy crowd, where law-office workers have lunch and young locals gather in the evening for drinks (quality wine by the glass) and little snacks (€2 mini-sandwiches). The price list is clear, and the youthful crowd seems to enjoy connecting with curious tourists (stand at bar or in square—there are no tables and no interior, Mon-Sat 10:00-14:30 & 18:00-21:00, closed Sun, on Campo Cesare Battisti, San Polo 213).

$$ Ristorante Vini da Pinto is a tourist-friendly eatery facing the fish market, with a large menu and relaxing outdoor seating (and easily confused with the restaurant next door to it). Owner

The Stand-Up Progressive Venetian Pub-Crawl Dinner

My favorite Venetian dinner is a pub crawl *(giro d'ombra)*— a tradition unique to Venice, where no cars means easy crawling. (*Giro* means stroll, and *ombra*—slang for a glass of wine—means shade, from the old days when a portable wine bar scooted with the shadow of the Campanile bell tower across St. Mark's Square.)

Venice's residential back streets hide plenty of characteristic bars *(bacari)*, with countless trays of interesting toothpick munchies *(cicchetti)* and blackboards listing the wines that are uncorked and served by the glass. This is a great way to mingle and have fun with the Venetians. Bars don't stay open very late, and the *cicchetti* selection is best early, so start your evening by 18:00. Many bars are closed on Sunday. For a stress-free pub crawl, consider taking a tour with the charming Alessandro Schezzini (see page 26).

The *Cicchetti* Experience

Cicchetti bars have a social stand-up zone and a cozy gaggle of tables where you can generally sit down with your *cicchetti* or order from a simple menu. In some of the more popular places, the crowds happily spill out into the street. Food generally costs the same price whether you stand or sit. I've listed plenty of pubs in walking order for a quick or extended crawl.

Look for a place that's more "bar" than "restaurant." Make sure they have *cicchetti* on display. Bar-hopping Venetians enjoy an *aperitivo,* a before-dinner drink. You may have to pay for it up front (but probably not—it varies). Then chill. Sip your drink and

Giorgio visits the market each morning to select the day's best catch. Enjoy the lunch-only, fixed-price, three-course seafood meal for €18, including a pasta, seafood sampler plate, veggies, and dessert. Grander versions cost €20-25. Rick Steves readers receive a welcoming prosecco and a farewell *limoncello* and homemade cookie (daily 11:00-23:00, Campo de le Becarie, San Polo 367a, tel. 041-522-4599).

$$ Osteria al Ponte Storto, a little family-run place on a quiet canalside corner a block off the main drag, is worth seeking out for its good-value main dishes, daily specials, and peaceful location.

make the scene while standing at the bar. Next, order a *cicchetti* or two by pointing. Chill some more, while munching and sipping. Then order another one or two. Find a stool or table nearby where you can sit (but don't sit at tables with tablecloths—those are for diners). Pay when you're ready to leave. If you've crawled enough, most of my recommended bars make a fine one-stop, sit-down dinner.

What to Eat (and Drink)

While you can order a plate, Venetians prefer going one-by-one... sipping their wine and trying this...then give me one of those... and so on. Try deep-fried mozzarella cheese, gorgonzola, calamari, artichoke hearts, and anything ugly on a toothpick. *Crostini* (small toasted bread with a topping) are popular, as are marinated seafood, olives, and prosciutto with melon. Meat and fish (*pesce;* PESH-ay) munchies can be expensive; veggies *(verdure)* are cheap, at about €3 for a meal-sized plate. In many places, there's a set price per food item (for example, €1.50). To get a plate of assorted appetizers for €8 (or more, depending on how hungry you are), ask for *"Un piatto classico di cicchetti misti da €8"* (oon pee-AH-toh KLAH-see-koh dee cheh-KET-tee MEE-stee dah OH-toh eh-OO-roh). Bread sticks *(grissini)* are free for the asking.

For drinks, start with an *aperitivo:* Order a Bellini, a *spritz con Aperol,* or a prosecco, and draw approving looks from the natives. Enjoy the house wines with the food. An *ombra* ("shadow") is a small glass of wine often offered with *cicchetti.* An *ombra rosso* (red) or *ombra bianco* (white), or a small beer *(birrino)* costs about €1. The house keg wine is cheap—€1 per glass, about €4 per liter. *Vin bon,* Venetian for fine wine, may run you from €2 to €6 per little glass. There are usually several fine wines uncorked and available by the glass. A good last drink is *fragolino,* the local sweet wine—*bianco* or *rosso.* It often comes with a little cookie *(biscotto)* for dipping.

Rather than a romantic place, it feels like the corner favorite of the neighborhood (Tue-Sun 12:00-15:00 & 18:00-21:45, closed Mon, down Calle Bianca from San Aponal church, San Polo 1278, tel. 041-528-2144, Nicola is the chef/owner).

Between the Rialto Bridge and Frari Church

$$$$ Trattoria Antiche Carampane is a dressy, family-run place with an open kitchen and a local following. They have a passion for fish (and make a point: no pizza) and serve traditional Venetian dishes with a fresh twist that change with the season. It's small—

there are just 30 seats with six tables on the street (Tue-Sat 12:45-14:30 & 19:30-22:30, closed Sun-Mon, reservations necessary, Rio Tera delle Carampane, San Polo 1911, tel. 041-524-0165, www.antichecarampane.com, Francesco).

$$ Antica Birraria la Corte is an everyday eatery on the delightful Campo San Polo. Popular for its huge array of pizza—and smaller selection of hearty salads, pasta, and *secondi*—it fills the far side of this cozy, family-filled square. Although the interior is sprawling and modern, it's a joy to eat on the square, where metal tables teeter on the cobbles, the wind plays with the paper mats, and children run free (daily 12:00-15:00 & 18:00-22:30, on Campo San Polo at #2168—see map on page 252, tel. 041-275-0570).

NEAR ST. MARK'S SQUARE

Other than the first place, a more serious restaurant, the other eateries listed here are cheap-and-cheery options convenient to your sightseeing. For locations, see the map on page 242.

$$$$ Ristorante Antica Sacrestia is a classic restaurant where the owner, Pino, takes a hands-on approach to greeting guests. His staff serves creative fixed-price meals (€35, €55, or €80), a humdrum *menù del giorno,* and wonderful pizzas. You can also order à la carte; their antipasto spread looks like a lagoon aquarium spread out on a plate. My readers are welcome to a free *sgroppino* (lemon vodka after-dinner drink) upon request (Tue-Sun 11:30-15:00 & 18:00-23:00, closed Mon, behind San Zaninovo/Giovanni Novo Church on Calle Corona, Castello 4463, tel. 041-523-0749, www.anticasacrestia.it). There's no wine by the glass. Order carefully. Pizza is your only budget escape.

$$ Rossopomodoro Pizzeria is a big, fun, and practical pizzeria offering top quality, good prices, and a very handy location. They cook Naples-style pizzas in their wood oven and also offer a selection of hearty salads and pastas (long hours daily, Calle Larga San Marco 404, tel. 041-243-8949).

$$$ L'Ombra del Leone is a big, modern, and classy bar (with attached restaurant) featuring an outdoor terrace right on the Grand Canal. It's in the Biennale offices and is popular with gondoliers. Its bar menu of salads and sandwiches has reasonable prices for the elegance and location (long hours daily, in Ca' Giustinian, behind San Moisè Church at the end of Calle Ridotto, tel. 041-241-3519).

Sandwich Row: On Calle de le Rasse, just steps away from the tourist intensity at St. Mark's Square, is a handy strip I call "Sandwich Row." Lined with several **$** sandwich bars, it's the closest place to St. Mark's to get a decent sandwich at an affordable price with a place to sit down (most places open long hours daily, about €1 extra per item to sit; from the Bridge of Sighs, head down the Riva and take the second lane on the left). They all sell the *tramezzino* local-style sandwiches. **Birreria Forst** serves busy local workers a selection of meaty sandwiches with tasty sauce on wheat bread, or made-to-order sandwiches (daily 9:30-23:00, air-con, rustic wood tables, Castello 4540, tel. 041-523-0557). **Bar Verde** is a more modern sandwich bar with fun people-watching views from its tables outside on the corner (also splittable salads, fresh pastries, at the end of Calle de le Rasse facing Campo Santi Filippo e Giacomo, Castello 4526).

Picnicking: Though you can't picnic on St. Mark's Square, you can legally take your snacks to the nearby Giardinetti Reali, the small park along the waterfront west of the Piazzetta.

North of St. Mark's Square, near Campo Santa Maria Formosa

For a (marginally) less touristy scene, walk a few blocks north to the inviting Campo Santa Maria Formosa. For locations, see the "Hotels & Restaurants near the Rialto Bridge" map, earlier in this chapter.

$$$$ Osteria alle Testiere is my top dining splurge in Venice. Hugely respected, Luca and his staff are dedicated to quality, serving up creative, artfully presented market-fresh seafood (there's no meat on the menu), homemade pastas, and fine wine in what the chef calls a "Venetian Nouvelle" style. With only 22 seats, it's tight and homey, with the focus on food and service. They have daily specials, 10 wines by the glass, and one agenda: a great dining experience. This is a good spot to let loose and trust your host. They're open for lunch (12:00-15:00), and reservations made via email only are a must for their two dinner seatings: 19:00 and 21:30 (plan on spending €60 for dinner, closed Sun-Mon, on Calle del Mondo Novo, just off Campo Santa Maria Formosa, Castello 5801, tel. 041-522-7220, www.osterialletestiere.it, info@osterialletestiere.it).

$$$ Osteria al Mascaron is a rustic little bar-turned-restaurant where I've gone for years to watch Gigi, Momi, and their food-loving band of ruffians dish up rustic-yet-sumptuous pastas with steamy seafood to salivating foodies. The *antipasto misto* fish and vegetable plate—have fun pointing—and two glasses of wine make a terrific light meal (Mon-Sat 12:00-15:00 & 18:00-23:00, closed Sun, reservations smart Fri-Sat; on Calle Lunga Santa Maria Formosa, a block past Campo Santa Maria Formosa, Castello 5225; tel. 041-522-5995, www.osteriamascaron.it).

Fast and Cheap Eats: The veggie stand on Campo Santa Maria Formosa is a fixture. For *döner kebabs* and pizza to go, head down Calle Lunga Santa Maria Formosa to **$ Peter Pan** at #6249 (daily 11:30-23:00, Castello).

DORSODURO

All of these recommendations are within a 10-minute walk of the Accademia Bridge (for locations, see the map on page 249). This area, called Dorsoduro, is great for restaurants and well worth the walk from the more touristy Rialto and San Marco areas. The first listings, near the Accademia, are best for lunch. The places in Zattere overlook the Giudecca Canal. Best for dinner are the restaurants near Campo San Barnaba. Last are a handful of pizzerias and *cicchetti* bars on Campo Santa Margarita. My top Dorsoduro listing, **Ristorante Lineadombra,** is described later in "Splurging on a Water (or Otherwise Great) View."

Near the Accademia Bridge

$$ Bar Foscarini, next to the Accademia Bridge and Galleria, offers decent pizzas and *panini* in a memorable Grand Canal-view setting. The food is forgettable and drinks are pricey. But you're paying a premium for this premium location. On each visit to Venice, I grab a pizza lunch here while I ponder the Grand Canal bustle. They also serve breakfast (daily 8:00-23:00, Nov-April until 20:30, on Rio Terà A. Foscarini, Dorsoduro 878c, tel. 041-522-7281, Paolo and Simone).

$ Enoteca Cantine del Vino Già Schiavi, with a wonderfully characteristic *cicchetti*-bar ambience, is much loved for its inexpensive *cicchetti,* sandwiches (order from list on board), and wine. You're welcome to enjoy your wine and finger food at the bar, in the back room surrounded by wine bottles, or out on the sidewalk (specify "*fuori*" to sit outside and they'll provide plastic cups; please don't sit on the bridge). This is primarily a wine shop with great prices for bottles to go (Mon-Sat 8:30-20:30, closed Sun, 100 yards from Accademia art museum on San Trovaso canal; facing the Accademia, take a right and then a forced left at the canal to the second bridge—it's at Dorsoduro 992, tel. 041-523-0034; they have no WC).

$ Bar al Maraveje is handy for a sandwich, with quiet, comfy tables just minutes from the Accademia. They serve a range of fresh sandwiches, from less expensive *topolini* (four-bite sandwiches) and *tramezzini* to heartier ciabatta sandwiches (daily, 100 yards west of the Accademia, just over a bridge on Calle de la Toletta, Dorsoduro 1185, tel. 041-523-5768). **$ Bar Toletta,** a few doors down (#1191), has similar offerings and better *tramezzini.* Like other bars around town, avoid their frozen, microwaved pasta, as evidenced by the laminated pictures out front.

$$$ Al Vecio Marangon Ristorante glows like a dream come true on its corner tucked away from the frenzy of Venice, about 100 yards west of the Accademia. This stylishly rustic restaurant serves *cicchetti*-style dishes and pastas within its tight and picturesque interior or at a line of outdoor tables. It's super romantic. Consider their splittable *piatto di cicchetti misti,* a sampler of sardines, octopus, codfish, and seafood salad. As they take no reservations, arrive early or be prepared to wait (daily 12:00-22:00, on Calle de la Toletta, Dorsoduro 1210, tel. 041-277-8554).

Zattere

The far south side of Dorsoduro has a wide promenade along the canal that, on warm summer evenings, has a special charm. Next to the Zattere vaporetto stop is **Pizzeria Zattere,** where you can enjoy your pizza on a floating dining barge. Nearby is the popular **Nico Gelateria** (also with floating seating on the canal). These two places are also worth consideration:

$$$ Terrazza dei Nobili takes full advantage of the warm, romantic evening sun. They serve regional specialties and pizza at tolerable prices. The breezy and beautiful seaside seating comes with formal service and the rumble of vaporetti from the nearby stop. The interior is bright and hip (daily 12:00-24:00; at the Zattere vaporetto stop, turn left to Dorsoduro 924; tel. 041-520-6895).

$$ Pizzeria Oke is playful, with casual tables on the embankment and a sprawling pizza-parlor interior. It's a hit with young Venetians for its fun atmosphere. While the energy and food are great, be careful to understand the bill—and be warned that dishes presented as free may end up on your check (daily 11:30-23:00, a couple hundred yards from the Zattere vaporetto stop, Dorsoduro 1414, tel. 041-520-6601).

On or near Campo San Barnaba

This small square is a delight—especially in the evening. As these places are within a few steps of each other—and the energy and atmosphere can vary—I like to survey the options before choosing (although reservations may be necessary to dine later in the evening).

$$$ Ristoteca Oniga has an eclectic yet cozy interior, great tables on the square, and is run by the enthusiastic Raffaele. The menu has a few vegetarian and meat dishes but focuses on fresh fish and other sea creatures, highlighted by their specialty, *bucintoro*—a pan full of mussels, clams, prawns, calamari, and spaghetti (daily 12:00-14:30 & 19:00-22:30, reservations smart, Campo San Barnaba, Dorsoduro 2852, tel. 041-522-4410, www.oniga.it).

Venetian Cuisine

Even more so than the rest of Italy, Venetian cuisine relies heavily on fish, shellfish, risotto, and polenta. Along with pizza and pasta, here are some typical foods you'll encounter. For more on Italian food, see the "Eating" section of the Practicalities chapter.

Sandwiches

Panini: Sandwiches made with rustic bread, filled with meat, vegetables, and cheese, served cold or toasted *(riscaldato)*.

Piadini: Flatbread or wrap-like sandwiches.

Tramezzini: Crustless white sandwiches, served cold (various fillings, such as egg, tuna, or shrimp mixed with mayonnaise).

Antipasti (Appetizers)

Venetians start a meal with a light *antipasti* or some *cicchetti*—finger-food appetizers sold in many bars.

Antipasto di mare: Marinated mix of chilled fish and shellfish.

Asiago cheese: A regional specialty, this cow's-milk cheese is either *mezzano* (young, creamy) or *stravecchio* (aged, pungent).

Sarde in saor: Sardines marinated with onions.

Risi (Rice), Pasta, and Polenta

Bigoli in salsa: Long, fat, whole-wheat noodle in anchovy sauce.

Pasta alla buzzara: Pasta in a rich seafood-tomato sauce, generally with shrimp.

Pasta al pomodoro: Pasta in a simple tomato sauce.

Pasta al vongole: Pasta with clams.

Pasta e fagioli: Bean-and-pasta soup.

Polenta: Thick cornmeal porridge served soft or cut into firm slabs and grilled.

Risi e bisi: Rice and peas.

Risotto: Short-grain rice simmered in broth and flavored with seafood, meat, or veggies. *Risotto nero* is made with squid and its ink.

Frutti di Mare (Seafood)

Venetian fish are generally smaller than American salmon and trout (think sardines and anchovies). The weirder the seafood (eel, octopus, frogfish), the more local it is.

Baccalà: Atlantic salt cod that's rehydrated and served with polenta; or chopped up and mixed with mayonnaise as a topping for *cicchetti* (appetizers), called *baccalà mantecato*.

Branzino: Sea bass, grilled and served whole.

Calamari: Squid, often cut into rings and deep-fried or marinated.

Cozze: Mussels, often steamed in an herb broth with tomato.

Gamberi: Shrimp—*gamberetti* are small, and *gamberoni* are large.

Moleche col pien: Fried soft-shell crabs.

Orata: Sea bream (usually farmed).

Pesce fritto misto: Deep-fried seafood (often calamari and prawns).

Pesce spada: Swordfish.

Rombo: Turbot, a flatfish similar to flounder.

Rospo: Frogfish, a small marine fish.

Salmone: Salmon (typically farm-raised).

Seppia: Cuttlefish, a squid-like creature. *Nero di seppia* is the squid served in its own ink, often over spaghetti.

Sogliola: Sole, served poached or oven-roasted.

Vitello di mare: "Sea veal," like swordfish—firm, mild, and grilled.

Vongole: Clams, often steamed with fresh herbs and wine, or served as *spaghetti alle vongole.*

Zuppa di pesce: Seafood stew.

Dolci (Desserts)

Rather than order dessert in a restaurant, I like to stroll with a cup or cone of gelato from one of Venice's popular *gelaterie.* Cookies are also popular. The numerous varieties are due perhaps to Venice's position in trade (spices) and love of celebrations.

Bisse: Seahorse-shaped cookies.

Bussola: Ring-shaped cookies made for Easter.

Croccante: Toasted almond confection, similar to peanut brittle.

Fritole: Tiny doughnuts associated with Carnevale (Mardi Gras).

Pinza: Rustic cornmeal and wheat-flour cake filled with dried fruit; made for Epiphany, January 6.

Tiramisù: Spongy ladyfingers soaked in coffee and Marsala, layered with mascarpone cheese and bitter chocolate.

Cocktails and Local Wines

Amarone: Rich and intense red, made from dried Valpolicella grapes that yield a wine high in alcohol—often around 15 percent.

Bardolino: Beaujolais-like wine made from Valpolicella grapes.

Bellini: Cocktail of prosecco and white-peach puree (invented at the pricey Harry's American Bar near St. Mark's Square).

Fragolino: A sweet, slightly fizzy dessert wine made from a strawberry-flavored grape.

Prosecco: Sparkling white wine. Connoisseurs say the best hails from Valdobbiadene.

Recioto: Dessert wine made with dried, aged Valpolicella grapes.

Sgroppino: Traditional after-dinner drink of squeezed lemon juice, lemon gelato, and vodka.

Soave: Crisp, dry white wine, great with seafood.

Spritz: White wine and soda or prosecco mixed with Campari (bitter) or Aperol (sweeter), over ice.

Tiziano: Grape juice and prosecco.

Valpolicella: Light, dry, fruity red wine, often served as the *vino della casa* (house wine).

EATING

$$$ Osteria Enoteca Ai Artisti serves well-presented quality dishes, with seating within its tight little wine-snob interior or at a few petite, romantic canalside tables. They serve good wines by the glass. When reserving, make sure they know your preference—a table on the canal or inside (Mon-Sat 12:45-14:30 & 19:00-22:00, closed Sun, Fondamenta de la Toletta, Dorsoduro 1169a, tel. 041-523-8944, www.enotecaartisti.com, Vicenzo and chef Francesca).

$$ Pizzeria al Profeta is a casual place popular with tourists for great pizza. Its sprawling interior seems to stoke conviviality, as does its leafy garden out back (daily 12:00-14:30 & 19:00-23:30; from Campo San Barnaba, a long walk down Calle Lunga San Barnaba to #2671; tel. 041-523-7466).

$$$ Enoteca e Trattoria la Bitta is dark and woody, with a soft-jazz bistro feel, tight seating, and a small back patio. They serve beautifully presented, traditional Venetian food with—proudly—no fish. Their helpful wait staff and small, handwritten daily menu are focused on local ingredients (including rabbit) and a "slow food" ethic. As it has an avid following, they do two dinner seatings (19:00 and 21:00) and require reservations (dinner only, closed Sun, cash only, just off Campo San Barnaba on Calle Lunga San Barnaba, Dorsoduro 2753a, tel. 041-523-0531, Debora and Marcellino).

On Campo Santa Margarita

For a fresh, youthful, and neighborhood vibe away from the tourist crowds and cutesy Venice, hike out to Campo Santa Margarita, where you'll find a multigenerational slice-of-life scene by day and a trendy college-bar scene after dark. The square is ringed by bakeries, pubs, pizzerias, and fruit stands offering options for everything from picnics to finer dining. If slumming, a picnic or takeout pizza on this square (with fine benches and trees) is great. The area gets a little sketchy late at night.

$$ Osteria alla Bifora is a former butcher shop, serving creative plates of mixed cold cuts in their candlelit woody interior and at tables on the square. For rustic *cicchetti* plates ranging from sardines, anchovies, and cod to platters of fine salamis and cheeses, this is a good choice (daily, #2930, tel. 041-523-6119, Franco and Mirella).

$$$ Osteria Do Torri is a family affair delightfully situated with tables overlooking the square. Loretta and Paolo offer classic Venetian dishes (daily, #3408, tel. 041-522-0686).

$$ Pier Dickens Ristorante-Pizzeria, next door, also has good tables on the square and serves a selection of pizzas as well as three-course fixed-price meals (daily, #3410, tel. 041-241-1979).

Various **hole-in-the-wall** *cicchetti* **bars** (on the square and just off it) serve drinks and *cicchetti* plates to local eaters with a contagious love of life. For the best gelato on the square, find **Gelateria Il Doge.**

CANNAREGIO

Diners wanting to get off the beaten path can head to Cannaregio, located along the fish's "back," just northeast of the train station. I've listed restaurants both near the Jewish Ghetto and near a main thoroughfare (see the map on page 252; these zones are about a 10-minute walk apart).

Near the Jewish Ghetto

This sleepy neighborhood—more residential than touristic—features a grid layout with straight and spacious canalside walks (part of an expansion from the 1400s). Although it lacks the higgledy-piggledy feel of the older part of town, it's worth the long walk for a look. Instead of coming here just for a meal, I'd make time to explore and then grab a bite while in the neighborhood. Cannaregio is most peaceful at sunset.

$$$ Osteria L'Orto dei Mori is a chic place serving nicely presented, creative Venetian cuisine. You can eat in the elegant, modern interior or on a great neighborhood square with 10 tables surrounded by a classic scene of wellhead, bridges, and canal (smart to reserve for dinner, Wed-Mon 12:30-15:30 & 19:00-24:00, closed Tue, on Campo dei Mori, facing a bridge on Fondamenta dei Mori, Cannaregio 3386; tel. 041-524-3677, www.osteriaortodeimori. com).

$$ Osteria Ai 40 Ladroni ("The 40 Thieves") is a characteristic, unpretentious old standby with a few tables on the canal, a rustic interior, and a convivial garden out back. The action is near the bar (they're proud of their mixed seafood *antipasti,* Tue-Sun 12:00-14:30 & 19:00-22:15, closed Mon, on Fondamenta de la Sensa near the corner of Calle del Capitello, Cannaregio 3253, tel. 041-715-736).

$$ Osteria Enoteca Timon, while nothing earthshaking, has a relaxing canalside setting with a hipster vibe, nice wines, and *cicchetti* (a block past the Jewish Ghetto on Fondamenta Ormesini near the corner of Calle de la Malvasia, Cannaregio 2754, tel. 041-524-6066).

$$ Trattoria Al Mariner, just one bridge east of Osteria Timon, is another fun eatery, with a rustic interior and romantic canalside tables serving delightful local dishes (Mon-Sat 7:00-24:00, closed Sun, Cannaregio 2679, tel. 041-720-036).

$$ Gam Gam Kosher is your best bet for all-kosher Venetian dishes with canalside seating near the Ghetto. While the interior seating is forgettable, the canalside tables will make the meal memorable (great vegetarian options; Sun-Thu 12:00-22:00, Fri 12:00-

Romantic Canalside Settings

If you want a meal with a canal view, it generally comes with lower quality and/or a higher price. But if you're determined to take home a canalside memory, these places can be great.

Recommended Canalside Eateries

The following spots are all described in detail elsewhere in this chapter.

Near the Rialto Bridge: The five places I call the "Bancogiro Stretch" offer wonderful canalside dining and a great place to enjoy a drink and/or a snack between meals or after dinner.

Near the Accademia: For decent pizzas overlooking the canal with no cover or service charge, head to **Bar Foscarini**, next to the Accademia Bridge.

Overlooking the Giudecca Canal: Particularly nice just before sunset, Terrazza dei Nobili is located in Zattere—on the Venice

side of the wide Giudecca Canal (for a cheaper perch on the same canal, consider Pizzeria Oke). I Figli delle Stelle Ristorante, on the island of Giudecca, is a classy restaurant offering romantic canalside seating and a wonderful experience. Ristorante Lineadombra, with a terrace on the Giudecca Canal, serves gourmet dishes to a dressy crowd.

In Cannaregio, near the Jewish Ghetto: Find memorable canalside dining at Gam Gam Kosher. And nearby, just north of the ghetto, a number of rustic eateries with rickety tables are set up along a peaceful canal, including Osteria Enoteca Timon and Trattoria Al Mariner.

two hours before Shabbat, Sat one hour after Shabbat-23:00, just underneath the Sotoportego del Gheto Vechio at #1122, tel. 366-250-4505).

Along the Main Drag

Closer to the Grand Canal than the options listed above, the following places are a few steps from the main drag that connects the

Other Places with a Canal View

Here are some other canalside dining options.

Rialto Bridge Tourist Traps: Venetians are embarrassed by the lousy food and aggressive "service" at the string of joints dominating the best romantic, Grand Canal-fringing real estate in town. Still, if you want to linger over dinner with a view of the most famous bridge and the songs of gondoliers oaring by (and don't mind eating with other tourists), this can be enjoyable. Don't trust the waiter's recommendations for special meals. The budget ideal would be to get a simple pizza or pasta and a drink for €15, and savor the ambience without getting ripped off. But few restaurants will allow you to get off that easy. To avoid a dispute over the bill, ask if there's a minimum charge before you sit down (most places have one).

Ponte dei Greci, East of St. Mark's Square: Two delightful canals meet at the Ponte dei Greci. Restaurants have gobbled up every inch of canalside real estate to feed tourists forgettable food—and great memories. Several touristy restaurants and pizzerias compete for business along Canal San Provolo. For nicer fare, **Ristorante alla Conchiglia** and **Trattoria da Giorgio ai Greci** (on Fondamenta San Lorenzo) are pricier, but have cheaper fixed-price menu options. They're lit up like Christmas trees after dark, and with gondolas gliding by, you can't argue with the setting (see the map on page 242 for locations).

Away from the Center

These recommended view eateries are good options if touring the lagoon.

On Fondamente Nove with a View of the Open Lagoon: Eat well while overlooking the north lagoon at **Ristorante Algiubagiò;** see "Splurging on a Water (or Otherwise Great) View," later.

On Burano: The setting is sublime at **Trattoria al Gatto Nero da Ruggero,** which sits on a tranquil canal under a tilting bell tower in the pastel townscape of Burano. If you're touring the lagoon and want to enjoy Burano without the crowds, go late and consider a dinner here (see page 211).

train station to the Rialto/San Marco area. All are near the San Marcuola vaporetto stop.

$$ Pizzeria Vesuvio, a neighborhood favorite, has classy indoor seating and pleasant tables outside (daily 11:00-23:00 except closed Wed Oct-April, on Rio Terà Farsetti, Cannaregio 1837, tel. 041-795-688).

$$ Enoteca Cicchetteria Do Colonne is a local dive with a loyal following and a good spread of *cicchetti* and sandwiches (no hot food). It's handy for a drink and a snack. While the food is mediocre, the scene—both at the bar and at the tables outside—feels real and is fun (daily 10:00-21:30, on Rio Terà del Cristo, Cannaregio 1814, tel. 041-524-0453).

SPLURGING ON A WATER (OR OTHERWISE GREAT) VIEW

Overlooking the Giudecca Canal: Peacefully situated on the Giudecca Canal, **$$$$ Ristorante Lineadombra,** immediately behind La Salute Church, has commanding lagoon views from their big floating terrace and a spacious, modern, and dressy interior. This is a gourmet treat, with gorgeously presented dishes that are local and modern at the same time. Each dish is a memory, and even though plates are pricey, you are welcome to share. The appetizers especially are big and are happily served on two smaller plates. Reserve ahead and choose seating inside or on their terrace. Service is friendly yet professional (daily 12:00-15:00 & 19:00-22:00, closed Tue off-season, a short walk behind La Salute Church, directly across the island from the Salute vaporetto stop, Dorsoduro 19, tel. 041-241-1881, www.ristorantelineadombra.com).

On Fondamente Nove, with a Lagoon View: Handy to the islands of Murano and Burano, **$$$$ Ristorante Algiubagiò** is a good place to eat as you look over the northern lagoon. The name joins the names of the four owners—Alberto, Giulio, Barbara, and Giovanna—who strive to impress visitors with quality, creative Venetian cuisine made with the best ingredients. Reserve a waterside table or sit in their classy cantina dining room (daily 12:00-15:00 & 19:00-22:30, between the two sets of vaporetto docks on Fondamente Nove, Cannaregio 5039—see map on page 201, tel. 041-523-6084, www.algiubagio.net).

On Giudecca Island: Sit canalside with a view of St. Mark's Square at **$$$ I Figli delle Stelle Ristorante,** which offers a delightful dining experience and an excuse to ride the boat from St. Mark's Square to the island of Giudecca. While they have inside seating, the reason to venture here is to enjoy fine views of Venice across the broad Giudecca Canal and all the water traffic. Reserve ahead to specify "first line" seating along the water, "second line" seating a few steps away, or a table inside (daily 12:30-14:30 & 19:00-23:00, 50 yards from Zitelle vaporetto dock—from San Marco, ride line #4.2, #4.1, or #2, Giudecca 70/71, tel. 041-523-0004).

A bit farther west on Giudecca Island (around the Palanca vaporetto dock), several **$$$** eateries offer similar canal views, even if St. Mark's Square isn't in the panorama. These are often less touristy (take vaporetto line #2 from Zattere to Palanca). Listen to the hum of the boats with a glass of wine.

On St. Mark's Square: For fancy dining on Venice's famous square, **$$$$ Gran Caffè Quadri** (a.k.a. Bistro ABC Quadri) is the place to go. Upstairs is their Michelin star restaurant, but this bistro, also dressy and a bit pretentious, shares the same kitchen, with a more traditional and accessible menu, and prices that won't ruin your appetite. While its 15 tables are all inside, the orchestra is just out the window (daily 12:00-15:00 & 19:00-22:30, reservations smart, San Marco 121, tel. 041-522-2105, www.alajmo.it/grancaffe-quadri).

PICNICS AND SWEETS
Picnicking

You're legally forbidden from picnicking anywhere on or near St. Mark's Square except for Giardinetti Reali, the waterfront park near the San Marco vaporetto docks. Though it's legal to eat outdoors elsewhere around town, you may be besieged by pigeons who are, in turn, besieged by aggressive seagulls.

Venice has one main produce market and several convenient supermarkets:

Outdoor Market near the Rialto Bridge: Assemble a fun picnic at the **fruit and vegetable market** that sprawls for a few blocks to the north of the Rialto Bridge (best Mon-Sat 8:00-13:00, liveliest in the morning, closed Sun). The adjacent **fish market** is wonderfully slimy (closed Sun-Mon). Side lanes in this area are speckled with fine hole-in-the-wall munchie bars, bakeries, and cheese shops. The Rialto Mercato vaporetto stop is convenient to both.

Produce Stands: Many larger squares have a produce stand. To find the one nearest St. Mark's Square, face St. Mark's Basilica, then walk along its left side, heading east down Calle de la Canonica. Cross the bridge and turn left at Campo Santi Filippo e Giacomo. There are also stands on Campo Santa Maria Formosa and Campo Santa Margarita.

Supermarket near St. Mark's Square: A handy **Co-op** supermarket is between St. Mark's and Campo Santa Maria Formosa, on the corner of Salizada San Lio and Calle del Mondo Novo at Castello 5817. It has a deli counter and a great selection of picnic supplies, including packaged salads and fresh sandwiches (daily 8:30-22:00).

Other Supermarkets: The largest supermarket in town is the **Co-op** at Piazzale Roma, next to the vaporetto stop at Santa Croce 504. It's an easy walk from the train station, as is a smaller **Co-op** on Campo San Felice (along the Strada Nova between the train station and Rialto area, Cannaregio 3660). A **Conad** supermarket is convenient for those staying in Dorsoduro: It's at #1492, as far west as possible on the Zattere embankment, by the San Basilio vaporetto stop and the cruise-ship docks. And just beyond the Rialto vaporetto stop is another handy **Co-op** (facing the Grand Canal on Riva del Carbon). All are open long hours daily. They cater to huge Airbnb demand with ready-to-eat packaged meals.

Good Gelato and Chocolate Spots

Venice isn't known for its quality gelato but you'll still find good *gelaterie* in every neighborhood, typically offering one-scoop cones for about €2 (€1 per extra scoop). The words *artigianale* or *produzione propria* indicate that a shop makes its own gelato, although sometimes from powder or paste bases (avoid brightly colored gelato or places that have overflowing tubs). The following places are all open long hours daily.

St. Mark's Side of the Rialto Bridge: A gourmet gelato shop, **Gelatoteca Suso,** serves delectable flavors in bowls you can eat (next to Campo San Bartolomeo on Calle de la Bissa, San Marco 5453a).

St. Mark's Square: Both **Gran Caffè Lavena** at #134 and **Todaro** (on the corner of the Piazzetta at #5, near the water just under the crocodile-topped column) are cafés that have gelato counters in summer. They won't win any awards, but they are convenient if you want something to lick while enjoying the San Marco orchestras.

On Campo Santa Margarita and Campiello San Tomà: Along with all the regular flavors, **Gelateria Il Doge,** with two locations, has Sicilian-style *granita*—slushy ice flavored with fresh fruit.

Near Campo Santa Maria Formosa: On Salizada San Lio is the popular **La Boutique del Gelato** (next to Hotel Bruno, run for many years by Alessandra). And nearby is a hit with chocolate lovers: **Cioccolateria VizioVirtù** (Vice and Virtue). Across from the recommended Osteria al Portego, it's a modern lab of deliciousness with fine gelato as a bonus (closed Mon, Castello 5988).

VENICE WITH CHILDREN

Some of the best fun I've had with my kids has been in Venice. The city doesn't need an amusement park...it is one big fantasy world. It's safe, friendly, and like nothing else your kids have ever seen. Though there's lots of pavement and few parks or playgrounds, just being there—and free to wander—can be delightful.

However, while Venice is great for older children and teens, it presents challenges if you're traveling with toddlers or infants. You'll need to keep small children safely in hand, as passageways are narrow and crowded, and there are rarely any fences or walls between the sidewalk and the water. (Campo Santa Maria Formosa is a rare place with railings, because a preschool uses it as their playground.)

With hundreds of stepped bridges, Venice is a frustrating obstacle course for strollers. But considering the dangers, bringing a lightweight stroller is still a good tactic for navigating Venice with a wily preschooler. Parents of infants might find a baby carrier less hassle.

Trip Tips

PLAN AHEAD
Involve your kids in trip planning. Have them read about the places that you may include in your itinerary (even the hotels you're considering), and let them help with your decisions.

Where to Stay
- If your kids love playing in the sand, consider staying in a hotel or apartment near the Lido. Easy beach access offers a convenient daily activity.
- Apartments can save money over hotel rooms, and having

a kitchen can eliminate the stress of restaurant dining with small children. See "Sleeping" in the Practicalities chapter for more on short-term rentals.

What to Bring

- If traveling with infants, bring a light stroller and/or a baby carrier.
- Pack your own drawing supplies and books, as these items are pricey in Italy.
- For a touch of home at the hotel, bring some favorite movies.
- Give your kid a cheap camera. Venice turns anyone into a photographer.

EATING (AND DRINKING)

Venetian fare can be different from the "Italian food" you have at home. While there's plenty of pasta, it's often prepared with seafood rather than tomatoes or meat. Picky eaters will want to avoid local seafood dishes such as eel *(anguilla)* and cuttlefish *(seppia)*. Here are more tips to keep your kids content and well-fed.

- For lunch or a snack, it's fun to buy pizza by the slice, fold it in half, and eat it as you stroll...or find a perch on a nearby square. Favorite pizza choices for kids include *margherita* (tomato sauce, cheese, and basil) and spicy *diavola* or *salame piccante,* which are the closest things on the menu to pepperoni (if you ask for *peperoni,* you'll get bell peppers).
- For ready-made sandwiches and other portable food, drop by an *alimentari* (deli) or a supermarket. Be aware that you can't picnic on St. Mark's Square (but you can at Giardinetti Reali, the nearby waterfront park; see the sidebar on page 75).
- Choose easy eateries. For good old American food, check out one of the American hamburger joints between the Rialto Bridge and St. Mark's Square.
- Having food on hand can avoid meltdowns. Stock your day bag with snacks, and plan to buy plenty of gelato.
- Eat dinner early (19:00 at restaurants), and skip the romantic places. If you eat early, you'll find that children are more welcome in nicer restaurants. Eating *al fresco* is great with kids. Try places on squares where kids can run free while you dine. You can nearly always order some kind of plain noodles.
- While the official drinking age in Italy is 18, teens 16 and over are sometimes offered wine or beer in restaurants, especially when accompanied by a parent. It's best to decide on a family policy beforehand.

CHILDREN

SIGHTSEEING

The key to a successful Venetian family vacation is to
slow down. Tackle one or two
key sights each day, mix in a
healthy dose of pure fun in a
square or on a boat, and take
extended breaks when needed.
A vaporetto ride is a great way
to start your visit.

Planning Your Time

- Incorporate your child's interests into each day's plans. Let
  your kids make some decisions: choosing lunch spots or decid-
  ing when to take a gondola ride. Let them lead you through
  the maze of Venice's back streets. Get lost together.
- Older kids and teens can help plan the details of a museum
  visit, such as what to see, how to get there, and ticketing details.
- Follow this book's crowd-beating tips to a T to avoid long
  waits in line.
- While Venice is short on parks, its many small squares have
  served as playgrounds for local children for centuries. Take
  breaks and let your kids run around while you take a seat at a
  café or bench.

Successful Sightseeing

- Italy's national museums generally offer free admission to children under age 18—always ask before buying tickets for your
  kids.
- Look for family and child discounts. If buying the Doge's Pal-
  ace/Correr Museum combo-ticket or a Museum Pass, ask for
  the family discount. A family ticket is also available for the
  Chorus Pass, which covers church visits. The **Rolling Venice**
  youth discount pass gives discounts on many sights and transportation for young travelers (for details, see page 29).
- If your children are old enough, they can be the tour guides
  and read this book's self-guided tours. (Standard tip for good
  guides: a two-scoop gelato.)
- Seek out museums with kid appeal, such as the Peggy Guggenheim Collection—though be aware that art may feature
  nudes or erotic themes.
- If you're visiting art museums with younger children, hit the
  gift shop first so you can buy postcards; then hold a scavenger
  hunt to find the pictured artwork. When boredom sets in, try
  "I spy" games or have them count how many babies or dogs

they can spot in all the paintings in the room. Museum audioguides are great for older children.

Making or Finding Quality Souvenirs

- Buy your kids a trip journal, and encourage them to write down their observations, thoughts, and favorite memories. This journal could end up being their favorite souvenir.
- For a group project, keep a family journal. Pack a small diary and a glue stick. While relaxing over a gelato, take turns writing or drawing about the day's events and include mementos such as ticket stubs from museums and postcards.
- Teens might love shopping (or even window-shopping). See the Shopping in Venice chapter for fun areas.

MONEY AND SAFETY

Before your trip gets underway, talk to your kids about safety and money.

- Give your child a money belt and an expanded allowance; you are on vacation, after all. Let your children budget their funds and compare and contrast the dollar and euro. Allowing your children the freedom to buy whatever they want will teach them responsibility, and it will be fun for them.
- It's good to have a "what if" procedure in place in case something goes wrong, such as getting separated in a crowd. Give your kids a business card from your hotel, along with your contact information and some euros, just in case. If they don't have a mobile phone, let them know to ask to use the phone at a hotel if they are lost.
- If you allow kids to explore a museum or neighborhood on their own, be sure to establish a clear meeting time and place.

STAYING CONNECTED

- If your kids have mobile phones, show them how to make calls in Italy (see "Staying Connected" in the Practicalities chapter).
- Most parents find it worth the peace of mind to buy supplemental messaging and data plans for the whole family. Adults can stay connected to teenagers while allowing them maximum independence, and teens can keep in touch with friends both old and new via apps such as WhatsApp, Snapchat, Google Talk, FaceTime, or Skype.
- Readily available Wi-Fi (at hotels and some cafés) makes bringing a mobile device worthwhile.

CHILDREN

Top Sights and Activities

KID-CENTRIC ATTRACTIONS

Boat Rides

Ride lots of boats (vaporetto, gondola, *traghetto,* or speedboat tours of the lagoon). If you can, try to sit in the front seat of a vaporetto for my Grand Canal Cruise. See how many kinds of service boats you can spot while on the canal (UPS, police, fire, garbage, and so on). Venice feels safe; if you have responsible teenagers, you could turn them loose with your hotel card, some euros for lunch, and a vaporetto pass (consider a Rolling Venice pass—see page 29). Note that vaporetti are free for kids under age 6, but everyone else pays full fare, and there is no discount-pass option for those between 6 and 13.

St. Mark's Square

This grand square is surrounded by splashy historic buildings and sights: St. Mark's Basilica, the Doge's Palace, the Campanile bell tower, and the Correr Museum. The square is filled with music, romantics, pigeons, and tourists by day. By night, the historical buildings are lit up, small orchestras put on free concerts, and good gelato is only a walk away. Anyone of any age will enjoy the magic of St. Mark's Square day or night.

The **pigeons** on the square offer a new breed of bird-watching. (Though feeding them is against the law, most tourists don't realize that—and enjoy trying to lure as many birds to drape over their kids as possible.) If you yell, the birds will just ignore you, but tossing a sweater into the air will cause a flocking flurry in a hurry.

Elevator Ride

Ride the elevator to the top of the Campanile bell tower to enjoy the grand view, and be there as the huge bells whip into ear-shattering action at the top of each hour. Some prefer the better view from the bell tower on the island of San Giorgio Maggiore. For details, see the 🔲 St. Mark's Square Tour and the San Giorgio Maggiore Tour chapters.

Glassblowing Demonstration

For a quick and entertaining demo of Venice's favorite craft, stop by the **Vetri d'Arte** showroom in Palazzo Rota (for details, see the Shopping in Venice chapter).

Venetian Adventures

To help your kids realize the magic of Venice, stoke their imagination with some of these recommended books, films, and video clips.

Books

Daughter of Venice (Donna Jo Napoli). A young girl disguises herself as a beggar boy to avoid entering a convent in 16th-century Venice.

The Dragon's Pearl (Devin Jordan). Fictional early adventures of 16-year-old Venetian Marco Polo.

Kids Go Europe: **Treasure Hunt Venice** (Ellen and Marvin Mouchawar). This tiny, spiral-bound book takes kids on a scavenger hunt through Venice.

Stones in Water and its sequel, **Fire in the Hills** (Donna Jo Napoli). Fictional account of a young Venetian boy sent to a Nazi labor camp, and his struggles to return to his beloved Venice.

Stravaganza: **City of Masks** (Mary Hoffman). First in the time-traveling series set in 16th-century "Talia," an alternate-universe Italy.

This Is Venice (Miroslav Slasek). This classic 1960s picture book captures Venice's charm with witty illustrations.

Venice: A 3D Keepsake Cityscape (Sarah McMenamy). Illustrated foldouts of Venice's top sights, with brief descriptions of their significance.

Venice for Kids (Elisabetta Pasqualin). Great guidebook for tweens and up, available at many museum bookshops.

VivaVenice: **A Guide to Exploring**, **Learning**, **and Having Fun** (Paola Zoffoli). Full of interesting facts, and sold at many bookstores in the city.

Films and Clips

Crash Course World History: Venice and the Ottoman Empire (YouTube). Commercial and cultural history of Venice with young-adult author and YouTuber John Green.

The Last Crusade (1989). Third Indiana Jones installment featuring scenes in the Venetian catacombs and a boat chase through the city's canals.

The Thief Lord (2006). Orphaned brothers run away to Venice, meet a band of child thieves, and discover the hidden secrets of Venice.

Rialto Bridge and Fish Market

The Rialto fish market is as fishy as they get (on the canal two blocks west of Rialto Bridge). Get there early in the day to watch people unload the boats at the market. You can leave by *traghetto* and cross the Grand Canal (*traghetto* dock at market). For more on the market, see the ◫ Rialto to Frari Church Walk chapter.

MUSEUMS AND EXHIBITS

Be choosy when taking kids to museums. The venerable and fascinating (to adults) Accademia will probably bore children. But the following museums may be enjoyable to kids.

Doge's Palace

The building is more impressive than the art inside. If your children aren't wowed by the architecture, they may still enjoy the tour of the dark, dank prison. The dungeon held the notorious lover Giacomo Casanova, sentenced to prison for being a magician. In his memoirs, he describes how he used an iron rod and the help of a fellow prisoner to make his escape. Young swashbucklers may like the swords and crossbows in the Armory. ◫ See the Doge's Palace Tour chapter.

Scuola San Rocco

This museum houses some of the best paintings by Tintoretto, which cover not only the walls, but also the ceilings. Your kids may get a kick out of using the provided mirrors to look at the paintings on the ceiling. ◫ See the Scuola San Rocco Tour chapter.

Peggy Guggenheim Collection

This museum shows major works from the first half of the 20th century, including pieces by Picasso, Pollock, Chagall, Magritte, and Dalí. Your children may not understand Surrealism, Futurism, or Abstract Expressionism, but there's enough variety here that they'll find something "cool." For younger kids, the outdoor sculpture garden is a rare green space in Venice where they can burn off some energy. Free workshops every Sunday from 15:00 to 16:30 give kids ages 4-10 a chance to experiment with techniques; though usually in Italian, the activity is sometimes offered in English. ◫ See the Peggy Guggenheim Collection Tour chapter.

San Giorgio Maggiore

Located on an island a short boat ride away, this is a great church to visit after battling the hordes of St. Mark's Square. Enjoy a lagoon ride to the island, then take an elevator to the top of the bell tower. ◫ See the San Giorgio Maggiore Tour chapter.

OUTDOOR ACTIVITIES AND OTHER EXPERIENCES

Parks

Venice doesn't have a lot of green spaces or playgrounds, but there are a few parks for kids.

Giardino Papadopoli: This tiny park, next to Venice's bus station, has one of the city's rare playgrounds. The nearest vaporetto stop is Piazzale Roma. Coming from the train station, take the Calatrava Bridge across the Grand Canal, turn left, and take the next bridge over a side canal to the park.

Giardini Pubblici (Public Gardens): An ideal spot for children who want an American park experience, the Public Gardens have swings, slides, a play area, and big trees (unusual in Venice). It's about a 20-minute walk along the water from St. Mark's Square, past the Arsenale, going toward the tail of the fish (vaporetto: Giardini).

Parco Delle Rimembranze (Memorial Park): Farther out on the tail, in the Sant'Elena neighborhood, this park contains a soccer field, along with basketball and tennis courts. It's one of the largest open spaces in Venice (vaporetto: S. Elena).

Lido Beach

The Lido has a fun, free, clean, sandy beach that's good for swimming, with an affordable self-service café, a bar, rentable umbrellas, and a well-priced beach-gear shop. Even the ride across the lagoon is enjoyable (vaporetto: Lido S.M.E., walk 10 minutes on Gran Viale S. Maria Elisabetta to beach entry).

Soccer

Consider attending a Venezia FC soccer game at the Pier Luigi Penzo stadium, located in the Sant'Elena neighborhood. Matches take place on Sundays (see www.veneziafc.it for schedule and ticket info). Buy a scarf with the team colors—black, orange, and green—and join the fun.

Signor Blum

This shop, on Campo San Barnaba—about a 10-minute walk northwest of the Accademia—has an array of colorfully painted wooden decorations. It's a good place to shop for kid-friendly souvenirs (for details, see the Shopping in Venice chapter).

CHILDREN

SHOPPING IN VENICE

The merchants of Venice are abundant, making this a fun city for window-shoppers. Long a city of aristocrats, luxury goods, and trade, Venice was built to entice. Around the train station and the Rialto Bridge, the city feels like one big open-air shopping mall. Trinket stands tuck themselves between internationally famous designer stores and hole-in-the-wall artisan workshops.

Carnevale masks, lace, glass, antique paper products, designer clothing, one-of-a-kind jewelry, custom-made shoes, fancy accessories, hand-painted or printed velvet and silk tapestries, and paintings are all popular with tourists visiting Venice. While no one claims Venice is great for bargains, it has a shopping charm that makes paying too much strangely enjoyable. Anything not made locally is brought in by boat—and therefore generally more expensive than elsewhere in Italy. The shops near St. Mark's Square charge the most.

In touristy areas, shops are typically open from 9:00 to 19:30 (sometimes with a break at midday), and some stores are open on Sunday. If you're buying at a market, bargain—it's accepted and almost expected. In shops, you may save by offering to pay cash.

For information on VAT refunds and customs regulations, see page 419.

For a private tour focusing on shopping and crafts, contact Walks Inside Venice, which offers several different itineraries (www.walksinsidevenice.com).

SHOPPING NEIGHBORHOODS

St. Mark's Square and Nearby: The streets closest to St. Mark's Square, and those along the Mercerie (the route between St. Mark's and the Rialto Bridge, also called "Marzaria"), are the most-trafficked, the highest-rent, and the highest-priced in town. This is where you'll see all of the big international names.

The neighborhood to the west of St. Mark's, going toward the Accademia Bridge, is more elegant and exclusive, with high-fashion shops along Calle Vallaresso (southwest of St. Mark's). While you'll see many tourists in these shops, you'll also encounter locals. Italians shop for quality; they tend to spend less on entertainment and more on looking good. With their limited budgets, they'd rather buy three top-quality shirts than ten mediocre ones. They don't impulse buy: Italian shoppers are on a strategic mission. For example, "I need this belt to match this outfit." Watch them in action and appreciate the difference.

As you get closer to the Accademia Bridge (around Campo San Stefano and Salizzada San Samuele), you'll find more characteristic and affordable stores, such as textile shops, art boutiques, and galleries.

Dorsoduro: Across the Accademia Bridge, the area immediately around the Accademia and Peggy Guggenheim Collection is touristy and can feel tacky, but does have some worthwhile places selling glass and/or jewelry with an artistic bent. In the opposite direction, a 10-minute walk past the Accademia, is the somewhat lower-rent area around Campo San Barnaba that attracts more innovative, less established artisans; this is a great place to window-shop.

Rialto Bridge and Nearby: Right by the bridge, Venice's historic market area is a cancan of shopping opportunities. Many of the products here are edible, but there are lots of hole-in-the-wall jewelry and trinket stores on the bridge, under the arcades to the north, and on the Ruga (the street running from the Rialto toward Campo San Polo and the Frari Church).

The route from the east side of the **Rialto Bridge to the train station** is where you're most likely to find two-euro stores, discount joints with cheap plastic goods, and—at holiday times—shops selling Easter or Christmas decorations. You'll see peddlers who lay out knockoff handbags on sheets that can be gathered up quickly if the police happen by. Near the Rialto end of this stretch is the luxury shopping mall T Fondaco dei Tedeschi.

WHAT TO BUY

Popular souvenirs and gifts include Murano glass, Burano lace, Carnevale masks, prints of Venetian scenes, traditional stationery (pens and marbled paper products of all kinds), calendars with Venetian scenes (and sexy gondoliers), and plenty of goofy knickknacks (Titian mouse pads, gondolier T-shirts, and little plastic gondola condom holders).

But beyond the typical souvenirs, Venice has a wealth of unique and locally made items, such as artisan jewelry, handcrafted fabrics, and made-to-order shoes. Although shops selling artisan goods can be quite expensive, they are atmospheric, engaging places to window-shop and daydream. If you're curious about the product, dip into a shop and ask a few questions. The vendor never knows when browsing might turn to buying...and neither do you.

Venetian Glass

Popular Venetian glass is available in many forms: vases, tea sets, decanters, glasses, jewelry, lamps, mod sculptures, and on and on.

Shops will ship it home for you, but you're likely to pay as much or more for the shipping as you are for the item(s), and you may have to pay duty on larger purchases. Make sure the shop insures their merchandise *(assicurazione),* or you're out of luck if it breaks.

Some visitors feel that because they're in Venice, they ought to grab the opportunity to buy glass. Remember that you can buy fine glass back home, too (Venice stopped forbidding its glassblowers from leaving the republic a few centuries ago)—and under less time pressure.

It's important to be an educated shopper if you are interested in buying glass. You'll want to avoid the cheap glass you'll see—most of it is imported from China or Mexico. Genuine, high-end Venetian glass comes with the signature of the artist etched directly into the glass, along with a number if it's a limited edition piece (for example, 14/30—number 14 of a total of 30 pieces made).

If you're serious about glass, visit the island of **Murano,** its glass museum, and its many shops—you'll find greater variety on the island (see Venice's Lagoon Tour chapter).

To learn more about glass art, consider a free glassblowing demo at the **Vetri d'Arte** showroom in Palazzo Rota. Tour groups come and go all day long for the entertaining little demonstration followed by a sales pitch, but individuals are welcome to sit in on the show. From Gran Caffè Quadri on St. Mark's Square, Sottoportico dei Dai leads over a bridge and, 30 yards later, directly into a lobby (it's unsigned, look for the ATM) where stairs lead up to the showroom (RS%—20 percent discount on glass with this book, daily 8:30-17:00, San Marco 834, tel. 041-241-2664).

Shopping in Venice

Masks
1 Ca' del Sol
2 Mask Maker
3 Papier Mâché
4 Tragicomica
5 Ca' Macana

Glass & Jewelry
6 Vetri d'Arte
7 Attombri
8 Marina e Susanna Sent (3)
9 Caron
10 Rialto 79

Lace & Textiles
11 Il Merletto
12 Annelie
13 Venetia Studium
14 Bevilacqua (2)

Stationery
15 Il Pavone (2)
16 Il Prato
17 Il Papiro
18 Gianni Basso Stampatore

Shoes
19 Daniela Ghezzo
20 Dittura

Books
21 Libreria Studium
22 Acqua Alta
23 Marco Polo

SHOPPING

SHOPPING

Gondola Workshops
- ㉔ Paolo Brandolisio
- ㉕ Le Fórcole di Saverio Pastor

Other
- ㉖ T Fondaco dei Tedeschi
- ㉗ Guadagni Design & Livio de Marchi
- ㉘ Signor Blum
- ㉙ Madera
- ㉚ Canestrelli

Mask Making

In the 1700s, when Venice was Europe's party town, masks were popular—sometimes even mandatory—to preserve the anonymity of visiting nobles doing things forbidden back home. At Carnevale (the weeks-long Mardi Gras leading up to Lent), everyone wore masks. The most popular were based on characters from the lowbrow comedic theater called commedia dell'arte. We all know Harlequin (simple, Lone Ranger-type masks), but there were also long-nosed masks for the hypocritical plague doctor, pretty Columbina masks, and so on.

Masks are made with the simple technique of papier-mâché, formed on a clay mold from layers of paper and glue. You'll see mask shops all over town. Just behind St. Mark's Square, on a quiet canal just inland from the Church of San Zaccaria (on Fondamenta de l'Osmarin), is the fascinating mask shop **Ca' del Sol,** at #4964 (with two showrooms to either side of a little bridge, www.cadelsolmascherevenezia. com) and another mask shop at #4968. Just a bit north, a block off Campo Santa Maria Formosa (next to the Acqua Alta bookstore) is the **Papier Mâché** mask shop of Stefano Gottardo, who proudly sells both traditional and modern masks. You're welcome to watch the artisans at work (at the end of Calle Lunga Santa Maria Formosa, Castello 5174b, tel. 041-522-9995, www.papiermache.it).

Out near the Frari Church is the well-respected **Tragicomica** mask shop (200 yards past Church of San Polo on Calle dei Nomboli at #2800, tel. 041-721-102, www.tragicomica.it; for details see page 229). Another good option is **Ca' Macana,** near Campo San Barnaba, a shop that's open to anyone who wants to see how traditional Venetian masks are made (they also offer mask-painting classes—arrange in advance; Dorsoduro 3172, tel. 041-520-3229, www.camacana.com).

Jewelry

Jewelers abound in Venice. Not surprisingly, glass jewelry and beadwork are particularly popular—you'll see references to *perle di Venezia* or *perle veneziane*, colorfully speckled glass beads. In addition to buying premade pieces, at many shops you can select the beads you like to create your own masterpiece. As with other glass, it's smart to ask where it was made.

Several jewelers can be found under the arcades (behind the chintzy souvenir stands) on the west (market) side of the Rialto

Bridge, including **Attombri,** selling pieces with a classic, fili-gree-plus-beads look (Sotoportego de Rialto, San Polo 65, www. attombri.com). **Marina e Susanna Sent** sells contemporary designs in three upscale showrooms (near St. Mark's next to Campo San Moisè at San Marco 2090, near the Accademia on Campo San Vio at Dorsoduro 681, and across Rialto Bridge at Sotoportego dei Oresi San Polo 70, www.marinaesusannasent.com). **Caron** sells handmade glass jewelry, west of the Accademia along Calle de la Toleta (Dorsoduro 1195). **Rialto 79** has wonderful glass beads, all made in the Lagoon and hand-crafted into lovely (and afford-able) jewelry (at the foot of the Rialto Bridge, San Polo 79, www. rialto79.com).

Lace

Lace, made from cotton or silk thread, is another Venetian spe-cialty. Prior to the Industrial Revolution, the city was a major trad-ing point for luxury fabrics like lace, silk, and satin, and Venetian Burano lace adorned the clothing of royalty. Venice is particularly known for "needle lace," with intricate flowers, leaves, and curling stems, which was used for cuffs, gowns, and frilly collars.

Lace lovers will find the journey out to Burano worthwhile. Here you'll find many shops such as **Merletti d'Arte dalla Lidia** and the **Lace Museum** (see Venice's Lagoon Tour chapter for more details). Today, much of the lace is machine-made, but Burano residents cherish the traditional art form and are attempting to re-vive it, producing tablecloths, doilies, handkerchiefs, and clothing. Stick to reputable shops to ensure that you are buying an authentic product.

In Venice, the **Il Merletto** shop just off St. Mark's Square is convenient, and sells pieces crafted by students of the Scuola dei Merletti, the local lace-making school in Burano (exit the square near the northwest corner through Sotoportego del Cavaletto, then cross the little bridge to the right, San Marco 95, tel. 041-520-8406). Ariana has a special treat for visitors. **Annelie,** in the Dor-soduro district, is another well-respected shop (on Calle Lunga San Barnaba, Dorsoduro 2748).

Textiles

Venetia Studium carries on the Venetian tradition for hand-paint-ed and woodblock-printed fabrics. In addition to velvet cushions and runners, they specialize in hanging lamps decorated with deli-cate hand-painted silk shades (just east of Campo Santa Maria Zo-benigo, San Marco 2425, tel. 041-523-6953, www.venetiastudium. com).

Bevilacqua is a big and well-established producer of velvet cushions, tapestries, and so on. Mario and Paola have a few high-profile shops around Venice, as well as an 18th-century, hand-operated loom that they still use. For the budget-conscious, they also sell equally fine machine-made products (easiest to find at the Canonica Bridge behind St. Mark's Basilica at San Marco 337b, another location just to the right as you look at the Church of Santa Maria Zobenigo at San Marco 2520; tel. 041-528-7581, www. bevilacquatessuti.com).

Stationery

A number of shops around town sell handmade paper, colorfully bound books, custom stamps and seals, and fine prints. **Il Pavone** is known for its marbleized paper and custom stamps (locations at Campiello dei Meloni, San Polo 1478, near Campo San Polo, sign says *Zaga;* and at Fondamenta Venier, Dorsoduro 721, near the Guggenheim; closed Wed, www.ilpavonevenezia.com). **Il Prato** specializes in vividly bound books, trays, and other items, as well as glass (on Calle de le Ostreghe, San Marco 2456, on a side corner of Campo Santa Maria Zobenigo west of St. Mark's Square, www. ilpratovenezia.com). A couple of blocks away is a branch of the Italy-wide chain **Il Papiro** (Calle del Piovan, San Marco 2764, www. ilpapirofirenze.it). **Gianni Basso Stampatore** produces beautiful letter-pressed note cards, bookplates, and stationery (closed Sun, on Calle del Fumo 5306, in the Cannaregio district).

Handmade Shoes

Fashion-conscious travelers may find it worth the splurge to indulge in custom-made shoes from a trained Venetian cobbler. Some well-regarded options include **Daniela Ghezzo** (tucked in an adorably cluttered hole-in-the-wall on Calle dei Fuseri near St. Mark's Square, San Marco 4365, www.danielaghezzo.it). For something distinctly Venetian, check out **Dittura,** which makes and sells velvet gondolier's slippers (on the main drag between the Accademia and Guggenheim, Dorsoduro 871).

Art Galleries and Boutiques

You'll find a fascinating smattering of art boutiques in the zone north and west of Campo San Stefano (on the St. Mark's side of the Accademia Bridge). From that square, head west on Calle Botteghe, which becomes Crosera before it runs into the skinny square called Salizzada San Samuele. Fronting this square are a half-dozen low-profile galleries worth a browse. At the bottom of the square, peek into the shop of **Livio de Marchi** and marvel at his meticulously detailed wood replicas of everything from handbags and ballet shoes to gloves and teddy bears (at #3157a, www. liviodemarchi.com).

Other Goods

Department Store: The designer shopping mall **T Fondaco dei Tedeschi** sells international brands that have nothing to do with

Venice at premium prices (Calle del Fontego dei Tedeschi, near the Rialto Bridge).

Housewares: Guadagni Design sells sleek and unique housewares, halfway down Salizzada San Samuele (San Marco 3336, www.guadagnidesign.it).

Toys: Fun for kids and grown-ups, **Signor Blum** makes and sells delightfully colorful wood-carved letters, symbols, mobiles, and scenes of Venice. It's located at the bottom corner of Campo San Barnaba, overlooking the canal (at #2840, www.signorblum. com).

Accessories: Located on Campo San Barnaba, next to the Grom *gelateria,* **Madera** is an attractive boutique with high-quality jewelry and handbags (closed Sun-Mon, Dorsoduro 2762, www. maderavenezia.it). They've also got a chic home and design showroom just a few short blocks down Calle Lunga San Barnaba.

Mirrors: At **Canestrelli,** soft-spoken Stefano Coluccio makes unique convex mirrors in circular frames, like the ones in old paintings. It's along Calle de la Toleta, between the Accademia Bridge and Campo San Barnaba (Dorsoduro 1173, www.venicemirrors. com).

NIGHTLIFE IN VENICE

You must experience Venice after dark. The city is quiet at night, as many tour groups (not mine) stay in the cheaper hotels of Mestre on the mainland, and the masses of day-trippers return to their beach resorts and cruise ships.

Do what you must to reserve energy for the evening: Take a nap, or skip a few sights during the day. When the sun goes down, a cool breeze blows in from the lagoon, the lanterns come on, the peeling plaster glows in the moonlight, and Venice resumes its position as Europe's most romantic city.

Though Venice comes alive after dark, it does not party into the wee hours. By 22:00, restaurants are winding down; by 23:00, many bars are closing; and by midnight, the city is shut tight. Evenings are made for wandering—even Venice's dark and distant back lanes are considered safe after nightfall. Enjoy the orchestras on St. Mark's Square. Experience Vivaldi's *Four Seasons* in a candlelit 17th-century church. Pop into small bars for an appetizer and a drink. Lick gelato. As during the day, it's the city itself that is the star. But Venice under a cloak of darkness has an extra dose of magic and mystery—the ambience that has attracted visitors since the days of Casanova.

GONDOLA RIDES

Riding a gondola is simple, expensive, and one of the great experiences in Europe. Gondoliers hanging out all over town are eager to have you hop in for a ride. While this is a rip-off for some, it's a traditional must for romantics.

The price for a gondola starts at €80 for a 35-minute ride during the day. You can divide the cost—and the romance—among up to six people per boat, but only two get the love seat. Prices jump to €100 after 19:00—when it's most romantic and relaxing. Adding a singer and an accordionist will cost an additional €120. If you value budget over romance, you can save money by recruiting fellow travelers to split a gondola. Prices are standard and listed on the gondoliers' association website (go to www.gondolavenezia.it, click on "Using the Gondola," and look under "charterage").

Dozens of gondola stations *(servizio gondole)* are set up along canals all over town. Because your gondolier might offer narration or conversation during your ride, talk with several and choose one you like. You're welcome to review the map and discuss the route. Doing so is also a good way to see if you enjoy the gondolier's personality and language skills. Establish the price, route, and duration of the trip before boarding, enjoy your ride, and pay only when you're finished. While prices are pretty firm, you might find them softer during the day. Most gondoliers honor the official prices, but a few might try to scam you out of some extra euros, particularly by insisting on a tip. (While not required or even expected, if your gondolier does the full 35 minutes and entertains you en route, a 5-10 percent tip is appreciated; if he's surly or rushes through the trip, skip it.)

If you've hired musicians and want to hear a Venetian song *(un canto Veneziano),* try requesting "Venezia La Luna e Tu." Asking to hear "O Sole Mio" (which comes from Naples) is like asking a Chicago lounge singer to sing "Swanee River."

Glide through nighttime Venice with your head on someone's shoulder. Follow the moon as it sails past otherwise unseen buildings. Silhouettes gaze down from bridges while window glitter spills onto the black water. You're anonymous in the city of masks, as the rhythmic thrust of your striped-shirted gondolier turns old crows into songbirds. This is extremely relaxing (and, I think, worth the extra cost to experience at night). Suggestion: Put the camera down and make it a point for you and your partner to enjoy a threesome with Venice. Women, beware...while gondoliers can be extremely charming, locals say that anyone who falls for one of these Venetian Romeos "has slices of ham over her eyes."

For cheap gondola thrills during the day, stick to the one-minute ferry ride on a Grand Canal *traghetto*. At night, vaporetti are nearly empty, and it's a great time to cruise the Grand Canal on the slow boat #1. Or hang out on a bridge along the gondola route and wave at romantics.

Gondolas

Two hundred years ago, there were 10,000 gondolas in Venice. Although the aristocracy preferred horses to boats through the early Middle Ages, beginning in the 14th century, when horses were outlawed from the streets of Venice, the noble class embraced gondolas as a respectable form of transportation.

The boats became *the* way to get around the lagoon's islands. To navigate over the countless shifting sandbars, the boats were flat (no keel or rudder) and the captains stood up to see. During the Age of Decadence, wannabe Casanovas would enjoy trysts in gondolas. Part of the gondolier's professional code was to never reveal what happened under the canopy of his little love boat.

Today, there are about 400 gondolas in service, used only for tourists. The boats are prettier now, but they work the same way they always have. Single oars are used both to propel and to steer the boats, which are built curved a bit on one side so that an oar thrusting from that side sends the gondola in a straight line.

These sleek yet ornate boats typically are about 35 feet long and five feet wide, and weigh about 1,100 pounds. They travel about three miles an hour (same as walking) and take the same energy to row as it does to walk. They're always painted black (six coats)—the result of a 17th-century law a doge enacted to eliminate competition between nobles for the fanciest rig. But each has unique upholstery, trim, and detailing, such as the squiggly shaped, carved-wood oarlock *(fórcola)* and metal "hood ornament" *(ferro)*. All in all, it takes about two months to build a gondola.

The boats run about €35,000-50,000, depending on options (air-con, cup holders, etc.). Every so often, the boat's hull must be treated with a new coat of varnish to protect against a lagoon-dwelling creature that eats into wood. A gondola lasts

ST. MARK'S SQUARE

For tourists, St. Mark's Square is the highlight, with lantern light and live music echoing from the cafés. Just being here after dark is a thrill, as **dueling café orchestras** entertain. The ultimate Venetian music scene is at the venerable Caffè Florian. But Gran Caffè Chioggia (facing the Doge's Palace) doesn't charge extra for music and has good jazz nightly (see the sidebar on page 72). Every night, enthusiastic musicians play the same songs, creating the same irresistible magic. Hang out for free behind the tables (allowing you to move easily on to the next orchestra when the musicians take a about 15 years, after which it can be refinished (once) to last another 10 years.

You can see Venice's most picturesque gondola workshop (from the outside; it's not open to the public) in the Accademia neighborhood. (Walk down the Accademia side of the canal

called Rio San Trovaso; as you approach Giudecca Canal, you'll glimpse the beached gondolas on your right across the canal.) The workmen, traditionally from Italy's mountainous Dolomite region (because they need to be good with wood), maintain this refreshingly alpine-feeling little corner of Venice.

Carving the uniquely curvy oarlock is an art form. To see the work in action, visit the wood-carving shop of **Paolo Brandolisio** (just behind St. Mark's Square, inland from the Church of San Zaccaria on Fondamenta de l'Osmarin—look for it down an alley from the Ca' del Sol mask shop). You can peek through the window to watch Paolo carving both *fórcole* and traditional oars (Mon-Fri 9:30-13:00 & 15:30-19:00, closed Sat-Sun, on Calle Corte Rota at #4725 just off Ponte dei Carmini). Look up Paolo on YouTube to watch him at work.

In the Dorsoduro district, you can visit the workshop of **Saverio Pastor,** another *fórcola* maker, who has scale models for sale (Mon-Fri 8:00-18:00, closed Sat-Sun, one canal east of the Peggy Guggenheim Collection, detour south along Fondamenta Soranzo de la Fornace to #341, www.forcole.com).

There are about 400 licensed gondoliers. When one dies, the license passes to his widow. And do the gondoliers sing, as the popular image has it? My mom asked our gondolier that very question, and he replied, "Madame, there are the lovers and there are the singers. I do not sing."

break), or spring for a seat and enjoy a fun and gorgeously set concert. If you sit a while, expect to pay €15 and up (for a drink and the cover charge for music)—money well spent. Dancing on the square is free—and encouraged.

Several venerable cafés and bars on the square serve expensive drinks outside but cheap drinks inside at the bar. The scene in a bar like **Gran Caffè Lavena** (despite its questionable chandelier) can be great. You'll hear people talking about the famous **Harry's American Bar,** which sells overpriced food and American cocktails to dressy tourists near the San Marco-Vallaresso vaporetto stop. But it's a rip-off...and the last place Hemingway would drink today. It's far cheaper to get a drink at any of the hole-in-the-wall bars just off St. Mark's Square; you can get a bottle of beer or even prosecco-to-go in a plastic cup.

Wherever you end up, streetlamp halos, live music, floodlit history, and a ceiling of stars make St. Mark's magic at midnight. You're not a tourist, you're a living part of a soft Venetian night...an alley cat with money. In the misty light, the moon has a golden hue. Shine with the old lanterns on the gondola piers, where the sloppy lagoon splashes at the Doge's Palace...reminiscing.

ENTERTAINMENT

Venice has a busy schedule of events, church concerts, festivals, and entertainment. Check at the TI or the TI's website (www.veneziaunica.it) for listings. The free monthly *Un Ospite di Venezia* lists all the latest happenings in English (free at fancy hotels, or check www.unospitedivenezia.it). For locations of these venues, see the maps in the Sleeping in Venice chapter.

Baroque Concerts: Venice is a city of the powdered-wig Baroque era. For about €25, you can take your pick of traditional Vivaldi concerts in churches through-out town. Homegrown Vivaldi is as ubiquitous here as Strauss is in Vienna and Mozart is in Salzburg. In fact, you'll find frilly young Vivaldis hawking concert tickets on many corners. Most shows start at 20:30 and generally last 1.5 hours. You'll see posters in hotels all over town (hotels sell tickets at face-value).

Tickets for Baroque concerts in Venice can usually be bought the same day as the concert, so don't bother with websites that sell tickets with a surcharge. The general rule of thumb: Musicians in wigs and tights offer better spectacle; musicians in black-and-white suits are better performers.

The **Interpreti Veneziani orchestra,** considered the best group in town, generally performs 1.5-hour concerts nightly at 21:00 inside the sumptuous San Vidal Church (€28, church ticket booth open daily 9:30-21:00, north end of Accademia Bridge, tel. 041-277-0561, www.interpretiveneziani.com).

If you just want a quick, free Vivaldi moment, stop by the **Music Museum** inside the San Maurizio Church, which Interpreti Veneziani has turned into a bilingual exhibition on the music and instruments of Vivaldi's time (free, daily 9:30-19:00, between St. Mark's Square and the Accademia on Campo San Maurizio, tel. 041-241-1840, www.museodellamusica.com).

Other Performances: Venice's most famous theaters are **La Fenice** (grand old opera house, box office tel. 041-2424, see page 37), **Teatro Goldoni** (mostly Italian live theater), and **Teatro Fondamenta Nuove** (theater, music, and dance).

Musica a Palazzo is a unique evening of opera at a Venetian palace on the Grand Canal. You'll spend about 45 delightful minutes in each of three sumptuous rooms (about 2.25 hours total) as seven musicians (generally three instruments and four singers) perform. They generally present three different Italian operas on successive nights—enthusiasts can experience more than one. With these kinds of surroundings, and under Tiepolo frescoes, you'll be glad you dressed up. As there are only 70 seats, you must book by phone or online in advance (€85, nightly at 20:30, Palazzo Barbarigo Minotto, Fondamenta Duodo o Barbarigo, vaporetto: Santa Maria del Giglio, San Marco 2504, mobile 340-971-7272, www.musicapalazzo.com).

Movies: Venetian cinema is rarely in the original language; expect to hear it in Italian. Every September, Venice's **film festival** (with some English-language films, www.labiennale.org) doubles the viewing choices and brings the stars out to Venice's Lido, a 10-minute vaporetto ride from St. Mark's Square.

PUBS, CLUBS, AND LATE-NIGHT SPOTS

Unlike other Italian cities, Venice doesn't have a good dance scene. The close proximity of apartments means loud music isn't tolerated late at night. The few *discoteche* are overpriced and exclusive (not tourist-friendly), with expensive drinks and little actual dancing. But there are plenty of zones where people gather to enjoy the late hours. The scene in front of St. Mark's Basilica is seductive (described earlier), but also consider the following options. For locations of these places, see the maps in the Sleeping in Venice chapter.

Near the Rialto Market: Each night, but especially on weekends, young Venetians and local night owls congregate in bars near the Rialto Market and along a nearby section of the Grand Canal. A strip of canalside restaurants I've dubbed the "Bancogiro Stretch" is a great place to enjoy a drink and the scene late at night (see page 265).

Between the Rialto and St. Mark's Square: Perhaps the best place to drink beer with an Italian is in an Irish pub—and Venice has several near the Rialto Bridge, including **Devil's Forest Pub** (a block off Campo San Bartolomeo on Calle dei Stagneri at San Marco 5185, tel. 041-520-0623, www.devilsforestpub.com) and **Inishark Pub** (closed Mon, on Calle del Mondo Novo, just west of Campo Santa Maria Formosa off Salizada San Lio, at Castello 5787, tel. 041-523-5300, www.inisharkpub.com).

Zattere: At the south end of Dorsoduro, a canalfront strip called Zattere (near the Zattere vaporetto stop) has a youthful vibe, with fun-loving pizzerias, *gelaterie*, and bars open late in season. **El Chioschetto alle Zattere** is a simple outdoor bar right on the promenade (just west of Zattere vaporetto dock; mobile 348-396-8466). The popular **Gelateria Nico** has a floating terrace for views with your dessert.

Campo Santa Margarita: The university student zone of Campo Santa Margarita, near the Accademia Bridge, is popular with young Venetians. It has a good restaurant, café, and bar scene—especially from May through September. **Caffè Rosso** is a favorite (unsigned at #2963—with a tiny interior and tons of outdoor seating, tel. 041-528-7998). A few doors down (at #2944), **Pizza al Volo** sells cheap, hearty slices to go until late. Across the square, find the excellent **Il Doge** *gelateria*. For more suggestions, see page 280.

A block away, facing the canal (across Campo San Barnaba), the **Venice Jazz Club** has live music from 21:00 to 23:00 (nightly except Thu and Sun). Doors open at 19:00 and light meals are served before the music starts (€20 includes first drink, no smoking, near Ponte dei Pugni, Dorsoduro # 3102, tel. 041-523-2056, mobile 340-150-4985, www.venicejazzclub.com, Federico).

Cannaregio: In the back streets of Cannaregio, **Il Paradiso Perduto** ("Paradise Lost") is notorious for being noisy late at night. When locals complain, night owls say there's got to be someplace in Venice that stays open late. The restaurant and bar has a huge following for its good casual food and ambience; there are often live concerts on Monday nights (closed Tue-Wed, on Fondamenta della Misericordia, Cannaregio 2540, vaporetto: San Marcuola, tel. 041-720-581).

VENICE CONNECTIONS

This chapter addresses your arrival and departure from Venice—by train, plane, car, bus, and cruise ship.

A two-mile-long causeway (with highway and train lines) connects Venice to the mainland. Mestre, the sprawling mainland section of Venice, has fewer crowds, cheaper hotels, and plenty of inexpensive parking lots, but zero charm. Don't stop in Mestre unless you're changing trains, parking your car, or sleeping there.

By Train

Be aware that there are two train companies: Trenitalia, with most connections (tel. 06-6847-5475, www.trenitalia.it), and Italo, with high-speed routes between larger cities (no rail passes accepted, outside Italy or from Italy with mobile phone, tel. 06-8937-1892; www.italotreno.it).

For travel within Italy, it's quick and easy to buy tickets online or through their apps. If you buy tickets at the station, take advantage of the ticket *(biglietti)* machines that display schedules, issue tickets, and even make reservations for rail-pass holders (found under the "Global Pass" ticket type). Some take only credit cards; others take cards and cash. Using them is easy—just select "English." Both Trenitalia and Italo have bright-red machines, so be sure you use the right one. Note that you can only buy tickets for Italian destinations from machines. An open ticket (generally for a *regionale* train) bought from a ticket desk or machine must be validated before boarding (stamp it in the machine near the track).

For some international destinations, you'll need to either go to a ticket window or visit a travel agency (also helpful if you need assistance buying tickets). For general information on train travel in

Italy—including ticket-buying options—see the "Transportation" section of the Practicalities chapter.

SANTA LUCIA TRAIN STATION

All trains to "Venice" stop at Venezia Mestre (on the mainland). Most continue on to Santa Lucia Station (a.k.a. Venezia S.L.) on the island of Venice itself. If your train happens to terminate at Mestre, you'll need to buy a €1.25 Mestre-Santa Lucia ticket and validate it before hopping any nonexpress, regional train (with an R or RV prefix) for the ride across the causeway to Venice (6/hour, 10 minutes).

Santa Lucia train station plops you right into the old town on the Grand Canal, an easy vaporetto ride or fascinating 45-minute walk (with a number of bridges and steps) to St. Mark's Square.

The station has a **baggage check** (daily 6:00-23:00, no lockers; along track 1). Pay **WCs** are at track 1 and in the back of the big bar/cafeteria area inside the station. You'll find the **TI** across from track 2. If the station TI is crowded when you arrive, visit the TI at St. Mark's Square instead.

Confirm your departure plan (at the station you can use the ticket machines or study the *partenze*/departures posters on walls). The banks of user-friendly ticket machines are handy (but cover Italian destinations only). They take euros and credit cards, display schedules, and issue tickets.

For international tickets or live help, head to the ticket windows in the corner, near track 14 (Trenitalia open 6:00-21:00; Italo open 7:30-20:00). Or take care of these tasks online or at a travel agency (ticket fee, ask your hotel for the nearest one).

Getting from the Train Station to Central Venice

It's best by **vaporetto.** Walk straight out of the station to the canal, where you'll see five vaporetto docks (A, B, C, D, and E), each serving different boats. Electronic signboards show which boats are leaving when and from which dock (for example, boat #2 to San Marco, from dock B). Most tourists want the fast boat #2 down the Grand Canal to Rialto and San Marco (generally from dock B) or the slow boat #1 down the Grand Canal, making every stop all the way to Rialto and San Marco.

Buy a €7.50 ticket before you board. If ticket-window lines by the docks are too long, you can also buy from self-service machines nearby (English-language option, major credit cards accepted), or inside the station at the TI or a newsstand. Before buying a single-ride vaporetto ticket, consider getting a transit pass (see page 19). Find your dock and validate your ticket/pass by touching it to the circular pad on the dock; the gates will open to let you onto the dock. Because docks serve multiple lines, before you hop on the vaporetto, confirm with the conductor this particular boat is going to your stop ("Rialto?").

A **water taxi** from the train station to central Venice costs about €60-80 (the taxi dock is straight ahead).

From Venice by Train to Other Destinations

When taking the train to nearby cities such as Padua and Verona, prices and journey times vary greatly depending on whether you take an express or regional train. Unless otherwise specified, the following connections are for Trenitalia.

Destinations in Italy: Padua (30 minutes, Trenitalia: 2/hour, Italo: hourly), **Vicenza** (45 minutes, Trenitalia: 2/hour, Italo: 7/day), **Verona** (1.5 hours, Trenitalia: 2/hour, Italo: 7/day), **Ravenna** (roughly hourly, 3 hours, transfer in Ferrara or Bologna), **Florence** (Trenitalia: hourly, 2-3 hours, may transfer in Bologna, often crowded—reserve ahead; Italo: 4/day, 2 hours, reservations required), **Bolzano/Dolomites** (to Bolzano about hourly, 3 hours, transfer in Verona; catch bus from Bolzano into mountains), **Milan** (Trenitalia: 2/hour, most direct on high-speed ES trains, 2.5 hours; Italo: 7/day, 2.5 hours), **Cinque Terre/Monterosso** (5/day, 6 hours, change in Milan), **Rome** (Trenitalia: hourly, 4 hours; direct night train, 7 hours, reserve ahead; Italo: 4/day, 3.5 hours, reservations required), **Naples** (Trenitalia: almost hourly, 5.5 hours, some change in Bologna or Rome, reserve ahead; Italo: 3/day, 5.5 hours, reservations required), **Brindisi** (5/day, 9 hours, change in Rome or Bologna).

International Destinations: Interlaken (4/day, 6 hours with 2 changes), **Munich** (1/day direct, 6.5 hours, more with change in Verona; reservable only at ticket windows or via www.bahn.com), **Innsbruck** (1/day direct, 5 hours, more with change in Verona; reservable only at ticket windows or via www.bahn.com), **Salzburg** (4/day, 6.5 hours with change in Villach), **Paris** (2/day, 11 hours, change in Turin; 1 direct night train, 14.5 hours, reserve up to 4 months in advance, no rail passes accepted, www.thello.com), **Geneva** (1/day direct, 2/day with change in Milan, 7-8 hours), **Vienna** (2/day direct, 8 hours; direct night train, 11 hours), **Ljubljana** (4/day, 5 hours, train to Trieste, then bus or train to Ljubljana). To Ljubljana, there's also a direct DRD bus from Mestre (1/day, 3 hours, www.drd.si) and a private shuttle service (www.goopti.com).

By Plane

MARCO POLO AIRPORT

Venice's surprisingly large, modern airport is on the mainland shore of the lagoon, six miles north of the city (airport code: VCE, tel. 041-260-9260, www.veniceairport.it). There's one sleek terminal, with a TI (daily 9:00-20:00), car-rental agencies, ATMs, a bank, and plenty of shops and eateries.

Getting Between the Airport and Venice

You can get between the airport and central Venice in any of four ways: by Alilaguna boat, water taxi, airport bus, or land taxi.

Type	Speed	Cost	Notes
Alilaguna boat	Slow	Moderate	No transfer
Water taxi	Fast	Expensive	No transfer
Airport bus to Piazzale Roma	Medium	Cheap	Transfer to vaporetto
Land taxi to Piazzale Roma	Medium	Moderate	Transfer to vaporetto

Alilaguna boats reach most of this book's recommended hotels very simply, with no changes. Hotels near the train station, however, are better served by the bus to Piazzale Roma.

Both Alilaguna boats and water taxis leave from the airport's boat dock, an eight-minute walk from the terminal, following signs along a sleek series of (indoor) moving sidewalks. Ticket offices are at the docks.

When flying out of Venice, allow plenty of time to get to the airport. From your hotel to the airport can take two hours. Alilaguna boats are small and can fill up. In an emergency, you can always hop in a water taxi and get to the airport in 30 minutes.

Alilaguna Airport Boats

These boats make the scenic journey across the lagoon, shuttling passengers between the airport and the island of Venice (€15, €27 round-trip, €1 surcharge if bought on boat, includes 1 suitcase and 1 piece of hand luggage, additional bags—€3 each, roughly 2/hour, 1-1.5-hour trip depending on destination). Alilaguna boats are not covered by city transit passes, but they do use the same docks and ticket windows as the regular vaporetti. You can buy Alilaguna tickets online for a slight discount, but it does not ensure a reservation as you must still exchange the voucher for a ticket (www. alilaguna.it or www.venicelink.com).

There are three key Alilaguna lines for reaching St. Mark's Square. From the airport, the **orange line** *(linea arancio)* runs down the Grand Canal, reaching Guglie (handy for Cannaregio hotels, 45 minutes), Rialto (1 hour), and San Marco (1.25 hours). The **blue line** *(linea blu)* heads first to Fondamente Nove (40 minutes), then loops around to San Zaccaria and San Marco (about 1.5 hours) before continuing to Zattere and the cruise terminal (almost 2 hours). In high season, the **red line** *(linea rossa)* runs to St. Mark's in just over an hour. It circumnavigates Murano and then runs parallel to the blue line, ending at Giudecca Zitelle.

For a full schedule, see www.alilaguna.it, visit the TI, call 041-240-1701, ask your hotelier, or scan the schedules posted at the docks.

From the Airport to Venice: Buy Alilaguna tickets at the ticket windows at the docks. Any ticket seller can tell you which line to catch to get to your destination. Blue- and orange-line boats from the airport run roughly twice an hour and go all day (until about midnight); red goes once an hour (runs 9:40-18:40). Ask your hotelier (when you reserve your room) which stop in Venice is best.

From Venice to the Airport: Ask your hotelier which dock and which line is best. Blue-line boats start leaving Venice as early as 3:50 in the morning. Scope out the dock and buy your ticket in advance to avoid last-minute stress. Get there 10 minutes early to assure yourself a seat.

Water Taxis

Luxury taxi speedboats zip directly between the airport and the closest dock to your hotel, getting you within steps of your destination in about 30 minutes. The official price is €110 for up to four people; add €10 for every extra person (10-passenger limit). You may get a higher quote—politely talk it down. A taxi can be a smart investment for small groups and those with an early departure.

From the airport, arrange your ride at the water-taxi desk or with the boat captains at the dock. From Venice, book your taxi trip the day before your departure, either through your hotel or directly with the Consorzio Motoscafi water taxi association (tel. 041-522-2303, www.motoscafivenezia.it).

Airport Shuttle Buses

Buses between the airport and Venice are fast, frequent, and cheap. They drop you at Venice's bus station, at the square called Piazzale Roma. From there, you can catch a vaporetto down the Grand Canal—convenient for hotels near the Rialto Bridge and St. Mark's Square. If you're staying near the train station, you can walk from Piazzale Roma to your hotel.

Two bus companies serve this route: ACTV and ATVO. ATVO buses take 20 minutes and go nonstop. ACTV buses make a few stops en route and take slightly longer (30 minutes), but you get a discount if you buy a Venice vaporetto pass at the same time (see page 19). The service is equally good (either bus: €8 one-way, €15 round-trip; ACTV bus with transit-pass discount: €6 one-way, €12 round-trip; runs about 5:00-24:00, 2/hour, drops to 1/hour early and late, check schedules at www.atvo.it or www.actv.it).

From the Airport to Venice: Buses leave from just outside the arrivals terminal. Buy tickets from the TI, the ticket desk in the terminal, the kiosk near baggage claim, or ticket machines. ATVO tickets are not valid on ACTV buses and vice versa. Double-check the destination; you want Piazzale Roma. If taking ACTV, you want bus #5.

From Venice to the Airport: At Piazzale Roma, buy your ticket from the ACTV windows (in the building by the bridge) or the ATVO office (at #497g) before heading out to the platforms (although sometimes an attendant sells tickets near the buses). The newsstand in the center of the lot also sells tickets.

Land Taxi or Private Minivan

It takes about 20 minutes to drive from the airport to Piazzale Roma or the cruise port. A **land taxi** can do the trip for about €50. To reserve a private minivan, contact **Treviso Car Service** (minivan—€55, seats up to 8; car—€50, seats up to 3; mobile 338-204-4390 or 333-411-2840, www.trevisocarservice.com).

TREVISO AIRPORT

Several budget airlines use Treviso Airport, 12 miles northwest of Venice (code: TSF, tel. 042-231-5111, www.trevisoairport.it). The fastest option into Venice (Tronchetto parking lot; convenient if taking vaporetto line #2) is on the **Barzi express bus,** which does the trip in just 40 minutes (€12, buy tickets on board, every 1-2 hours, www.barziservice.com). From Tronchetto, hop on a vaporetto, or take the People Mover monorail to Piazzale Roma for €1.50. **ATVO buses** are a bit more frequent and drop you right at Piazzale Roma (saving you the People Mover ride), but take nearly twice as long (€12 one-way, €22 round-trip, about 2/hour, 70 minutes, www.atvo.it; buy tickets at the ATVO desk in the airport and stamp them on the bus). **Treviso Car Service** offers minivan service to Piazzale Roma (minivan—€75, seats up to 8; car—€65, seats up to 3; for contact info, see listing earlier).

By Bus

PIAZZALE ROMA BUS STATION

Venice's "bus station" is an open-air parking lot called Piazzale Roma. The square itself is a jumble of different operators, platforms, and crosswalks over busy lanes of traffic. But bus stops are well-signed. The ticket windows for ACTV (including #5 to Marco Polo Airport) are in a building between the bridge and vaporetto stop. The ATVO ticket office (express buses to Marco Polo and Treviso airports and to Padua) is at #497g in the big, white building, on the right side of the square as you face away from the canal (office open daily 6:45-19:30).

Piazzale Roma also has two big parking garages and the People Mover monorail (€1.50, links to the cruise port and then the parking-lot island of Tronchetto). A baggage-storage office is next to the monorail at #497m (€7/24 hours, daily 6:00-21:00).

If you arrive here, find the vaporetto docks (just left of the modern bridge) and take #1 or the faster #2 down the Grand Canal to reach the Rialto, Accademia, or San Marco (St. Mark's Square) stops. Electronic boards direct you to the dock you want. Before buying a single-ride vaporetto ticket, consider getting a transit pass (see page 19). If your hotel is near here or near the train station, you can get there on foot.

By Car

PARKING IN VENICE

The freeway (monitored by speed cameras) dead-ends after crossing the causeway to Venice. At the end of the road you have two parking-garage choices: Tronchetto or Piazzale Roma. As you drive into the city, signboards with green and red lights indicate which lots are full. (You can also park in Mestre, on the mainland, but this is less convenient.)

Parking at Tronchetto: This big garage is a bit farther out, but it's a little cheaper and well-connected by vaporetto (€3-5/hour, €21/24 hours, tel. 041-520-7555, www.veniceparking.it).

From the garage, cross the street to the brick building and go right to the vaporetto dock (not well signed, look for *ACTV*). At the dock, catch vaporetto #2 in one of two directions: via the Grand Canal (more scenic, stops at Rialto, 40 minutes to San Marco), or via Giudecca (around the city, faster, no Rialto stop, 30 minutes to San Marco).

Don't be waylaid by aggressive water-taxi boatmen. They charge €100 to take you where the vaporetto will for far less. Also avoid the travel agencies masquerading as TIs; deal only with the ticket booth at the vaporetto dock or the VèneziaUnica public transport office. If you're going to buy a local transit pass, do it now.

If you're staying near the bus or train station, you can take the €1.50 **People Mover** monorail, which brings you from Tronchetto to the bus station at Piazzale Roma. From there, it's a five-minute walk across the modern Calatrava Bridge to the train station (buy tickets with cash or credit card from machine, 3-minute trip).

Parking at Piazzale Roma: The two garages here are more convenient but a bit more expensive and likelier to be full. Both face the busy Piazzale Roma, where the road ends. The big white building on your right is the **Autorimessa Comunale** city garage (€26/24 hours, TI office in payment lobby open daily 7:30-19:30, tel. 041-272-7211, www.avmspa.it). In a back corner of the square is the private **Garage San Marco** (€32/24 hours, tel. 041-523-2213, www.garagesanmarco.it). At either, you'll have to give up your keys. Near the Garage San Marco, avoid the Parcheggio Sant'Andrea, which charges higher rates.

Parking in Mestre: The **Parcheggio Stazione** garage across from the train station in Mestre (on the mainland) makes sense if you have light bags and are staying within walking distance of Santa Lucia Station (€2.50/hour, €14/day, www.sabait.it).

By Cruise Ship or Boat

Most cruise ships dock at Venice's Stazione Marittima, at the west end of town. From the cruise port, the most direct way to reach St. Mark's Square is to take the Alilaguna **express boat** (2/hour in each direction, 30 minutes, www.alilaguna.it).

Another option is to take the **People Mover** monorail from the port to Piazzale Roma, then hop on a **vaporetto.** It's about a five-minute walk to the People Mover, then a three-minute ride to Piazzale Roma, where you'll find a stop for vaporetti to Rialto, Accademia, or San Marco (boat #1 or the faster boat #2).

Other options for getting to the center from the cruise port include **walking** (about an hour to St. Mark's Square) or an expensive **water taxi** ride (at least €70-80).

For more details, see my *Rick Steves Mediterranean Cruise Ports* guidebook.

A 31-hour boat ride can take you to **Patras** in Greece, if you have the patience (about 4/week, fewer off-season; Minoan Lines, www.minoan.gr; or Anek Lines, www.anek.gr).

NEAR VENICE

Venice is just one of many towns in the Italian region of Veneto (VEHN-eh-toh), but few visitors venture off the lagoon. That's a shame, as there's much to see within a very short hop of Venice: the important and worthwhile towns of **Padua, Verona, Vicenza,** and **Ravenna.**

If you can't make it to all four, pick the one that interests you. Art lovers will want to head to **Padua** to see Giotto's celebrated Scrovegni Chapel or to **Ravenna** for its sumptuous Byzantine mosaics. History buffs should see **Verona**'s impressive Roman ruins. Verona is also the pick for star-crossed lovers retracing Romeo and Juliet's steps. Architecture fans could consider a quick stop in Palladio-designed **Vicenza,** located about halfway between Padua and Verona.

If you're Padua-bound, remember that you need to reserve ahead to see the Scrovegni Chapel. Don't bother visiting Vicenza on a Monday, when many of the top sights are closed; in Verona, several sights are only open in the afternoon on Mondays.

Spending a day at one of these towns as a side-trip from Venice is exciting and efficient. Padua, Verona, and Vicenza are on the same train line. Connected by at least two trains per hour, they're easy to visit. Only Ravenna is not on the main Venice-Milan train line. To reach Ravenna, you'll need to make at least one change, either in Bologna or Ferrara.

Trenitalia operates Regional (R), "Fast Regional" (RV), and Frecce (Express) trains. Italo runs their own trains equivalent to the Frecce, but these don't work with Eurail passes. Train travelers find that the "fast regional" trains (marked with an RV prefix on schedules and ticket machines) offer the best mixture of speed, convenience, and savings. Frecce and Italo trains cost quite a bit more—and though rail-pass holders don't have to pay the fare, they do have to commit to a time and pay to reserve a seat. Regional trains don't require (or even accept) seat reservations. The regular regional trains (R prefix) offer the same savings as the RV ones but are much slower.

Type of Train	Venice-Padua	Venice-Verona	Venice-Ravenna
R (Regional)	€4.50, 50 minutes	€9.25, 2 hours	none
RV (Fast Regional)	€4.50, 30 minutes	€9.25, 1.5 hours	€14.50-19, 3-3.5 hours (includes regional train)
Frecce (Express)	€19, 30 minutes	€28, 70 minutes	€23-44, 2.5-3 hours (includes regional train)
Italo	€15, 30 minutes	€20, 70 minutes	none

PADUA

Padova • Vicenza

This inexpensive, easily appreciated city is a fine destination on its own and a convenient base for day trips all around the region. Nicknamed "The brain of Veneto," Padua (*Padova* in Italian) is home to the prestigious university (founded in 1222) that hosted Galileo, Copernicus, Dante, and Petrarch. Pilgrims know Padua as the home of the Basilica of St. Anthony, where the reverent assemble to touch his tomb and ogle his remarkably intact lower jaw and tongue. And lovers of early Renaissance art come here to make

a pilgrimage of their own: to gaze at the remarkable frescoes by Giotto in the Scrovegni Chapel. But despite the fact that Padua's museums and churches hold their own in Italy's artistic big league, its hotels are reasonably priced, and the city doesn't feel touristy. Padua's old town center is elegantly arcaded, filled with students, and sprinkled with surprises, including some of Italy's most inviting squares for lingering over an *aperitivo* as the sun slowly dips low in the sky.

From Padua, architecture fans can ride by train (15-25 minutes) to Vicenza and its celebrated Palladian buildings (see the end of this chapter). And Venice is just a half-hour away in the other direction.

PLANNING YOUR TIME: PADUA IN A DAY

Day-trippers can do a quick but enjoyable blitz of Padua—including a visit to the Scrovegni Chapel—in as little as six hours. Trains from Venice are cheap, take 30 minutes, and run frequently. Once in Padua, everything is a 10-minute walk or a quick tram ride apart.

To see Giotto's Scrovegni Chapel, you need to make a reservation; your entry time will dictate the order of your sightseeing (see "Reservations" on page 330). When planning your day, also consider these factors: The station has a reliable baggage-check desk; the open-air markets are vibrant in the morning; student life is best at the university late in the day; and the Basilica of St. Anthony is open all day, but the reliquary chapel closes midday, from 12:45 to 14:30.

Ideally, I'd do it this way: 9:00—market action and sightseeing in town center, 11:00—Basilica of St. Anthony, 13:00—lunch, 15:00—Scrovegni Chapel tour. Then, cap off your day with a *spritz* on the main square.

Orientation to Padua

Padua's main tourist sights lie on a north-south axis through the heart of the city, from the train station to Scrovegni Chapel to the market squares (the center of town) to the Basilica of St. Anthony. It's roughly a 10-minute walk between each of these sights, or about 30 minutes from end to end. I've designed this chapter around Padua's wonderful, single tram line, which makes lacing things together quick and easy (see "Getting Around Padua," later).

TOURIST INFORMATION

Padua has two TIs: in the **center** (in the alley behind Caffè Pedrocchi at Vicolo Cappellatto Pedrocchi 9, Mon-Sat 9:00-19:00, Sun 10:00-16:00) and at the **train station** (same hours, tel. 049-520-7415, www.turismopadova.it).

The **Padova Card** includes entry to all the recommended sights in this chapter—except the university's Anatomy Theater and the Oratory of St. George—plus unlimited tram rides (€16/48 hours, €21/72 hours, buy at either TI, the Scrovegni Chapel, or online at www.padovacard.it). If you go through the chapel website (www.cappelladegliscrovegni.it), you can buy the card and make a chapel reservation at the same time. Show your receipt to collect your pre-purchased card at either TI or at the chapel. Also, there's a chance the TI can book same-day reservations to the Scrovegni Chapel (no less than three hours in advance) with a Padova Card purchase.

ARRIVAL IN PADUA

By Train: The efficient station is a user-friendly shopping mall, including a Despar supermarket (daily until 21:00). Along track 1, on the far right as you face the tracks, are pay WCs and baggage storage (daily 6:30-20:00, bring photo ID). Avoid long lines by purchasing train tickets from machines.

To get downtown, simply hop on Padua's handy **tram** (see

Padua

See Padua Center detail map

To A-4
Autostrada
(Venice &
Verona)

**TRAIN
STATION**

VIA FRA PAOLO SARPI

V. CODALUNGA

Stazione

VIA B. CAIROLI

CITY
BUSES

BUSES TO
AIRPORT &
VENICE

VIA N. TOMMASEO

VIA BEATO GIOVANNI VERDARA

VIA DELLA ROTONDA

VIALE CODALUNGA

VIA GIOTTO

V. DIEGO VALERI

V. FOSCOLO

C. DEL POPOLO

Piazza Alcide
de Gasperi

VIA TRIESTE

Trieste

VIA SAN PELLEGRINO

V. DEL CARMINE

CARMINE
CHURCH

OLD CITY
WALLS

GARIBALDI

See Padua Center detail map

VIA DEI SAVONAROLA

Piovego

Eremitani

**SCROVEGNI
CHAPEL**

Canale

VIA SAN PIETRO

PALAZZO
ZUCKERMANN

**CIVIC
MUSEUMS**
(SCROVEGNI
TICKETS)

V. CARLO LEONI

CORSO MILANO

VIA DANTE

VIA SAN FERMO

CORSO

ERMITAGE
CHURCH

V. VERDI

Piazza dell'
Insurrezione

VIA SANTA LUCIA

S. NICOLÒ

V. PATRIARCATO

Piazza
Capitaniato

**MARKET
SQUARES**

PEDROCCHI
BLDG.

CAVOUR

R. CONTI ROMANI

ZABARELLA

VIA ALTINATE

BAPTISTERY

Piazza
Signori

Piazza
Frutta

Piazza
Cavour

Ponti
Romani

V. DEI TADI

Piazza
Duomo

PALAZZO
RAGIONE

DUOMO

VIA MANIN

Piazza
Erbe

V. SONCIN

UNIVERSITY
(PALAZZO BO)

VIA CESARE BATTISTI

VIA DEI VESCOVADO

SOLFERINO

Piazza
Antenore

VIA DEL SANTO

VIA SAN SANTO

VIA SANTA ROSA

MARSALA

RIVIERA TITO LIVIO

Tito
Livio

**SAN
FRANCESCO**

VIA GALILEO GALILEI

SPERONI

V. S. GREGORIO BARBARIGO

VIA ROMA

S. MARIA
SERVI

VIA SAN TOMASO

20 SETTEMBRE

Piazzetta
Palatucci

VIA SANTA
CHIARA

VIA SAN FRANCESCO

Piazza
del Castello

VIA

Piovego

VIA UMBERTO I

RIVIERA RUZANTE

Canale

R. TISO CAMPOSAMPIERO

VIA DEI ROGATI

V. SEMINARIO

Piazza
del
Santo

V. CESAROTTI

V. TORRESINO

VIA ACQUETTE

Prato
della Valle

Santo

**BASILICA OF
ST. ANTHONY**
See detail map

V. BELLUDI

V. BRIOSCO

VIA ALBERTO

CAVALLETTO

VIA DIMESSE

**Prato
della Valle**

**Botanic
Garden**

200 Meters

200 Yards

"Getting Around Padua," below). Purchase your ticket (€1.30, or €3.80 day pass) from shops inside the station or in the low brown rectangular booth in front of the station, which has both machines and a staffed window. Leaving the station, the tram stop is 100 yards to the right at the foot of the bridge (direction: Capolinea Sud). Note that thieves like this tram when it comes to picking the pockets of tourists. A **taxi** into town (a good option after dark) costs about €8-10.

By Bus: The bus station is 100 yards east of the train station. Buses arrive here from Venice's Piazzale Roma and Marco Polo Airport.

By Car: Padua has a smart park-and-ride system near each end of the tram line, providing cheap parking and convenient access to town using the tram. The north lot is at the Pontevigodarzere stop, the south lot at the Capolinea Guizza stop. At either lot, buy parking tickets from machines or at the nearby café (€1 for all day and free overnight).

For more costly parking closer to town, try **Padova Centro Park** (near the train station and the Scrovegni Chapel, €6/24 hours) or **Piazza Isaac Rabin** (near Prato della Valle, €12/24 hours).

HELPFUL HINTS

Pronunciation: You say Padua (PAD-joo-wah), they say Padova (PAH-doh-vah). The city's top sight, Scrovegni Chapel, is pronounced skroh-VEHN-yee.

Bookstore: Feltrinelli, with books in English, is one block from the main university building (daily 9:00-19:45, Via San Francesco 7, tel. 199-151-173).

Launderette: Self-service **Lavami** is central, tiny, and modern with English instructions on flip cards (daily 7:00-21:30, Via Marsala 22 near intersection with Via dell'Arco, tel. 049-876-4532).

Local Guide: Charming and helpful **Cristina Pernechele** is a great teacher who is passionate about her hometown (€120/half-day, mobile 338-495-5453, cristina@pernechele.eu). If she's booked, she can suggest other good local guides.

GETTING AROUND PADUA

Ignore the city buses; pretend there is only the **tram** and rely on it. There's just one line, which efficiently and without stress connects everything you care about. With a Padova Card you get unlimited tram use; just show the card to security upon request. Or, buy tickets from tobacco shops, newsstands, or the booth on the square in front of the train station and validate them on board; there are also ticket machines at some stops, but they sell only single tickets and don't give change (€1.30 single ticket good for 75 minutes, €3.80

biglietto giornaliero good for one calendar day; departs every 8 minutes during the day Mon-Sat, every 20 minutes evenings and Sun). The rubber-wheeled trams run on a single rail.

Before boarding, note the tram direction on posted schedules and above the front window (Pontevigodarzere is northbound, Capolinea Sud is southbound). Stops that matter to tourists include Stazione FS (train and bus stations), Eremitani (Scrovegni Chapel), Ponti Romani (old town center, market squares, university), Tito Livio (ghetto, old town center, Hotel Majestic Toscanelli), and Santo (both for Basilica of St. Anthony and neighborhood hotels).

Padua's **hop-on, hop-off tour buses** are not worth the time or money.

Sights in Padua

IN THE CENTER

Padua's two main sights (Basilica of St. Anthony and Scrovegni Chapel) are, respectively, at the southern and northern reaches of downtown. But its atmospheric, cobbled core—with bustling markets, vibrant student life, and inviting sun-and-café-speckled piazzas—is its own ▲▲▲ attraction. You could simply stroll the area aimlessly or seek out some of the following spots.

▲▲Market Squares

The stately Palazzo della Ragione (described later) provides a dramatic backdrop for Padua's almost exotic-feeling produce market, which fills the surrounding squares—**Piazza delle Erbe** and **Piazza della Frutta**—each morning and all day Saturday (Mon-Fri roughly 8:00-13:00, Sat 8:00-19:00 but a bit quieter in the afternoon, closed Sun). Second only to the produce market in Italy's gastronomic capital of Bologna, this market has been renowned for centuries as having the freshest and greatest selection of herbs, fruits, and vegetables. The presentation is an art in itself. As you wander, appreciate the local passion for good food: Residents can tell the month by the seasonal selections, and merchants share recipe tips with shoppers. You'll notice quite a few Sri Lankans working here (Italy took in many refugees from Sri Lanka's civil war).

Don't miss the **indoor market** zone on the ground floor of the Palazzo della Ragione. Wandering through this H-shaped arcade—where you'll find various butchers, *salumerie* (delicatessens), cheese shops, bakeries, and fishmongers at work—is a sensuous experience. For centuries, this was a market for luxury items (furs, fine fabrics, silver, and gold—notice the imposing iron gates used to lock it up each evening). Then, the devastating loss to the French in 1797 marked the end of good times, and with no market for luxury items, the arcade was used to sell perishables—meat and cheese—out of the sun.

The building with the flags overlooking Piazza delle Erbe is the Renaissance city hall with a Rationalist (fascist-era) wing on the right. (Notice the relief from the 1930s celebrating Mussolini's pathetic little empire—Libya, Albania, Somalia, and Ethiopia.) And opposite the big Palazzo della Ragione is the Jewish quarter and a charming zone of arcaded lanes (some of about 15 miles of lanes in the city that provided protection from sun and rain in the Middle Ages, giving the city an extra boost of elegance).

Students gather in the squares after the markets have closed, spilling out of colorful bars and cafés, drinks in hand (see sidebar). Bars and food stalls offer plenty of refreshments and fun food. Pizza by the slice is dirt-cheap. For pointers on a recommended local sandwich stand, **Bar dei Osei,** and a neighboring squid stand, see "Eating in Padua," later.

Just a few steps away from these is a classic old pharmacy that dates to 1841: The licorice-perfumed **Ai Due Cantini d'Oro,** which stocks retail items like it did before World War II, sells odd foods and specialty items for every dietary need (Tue-Sun 9:00-13:00 & 16:00-19:30, closed Mon, Piazza della Frutta 46, tel. 049-875-0623).

▲Palazzo della Ragione

Looming over Padua's two big central market squares (Piazza delle Erbe and Piazza della Frutta), this grand 13th-century palazzo—commonly called *il Salone* (the great hall)—once held the medieval law courts.

Cost and Hours: €6; Tue-Sun 9:00-19:00, Nov-Jan until 18:00, closed Mon year-round; Ponti Romani tram stop, tel. 049-820-5006.

Visiting the Palazzo: Facing the palazzo from Piazza delle Erbe, climb the grand staircase on the palazzo's far right side, buy your ticket (and pick up the English info flier), and go to the loggia overlooking Piazza delle Erbe. Enjoy the view and the fine vaulting that was painted in the 1300s to celebrate

PADUA

Padua Center

Piovego

VIA DEI SAVONAROLA

Canale

VIA SAN PIETRO

V. CARLO LEONI

CORSO MILANO

VIA DANTE

Piazza
dell'
Insurrezione

VIA DEI LIVELLO

VIA VERDI

VIA

RIVIERA SAN BENEDETTO

V. PATRIARCATO

SAN
NICOLÒ

VIA SANTA LUCIA

VIA ACC.

VIA A. DONDI

VIA BREDA

2

Piazza
Capitaniato

LION

Piazza
Signori

11

16

14

**Piazza
Frutta**

12 **23**

VIA DEI TADI

BAPTISTERY

VIA MANIN

PALAZZO
RAGIONE

STAIRS

15

**Piazza
Erbe**

S. CANZ.

Piazza
Duomo

8

V. SONCIN

DUOMO

7

VIA S. MARTIN E SOLFERINO

VIA S. MART. SOLF.

VIA FABBRI

VIA DEI VESCOVADO

VIA SPERONI

VIA S. GREGORIO BARBARIGO

1

VIA ARCO

13

22

9

MARSALA

VIA SANTA ROSA

S. MARIA
SERVI

VIA ROMA

VIA SAN TOMASO

Piazza
del Castello

Piazzetta
Palatucci

20 SETTEMBRE

Piovego

VIA

VIA DEI ROGATI

VIA UMBERTO I

10

Canale

R. TISO CAMPOSAMPIERO

V. A. ALFARIT

V. SEMINARIO

V. ROBERTO MARIN

VIA ACQUETTE

V. TORRESINO

VIA ANDREA MEMMO

VIA DIMESSE

To Prato della Valle,
Piazza Isaac Rabin Parking
& A-13 Autostrada
(Florence)

20

PADUA

PADUA

Accommodations
1. Hotel Majestic Toscanelli
2. Albergo Verdi
3. Hotel Belludi 37
4. Hotel Al Fagiano
5. Hotel Al Santo
6. Hotel Casa del Pellegrino

Eateries
7. Osteria L'Anfora
8. Osteria dal Capo
9. Enotavola Pino
10. Enoteca Antonio Ferrari
11. La Lanterna Ristorante
12. Bar dei Osei & La Folperia
13. Bar Corte Sconta
14. Bar All'Ombra della Piazza
15. Pastasuta & Cristina e Massimo
16. Gnam Gnam Gelato
17. Antica Trattoria dei Paccagnella
18. Pizzeria Pago Pago
19. Pollodoro la Gastronomica
20. Portogallo Gelateria

Other
21. Feltrinelli Bookstore
22. Launderette
23. Ai Due Cantini d'Oro (Old Pharmacy)

Note: Much of central Padua is pedestrian & bike-friendly

Drinking a *Spritz* with the Student Crowd

Each early evening, before dinner, students enliven Padua by enjoying a convivial drink in their favorite places. Piazza dei Signori is trendier, with people of all ages, while the scene on Piazza delle Erbe is more bohemian and alternative. Or you could sit in front of the university, nurse your drink, and watch the graduates get roasted with their crazy gangs of friends.

The drink of choice is a *spritz,* an aperitif generally made with Campari (a red liqueur infused with bitter herbs), white wine or prosecco, and sparkling water, and garnished with a blood-orange wedge. Another version is a sweeter and lighter *spritz* made with Aperol (an orange-flavored liqueur), which has a lower alcohol content and is not as bitter as the heavier Campari *spritz.* Padovans brag that Aperol was created here in 1919.

Grab a table and be part of the scene. This is a classic opportunity to enjoy a real discussion with smart, English-speaking students who see tourists not as pests, but as interesting people from far away. For an instant conversation starter, ask about the current political situation in Italy, the right-wing party's policy on immigrants, or the cultural differences between Italy's North and South. A question they might ask you: "What the hell is the electoral college?"

the city's wealth when Padua was an independent city-state (one of many little states in "the land of a thousand bell towers" that ultimately formed Italy).

Step into the great hall and head right, to the back of the room opposite the giant horse to take it all in. This huge hall—265 feet by 90 feet—was at one time adorned with frescoes by Giotto. A fire in 1420 destroyed those paintings, and the palazzo was redecorated with the 15th-century art you see today: a series of 333 frescoes depicting the signs of the zodiac, labors of the month, symbols representing characteristics of people born under each sign, and, finally, figures of the 12 apostles and favorite saints to legitimize the power of the courts in the eyes of the Church.

The hall is topped with a hull-shaped roof, which helps to support the structure without the use of columns—quite an architectural feat when built in 1306, considering the building's dimensions.

The biggest thing in the hall is the giant, very anatomically correct horse. Its prominent placement represents the pride locals feel for the Veneto's own highly respected breed of horse. (After the bronze ones in St. Mark's Basilica in Venice, these are the favorite horses in the region.)

The curious black stone in the corner (behind you on the right) is the "Stone of Shame," which was the seat of debtors being punished during the Middle Ages. It was introduced as a compassionate alternative to prison by St. Anthony in 1230. Instead of being executed or doing prison time, debtors sat upon this stone, surrendered their possessions, and denounced themselves publicly before being exiled from the city.

Behind it on the left is a Foucault pendulum that demonstrates the rotation of the earth (well described in English). Computers display information that helps give meaning to the building. After enjoying the paintings and getting a closer look at the horse, leave through the door you entered.

Piazza dei Signori

Just a block away from Palazzo della Ragione, this square is a busy clothing market in the morning and the most popular gathering

place in the evening for students out for a drink. The circa-1400 clock decorates the former palace of the ruling family. The aggressive lion with unfurled wings on the column was a reminder of the Venetian determination to assert its control. Today that lion can be seen as representing the Veneto region's independence from Rome: Italy's North (Veneto and Lombardy) is tired of subsidizing the South. Grumbling about this issue continues to stir talk of splitting the country.

▲Caffè Pedrocchi

The white-columned, Neoclassical Pedrocchi building is much more than just a café on the ground floor. A complex of meeting rooms and entertainment venues, it stirs the Italian soul (or the patriotic Italian soul, at least). Built in 1831 during the period of Austrian rule, Caffè Pedrocchi was inaugurated for the fourth Italian Congress of Scientists, which convened during the mid-19th century to stir up nationalistic fervor as Italy struggled to unite as a single country. In 1848, this symbol of patriotic hope was the target (no surprise) of those repressing a student uprising that was being plotted here. (For more on the story of Italy's unification, visit the upstairs Museum of the Risorgimento; see the next listing.)

Cost and Hours: Café interior free, daily 8:00-23:00, across from Via VIII Febbraio near Ponti Romani tram stop, tel. 049-878-1231, www.caffepedrocchi.it.

Visiting the Café: Each of the café's three dining rooms is decorated and furnished in a different color (denoted by the hue of velvet on the chairs): red, white, or green—representing the colors of the Italian flag. In the outer, unheated **Sala Verde** (Green Room), people are welcome to sit and relax without ordering anything or having to pay. This is where Italian gentlemen read their newspapers and gather with friends to chat about the old days. In the **Sala Rossa** (Red Room), the clock over the bar is flanked by marble reliefs of morning and night, a reminder that, back in the 19th century, the room was open 24 hours a day. In the rooms on either side, the maps of the hemispheres with south

up top reflect the anti-conventional spirit of the place. In the **Sala Bianca** (White Room), where one of the revolutionaries in that ill-fated 1848 uprising was killed, you can see a bullet hole in the wall (framed in tarnished silver).

The menu offers teahouse fare, including sandwiches and ice-cream sundaes, a variety of breakfast combos, and the writer Stendhal's beloved *zabaglione*, a creamy custard made with Marsala wine. A shiny new bar in the center of the building has a pastry counter and serves sandwiches at outdoor tables. Remember that in Italy, you can order a basic coffee standing up at the bar of any place, no matter how fancy, and pay the same low, government-regulated price.

▲Museum of the Risorgimento

Upstairs in Caffè Pedrocchi, this small museum tells the stirring story of Italy's unification in a series of fine 19th-century rooms. With good English descriptions, the museum traces Padua's role in Italian history, from the downfall of the Venetian Republic (1797) to the founding of the Republic of Italy (1946).

Cost and Hours: €4; Tue-Sun 9:30-12:30 & 15:30-18:00, closed Mon; entrance up staircase on Piazza Cavour side of café; tel. 049-878-1231.

Visiting the Museum: You'll pass through a series of rooms—all in different styles, such as Greek, Etruscan, or Egyptian—that were intended to evoke memories of the glory of past epochs, which a united Italy had hopes of reliving. Exhibits include uniforms, medals, weaponry, old artillery, fascist propaganda posters, and a 30-minute propagandistic video in Italian that also contains a lot of fascinating footage with no narration (runs on a loop in a small theater). The video is a "Luce" production (meaning a Mussolini production) and features great scenes of the town in the 1930s, including clips of Il Duce's visit and later WWII bombardments.

The war and propaganda posters in the last room are haunting. An old woman (what we would call a "gold star" mother) wears the medal of a son lost in battle and pleads to those who question the fascist-driven war effort: "Don't betray my son." Another (with a Nazi soldier offering a handshake) declares, "The Germans are truly our friends." And yet another asks, "And you...what are *you* doing?"

▲University of Padua

The main building of this prestigious university, known as Palazzo Bò, is adjacent to Caffè Pedrocchi. Founded in 1222, it's one of the first, greatest, and most progressive universities in Europe. Back when the Church controlled university curricula, a group of professors and students broke free from the University of Bologna to create this liberal school, which would be independent of Catholic constraints and accessible to people of other faiths.

A haven for free thought, the university attracted intellectuals from all over Europe, including the great astronomer Copernicus, who realized here that the universe didn't revolve around him. And Galileo—notorious for disagreeing with the Church's views on science—called his 18 years on the faculty here the best of his life.

Anyone can stroll through its two courtyards for free. And tours are given in English several times a day for a deeper look that includes the famed Anatomy Theater.

Cost and Hours: Grounds—free, closed Sun; University and Anatomy Theater tour—€5 (English tours Mon-Sat generally at 10:30, 12:30, 14:30, and 16:30, fewer tours in winter, no tours on Sun, maximum 40 people per tour); Via VIII Febbraio 7 (Ponti Romani tram stop), tel. 049-827-3939, www.unipd.it/en/guidedtours. Confirm tour times and availability on website or by phone, or stop by the ticket desk (in passage between two courtyards).

Visiting the Courtyards on Your Own: You can poke into two of the university's courtyards (or peer through the gate on Sunday when it's closed). Find the entrance on Via VIII Febbraio under the "Gymnasium" inscription (30 yards from Caffè Pedrocchi, facing City Hall). You'll pop into a 16th-century courtyard, the school's historic core.

It's littered with the coats of arms of important faculty and leaders of the university over the ages. Classrooms, which open onto the square, are still used. Today, students gather here, surrounded by memories of illustrious alumni, including the first woman in the world to receive a university degree (in 1678).

A passageway leads from here to an adjacent second courtyard, dating from the fascist era (c. 1938). The relief celebrates heroic students in World War I. Off this courtyard, notice the richly decorated stairway, frescoed fascist-style in the 1930s with themes celebrating art, science, and the pursuit of knowledge.

The tiny Da Mario Bar, just under the WWI mural in the second courtyard, is fun for its photos of the crazy rituals of university life (run by 80-year-old Mario, famed for his strong *spritzes*, open Mon-Fri only).

University and Anatomy Theater Tour: Students give 45-minute tours of the university that include a look at Europe's first great Anatomy Theater (from 1595). Despite the Church's strict ban on autopsies, more than 300 students would pack this theater to watch professors dissect human cadavers (the bodies of criminals from another town). This had to be done in a "don't ask, don't tell" kind of way, because the Roman Catholic Church only started allowing the teaching of anatomy through dissection in the late 1800s.

▲Baptistery

Located next to Padua's skippable Duomo, this richly frescoed little building was once the private chapel of Padua's ruling family, the Carraresi. In the 1370s, they hired Florentine artist Giusto de' Menabuoi to do a little interior redecoration. Later, in 1405, Venice conquered Padua and deposed the Carraresi; the building was turned into a baptistery, but the decorations survived.

Cost and Hours: €3, daily 10:00-18:00, on Piazza Duomo.

Visiting the Baptistery: The Baptistery's frescoes, like those in St. Mark's Basilica in Venice, show Byzantine influence. Almighty Christ, the Pantocrator, is in majesty on top, while approachable Mary and the multitude of saints provide the devout with access to God. Find the world as it was known in the 14th century (the disk below Mary's feet). It kicks off a cycle of scenes illustrating Creation (clockwise from the creation of Adam). The four evangelists (Matthew, Mark, Luke, and John) with their books and symbols fill the corners. A vivid Crucifixion scene faces a gorgeous An-

Graduation Antics in Padua

With 60,000 students, Padua's university always seems to be hosting graduation ceremonies. There's a constant trickle of happy grads and their friends and families celebrating the big event.

During the school year, every 20 minutes or so, a student steps into a formal room (upstairs, above the university court-yard) to officially meet with the leading professors of his or her faculty. When they're finished, the students are given a green laurel wreath. They pose for ceremonial group photos and family snapshots. It's a sweet scene. Then, craziness takes over.

The new graduates replace their somber clothing with raunchy outfits, as gangs of friends gather around them on Via VIII Febbraio, the street in front of the university. The roast begins. The gang rolls out a giant butcher-paper poster with a generally obscene carica-ture of the student and a litany of *This Is Your Life* photos and stories. The new grad, subject to various embarrassing pranks, reads the funny statements out loud. The poster is then taped to the university wall for all to see. (Find the plastic panels to the right of the main entry, facing Via VIII Febbraio. Gradua-tion posters are allowed to stay there for 24 hours. The panels are emptied each morning, but by nighttime a new set of post-ers is affixed to the plastic shields.)

During the roast, the friends sing the catchy but obscene local university anthem, reminding their newly esteemed friend not to get too huffy: *Dottore, dottore, dottore del buso del cul. Vaffancul, vaffancul* (loosely translated: "Doctor, doc-tor. You're just a doctor of the a-hole...go f-off, go f-off"). After you've heard this song (with its fanfare and oom-pah-pah catchiness) and have seen all the good-natured fun, you can't stop singing it.

The crazy show is usually staged late in the afternoon. Outdoor café tables afford great seats to enjoy the spectacle.

nunciation. And the altar niche features a dim, blue-toned, literal Apocalypse from the book of Revelation.

While the Baptistery was created 70 years after Giotto, it feels older. Because de' Menabuoi was working for a private family, he needed to be politically correct and not threaten or offend the fam-ily's allies—especially the Church. While still mind-blowing, the Baptistery's art seems relatively conservative compared to Giotto's

Scrovegni Chapel. Giotto, supported by the powerful Scrovegni family and the Franciscans, could get away with being more progressive and bold.

▲▲▲SCROVEGNI CHAPEL AND CIVIC MUSEUMS

Wallpapered with Giotto's beautifully preserved cycle of nearly 40 frescoes, the glorious Scrovegni Chapel holds scenes depicting the lives of Jesus and Mary. You must make reservations in advance to see the chapel. To protect the paintings from excess humidity, only 25 people are allowed in the chapel at a time. Every 20 minutes, a new group is admitted for a 15-minute video presentation in an anteroom, followed by 20 minutes in the chapel.

With a Scrovegni Chapel ticket you can also visit the adjacent Civic Museums (archaeology and paintings).

Cost and Hours: €13, covers the Scrovegni Chapel and Civic Museums. Reserve a timed-entry slot when you buy your ticket—see "Reservations," below. The **chapel** is open daily 9:00-19:00; the **museums** are open Tue-Sun 9:00-19:00, closed Mon. Special evening visits to the chapel are available in peak season (see below).

Information: Tel. 049-201-0020, www.cappelladegliscrovegni.it.

Reservations: Prepaid reservations are required, and your smartest move would be to reserve your ticket well in advance online (or by phone). Select the day you want to visit, then the time. Remember that for just a bit more, you can get the Padova Card that includes the Scrovegni plus other Padua sights and the tram—just make your chapel reservation when you buy the card online.

Unfortunate souls arriving in Padua without a Scrovegni reservation can sometimes buy a same-day ticket, but don't count on it. You could drop by the ticket office to see if anything is available. Or, check at the TI; with a Padova Card purchase they may be able to make same-day reservations no less than three hours (and up to 48 hours) in advance. You might also see local tour guides, who have to book blocks of tickets, trying to unload unneeded tickets. But why waste time hunting around for tickets when you can reserve in advance?

Evening Visit: Special 20-minute evening visits to the chapel only (not the Civic Museums) are available for €8 (April-Oct daily 19:00-22:00). To book this, go to the Scrovegni website and choose "Giotto Under the Stars."

Giotto di Bondone (c. 1267-1337)

Although details of his life are extremely sketchy, we know that the 12-year-old shepherd Giotto was discovered painting pictures of his father's sheep on rock slabs. He grew to become the wealthiest and most famous painter of his day. His achievement is especially remarkable because painters at that time weren't considered anything more than craftsmen—and weren't expected to be innovators.

After making a name for himself by painting frescoes of the life of St. Francis in Assisi, the Florentine tackled the Scrovegni Chapel (c. 1303-1305). At age 35, he was at the height of his powers. His scenes were more realistic and human than anything that had been done for a thousand years. Giotto didn't learn technique by dissecting corpses or studying the mathematics of 3-D perspective; he had innate talent. And his personality shines through in the humanity of his art.

The Scrovegni frescoes break ground by introducing nature—rocks, trees, animals—as a backdrop for religious scenes. Giotto's people, with their voluminous, deeply creased robes, are as sturdy and massive as Greek statues, throwbacks to the Byzantine icon art of the Middle Ages. But these figures exude stage presence. Their gestures are simple but expressive: A head tilted down says dejection, an arm flung out indicates grief, clasped hands indicate hope. Giotto created his figures not just by drawing outlines and filling them in with single colors; he filled the outlines in with subtle patchworks of lighter and darker shades, and in doing so pioneered modern modeling techniques. Giotto's storytelling style is straightforward, and anyone with knowledge of the episodes of Jesus' life can read the chapel like a comic book.

The Scrovegni represents a turning point in European art and culture—away from scenes of heaven and toward a more down-to-earth, human-centered view.

Helpful Hint: If you packed binoculars, bring them along for a better—and more comfortable—view of the uppermost frescoes.

Getting There: From either the town center or the train station, it's a 10-minute walk, or a quick tram ride to the Eremitani stop.

Getting In: To reach the chapel, enter through the Eremitani building, where you'll find the Civic Museums, ticket office, and the free and mandatory bag check. Though you're instructed to pick up your tickets at the ticket office one hour before your visit,

in practice, 30 minutes is enough
to weather any commotion at the
desk. Present your confirmation
number at the ticket desk, verify
your time, pick up your ticket,
and check any bags or purses.

While waiting for your
reserved time, blitz the Pinacoteca and Multimedia Room
(described later). Read the chapel description below before you
enter, since you'll only have a short time in the chapel itself.

From the ticket office, follow the signs, go outside, and walk
100 yards down the path, passing some ruins of Roman Padua. Be
at the chapel doors at least five minutes before your scheduled visit.
The doors are automatic, and if you're even a minute late, you'll
forfeit your visit with no recourse.

At your appointed time, you first enter an anteroom to watch
an instructive 15-minute video (with English subtitles) and to establish humidity levels before continuing into the chapel. Although
you have only a short visit inside the chapel, it is divine. You're
inside a Giotto time capsule, looking back at an artist ahead of his
time.

Scrovegni Chapel (Cappella degli Scrovegni)

Painted by Giotto and his assistants from 1303 to 1305 and considered by many to be the first piece of modern art, this work
makes it clear: Europe was breaking out of the Middle Ages. A
sign of the Renaissance to come, Giotto placed real people in real
scenes, expressing real human emotions. These frescoes were radical for their 3-D nature, lively colors, light sources, emotion, and
humanism.

The chapel was built out of guilt for white-collar crimes. Reginaldo degli Scrovegni charged sky-high interest rates at a time
when the Church forbade the practice. He even caught the attention of Dante, who placed him in one of the levels of hell in his
Inferno. When Reginaldo died, the Church denied him a Christian
burial. His son Enrico tried to buy forgiveness for his father's sins
by building this superb chapel. After seeing Giotto's frescoes for
the Franciscan monks of St. Anthony, Enrico knew he'd found the
right artist to decorate the interior (and, he hoped, to save his father's soul). The Scrovegni residence once stood next to the chapel,
but it was torn down in 1824.

Giotto's Frescoes: Giotto painted the entire chapel in 200
working days over two years, but you'll get only 15 minutes to see it.

As you enter the long, narrow chapel, look straight to the far

Scrovegni Chapel

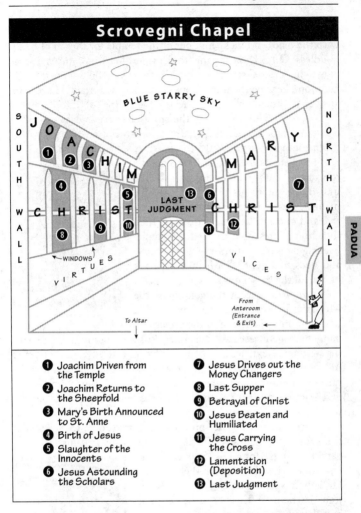

BLUE STARRY SKY

S O U T H   W A L L

N O R T H   W A L L

J O A C H I M

M A R Y

C H R I S T

C H R I S T

1 **2** **3**

4

5

8 **9** **10**

13 **6**

11 **12**

7

LAST JUDGMENT

← WINDOWS →

VIRTUES

VICES

From Anteroom (Entrance & Exit) ←

To Altar ↓

1 Joachim Driven from the Temple

2 Joachim Returns to the Sheepfold

3 Mary's Birth Announced to St. Anne

4 Birth of Jesus

5 Slaughter of the Innocents

6 Jesus Astounding the Scholars

7 Jesus Drives out the Money Changers

8 Last Supper

9 Betrayal of Christ

10 Jesus Beaten and Humiliated

11 Jesus Carrying the Cross

12 Lamentation (Deposition)

13 Last Judgment

end—the rear wall is covered with Giotto's big *Last Judgment*. Christ in a bubble is flanked by crowds of saints and by scenes of heaven and hell. This is the final, climactic scene of the story told in the chapel's 38 panels—the three-generation history of Jesus, his mother Mary, and Mary's parents.

The story begins with Jesus' grandparents, on the long south wall (with the windows) in the upper-left corner. **1** In the first frame, a priest scolds the man who will be Mary's father (Joachim, with the halo) and kicks him out of the temple for the sin of being childless. ❷ In the next panel to the right, Joachim returns dejectedly to his sheep farm. ❸ Meanwhile (next panel), his wife is in the bedroom, hearing the miraculous news that their prayers have been answered—she'll give birth to Mary, the mother of Jesus.

From this humble start, the story of Mary and Jesus spirals clockwise around the chapel, from top to bottom. The top row (both south and north walls) covers Mary's birth and life.

Jesus enters the picture in the middle row of the south (windowed) wall. ❹ The first frame shows his birth in a shedlike manger. In the next frame, the Magi arrive and kneel to kiss his little toes. Then the child is presented in the tiny temple. Fearing danger, the family gets on a horse and flees to Egypt. ❺ Meanwhile, back home, all the baby boys are slaughtered in an attempt to prevent the coming of the Messiah (*Slaughter of the Innocents*).

Spinning clockwise to the opposite (north) wall, you see (in a badly damaged fresco) ❻ the child Jesus astounding scholars with his wisdom. Next, Jesus is baptized by John the Baptist. His first miracle, at a wedding, is turning jars of water into wine. Next, he raises a mummy-like Lazarus from the dead. Riding a donkey, he enters Jerusalem triumphantly. ❼ In the temple, he drives out the wicked money changers.

Turning again to the south wall (bottom row), we see scenes from Jesus' final days. ❽ In the first frame, he and his followers gather at a table for a Last Supper. Next, Jesus kneels humbly to wash their feet. ❾ He is betrayed with a kiss and arrested. Jesus is tried. ❿ Then he is beaten and humiliated.

⓫ Finally (north wall, bottom row), he is forced to carry his own cross, crucified, and prepared for burial, while his followers mourn (⓬ *Lamentation*). Then he is resurrected and ascends to heaven, leaving his disciples to carry on.

⓭ The whole story concludes on the rear wall, where Jesus reigns at the Last Judgment. The long south wall (ground level) features the Virtues that lead to heaven, while the north wall has the (always more interesting) Vices. And all this unfolds beneath the blue, starry sky overhead on the ceiling.

Some panels deserve a closer look:

Joachim Returns to the Sheepfold (south wall, upper left, second panel): Though difficult to appreciate from ground level, this oft-reproduced scene is groundbreaking. Giotto—a former shepherd himself—uses nature as a stage, setting the scene in front of a backdrop of real-life mountains and adding down-home details like Joachim's jumping dog, frozen in midair.

Betrayal of Christ, a.k.a. *Il Bacio,* "The Kiss" (south wall, bottom row, center panel): Amid the crowded chaos of Jesus' arrest, Giotto skillfully creates a focus upon the central action, where Judas ensnares Jesus in his yellow robe (the color symbolizing envy), establishes meaningful eye contact, and kisses him.

Lamentation, a.k.a. *Deposition* (north wall, bottom row, middle): Jesus has been crucified, and his followers weep and wail over the lifeless body. John the Evangelist spreads his arms wide and shrieks, his cries echoed by anguished angels above. Each face is a study in grief. Giotto emphasizes these saints' human vulnerability.

Last Judgment (big west wall): Christ in the center is a glorious vision, but the real action is in hell (lower right). Satan is

a Minotaur-headed ogre munching on sinners. Around him, demons give sinners their just desserts in a scene right out of Dante... who was Giotto's friend and fellow Florentine. Front and center is Enrico Scrovegni, in a violet robe (the color symbolizing penitence), donating the chapel to the Church in exchange for forgiveness of his father's sins.

Before the guard scoots you out, take a look at the actual altar. Though Enrico's father's tomb is lost, Enrico Scrovegni himself is in the tomb at the altar. The three statues are by Giovanni Pisano—Mary (in the center) supports Baby Jesus on her hip with a perfectly natural, maternal S-shape. She's flanked by anonymous deacons.

Nearby: Between the museum and the chapel are the scant remains of **Roman Padua.** The remnants are from the wall of an arena (with a reconstructed grand entry gate) and include nicely fitting pipes that once channeled water so that the arena could be flooded for special spectacles.

Civic Museums (Musei Civici agli Eremitani)
The Eremitani, the building that functions as the entry for the adjacent Scrovegni Chapel, was once an Augustinian hermit's monastery and now houses the Civic Museums: archaeology on the ground floor and paintings upstairs in the Pinacoteca (all included with your Scrovegni Chapel ticket).

Archaeology Museum: Filling the ground floor around the

monastery's cloister courtyard is an impressive collection of ancient statues and artifacts—Egyptian, Venetian, and Roman. Sadly, there are no English descriptions.

Pinacoteca: The entire upper floor of the monastery, also facing the cloister, is the Pinacoteca (picture gallery). The collection has 13th- to 18th-century paintings by Titian, Tintoretto, Giorgione, Tiepolo, Veronese, Bellini, Canova, and other Veneto artists.

Start your visit by going directly to its highlight: the **Giotto crucifix.** Climb to the top of the stairs, take a few steps to the right through the cloister's gallery, and into a room featuring a precious crucifix. Ask for *"La Croce di Giotto?"* (lah KROH-cheh dee JOH-toh?)

The remarkable crucifix, painted by Giotto on wood, originally hung in the Scrovegni Chapel between the Scrovegni family's private zone and the public's worshipping zone. If you kneel on the floor and look up, the body really pops. The adjacent "God as Jesus" *(L'Eterno)* was the only painting in the otherwise frescoed chapel. (The original hangs here for conservation purposes; its copy is the only nonoriginal art in the chapel.) Studying these two masterpieces affirms Giotto's greatness.

Behind the crucifix room is a collection of 14th- and 15th-century art. While the works here are exquisite—and came well after Giotto—they're clearly done by artists without the genius of Giotto.

Rest of the Civic Museums: The **Multimedia Room** in the basement (take stairs down from the cloister) is a children's exhibit giving more meaning to the Scrovegni Chapel frescoes with a 15-minute video in a small theater (pick up headphones for English), and fun computer teaching programs. Across the busy street is the **Palazzo Zuckermann,** with a commotion of applied and decorative arts (clothing, furniture, and ceramics) from the Venetian Republic (1600s and 1700s) and a collection of 19th-century coins and local Impressionist paintings.

▲▲▲BASILICA OF ST. ANTHONY

Friar Anthony of Padua, "Christ's perfect follower and a tireless preacher of the Gospel," is buried here. Construction of this impressive Romanesque/Gothic church (with its Byzantine-style domes) started immediately after St. Anthony's death in 1231. As a mark of his universal appeal and importance

St. Anthony of Padua (1195-1231)

One of Christendom's most popular saints, Anthony is known as a powerful speaker, a miracle worker, and the finder of lost articles.

Born in Lisbon to a rich, well-educated family, his life changed at 25, when he saw the mutilated bodies of some Franciscan martyrs. Their sacrifice inspired him to join the poor Franciscans and dedicate his life to Christ. He moved to Italy and lived in a cave, studying, meditating, and barely speaking to anyone.

One day, he joined his fellow monks for a service. The appointed speaker failed to show up, so Anthony was asked to say a few off-the-cuff words to the crowd. He started slowly, but, filled with the Spirit, he became more confident and amazed the audience with his eloquence. Up in Assisi, St. Francis heard about Anthony and sent him on a whirlwind speaking tour.

Anthony had a strong voice, knew several languages, had an encyclopedic knowledge of theology, and could speak spontaneously as the Spirit moved him. It's said that he even stood on the shores of the Adriatic Sea in Rimini and enticed a school of fish to listen. Anthony also was known as a prolific miracle worker.

In 1230, Anthony retired to Padua, where he founded a monastery and initiated reforms for the poor. An illness cut his life short at 36. Anthony said, "Happy is the man whose words issue from the Spirit and not from himself!"

PADUA

in the medieval Church, he was sainted within a year of his death. Speedy. And for nearly 800 years, his remains and this glorious church have attracted pilgrims to Padua.

Cost and Hours: The **basilica** is free and open daily 6:20-19:45 (Nov-March Mon-Fri closes at 18:45). The **Chapel of the Reliquaries** is also free and keeps the basilica's hours but closes for lunch (12:45-14:30). The nearest tram stop is Santo.

Information: Tel. 049-822-5652, www.santantonio.org.

Other Basilica Sights: A €7 combo-ticket gets you into the basilica's museum, Oratory of St. George, and Scuola del Santo. These sights are generally open daily 9:00-13:00 & 14:00-18:00. Tickets are sold at the info desk at the cloisters (just to the right of the church entry) and include an excellent audioguide that covers the basilica and all related sights (you must provide your own earbuds).

Dress Code: A modest dress code is enforced.

Church Services: The church hosts six separate Masses each morning (the last at 11:00), as well as at 17:00 and 18:00 in sum-

Basilica of St. Anthony

- **1** View of Basilica
- **2** St. Anthony's Tomb
- **3** Original Chapel
- **4** Chapel of the Reliquaries
- **5** Cloisters
- **6** Oratory of St. George & Scuola del Santo

mer and on Sunday year-round, plus additional Sunday services at 12:15, 16:00, and 19:00.

Self-Guided Tour

Stand outside to view the basilica's red-brick facade. St. Anthony looks down and blesses all. He holds a book, a symbol of all the knowledge he had accumulated as a quiet monk before starting his preaching career.

A golden angel—the weathervane atop the spire—points her trumpet into the wind. (While you can never really be sure with angels, locals say they know it's a woman because she always tells the truth.)

Guarding the church is Donatello's life-size equestrian statue of the Venetian mercenary general, Gattamelata. Though it looks like a thousand other man-on-a-horse statues, it was a landmark in Italy's budding Renaissance—the first life-size, secular, equestrian statue cast from bronze in a thousand years.

The church is technically outside Italy. When you pass the banisters that mark its property line, you're passing into Vatican territory.

• *Enter the basilica and grab a pew in the center of the nave. Let your eyes adjust.*

Sit and appreciate the space. Gaze past the crowds and through the incense haze to Donatello's glorious crucifix rising from the altar, and realize that this is one of the most important pilgrimage sites in Christendom. Along with the crucifix, Donatello's bronze statues—Mary with Padua's six favorite saints—grace the high altar. Late in his career, the great Florentine sculptor spent more than a decade in Padua (1444-1455), creating the altar and Gattamelata.

• *Head to the left side of the nave to find the gleaming marble masterpiece that is the focus of the visiting pilgrims—the tomb of St. Anthony.*

St. Anthony's Tomb: Pilgrims file slowly through this side chapel around the tomb, so focused on the saint that they hardly notice the nine fine marble reliefs. (While the long queue looks intimidating, these folks are just waiting their turn to touch the tomb; you can easily skirt around the side of this group for a closer look at each panel.) These Renaissance masterpieces were carved during the 16th century and show scenes and miracles from the life of the saint. As you enjoy each scene, notice the Renaissance mastery of realism and 3-D perspective and the intricate frames, which celebrate life with a burst of exuberance. Note also the vivid faces with their powerful emotions.

The **first relief** depicts St. Anthony receiving the Franciscan tunic. The architectural setting (such as the perspective of the arches on the left and the open door) illustrates the new ability to show depth by using mathematics. The cityscape above is Padua in about 1500.

In the **second relief,** a jealous husband has angrily stabbed his wife. Notice the musculature, the emotion, and the determination in the faces of loved ones. Above, in the clouds, Anthony intercedes with God to bring the woman back to life.

The **third panel** shows Anthony bringing a young man back to life. Above is the Palazzo della Ragione looking as it still does today.

The **fourth scene,** by the famous Florentine sculptor Jacopo Sansovino, shows three generations: a dead girl, her distraught mom, and a grandmother who's seen it all. A boy on the right realistically leans on his stick. Of course, Anthony will eventually change the mood, but right now it's pretty dire. Above is a relief of this basilica.

In the **fifth relief,** a fisherman holds a net, sadly having retrieved a drowned boy. The mother looks at Anthony, who blesses and revives the boy. Across from here is the saint's actual tomb. Under thoughtful lighting, it reads *Corpus S. Antonii.* Prayer letters are dropped behind the iron grill.

The **sixth relief** shows "the miracle of the miser's heart." Anthony's helper dips his hand into a moneylender's side to demonstrate the absence of his heart. At his foot, the square tray with coins and a heart illustrates the scriptural verse "for where your treasure is, there your heart will be also."

For the **seventh relief,** Anthony holds the foot of a young man who confessed to kicking his mother. Taking a lesson from the saint about respecting your mother a little too literally, the man had cut off his own foot. The hysterical mother implores Anthony's help, and the saint's prayers to God enabled him to reattach the foot.

Stand in the corner for a moment, observing the passionate devotion that pilgrims and Paduans alike have for Anthony. Touching his tomb or kneeling in prayer, the faithful believe Anthony is their protector—a confidant and intercessor for the poor. And they believe he works miracles. Believers leave offerings, votives, and written prayers to ask for help or to give thanks for miracles they believe Anthony has performed. By putting their hands on his tomb while saying silent prayers, pilgrims show devotion to Anthony and feel the saint's presence.

Popular Anthony is the patron saint of dozens of things: travelers, amputees, donkeys, pregnant women, infertile women, and flight attendants. Most pilgrims ask for his help in his role as the "finder of things"—from lost car keys to a life companion. You'll see dozens of photos posted on his tomb in prayer or as thanks, including many of fervently wished-for newborns.

The **eighth scene** makes the point that—unlike St. Francis, who was a rowdy youth—Anthony was holy even as a toddler. He tosses the glass (representing his faith), which, rather than shattering, breaks the marble floor.

In the **ninth relief,** a jealous husband (the bearded man behind Anthony) accuses his wife of cheating. The wife asks Anthony to identify her baby's father. Anthony asks the child, who speaks and says that the husband is his real dad and his mother was not messing around. Everyone is relieved—whew!

Before leaving, pause to appreciate how the entire chapel is an integrated artistic wonder.

• *Leave the chapel (between scenes eight and nine) and step into the oldest part of the church. This is the...*

Original Chapel: This is where Anthony was first buried in 1231. To the left of the altar, note the fine (and impressively realistic for the 1380s) view of medieval Padua, with this church outside the wall (finished by 1300 and looking like it does today). Below the cityscape, in a circa-1380 fresco, Anthony on his cloud promises he'll watch over Padua.

As you exit this chapel, you'll notice many tombs nearby. People wanted to be buried near a saint. If you could afford it, this was about the best piece of real estate a dead person could want. (The practice was ended with Napoleonic reforms in 1806.)

• *Continue your circuit of the church by going behind the altar into the apse, to the Chapel of the Reliquaries. Just before that is the Polish chapel with its ornate bronze gate and a painting of St. John Paul II (canonized in 2014). At busy times, you may have to line up and trudge slowly up the stairs past the reliquaries.*

Chapel of the Reliquaries: The most prized relic is in the glass case at center stage—Anthony's tongue. When Anthony's remains were exhumed 32 years after his death (in 1263), his body had decayed to dust, but his tongue was found miraculously unspoiled and red in color. How appropriate for the great preacher who, full of the Spirit, couldn't stop talking about God.

Entering the chapel, join the parade of pilgrims working their way clockwise around the chapel and up the stairs. First, on the left, look for the red, triangular vestment in which Anthony's body was wrapped. Next is his rough-hewn wood coffin. Then, up the stairs, is his pillow—a comfy rock (chest level in first glass case). The center display case contains (top to bottom) the saint's lower jaw with all his teeth impressively intact (*il mento,* located about 8 feet high), his uncorrupted tongue (*lingua,* at about eye level), and, finally, his vocal chords (*apparato vocale,* at about waist level) discovered intact when his remains were examined in 1981. In the last display case, a fragment of the True Cross *(la croce)* is held in a precious cross-shaped reliquary. Finally, descend the stairs and pass St. Anthony's holy, and holey, tunic *(tonaca)* in the center of the room. Pilgrims stop at a desk to pick up a small card with a tiny piece of blessed cloth that touched Anthony's tongue.

Above the relics, decorating the cornice, is the *Glorification of St. Anthony.* In this Baroque fantasy—made in 1691 of carved marble and stucco—a cloud of angels and giddy *putti* tumble to the left and right in jubilation as they play their Baroque-era musical instruments to celebrate Anthony's arrival in heaven.

• *Leaving this relic chapel, continue circling the apse. You'll come to the* **Chapel of Benediction.** *Here, under a powerful modern fresco of the*

Crucifixion (by Pietro Annigoni, painted in 1982), a priest is waiting to bless anyone who wishes to be blessed.

Next, past the sacristy (where you can peek in at priests preparing for Mass), is a door leading to the cloisters. But before heading out, walk just beyond this passage to the...

Chapel of St. James: Exactly opposite the tomb of St. Anthony, this chapel features an exquisite 14th-century fresco by Altichiero da Zevio. Study the vivid commotion around the Crucifixion, clearly inspired by Giotto (this was created 70 years after the Scrovegni Chapel). The faces are real—right off the streets of 14th-century Padua. From this chapel, look across the nave and appreciate how Anthony's massive tomb is so beautifully integrated into the church architecturally.

• *Next, exit out into the cloisters. From the right side of the nave as you face the altar, follow signs to* chiostro.

Cloisters: Of the four cloisters at the basilica, you can wander in three. The main cloister is dominated by an exceptionally bushy

magnolia tree, planted in 1810 (the magnolia was exotic for Europe when it was imported from America in 1760). Also in the cloister are the graves of the most illustrious Paduans, such as Gabriel Fallopius, the scientist who gave his name to his discovery, the Fallopian tube. When Napoleon decreed that graves should be moved out of cities, this once grave-covered courtyard was cleared of tombstones. But the bodies were left in the ground, perhaps contributing to the magnolia tree's fecundity. Today the tree remains an explosion of life.

In another cloister, the **multimedia exhibit** tells about the life of St. Anthony and the Franciscan mission in a slow, thoughtful, and evangelical way (free, 20 minutes, entry every 10 minutes). You move two times as you use headphones to listen to the story of each tableau.

At the far end of the cloister, a small **museum** (shares combo-ticket with the oratory and scuola) is filled with votives and folk art recounting miracles attributed to Anthony. The abbreviation *PGR* that you'll see on many votives stands for *per grazia ricevuta*—for answered prayers.

Other Basilica Sights: There are two other sights, covered by the same combo-ticket as the museum. The small but sumptuous **Oratory of St. George** faces the little square in front of the basilica. The oratory ("ora" means prayer) is not actually a church, though it's certainly a fine place to pray—it's filled with vivid, circa-1370 frescoes showing scenes not of Anthony but from the life of St. George, St. Lucia, and St. Catherine. Because many lovers credit St. Anthony with finding them their partners—and this is the closest place to St. Anthony where you can be married—it's popular for weddings.

Next door and upstairs is the skippable **Scuola del Santo** (a.k.a. La Scoletta), the former meeting hall of the Confraternity of Anthony. It has frescoes and paintings by various artists—including some by Titian.

NEAR THE BASILICA
Prato della Valle

The square is 150 yards southwest of the basilica (down Via Beato Luca Belludi). Once a Roman theater and later Anthony's preach-

ing grounds, this square claims to be the largest in Italy. It's a pleasant, 400-yard-long, oval-shaped piazza with fountains, walkways, dozens of statues of Padua's eminent citizens, and grass. It's also a lively **market** scene (though smaller than those previously listed): fruit and vegetables (Mon-Fri 8:00-13:00), clothing, shoes, and household goods (Sat 8:00-19:00), and antiques (third Sun 8:00-19:00). This place is often busy with special events and festivals. Ask at the TI or your hotel if anything's going on at Prato della Valle.

▲Botanic Garden (Orto Botanico)

Green thumbs, science fans, and anyone who wants a break from art or religious sights can appreciate this historic botanical garden, which contains the university's vast collection of rare plants. Founded in 1545 for the cultivation and study of medicinal plants, it's the world's oldest existing academic botanical garden. Because of the Venetian Republic's vast reach through trade and commerce, and the university's renown, exotic plants from all over the world made their way to Padua. It's believed that the first potato, sesame, lilac, and sunflower in Europe were planted in this city.

Cost and Hours: €10; daily 9:00-19:00, closes earlier off-season, last entry one hour before closing; the garden's free app is best suited to plant and science buffs; entrance 150 yards south of Basilica of St. Anthony—with your back to the facade, take a hard left; Santo tram stop, tel. 049-201-0222, www.ortobotanicopd.it.

Visiting the Garden: The botanical garden's original 16th-century square-within-a-circle configuration remains intact. Inside its circular wall, the garden is filled with elegant, geometrical plant beds. Wandering the paths, visitors can also admire a 340-year-old Oriental plane tree, a Southern magnolia that's only 10 years younger than the United States, and the garden's oldest specimen—a St. Peter's dwarf palm that was planted in 1585, and inspired Goethe to write his essay on the "Metamorphosis of Plants."

From the south end of the enclosed garden, find the path over a footbridge that leads to the striking and enormous **Biodiversity Garden.** The five greenhouse biomes take you on a journey through the world's major climate zones. Panels provide superb English descriptions of the environments and offer insight into how plant life has influenced the development of humankind—and vice versa.

Sleeping in Padua

Rooms in Padua's hotels are more spacious and a better value than those in Venice. I've listed a couple of hotels in the center and a group of accommodations near the basilica. All are reachable from the station by tram; only Albergo Verdi is more than a five-minute walk from the nearest tram stop.

IN THE CENTER

$$$ Hotel Majestic Toscanelli, an old-fashioned, ornate, family-run hotel with 34 rooms, owns a perfectly convenient location right in the town center—buried in the characteristic ghetto with wonderful cobbled ambience. At night, this area is popular with noisy students; request a quiet room on the back side (RS%, spacious attic "loft" rooms with kitchenettes and low beams, air-con, elevator, pay parking, Via dell'Arco 2, Tito Livio tram stop, tel. 049-663-244, www.toscanelli.com, majestic@toscanelli.com, Mario Morosi and family). From the tram stop, follow the passageway next to #26, then jog left down Via Marsala and turn right on Via dell'Arco.

$$ Albergo Verdi, an outdated Ikea-esque little place, is crammed into an old building on a small back street beyond Piazza dei Signori. While public spaces are tight, the 14 rooms are sufficient (air-con, tiny elevator, Via Dondi dall'Orologio 7, Ponti Romani tram stop, tel. 049-836-4163, www.albergoverdipadova. it, info@albergoverdipadova.it). From Piazza dei Signori, walk through the arch under the clock tower and go to the far end of Piazza del Capitaniato; the hotel is on the side street to your right.

NEAR THE BASILICA OF ST. ANTHONY

Santo is the nearest tram stop for the following hotels.

$$$ Hotel Belludi 37 is a slick, stylish place renting 16 chic rooms in an old building. The decor is dark, woody, and crisp. Owners Andrea and Mauro are friendly and attentive, as is their staff (RS%, some rooms with basilica view, air-con, lots of stairs with no elevator, apartments available nearby, a block from the Santo tram stop at Via Beato Luca Belludi 37, tel. 049-665-633, www.collezionebelludi.it, info@belludi37.it).

$$ Hotel Al Fagiano feels like an art gallery with crazy, sexy, modern art everywhere. The hotel is all about the union of a man and a woman (quite romantic). They rent 37 bright and cheery rooms, each uniquely decorated with Rossella Fagiano's creations (RS%, air-con, elevator, pay parking, 50 yards from the Santo tram stop at Via Antonio Locatelli 45, tel. 049-875-0073, www. alfagiano.com, info@alfagiano.com; Anita, Rossella, and Amato).

$ Hotel Al Santo, run with charm by Valentina and Antonio, offers 15 spacious rooms with essential comforts on two floors above their restaurant, a few steps from the basilica. Given the warm welcome and pleasant location, it's a fine value (family rooms, double-paned windows, quieter rooms off street, some rooms with basilica views, air-con, elevator, pay parking, Via del Santo 147, tel. 049-875-2131, www.alsanto.it, alsanto@alsanto.it).

$ Hotel Casa del Pellegrino, with 148 spotless, cheap, bare rooms and straight pricing, is owned by the friars of St. Anthony. It's home to the pilgrims who come to pay homage to the saint in the basilica next door. Any visitor to Padua is welcome, making it popular with professors and students. Some rooms with basilica views also come with more noise—both from the street and, starting at 6:00 in the morning, the church bells—while others are in *dipendenza,* the hotel's modern wing (cheaper rooms with shared bath, family rooms, ask for a room off the street, breakfast extra, air-con, elevator, pay parking, Via Melchiorre Cesarotti 21, tel. 049-823-9711, www.casadelpellegrino.com, info@casadelpellegrino.com).

Eating in Padua

The university population means cheap, good food abounds. My recommended restaurants are all centrally located in the historic core. You'd think there would be fine dining on the charming market squares, but on the piazzas it's a takeout-pizza and casual-bar scene (dominated by students after dark). La Lanterna, at the neighboring Piazza dei Signori, is the best on-square option—but they only offer functional Italian classics. The dreamily atmospheric ghetto neighborhood (just two blocks off the market squares) thrives after dark with trendy bars and a lively student *spritz* scene.

I've listed several serious restaurants (each with a distinct personality), plus a good pizzeria and a good gelateria at each end of town. And, if you want a fun and mobile multi-stop meal of bar

PADUA

food capped with some fine gelato, string together my recommendations under "Cheap Eats and Bars with Tapas in the Center."

DINING NEAR THE CENTER

$$ Osteria L'Anfora is a colorful if chaotic place serving classic dishes in an informal, fun-loving space. Don't be put off by the woody, ruffian decor, the squat toilet, and the fact that it's a popular hangout for a pre-meal drink. They take food seriously and serve it at good prices, and the fun energy and commotion add to the dining experience (meals served Mon-Sat 12:30-15:00 & 19:30-22:30, bar open 9:00-24:00, closed Sun, reservations smart for dinner, Via dei Soncin 13, tel. 049-656-629).

$$ Osteria dal Capo is a tight and jumbled little bistro with chandeliers and white tablecloths serving classic Veneto meat and fish dishes, home-cooking style (closed Sun-Mon, inside only, reserve for dinner, Via degli Obizzi 2, tel. 049-663-105, www.osteriadalcapo.it).

$$$ Enotavola Pino (*enotavola* means "wine table") is, in the front, a dressy, hip wine bar where owner/chef Pino offers scores of wines by the glass—each with a little plate of mortadella. The back is a sleek and youthful fish-only restaurant with a busy, open kitchen and bright, spacious seating. If you like the energy in the wine bar, you can order from the menu there, too (closed Mon like any serious fish restaurant, Via dell'Arco 37, tel. 049-876-2385).

$$$ Enoteca Antonio Ferrari is a top-end wine bar serving near-gourmet-level meat and cheese boards to a smart, young, and local foodie crowd. It's pricey but a good value and feels bright and youthful (daily, Via Umberto 1, tel. 049-666-375).

CHEAP EATS AND BARS WITH TAPAS IN THE CENTER

$$ Pizza on Piazza dei Signori: Though **La Lanterna** has a forgettable interior and a predictable menu of pizzas, pastas, and *secondi*, its prime location provides a rare-in-Padua chance to sit in a grand square under the stars, surrounded by great architecture. Locals know it as the first pizzeria in town (Fri-Wed 12:00-15:00 & 18:00-24:00, closed Thu, Piazza dei Signori 39, tel. 049-660-770, www.lalanternapadova.it).

$ Squid, *Porchetta*, and *Spritz* on Piazza della Frutta: Just a simple sandwich place, **Bar dei Osei** has some of the best outdoor seats in town. While Paduans love their delicate *tramezzini*—white-bread sandwiches with crusts cut off—I'd choose their *porchetta*—savory roasted pork sandwiches. You'll find a two-foot-long mother lode waiting on the counter for you; tell friendly Betty how big a slice you'd like. Wines are listed on the board (Mon-Sat 7:00-21:00, closed Sun, Piazza della Frutta 1, tel. 049-875-9606).

In the evenings, just a few feet away, **La Folperia squid stand** sells mostly boiled and spiced plates of squid by the weight—indicate small (€6) or big (€12) and request bread. Crowd your way up to the bar, and Massimiliano and Barbara will take care of you (Mon-Sat 17:00-20:30, closed Sun). Even with a plate of La Folperia seafood, you're welcome to grab a Bar dei Osei table and order a drink from the roaming server.

$ *Cicchetti* **Bars Popular with Students:** Surrounding Palazzo della Ragione you'll find lots of atmospheric bars jammed with students marked by the glowing orange glasses of *spritz*. These bars also serve little €1 and €2 bites (mostly fried gut bombs and enticing open-face sandwiches). While the tapas aren't advertised, the walls are scribbled with the various wines, vermouths, and cocktails for sale. Two classy holes-in-the-wall are particularly atmospheric (each about a block off the market squares): **Bar Corte Sconta** (across the street from the recommended Hotel Majestic Toscanelli, at Via dell'Arco 9) and **Bar All'Ombra della Piazza** (100 yards off Piazza della Frutta, down the tiny Via Pietro D'Abano at #16).

$ **Pasta and Vegetarian on Piazza della Erbe: Pastasuta** is a minimalist little pasta joint tucked away in the Palazzo della Ragione arcade (Piazza delle Erbe side). Choose your pasta and sauce combo or enjoy prepared options from their little *tavola fredda*. Seating is limited, but all of their dishes can be packed to go. Just say, *"Per portare via, per favore"* (Mon-Sat 8:00-21:00, closed Sun). **Cristina e Massimo,** just a few doors down from Pastasuta, serves seasonal and creative vegetarian dishes, from fancy salads to muffins to tarts (Mon-Sat 7:00-20:00, closed Sun).

Gelato: For your best dessert in the market square area, enjoy a high-end gelato at **Gnam Gnam** (that means "yum yum") on Piazza dei Signori (Via San Clemente 18).

NEAR THE BASILICA OF ST. ANTHONY

$$ **Antica Trattoria dei Paccagnella,** the most serious restaurant near the basilica, serves nicely presented, seasonal local dishes with modern flair and an impressive attention to ingredients. The place has friendly service, modern art on the walls, and no pretense. It's thoughtfully run by two brothers, Raffaele and Cesare (daily 12:00-14:00 & 19:00-22:00 except dinner only on Sun-Mon, Via del Santo 113, tel. 049-875-0549).

$ **Pizzeria Pago Pago** dishes up wood-fired Neapolitan pizzas (a local favorite) and daily specials depending on what's in season. They also have good salads, non-pizza dishes, and beer on tap in a bright and high-energy dining area (Wed-Mon 12:00-14:00 & 19:00-24:00, closed Tue; 2 blocks from basilica, up Via del Santo and right onto Via Galileo Galilei to #59; tel. 049-665-558, Gaetano and Modesto).

$ **Pollodoro la Gastronomica,** my pick of the takeout delis near the basilica, sells roast chicken, pastas, pizza, and veggies. They'll also make sandwiches (Wed-Mon 9:00-14:00 & 17:00-20:00, closed Tue, 100 yards from basilica at Via Belludi 34, tel. 049-663-718).

Gelato: Portogallo Gelateria is considered the best gelateria in town, with amazing and creative flavors (Via Umberto 1, Alberto).

Padua Connections

Unless otherwise specified, the following connections are for Trenitalia.

From Padua by Train to: Venice (Trenitalia: 2/hour, 30 minutes; Italo: hourly, 30 minutes), **Vicenza** (at least 2/hour, fewer on weekends, 15-25 minutes), **Milan** (Trenitalia: 1-2/hour, 2-3 hours; Italo 7/day, 2 hours), **Verona** (2/hour, 40-80 minutes), **Ravenna** (roughly hourly, change in Bologna or Ferrara, 2.5-3.5 hours), **Florence** (4/day direct, 2 hours, require reservations; otherwise 3 hours with connections). When taking the train to Venice, Vicenza, Verona, or Ravenna, buy a ticket on a regional train (R or RV). The Trenitalia Frecce or Italo express trains cost more and get you there only marginally faster (especially when compared to an RV train).

By Bus to: Venice's Marco Polo Airport (65 minutes, €8.50 from ticket windows, €10 on board, hourly at :25 past the hour from 6:25 to 21:25, leaves from platform 11 at Padua's bus station, next to the train station; recheck times at www.fsbusitaliaveneto. it). If flying into the airport, take this bus to get directly to Padua (buy tickets at windows in arrivals hall or at airport TI).

By Minibus to Airports: An Air Service minibus runs from Padua to **Marco Polo Airport** (€35/person) or **Treviso Airport** (€42/person), reservations required, tel. 049-870-4425, www. airserviceshuttle.it).

Vicenza

To many architects, Vicenza (vih-CHEHN-zah) is a pilgrimage site. Entire streets look like the back of a nickel. This is the city of Andrea Palladio (1508-1580), the 16th-century Renaissance architect who defined the Palladian style that is now so influential in countless British country homes. But as grandiose as Vicenza's Palladian facades may feel, there is little marble here because the city lacked the wealth to build with much more than painted wood and plaster.

If you're an architecture buff, Vicenza merits a quick day trip on any day but Monday, when major sights are closed. If you're packing light, it's an easy stop, located on the same train line as Padua, Verona, and Venice. However, because you can't store bags at the train station, it's not worth stopping here if you have lots of luggage (though in a pinch, the TI may be willing to store bags for you while you walk around town).

Tourist Information: The TI is next to the Olympic Theater at Piazza Matteotti 12 (daily 9:00-13:30 & 14:00-17:30, tel. 0444-320-854, www.visitvicenza.org). Ask for the free brochure on Palladio's buildings. Architecture fans appreciate the booklet titled *Vicenza and the Villas of Andrea Palladio.*

Arrival in Vicenza: From the **train station,** I'd head straight for the most distant sight, the Olympic Theater (with a TI next door) and then see other sights on the way back. Go straight out the train station's front door, and use the crosswalk on the right side of the roundabout. From here, it's a five-minute walk straight ahead up wide Viale Roma to the PAM supermarket at the bottom of Corso Palladio; turn right through the gate, and then it's a good 10 minutes more down the Corso to the Olympic Theater (a taxi costs €8). **Drivers** can park in one of the cheap parking lots (Parcheggio Bassano and Parcheggio Cricoli) and catch a free shuttle bus to the center.

Sights in Vicenza

Helpful bilingual signs in front of Palladio's buildings explain their history. Arrows around town point you to his major works.

All the sights mentioned (except the villas outside town) are covered by the **Museum Card** combo-ticket (€15, €18 family pass, good for 3 days, sold at Olympic Theater and Palazzo Leoni Montanari Galleries).

▲▲Olympic Theater (Teatro Olimpico)

Palladio's last work, one of his greatest, shouldn't be missed. This indoor theater is a wood-and-stucco festival of classical columns, statues, and an oh-wow stage bursting with perspective tricks. When you step back outside, take another look at the town's main drag—named after Palladio. It's the same main street you saw on the stage of his theater.

Cost and Hours: €12.50; Tue-Sun 9:00-17:00, closed Mon, very occasionally closed when theater is in use; audioguide available, entrance to left of TI at Piazza Matteotti 11, info tel. 0444-222-800, tickets tel. 044-496-4380, www.teatrolimpicovicenza.it.

▲Church of Santa Corona (Chiesa di Santa Corona)

A block away from the Olympic Theater, this "Church of the Holy Crown" was built in the 13th century to house a thorn from the Crown of Thorns, given to the Bishop of Vicenza by the French King Louis IX. The church has two artistic highlights: Paolo Veronese's *Adoration of the Magi* (1573) and Giovanni Bellini's fine *Baptism of Christ* (c. 1502).

Cost and Hours: Free, Tue-Sun 9:00-12:00 & 15:00-18:00, closed Mon, Contrà Santa Corona 2, tel. 0444-323-644.

Archaeological and Natural History Museum (Museo Naturalistico Archeologico)

Located next door to the Church of Santa Corona, this museum's ground floor features Roman antiquities (mosaics, statues, and artifacts excavated from Rome's Baths of Caracalla, plus swords) and a barbarian warrior skeleton complete with sword and helmet. Prehistoric scraps are upstairs. Look for English description sheets near exhibit entryways throughout.

Cost and Hours: €3.50, Tue-Sun 9:00-17:00, closed

Mon, Contrà Santa Corona 4, tel. 0444-222-815, www.museicivicivicenza.it.

Palazzo Leoni Montanari Galleries
(Gallerie di Palazzo Leoni Montanari)

Across the street from the Church of Santa Corona, this small museum is a palatial riot of Baroque, with cherub-cluttered ceilings jumbled like a preschool in heaven. A quick stroll shows off Venetian paintings and a floor of Russian icons.

Cost and Hours: €8.50, Tue-Sun 10:00-18:00, closed Mon, Contrà Santa Corona 25, tel. 800-578-875, www.palazzomontanari.com.

Piazza dei Signori

Vicenza's main square has been the center of town ever since it was the site of the ancient Roman forum. The commanding **Basilica Palladiana,** with its 270-foot-tall, 13th-century tower, dominates the square. This was once the meeting place for local big shots. It was young Palladio's proposal—to redo Vicenza's dilapidated Gothic palace of justice in the Neo-Greek style—that established him as the city's favorite architect. The rest of Palladio's career was a one-man construction boom. The basilica hosts special exhibitions that sometimes involve a fee, but you can often pop in for a free look.

Villas on the Outskirts of Vicenza

Vicenza is surrounded by dreamy Venetian villas. Venice's commercial empire receded in the 1500s when trade began to pick up along the Atlantic seaboard and dwindle in the Mediterranean. Venice redirected its economic agenda to agribusiness, which led to the construction of lavish country villas, such as **Villa la Rotonda,** the inspiration for Thomas Jefferson's Monticello (www.villalarotonda.it), and **Villa Valmarana ai Nani** (www.villavalmarana.com). Located southeast of the town center, both houses are furnished with period pieces (closed Mon). Pick up the free brochure on Palladio's villas from the TI if you plan to visit.

PADUA

Vicenza Connections

From Vicenza by Train to: Venice (Trenitalia: 2/hour, 45 minutes; Italo: 7/day, 45 minutes), **Padua** (at least 2/hour, fewer on weekends, 15-25 minutes), **Verona** (2/hour, 30 minutes), **Milan** (1-2/hour, 2 hours). You'll save money by taking the slow R or the faster RV trains to Vicenza instead of the speedy Freccia or ES trains.

VERONA

Romeo and Juliet made Verona a household word. Alas, a visit here has nothing to do with those two star-crossed lovers. You can pay to visit the house that falsely claims to be Juliet's (with an almost believable balcony and a courtyard swarming with tour groups), join in the tradition of rubbing the breast of Juliet's statue to help find a lover (or to pick up the sweat of someone who can't), and even make a pilgrimage to what isn't "La Tomba di Giulietta."

Fiction aside, Verona has been an important crossroads for 2,000 years and is, therefore, packed with genuine history. R&J fans will take some solace in the fact that two real feuding families, the Montecchi and the Cappellos, were the models for Shakespeare's Montagues and Capulets. And, if R&J had existed and were alive today, they would still recognize much of their "hometown."

Verona's main attractions are its wealth of Roman ruins; the remnants of its 13th- and 14th-century political and cultural boom brought about by its leading family, the Scaligeri; its 21st-century, pedestrian-only ambience; and its world-class opera festival, held each summer. After Venice's festival of tourism, the Veneto region's second city is a cool and welcome sip of pure Italy, where dumpsters are painted by schoolchildren as class projects and public spaces are primarily the domain of locals, not tourists. If you like Italy but don't need blockbuster sights, this town is a joy.

Orientation to Verona

Verona's old town fills an easy-to-defend bend in the River Adige. The vibrant and enjoyable core of Verona lies along Via Mazzini between Piazza Brà (pronounced "bra") and Piazza Erbe, Verona's market square since Roman times. Each evening the two main streets from Piazza Brà to Piazza Erbe, Via Mazzini and Corso Porta Borsari, are enlivened by a wonderful *passeggiata*...bustling with a slow and elegant parade of strollers. For a good day trip to Verona, take my self-guided walk, beginning with a visit to the Roman Arena.

TOURIST INFORMATION

Verona's helpful TI is just off **Piazza Brà**—from the square, head to the big yellow building with columns and cross the street to Via degli Alpini 9 (Mon-Sat 9:00-19:00, Sun 10:00-18:00, shorter hours off-season, tel. 045-806-8680, www.turismoverona.eu). If you're staying the night, ask the TI about concerts.

Sightseeing Passes: The **Verona Card** covers city transportation and entry to all recommended Verona sights. The card can save day-trippers quite a bit if you're intent on blitzing the city's sights (€20/24 hours, €25/48 hours, sold at TI and at participating sights, www.turismoverona.eu).

The €6 **Church Card,** sold at four churches that require admission (San Zeno, Duomo, Sant'Anastasia, and San Fermo, normally €3 each), pays for itself if you visit two (www.chieseverona.it).

Walking Tours: The TI organizes 90-minute tours in English (€12/person, Sat-Sun at 11:00, none in winter). Tours meet inside the Piazza Brà TI and stroll all the way through the old town (confirm schedule, no reservation necessary).

ARRIVAL IN VERONA

By Train: Verona's main train station is called Verona Porta Nuova. In the main hall, you'll find pay WCs and a baggage-check office (daily 8:00-20:00). Buses and taxis are immediately outside.

Avoid the boring 15-minute walk from the station to the center. Buses are cheap, easy, and leave every few minutes (although taxis are smart after sundown). Buy a ticket from the tobacco shop inside the station (€1.30/90 minutes, €4 day pass valid until midnight), or buy one on board using coin-op machines for €0.70 more. Leaving the station, angle right across the street to the bus stalls: For **Piazza Brà** (near the Roman Arena) and **San Fermo** (near the Ponte Navi bridge), find platform B1 and hop on a bus (#11, #12, #13, #51, and #52 run Mon-Sat until 20:00; #90, #92, and #98 run after 20:00 and all day Sun). For **Porta Borsari** (ancient city main gate), find platform D2 (buses #21, #22, #23, #24, #41, and #61 run Mon-Sat; #93, #94, and #95 run evenings and Sundays). If in doubt, confirm that your bus is headed to the city center by asking, *"Per il centro?"* (pehr eel CHEN-troh). Validate your ticket by stamping it in the machine on the bus.

If getting off at Piazza Brà, you'll see the can't-miss-it Roman

Arena (bus stops in front of big, yellow, Neoclassical building). The TI is near the bus stop, against the medieval wall. You can catch return buses to the station (same numbers) from the stop on the piazza side of the street, or from another bus stop on Piazza Brà, near the WCs.

Taxis pick up only at taxi stands (at Piazza Brà, Piazza Erbe, and the train station) and cost €10-12 for the quick ride between the train station and the center of town (€2 more on Sundays and after 22:00, €1/big bag).

By Car: The old town center (where nearly all my recommended hotels are located) is closed to traffic. Your hotel can get you permission to drive in—ask when you book. Otherwise your license plate will be photographed, and an expensive ticket might be waiting in the mail when you get home.

Drivers will find reasonably priced parking in well-marked lots and garages just outside the center. The underground **Cittadella garage,** at Piazza Cittadella (a block off Piazza Brà, behind the TI), is huge, convenient, and easy to find (€2/hour, €16/24 hours). The **Città di Nimes/Parking Stazione** lot is near the wall, a five-minute walk from the train station (€1.50/hour, €7/day). **Street parking** is limited to two hours and costs €1/hour (spaces marked with blue lines, buy ticket at a tobacco shop or ticket machine, place ticket on dashboard; some hotels can give you a free street-parking permit—ask).

By Plane: Efficient AeroBus shuttles connect Verona's airport (known as Catullo or Verona-Villafranca, 12 miles southwest of the city, airport code: VRN, tel. 045-809-5666, www.aeroportoverona.it) with its train station (€6, valid for 75 minutes on AeroBus and city buses, buy tickets on board or at tobacco shop, 3/hour, 15 minutes).

HELPFUL HINTS

Sightseeing Schedules: Most sights (except churches) are closed on Monday mornings and typically open after lunchtime. The churches are closed Sun morning to sightseers.

Opera: From mid-June through early September, Verona's opera festival brings the city to life, with 15,000 music fans filling the Roman Arena for almost nightly performances (cheap upper-level seats—€25-30, day-of-show tickets often available). The city is packed and festive—restaurants have prescheduled seatings for dinner, and hotels jack up their prices. You can book tickets at the TI or through the official box office (buy online at www.arena.it or call 045-800-5151; during opera season, box office open daily 10:00-17:45, or until 20:30 on performance days; Via Dietro Anfiteatro 6B).

Laundry: The self-service **Oblò** is a short walk from Porta Borsari

VERONA

VERONA

Verona

Accommodations

1. Hotel Antica Porta Leona
2. Hotel Aurora
3. B&B Casa Coloniale
4. To L'Ospite Apartments
5. Protezione della Giovane
6. Hotel Giulietta e Romeo & Hotel Milano
7. Hotel Colomba d'Oro
8. Aparthotel Verona House
9. To Pepita Lodge
10. Albergo Arena

Eateries & Other

11. Cangrande Ristorante & Enoteca
12. Darì Ristorante & Enoteca
13. Trattoria al Pompiere
14. Antico Caffè Dante
15. Bottega del Vino
16. Ristorante Torcolo
17. Osteria Caffè Monte Baldo
18. La Piazzetta
19. Osteria Sottoriva
20. Osteria del Bugiardo
21. Osteria Vini Zampieri
22. Pizzeria da Salvatore
23. Pizzeria Du de Cope
24. Döner Kebab Shop
25. Supermarket (2)
26. Salumeria Caliari & Salumeria Albertini
27. Gelateria Savoia
28. L'Arte del Gelato
29. Launderette

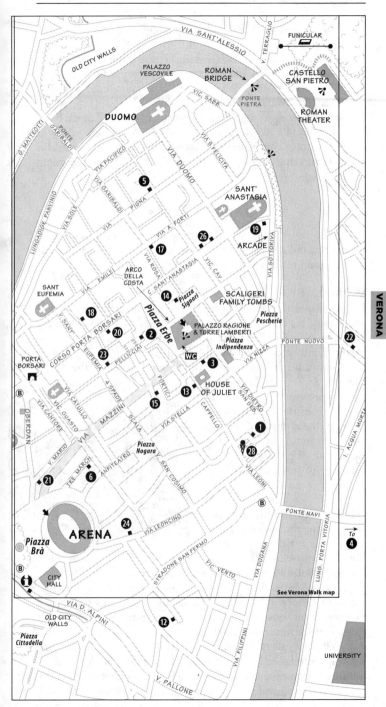

VERONA

in a tranquil neighborhood (daily 8:00-22:30, Via Mario To-deschini 18).

Private Guides: Three enthusiastic Verona guides give private tours of the town and region tailored to specific interests—villas, wine tasting, and so on (€125/2 hours, €265/5 hours). They are **Marina Menegoi** (mobile 328-958-1108, www.marinamenegoi.com, mmenegoi@gmail.com), **Valeria Biasi** (mobile 348-903-4238, www.aguideinverona.com or www.veronatours.com, valeria@aguideinverona.com), and **Franklin Baumgarten** (mobile 347-566-6765, franklin_baumgarten@web.de).

Verona Walk

This walk covers the essential sights in the town core, starting at Piazza Brà and ending at the cathedral. Allow two hours (including the tower climb and some dawdling).

❶ Piazza Brà

If you're wondering about the name, it comes from the local dialect and means "big open space." A generation ago this piazza was noisy with cars. Now it's open and people friendly—it's become the community family room and natural festival grounds.

Grab a bench near the central **fountain** called "The Alps." This was a gift from Verona's sister city Munich, which is just over the mountains to the north. You'll see in the middle of the fountain the symbols of the two cities separated by the Alps, carved out of pink marble from this region. In general, Verona has a bit of an alpine feel; historically it was the place where people rested and prepared before crossing the mountains, and to this day it's the place where the main west-east, Milan-Venice train line meets the north-south line up to Bolzano, the Dolomites, and Austria.

The ancient **arena** looming over the piazza is a reminder that the city's history goes back to Roman times. On this walk, we'll meander across what was the ancient city, from the arena on this side to the theater across the river.

With the fall of Rome in the fifth century, Verona became a favored capital of barbarian kings. In the Middle Ages, noble families had to choose sides in the civil struggles between emperors (Ghibellines) and popes (Guelphs). During this time (1200s),

Verona Walk

1. Piazza Brà
2. Roman Arena
3. Devotional Column
4. Porta Borsari & Corso Porta Borsari
5. Enoteca Oreste
6. Piazza Erbe
7. House of Juliet
8. Piazza dei Signori
9. Tombs of the Scaligeri Family
10. Groceries (2)
11. Church of Sant'Anastasia
12. Ponte Pietra & River View
13. Duomo

200 Meters
200 Yards

VERONA

VERONA

the town bristled with several hundred San Gimignano-type towers, built by different families to symbolize their power. When the Scaligeri family rose to power here in the 14th century, they established stability on their terms and made the other noble families lop off their proud towers—only the Scaligeri were allowed to keep theirs. To add insult to injury, the Scaligeri paved the city's roads with bricks from the other families' toppled towers. But interfamily feuds made it impossible for the Scaligeri to maintain a stable government, and in 1405 the town essentially gave itself to Venice, which ruled Verona until Napoleon stopped by in 1796. During the 19th century, a tug-of-war between France and Austria actually divided the city for a time, with the river marking the border of each country's domain. Eventually Verona, like Venice, fell into Austrian hands. Reminders of Austrian rule remain: The huge, yellow, Neoclassical **city hall** facing Piazza Brà (look for the flags) was built by the Austrians to serve as their 19th-century military headquarters. Their former arsenal stands just across the river, and an Austrian fortress caps the hill looking over the city. But the big **equestrian statue** is of Italy's first king, Victor Emmanuel II, celebrating Italian independence and unity, which was won in the 1860s. The **statue of a modern soldier** striking a *David* pose, with a machine gun instead of a sling over his shoulder, honors Verona's war dead.

Apart from all its history, Piazza Brà is about strolling—the evening *passeggiata* is a kind of national sport in Italy. The broad, shiny sidewalk (named "Liston" after a Venetian promenade; note the fine, Venetian-style marble pavement slabs) was built by 17th-century Venetians, who made it big and wide so that promenading socialites could see and be seen in all their finery.

❷ Roman Arena

The Romans built this stadium outside their town walls, just as modern stadiums are usually located outside downtown districts. With 72 aisles, this elliptical, 466-by-400-foot amphitheater is the third largest in Italy (and it was originally 50 percent taller). Most of the stone you see is original. Dating from the first century AD, it looks great in its pink marble. Over the centuries, crowds of up to 25,000 spectators have cheered Roman gladiator battles, medieval executions, rock concerts, and modern plays, all taking advantage of the arena's famous acoustics. This is also where the popular opera festival is held every summer. Started in 1913, the festival has run continuously ever since, except for brief breaks during both World Wars, when the arena was used as a bomb shelter. While there's little to see inside except the impressive stonework, it's memorable to visit a Roman arena that is still a thriving concert venue. If you climb to the top, you'll enjoy great city views.

The gladiators posing with tourists out front are mostly from Albania and part of a local gang; they're notorious for overcharging for photos. While they're a nuisance, the police say it's better that they're scamming a living here than finding even more disreputable ways to get by.

Cost and Hours: €10, don't bother with the combo-ticket that includes the unimpressive Maffei Museum; Tue-Sun 8:30-19:30, Mon from 13:30, closes earlier—likely around 16:00—during summer opera season, last entry one hour before closing; WC near entry, tel. 045-800-3204.

• *As you exit the arena, look to your right. Where the street splits you'll see the...*

❸ Devotional Column

In the Middle Ages, this column blessed a marketplace held here. Ten yards in front of it, a bronze plaque in the sidewalk shows the Roman city plan—a town of 20,000 placed strategically in the bend of the river, which provided protection on three sides. A wall enclosed the peninsula. The center of the grid was the forum, to-day's Piazza Erbe. (Look down Via Mazzini, the busy main pedestrian drag—the bell tower in the distance marks Piazza Erbe.)

• *After viewing the bronze plaque, turn with your back to the arena and head down Via Oberdan (bearing left at the fork). Continue a couple of blocks (passing a derelict fascist-era theater, the Astra, set back from the street on the left, at #13) until you see an ancient gate to your right.*

❹ Porta Borsari and Corso Porta Borsari

You're standing before the main entrance to Roman Verona; back then, this gate functioned as a tollbooth (*borsari* means purse, referring to the collection of tolls that once took place here). Carved into the rock below the spiral, fluted columns (which parents nickname *"tortiglioni"*—a pasta kids can relate to), is a tribute to the emperor who restored this gate. Outside the adjacent Caffè Rialto, the stone on the curb is from a tomb: In Roman times, the roads outside the walls were lined with tombstones, because burials were not allowed within the town itself. Turn around, look down Corso Cavour, and imagine it in Roman times, leading away from the city gate and lined with tombs. Step into the café. A glass panel in the floor shows the original Roman foundations and pavement stones.

Back outside, cross under the Roman gate and head into the ancient city. Walk down Corso Porta Borsari, the Roman main drag, toward what was the forum. Make it a scavenger hunt. As you walk, discover bits of the town's illustrious past—chips of Roman columns, medieval reliefs, fine old facades, fossils in marble—as well as its elegant present of fancy shops, in a setting that prioritizes pedestrians over cars. On the right, you'll pass the recommended Osteria del Bugiardo, a popular wine bar and a good place to take a break and hang out with Verona's young and trendy.

• *Between Corso Porta Borsari 13 and 15, detour right down Vicolo San Marco in Foro, following the Pozzo dell'Amore sign. Twenty yards ahead on your right, you'll find...*

❺ Enoteca Oreste

This funky wine-and-grappa bar is still run by Oreste (with his Chicagoan wife, Beverly) like a 1970s, old-style *enoteca*. Browse and sample and clown around with Oreste. This historic *enoteca* was once the private chapel of the archbishop of Verona. Traces of the past hide between the bottles—ask Beverly to tell you the story (light food, Vicolo San Marco in Foro 7, tel. 045-803-4369).

• *Return to Corso Porta Borsari and continue one block until you hit a big square.*

❻ Piazza Erbe

This bustling market square is a photographer's delight. Its pastel buildings corral the fountains, pigeons, and people who have congregated here since Roman times, when this was a forum. Notice the Venetian lion hovering above the square atop a column, reminding locals of the conquest of 1405. Wander into the market, to the fountain in the middle. A fountain has bubbled here for 2,000 years. The original Roman statue lost its head and arms.

VERONA

After a sculptor added a new head and arms, the statue became Verona's Madonna. She holds a small banner that reads, roughly, *"The city of Verona deserves respect and justice."* During medieval times, the stone canopy in the center of the square (past the fountain) held the scales where merchants measured the weight of goods they bought and sold, such as silk and wool.

If you were standing here in the Middle Ages, you would have been surrounded by proud noble-family towers. Medieval nobles showed off with towers. Renaissance nobles showed off with finely painted facades on their palaces. Find remnants of the 16th-century days when Verona was nicknamed "the painted city."

Locals like to start their evening with an *aperitivo* here. Each bar caters to a different market segment. Survey the scene and, if or when the time is right, choose the terrace that suits you and join in the ritual. It's simple: Grab a spot, adjust your seat for the best view, and order a *spritz* to drink (€4 with a plate of olives and chips).

• *At the far end of Piazza Erbe is a market column featuring St. Zeno, the patron of Verona, who looks at the crazy crowds flushing into the city's silly claim to touristic fame: the House of Juliet (100 yards down Via Cappello to #23, on the left—just follow the crowds). Side-trip there now (but watch your wallet—it's a pickpocket's haven).*

❼ House of Juliet

The tiny, admittedly romantic courtyard is a spectacle: Tourists from all over the world pose on the balcony, while those hoping for love wait their turn to polish Juliet's bronze breast. Residents marvel that each year, about 1,600 Japanese tour groups break their Venice-Milan ride for an hour-long stop in Verona just to see this courtyard (free, gates open roughly 8:30-19:30 or longer). It's fun to stand in the corner and observe the scene, knowing that all this commotion was started by a clever tour guide in the early 1970s as a way to attract visitors to Verona.

The courtyard walls have long been filled with amorous graffiti. The latest trend is to affix a paper note to the gates or walls with chewing gum. The wall of padlocks is another gimmick, enabling lovers to blow money in an attempt to prove that their hearts are thoroughly locked up. (The shop that sells the locks also sells pens to write on them.) The red mailbox is for love letters to Juliet.

There's actually a Juliet Club that reviews these—and all the letters mailed from around the world to "Juliet, Verona, Italy." Each year, the club awards the author of the sweetest letter a free vacation to Verona.

Even those who milk their living out of this sight freely admit, "While no documentation has been discovered to prove the truth of the legend, no documentation has disproved it either." The "museum," which displays art inspired by the love story, plus costumes and the bed from Franco Zeffirelli's film *Romeo and Juliet,* is certainly not worth the entry fee.

Was there ever a real Juliet Capulet? You just walked down Via Cappello, the street of the cap makers. Above the courtyard entry (looking out) is a coat of arms featuring a hat—representing a family that made hats and which would be named, logically, Capulet.

The public's interest in a fictional Romeo and Juliet—or at least Juliet—is a sign that there's a hunger for a Juliet in our world. Observing the mobs clamoring to polish her breast or blow kisses from her bogus balcony, I try to appreciate what she means to people, and to psychoanalyze what she provides to those who come to Verona specifically for this: the message that love will prevail. In love, you can lose, and still be a winner. Juliet is brave, tragic, honest, outspoken, timeless, and passionate. She's a mover and a shaker, a dreamer and a fighter. In a way, this is a pagan temple where the spirit of Juliet gives people something to believe in...or maybe it's just a bunch of baloney appreciated by a simple-minded crowd.

• *Return to Piazza Erbe. From the middle of the piazza, head right on Via della Costa and into the big square.*

❽ Piazza dei Signori

Literally the "Lords' Square," this is Verona's sitting room, quieter and more harmonious than Piazza Erbe. The buildings—which span five centuries—define the square and are all linked by arches. From one arch dangles a whale's rib. It was likely a souvenir brought home by a traveling merchant from a trip to the Orient, reminding the townspeople that there was a big world out there. The long portico on the left is inspired by a building in Florence: Brunelleschi's Hospital of the Innocents, considered the first Renaissance building.

Locals call the square Piazza Dante for the statue of the Italian poet **Dante Alighieri** that dominates it. Dante—always pensive, never smiling—seems to wonder why the tourists choose Juliet over him. Dante was expelled from Florence when that city sided with the pope (who didn't appreciate Dante's writing) and banished its greatest poet. Verona and its ruling Scaligeri family, however, were at odds with the pope (siding instead with the Holy Roman Emperor), and granted Dante asylum.

With the whale's rib behind you, you're facing the brick, crenellated, 14th-century Scaligeri residence. Behind Dante is the yellowish, 15th-century Venetian Renaissance-style Portico of the Counsel. At Dante's two o'clock is the 12th-century Romanesque Palazzo della Ragione.

Looking back the way you came, follow the white *toilette* signs into the courtyard of the **Palazzo della Ragione.** The impressive stairway is the only surviving Renaissance staircase in Verona. Within the palazzo you can visit the Gallery of Modern Art (skippable) and climb the 13th-century **Torre dei Lamberti** for a grand city view. The elevator saves you 243 steps—but you'll still need to walk up 46 more to get to the tower's first viewing platform (€8 ticket covers tower and Gallery of Modern Art, €4 for just the gallery, no individual tower tickets sold; Mon-Fri 10:00-18:00, Sat-Sun 11:00-19:00; ticket office next to staircase, tel. 045-800-1903, www.palazzodellaragioneverona.it).

• *Exit the courtyard the way you entered and turn right, continuing downhill. Within a block, you'll find the...*

❾ Tombs of the Scaligeri Family

These exotic and veritable Gothic 14th-century tombs, with their fine, original, wrought-iron protective cages, evoke the age when

one family ruled Verona. The Scaligeri were to Verona what the Medici family was to Florence. These were powerful people. They changed the law so that they could be buried within the town. They forbade the building of any noble family's new towers but their own. And, by building tombs atop pillars, they arranged to be looked up to, even in death.

• *Continue 15 yards to the next corner and take the first left on Vicolo Cavalletto. At the first corner, turn right along Corso Sant'Anastasia toward the big, unfinished brick facade of Verona's largest church. For a fragrant and potentially tasty diversion, pop into* ❿ *two classic grocery stores: Salumeria Caliari (at #33, closed Sun afternoon) and Salumeria Albertini (#41).*

⓫ Church of Sant'Anastasia

This church was built from the late 13th century through the 15th century. Although the facade was never finished (the builders ran out of steam), the interior was—and still is—brilliant. Step inside to see the delightful way this region's medieval churches were painted. Note the grimacing hunchbacks holding basins of holy water on their backs (near main entrance at base of columns). And don't miss Pisanello's fresco of *St. George and the Princess of Trebizond* (1438; at the

tip of the arch, high above chapel to right of altar). Once colorful, it has oxidized over time to its current monochrome state. For a closer look at its wonderful detail, check out the images on the computer terminal below the fresco. Ask for the English brochure, which describes the story of the church.

Cost and Hours: €3; Mon-Sat 9:00-18:00, Sun from 13:00, shorter hours in winter; www.chieseverona.it.

• *Leaving the church, make two lefts, and walk along the right side of the church to Via Sottoriva. To the right, the Sottoriva arcade was once busy with colorful wine bars and osterie, some of which still exist (see "Eating in Verona," later). But for now, head to the left on Via Sottoriva. In a block, you'll reach a small riverfront area with stone benches that usually have a few modern-day Romeos and Juliets gazing at each other rather than at the view. Belly up to the river view.*

⓬ Ponte Pietra and River View

The white stones of the Ponte Pietra footbridge are from the original Roman bridge that stood here. After the bridge was bombed in World War II, the Veronese fished the marble chunks out of the river to rebuild it. From here, you can see across the river to the Roman Theater, built into the hillside behind the green hedge (see "Sights in Verona," later). Way above the theater (behind the cypress trees) is the fortress, Castello San Pietro. The nearby funicular can take you there.

The wide spot in the river here was called the "Millers' Widening," where boats stopped and unloaded grain to be milled. Water wheels once lined the river and powered medieval Verona, employing technology imported from the Holy Land by 10th-century Crusaders.

Continue up the river toward the bridge. Walk to its high point and enjoy the view.

• *From the bridge, look back 200 yards at the tall white spire...that's where you're heading. Walk back off the bridge, then turn right, keeping an eye on the left for the steeple of the...*

⓭ Duomo

Started in the 12th century, this church was built over a period of several hundred years. Before entering, note the fine Romanesque carvings on its facade.

Cost and Hours: €3; Mon-Sat 10:00-17:00, Sun from 13:30, shorter hours off-season.

Visiting the Church: Step inside, pick up the leaflet that explains the church's highlights, and head to the back-left corner of the church. In the last chapel on the left is Titian's 16th-century *Assumption of the Virgin.* Mary calmly rides a cloud—direction up—to the shock and bewilderment of the crowd below. Notice a handful of tombs embedded in the walls about 15 feet above floor level—an unusual feature. (Generally, tombs are found in the floor of the church or in crypts below.)

Now head up the aisle to the last door on the left (left of high altar), where you'll find the **ruins** of an older church. These are the 10th-century foundations of the Church of St. Elena, turned intriguingly into a modern-day chapel featuring exposed fourth-century mosaic floors from the Roman church that originally stood here.

From there, pass through the little open-air courtyard into the adjacent **baptistery,** with its clean Romanesque lines, hanging 14th-century crucifix, and fine marble font. Try to identify the eight biblical scenes carved on its panels before referring to my answers. (Answers, starting with the panel just to the right of center and working counterclockwise: Annunciation; first Christmas, with animals licking Baby Jesus and giving him a barnyard welcome; announcement to shepherds of Jesus' birth, with their flock stacked on one side; Epiphany, with the Three Kings giving their gifts to Baby Jesus; Herod commanding that all male infants be killed; Slaughter of the Innocents; flight to Egypt; and finally, facing the entry door, John the Baptist baptizing Christ.)

Finally, after leaving the church, circle around its left side (as you face the main facade) to find the peaceful Romanesque **cloister** *(chiostro)*, with mosaics from a fifth-century Christian church exposed below the walk.

Sights in Verona

Several of Verona's main sights, including the Roman Arena, Church of Sant'Anastasia, and Duomo, are covered in my Verona Walk.

▲▲Evening *Passeggiata*

For me, the highlight of Verona is the *passeggiata* (stroll)—especially in the evening. Make a big circle from Piazza Brà through the old town on Via Mazzini (one of Europe's many "first" pedestrian-only streets) to the colorful Piazza Erbe, and then back down Corso Porta Borsari to Piazza Brà. This is a small town, where people know each other, and they're all out on parade. Like peacocks, the young and nubile spread their wings. The classy shop windows are integral to the *passeggiata* as, for many of the ladies, shopping is a sport. Their never-finished wardrobes are considered a work in progress, and this is when they gather ideas. If you're going to complement your stroll with a stop in a café or bar, the best plan is to enjoy a *spritz* drink—not on Piazza Brà, but on Piazza Erbe (the oldest and most elegant bars are on the end farthest from Juliet's balcony).

▲Castelvecchio

Verona's powerful Scaligeri family built this castle (1343-1356) as both a residence and a fortress. The castle, located west of Piazza Brà and the Roman Arena, has two parts: the family palace and the quarters for their private army (separated, for the nervous family's security, by a fortified wall and an internal moat). Today, it houses the city's art gallery, with an extensive, enjoyable collection of sculpture and paintings.

Cost and Hours: €6, Tue-Sun 8:30-19:30, Mon from 13:30, last entry 45 minutes before closing, Corso Castelvecchio 2, tel. 045-806-2611. Info sheets are available throughout, but the €4 audioguide (€6/2 people) is still worthwhile.

Visiting the Castle: Religious statues were Verona's medieval forte, while paintings were the city's Renaissance forte. From the entrance, you'll head right toward the **statues,** once brightly painted. Cross to the next wing and head upstairs to walk through two floors that trace the evolution of **painting** from the 13th through the 17th century, including minor works by many major masters (such as Bellini, Mantegna, and Veronese). You'll also pass by a small armory collection.

En route, watch for the chance to roam the **ramparts** with fine views of the city, river, and Ponte Scaligero. Kids (and kids at heart) enjoy scrambling across the delightfully crenellated parapets. Verona was an independent city-state from 1176 to 1387. Then came a long period of subjugation under other powers which, in more modern times, included the Austrians. From the ramparts you can see remnants of Austrian rule: the arsenal across the river and the castle atop the distant hill.

Nearby: Next to Castelvecchio, the picturesque red-brick bridge called **Ponte Scaligero**—fortified and crenellated, as if a continuation of the castle—is free, open to the public, and fun to stroll across. Destroyed by the Germans in World War II, it was rebuilt in the 1950s using many of its original bricks, which were dredged out of the river. Today it's understandably a favorite for wedding-day photos.

OUTSIDE THE CITY CENTER
▲Basilica of San Zeno Maggiore
This church, a 15-minute walk upriver beyond Castelvecchio, is dedicated to the patron saint of Verona, whose remains are buried in the crypt under the main altar. In addition to being a fine example of Italian Romanesque, the basilica features Mantegna's *San Zeno Triptych* (1456-1459) with its marvelous perspective, peaceful double-columned cloisters, and a set of 48 paneled 11th-century bronze doors nicknamed "the poor man's Bible." Pretend you're an illiterate medieval peasant and do some reading. Facing the altar, on the walls of the right-side aisle, you can see frescoes painted on top of other frescoes and graffiti dating from the 1300s. These were done by people who fled into the church in times of war or flooding and scratched prayers into the walls. Druidic-looking runes are actually decorated letters typical of the Gothic period, like those in illuminated manuscripts.

Cost and Hours: €3; Mon-Sat 8:30-18:00, Sun from

12:30, shorter hours off-season; on Piazza San Zeno, www.
chieseverona.it.

Roman Theater (Teatro Romano)

Dating from about the time of Christ, this ancient theater—located across the Roman Bridge, north of the city center—was dis-

covered in the 19th century and restored. Admission includes the Roman Museum, located high in the building above the theater (reach it via elevator—start at the stage and walk up the middle set of stairs, then continue straight on the path through the bushes).

The museum displays a model of the theater, a small chapel, and Roman artifacts, including mosaic floors, busts and other statuary, clay and bronze votive figures, and architectural fragments. There's not much to see. Unless you've never seen a Roman ruin, I'd skip it.

Cost and Hours: €4.50, Tue-Sun 8:30-19:30, Mon from 13:30, last entry one hour before closing, theater located across the river near Ponte Pietra footbridge, tel. 045-800-0360. From mid-June through August, the theater stages Shakespeare plays—only a little more difficult to understand in Italian than in Elizabethan English.

Giusti Garden (Giardino Giusti)

You'll see this picturesque Renaissance garden capping the steep hilltop just across the Roman Bridge at the northern edge of the city. It's a little oasis with manicured box hedges, towering cypress trees, and a city view from the top of its hill. For most people, however, it's not worth the hike, time, or money.

Cost and Hours: €8.50, daily 9:00-19:00, across the river, beyond Ponte Nuovo.

Sleeping in Verona

Hotel prices soar from mid-June through early September (opera season), in early April (during the Vinitaly wine festival—see "The Wines of Verona" sidebar, later), and during big trade fairs or major holidays. Unless your goal is opera, consider coming outside the summer months. For hotel locations, see the Verona map, at the beginning of this chapter.

NEAR PIAZZA ERBE

$$$$ Hotel Antica Porta Leona exudes refined elegance and is worth the splurge. Each of its 23 rooms is uniquely decorated, with some named for famous operas. Use of pool, gym, and spa facilities are included (air-con, elevator, some rooms in nearby annex, valet garage parking, Corticella Leoni 3, tel. 045-595-499, www. anticaportaleona.it, info@anticaportaleona.it).

$$ Hotel Aurora, at the corner of Piazza Erbe and Via Pelliciai, has friendly family management, attention to detail, a welcoming terrace with wonderful piazza views, and 18 straightforward rooms (family rooms, air-con, elevator, Piazzetta XIV Novembre 2, tel. 045-594-717, www.hotelaurora.biz, info@hotelaurora.biz, Rita).

$$ Casa Coloniale is just a stone's throw from Piazza Erbe. The four rooms all have balcony views and are furnished with a simple yet bright and stylish flair. Energetic owner Lucca runs the nearby Caffè Coloniale (Piazza Viviani Francesco 12), where breakfast is provided, along with B&B check-in after 15:00 (air-con, no elevator, Via Cairoli 6, tel. 393-940-8687, mobile 337-472-737, www.casa-coloniale.com, info@casa-coloniale.com).

$$ L'Ospite, a 10-minute walk across the river from Piazza Erbe, has six cozy, immaculate, fully equipped apartments and lots of stairs. The rooms, warmly managed by English-speaking Federica De Rossi, sleep two to four (family rooms, no reception or daily cleaning, air-con, Via XX Settembre 3, tel. 045-803-6994, mobile 329-426-2524, www.lospite.com, info@lospite.com). Coming from the station by bus (ride same buses as those headed downtown; see "Arrival in Verona" at the start of this chapter), get off three stops past Piazza Brà, just after crossing the bridge, at the XX Settembre stop (across the street from the apartments).

¢ Protezione della Giovane, run by an association that houses poor women, also rents rooms and dorm beds to female tourists (and their children, up to age 12 for boys). Buried deep in the old town and up several flights of stairs, this place offers 10 cheap beds in a clean, institutional, and peaceful setting (women only, no breakfast, 23:00 curfew, reception open 9:00-20:00, Wi-Fi in common

VERONA

areas, Via Pigna 7, tel. 045-596-880, www.protezionedellagiovane.it, info@protezionedellagiovane.it).

NEAR PIAZZA BRÀ

You'll find several options in the quiet streets just off Piazza Brà. From the square, white or yellow signs point you to the hotels. Most of these are big, fairly impersonal business-class places. Albergo Arena and Pepita Lodge are a little farther out, but still within a short walk to Piazza Brà.

$$$ Hotel Giulietta e Romeo is on a quiet side street 100 yards behind the Roman Arena. It's stylish and well-managed; 10 of its 37 sexy, ultra-modern rooms have balconies (air-con, elevator, free loaner bikes, fitness room, pay parking in garage or ask for free street parking permit, Vicolo Tre Marchetti 3, tel. 045-800-3554, www.hotelgr.it, info@hotelgr.it).

$$$ Hotel Colomba d'Oro is a sprawling place with old-school elegance, renting 50 spacious rooms with Baroque flourishes. It has generous public spaces, including a courtyard, and overlooks a quiet and central street (air-con, elevator to every other floor, stairs between the rest, Via C. Cattaneo 10, tel. 045-595-300, www.colombahotel.com, info@colombahotel.com).

$$$ Hotel Milano is an arty hotel with 56 rooms. The lobby and fancier rooms are tricked out in black and chrome. It has a wonderful terrace and hot tub overlooking the Roman Arena (air-con, elevator, pay parking in garage, Vicolo Tre Marchetti 11, tel. 045-596-011, www.hotelmilano-vr.it, info@hotelmilano-vr.it).

$$ Aparthotel Verona House is a good option if you want hotel amenities and residential comfort. The 23 apartments are swanky and stylish (some can fit up to eight people). The bright, spacious breakfast room has great views onto Castelvecchio and doubles as an honor bar in the afternoon and evening (air-con, elevator, pay parking, loaner bikes, Stradone Provolo 3, tel. 045-205-0366, www.veronahouse.com, info@hotels2go.it).

$$ Pepita Lodge is convenient for train travelers and a 10-minute walk from Piazza Brà. The artful and spacious rooms have a calm, contemporary, clean-lines vibe. Breakfast is provided across the street at a *pasticceria* (family rooms, air-con, elevator, pay parking, Corso Porta Nuova 103, reception at #99B, tel. 045-800-1393, www.pepitalodge.it, info@pepitalodge.it).

$$ Albergo Arena, with a contemporary feel and few frills, is just this side of dreary but a good value for those on a budget. Located in a peaceful courtyard off a busy street a few blocks from Piazza Brà, it offers 16 basic, quiet rooms (air-con, elevator, just west of Castelvecchio at Stradone Porta Palio 2, tel. 045-803-2440, www.albergoarena.it, info@albergoarena.it, Francesco and Elena).

Eating in Verona

Every restaurant listed here is within a 10-minute walk of the others. They're mostly small and intimate and found along side streets. It's tempting to grab a table next to the *passeggiata* action along Piazza Brà, but you'll be sacrificing service, value, and quality for your view of the floodlit Roman Arena and Verona on parade (perhaps a fair trade-off). Restaurants on the piazza tend to charge a cover and service fee, making even pizza a pricey choice. For restaurant locations, see the Verona map at the beginning of this chapter.

FINE DINING

$$$$ Cangrande Ristorante & Enoteca offers seating in an outdoor garden or in a plush little dining area inside. The star offering is a €49.50 set menu including *antipasti*, pasta, a meat or fish course, and dessert. They also offer a light à la carte menu at lunch (Wed-Mon 12:30-14:30 & 18:30-22:00, closed Tue, also closed Mon during opera season; a block off Piazza Brà at Via Dietro Liston 19D—if the equestrian statue jogged slightly right, he'd head straight here; tel. 045-595-022, www.cangranderistorante.it).

$$$$ Darì Ristorante & Enoteca, run by longtime Verona restaurateurs Corinna and Giuliano, has a lovely setting inside and out and beautifully presented food (Wed-Mon 12:00-15:00 & 18:30-22:30, closed Tue, Vicolo Cieco San Pietro Incarnario 5, tel. 045-595-022, www.ristorantedari.com).

$$$ Trattoria al Pompiere, which has a commitment to regional traditions, has formal waiters weaving among its tight tables and walls plastered with photos of big shots from the area. This bustling place is a favorite of local foodies. Marco and his gang serve gourmet meats and cheeses as *antipasti* from their larger-than-life back counter, ideal for a mixed plate to complement the huge selection of fine wines. Reservations are wise (Mon-Sat 12:40-14:00 & 19:40-22:30, closed Sun, chivalry lives—ladies' menus come without prices; halfway between Piazza Erbe and Juliet's courtyard—head down narrow side street next to Via Cappello 8 to Vicolo Regina d'Ungheria 5; tel. 045-803-0537, www.alpompiere.com).

$$$ Antico Caffè Dante is a high-end place with a 19th-century pedigree and elegant service on the coziest and classiest square in town. You can enjoy a memorable meal of classic Veneto cuisine either at romantic tables on the square or inside. While it's not cheap, if you want to dress up and enjoy a slow, romantic, memorable meal, this can be a good value. The kitchen has limited hours, but the café is open throughout the day (daily 12:00-15:00 & 18:00-23:00, closed Sun afternoon off-season; Piazza dei Signori 2, tel. 045-800-0083, www.caffedante.it).

$$$ Bottega del Vino is pricey, venerable, and a bit preten-

The Wines of Verona

Wine connoisseurs love the high-quality wines of the Verona area. The hills to the east are covered with grapes to make Soave; to the north is Valpolicella country; and Bardolino comes from vineyards to the west.

Valpolicella grapes, which are used to make the fruity, red Valpolicella table wine (found everywhere), are also the basis for full-bodied red Amarone and the sweet dessert wine Recioto. To produce Amarone, grapes are partially dried *(passito)* before fermentation, then aged for a minimum of four years in oak casks, resulting in a rich, velvety, full-bodied red. Recioto, which in local dialect means "ears," uses only the grapes from the top of the cluster (so they sort of look like the "ears" of the cluster's "head"). Because these grapes get the most sun, they mature the fastest and have the highest concentration of sugar. Before pressing, the grapes are dried for months until all moisture has gone out; the wine is then aged for one to three years.

Bardolino, from the vineyards near Lake Garda, is a light, fruity wine, like a French Beaujolais. It's a perfect picnic wine.

Soave, which might be Italy's best-known white wine, goes well with seafood and risotto dishes. While Soave can vary widely in quality, the best are called "Soave Classico" and come from the heart of the region, near the Soave Castle. Soave is sometimes aged in oak casks, giving it a mellow, rounded flavor.

Sample these and many others at the numerous *enoteche* (wine-tasting bars) or at any restaurant around town. In early April, Verona hosts Vinitaly, the most important international convention of domestic and international wines. Vintners vie for prestigious awards for the past year's vintage. Tourists are welcome to attend at the end of the week and are shuttled to the convention hall from Piazza Brà. Hotels book up months in advance. Check with the TI and Vinitaly.com for details.

If you're visiting the area in the fall, consider a day trip to nearby Monteforte d'Alpone, east of Verona. The town hosts a fun, raucous wine festival in September—ask at the TI for more information on this and other regional wine festivals.

VERONA

tious. Under a high ceiling and walls of wine bottles, brisk, black-vested waiters match traditional dishes (polenta, duck, game) with glasses of fine wine. Choose from 50 open bottles. The waitstaff, ambience, and food have deep roots in local culture. I like their front room best. Reservations are smart for dinner (good daily specials, daily 11:00-23:00—kitchen closed 14:30-19:00, bar open later, off Via Mazzini at Via Scudo di Francia 3, tel. 045-800-4535, www.bottegavini.it).

MODERATE RESTAURANTS

$$ Ristorante Torcolo is a family restaurant, with mom (Paola) running the kitchen, and father and son (Roberto and Luca) serving the meals. While it feels a bit dressy, it lacks pretense. They serve all the classics but with modern twists, and have an accessible menu and extensive wine list. Eat in their dining hall or on the tiny courtyard outside (daily 12:30-14:30 & 19:00-22:30, dinner from 17:00 in opera season, just behind the Piazza Brà scene on a quiet street, Via Carlo Cattaneo 11, tel. 045-803-3730).

$$ Osteria Caffè Monte Baldo has cafè-style bites plus a full menu with dishes typical of Verona like *risotto all'Amarone* for two or potato-less *gnocchi di malga*. If you want to share, go with the cold cuts and cheese boards. Or just pop into this cozy, rustic spot for a drink and snack on some *tartine* (small open-faced sandwiches; open daily 12:00-23:00, Via Rosa 12, tel. 045-803-0579). Their sister eatery, **La Piazzetta**, offers the exact same menu but in a more relaxed, boho-chic environment with terrace seating (daily 12:00-15:00 & 19:00-22:30, Corte San Giovanni in Foro 4/A, tel. 045-591-099).

EATING IN *OSTERIE* (OLD BARS)

Wandering around the old town, you'll see plenty of Verona's thriving little watering holes. While these traditional old bars focus more on wine than on food, most serve memorable, characteristic, and affordable plates. Menus are simple and rustic—sometimes just bar munchies and the daily pasta. Service is relaxed and the clientele is young and local. For drinks it's mostly wine or water—fine wines are served by the glass, with bottles open and prices listed on blackboards. (I saw one sign suggesting that patrons "don't drive too much to drink.")

I've listed three places below: a classic antique osteria with more of a menu; a trendy, more modern place in the old center; and a small one-man show just off Piazza Brà, where you're most likely to make a new friend.

$$ Osteria Sottoriva (not to be confused with nearby Ostregheteria Sottorviva 23) survives from an era when Verona's river served as the town thoroughfare, and business deals could be made over a glass of wine at rustic riverside eateries. Located in a fine old covered arcade (the portico of Via Sottoriva), with both cozy indoor and outdoor seating, Sottoriva serves simple Veneto fare that changes seasonally and with the owner's whim (daily 11:00-15:00 & 18:00-22:30—but open all day long in summer, closed Wed in winter, behind the Church of Sant'Anastasia at Via Sottoriva 9, tel. 045-801-4323).

$$ Osteria del Bugiardo is jammed with a hip young crowd that spills out into the pedestrian-filled Corso Porta Borsari. They

VERONA

A Mobile Feast Through Verona

Verona is a great town to sample the *aperitivo* ritual. All over town, locals enjoy a refreshing *spritz*, ideally on Piazza Erbe between 18:00 and 20:00. Choose a nice perch, and then, for about €4, you'll get the drink of your choice and a few nibbles (olives and/or potato chips) and a chance to feel very local as you enjoy the *passeggiata* scene.

Consider this for a fun sampling of many dimensions of the Verona eating and socializing scene: Start with an *aperitivo* on **Piazza Erbe,** then walk across Ponte Nuovo to **Pizzeria da Salvatore** and enjoy the town's best pizza. If you have to wait for a table, have another *spritz* at the neighboring bar. Then stroll along the river to **Osteria Sottoriva,** and enjoy a little sampling of bar food with a glass of Amarone (wine to meditate with) under the old arcade. Finish by meandering through the old center back to Piazza Brà for a gelato at **Gelateria Savoia.** *Buon appetito!*

have a buffet of little sandwiches, can whip up a plate of top-quality cheeses, and serve a good pasta-of-the-day. They showcase their own Buglioni wines and are proud to tell you more about them (daily 11:00-24:00, Corso Porta Borsari 17a, tel. 045-591-869).

$$ Osteria Vini Zampieri, with a tiny bar and a few tables, keeps a tradition of stoking conviviality with good wine since 1937. Its young and energetic manager, Leo, is passionate about organic wines, slow food, and his own home-brewed beer. As the drinks are their priority, they don't serve much food—just some bar munchies and a nice *antipasti* plate. Locals go for horse's balls *(polpettine di cavallo),* which are procured from the butcher down the street (daily 11:00-14:00 & 17:00-late except closed Mon for lunch, a few steps off Piazza Brà and next to Via Mazzini at Via Alberto Mario 23, tel. 045-597-053). You're welcome to play foosball downstairs on what Italians call the *calcio balilla* ("the little boy soldiers of Mussolini").

PIZZA, CHEAP EATS, AND SWEETS

$ Pizzeria da Salvatore, Verona's first pizzeria, opened in 1963, when pizza was considered a foreign food...from Naples. They serve the best pizza in town, and a visit here offers a nice excuse to stroll across the river into a part of town with no tourists. It's family-friendly, not fancy or romantic, and you'll squeeze into a tight row of tiny tables, rubbing elbows with your neighbors. While it's not quite Naples, it's justifiably popular—come early, or plan to leave your name on the list and wait awhile (Tue-Sat 12:30-14:30 &

19:00-23:00, Sun 19:00-23:00 only, closed Mon, no reservations, across Ponte Nuovo to Piazza San Tomaso 6, tel. 045-803-0366).

$$ Pizzeria Du de Cope is a colorful, high-energy, informal place (with paper placemats) that buzzes with smartly attired young waiters and locals who keep coming back for the pizza (daily 12:00-14:30 & 19:00-23:00, flamboyant desserts, families welcome, no reservations, at Galleria Pelliciai 10, tel. 045-595-562).

$ *Döner kebab* shops all over town serve hearty, cheap kebabs to munch on from a stool or to take out (most open daily roughly noon-midnight). *Piadine* (pita-bread) kebabs are worth the €4, and the super-sized kebabs can fill a couple on a very tight budget for a total of €7. The best kebabs, according to local assessments, are behind the Roman Arena at Via Leoncino 44. There's another good place on the other side of Piazza Brà at Via Teatro Filarmonico 6b. The benches in the center of Piazza Brà are handy for a scenic place to munch your cheap meal.

Groceries: The large **PAM supermarket chain** has two helpful locations (both generally open 8:00-21:00 with shorter hours on Sun). One is just outside the historic gate on Piazza Brà (exit Piazza Brà through the gate and take the first right to Via dei Mutilati 3). The other one is across the Adige River, beyond Ponte Vittoria (Via IV Novembre 6A). Near the Church of Sant'Anastasia are two classic grocery stores, **Salumeria Caliari** and **Salumeria Albertini** (as mentioned in the town walk, earlier).

Gelato: The venerable **Gelateria Savoia** has been in business since 1939. It's in an arcade just off Piazza Brà, marked by a crowd licking their distinctive *semi-freddo*—a specialty of bitter-almond amaretto, cream, and cookie (just off Piazza Brà at Via Roma 1b). Just next to the Porta Leoni Roman gate (and in front of an excavation of the foundations of the gate) is **l'Arte del Gelato**. The gelateria prides itself on using organic ingredients. Their Sicilian *granite* and their *semi-freddo* are nearly as popular as their gelato (Via Leoni 3).

Verona Connections

You have several options for getting train tickets in Verona: the standard station ticket office (with slow-moving lines, daily 6:00-21:00), a bank of modern machines (good English descriptions, cash and credit cards accepted), or the Deutsche Bahn ticket office (20 yards from baggage check office in the tunnel, offering tickets at the same cost as the station office but with German efficiency and no lines, Mon-Sat 8:00-18:00, closed Sun). Or you can buy tickets online with the train companies—Trenitalia or Italo (either via their websites or apps).

Every hour, at least two trains connect Verona with Venice,

Padua, and Vicenza. Choose one of the cheaper regional trains (R or RV) instead of the faster Italo or Frecce express trains, which get you there slightly sooner but cost much more. Unless otherwise specified, the following connections are for Trenitalia.

From Verona by Train to: Venice (2/hour, 70 minutes-2 hours), **Padua** (2/hour, 40-80 minutes), **Vicenza** (2/hour, 30-60 minutes), **Florence** (*Firenze*, Trenitalia: about hourly, 1.5 hours direct or 2.5 hours with transfer in Bologna; Italo: 4/day, 1.5 hours), **Bologna** (hourly, 1.5 hours), **Milan** (Trenitalia: 2/hour, 1.5-2 hours; Italo: 7/day, 1.5 hours), **Rome** (Trenitalia: at least hourly, 4-5 hours, often with transfer in Bologna, also 1 direct night train, 6.5 hours; Italo: 4/day, 3.5 hours), and **Bolzano** (about hourly, 2.5 hours).

RAVENNA

Ravenna is on the tourist map for one reason: its 1,500-year-old churches, decorated with best-in-the-West Byzantine mosaics. The city's churches and mosaics date from the time (c. AD 400-600) when it was the center of Western civilization—a civilization in transition, from Roman to barbarian to Byzantine to medieval. You'll see all these layers in Ravenna.

In 402, barbarian tribes were zeroing in on the city of Rome. The Roman emperor moved his capital to Ravenna, a city well-known as a home port for the imperial navy (today's Classe). Because of its location, Ravenna kept close ties with the other Roman capital at Constantinople (called Byzantium).

Ravenna was conquered by the Goths (via Hungary) in 476, and the 1,000 years of the Roman Empire came to an end. But Ravenna continued on as the Goths' capital. They kept much of the Roman infrastructure and legitimized their rule by building sophisticated palaces and churches in the Roman style.

In 540, the Byzantine emperor Justinian conquered the Goths. This reunited Italy with the still-thriving Empire to the east. Justinian turned Ravenna into a pinnacle of civilization. It remained a flickering light in Europe's Dark Ages for another 200 years, until the Lombard tribes of Germany booted out the Byzantines (in 751). Ravenna then melted into the backwaters of medieval Italy, staying out of historical sight for a thousand years.

In your sightseeing, you'll see art from each of these periods: Roman (Mausoleum of Galla Placidia, Neonian Baptistery), barbarian/Gothic (Arian Baptistery, Basilica di Sant'Apollinare in Nuovo), Byzantine (Basilica di San Vitale, House of Stone Carpets, Church of Sant'Apollinare in Classe), and medieval (Tomb of Dante, Basilica di San Francesco).

Today, Ravenna's economy booms with a big chemical industry, the discovery of offshore gas deposits, and the construction of a new ship canal. More cruise ships than ever are stopping here, six miles from the town center.

From a traveler's perspective, Ravenna has a delightful workaday quality, providing relief from the touristic intensity of Venice and Florence. The bustling town center is Italy's best for bicyclists. Residents go about their business, while busloads of tourists (mostly cruise-ship passengers and Italian school groups) slip quietly in and out of town for the best look at the glories of Byzantium this side of Istanbul—specifically, the richest collection anywhere of mosaics from the fifth and sixth centuries. Many are pleasantly surprised by the peaceful charm of this low-key town. If it seems less prettied-up than some of the more famous Italian towns, well... that's sort of the point.

PLANNING YOUR TIME

While the highlights of Ravenna can be seen in a four-hour stopover, the city can provide an entire day of relaxing and enjoyable sightseeing—particularly for mosaic lovers. Its inexpensive lodgings and restaurants offer good value for your money. The town is a doable, though long, day trip from Venice or Padua (about three hours by train each way). It's more pleasant to spend the night. You could also stop here on your way from Venice or Padua to Florence. Ravenna is busiest between March and mid-June—prime field-trip season.

Famous but Skippable: Nearly all train travelers to Ravenna change in the regional capital of **Bologna.** While it might be tempting to check your bag at Bologna's station and spend a few hours in town, I'd resist—Ravenna is much more pleasant. Though well-preserved, Bologna is huge (three times the size of Ravenna), congested, and relatively charmless. If you decide to stop off here anyway, head straight to Piazza Maggiore (a 20-minute walk from the station), home to the Town Hall, the TI, and a famous statue of Neptune. The big Gothic building across the square is the unfinished 14th-century Basilica di San Petronio—destined to be one of the biggest churches in Christendom until the Vatican put the brakes on the project. A few blocks west are Bologna's twin symbols, a pair of leaning brick towers.

The nearby beach town of **Rimini** is an overrated, crowded mess.

Orientation to Ravenna

Particularly because its sights are concentrated right downtown, Ravenna feels small for a city of 160,000. Central Ravenna is quiet, with a pedestrian-friendly core and more bikes than cars. Subtle white-brick paving down the center of "pedestrian" streets indicates the bike lane: Keep to the sides and listen for the outta-my-way bells (while watching local pedestrians flagrantly stroll right down the middle).

On a quick visit to Ravenna, follow my self-guided walk and visit the Basilica di San Vitale, its adjacent Mausoleum of Galla Placidia, and the Basilica di Sant'Apollinare Nuovo (all covered by one combo-ticket—see "Helpful Hints," below).

TOURIST INFORMATION

The TI is a 15-minute walk (or a 5-minute pedal) from the train station (Mon-Sat 8:30-19:00, Sun 9:30-17:30, shorter hours off-season; Piazza San Francesco 7, tel. 0544-35404, www.turismo.ra.it). Pick up their quarterly *Welcome to Ravenna* publication for a review of events and activities in town.

ARRIVAL IN RAVENNA

By Train: The compact, manageable train station has all the basic services, including ticket windows and machines, pay WCs, fast food, and a newsstand. While there's no baggage storage inside the station, if you exit to the left and walk two minutes, you can pay to **check your bag** at the Co-op San Vitale bike-rental shop, listed later.

The station is just a few minutes' walk east of the main pedestrian street: Exit through the front of the station and keep going straight ahead until you hit the main square, Piazza del Popolo (my self-guided walk begins with this same stroll from the station). If you prefer to bike, you can rent wheels at the Co-op San Vitale.

By Car: Don't drive into the center, as you'll be fined. Two inexpensive lots are near the historic core: one accessible from the west side of Via Roma, at Piazzale Torre Umbratica (€1.80/day), and another at Largo Giustiniano just north of the Basilica di San Vitale (€3/day). Or find a free lot south of the station, on Circonvallazione Piazza d'Armi; another is north of the Piazzale Torre Umbratica lot, on Via Monsignore F. Lanzoni. Many lots and places on the street are free overnight (20:00-8:00), and most are free on Sunday.

HELPFUL HINTS

Combo-Ticket: Five of Ravenna's best mosaic sights are covered by a single €11.50 combo-ticket that's good for seven days; just buy it at the first sight you visit. Included are the Basilica di San Vitale, Mausoleum of Galla Placidia, Basilica di Sant'Apollinare Nuovo, Archiepiscopal Museum (with its Chapel of Sant'Andrea), and Neonian Baptistery. All five

Ravenna

sights are church-run, distinctly different, and well worth visiting.

Laundry: The self-service **LavaFlash,** 10 minutes south of the train station, is next door to a bountiful produce store (daily 7:00-23:00, 400 yards south of Via Candiano on right-hand side of Circonvallazione Piazza d'Armi, mobile 0544-182-4601).

Accommodations

1. Hotel Bisanzio
2. M Club B&B
3. Casa Masoli B&B
4. Villa Noctis
5. A Casa di Paola
6. Hotel Italia
7. Albergo I Cherubini

Eateries & Other

8. Ca' de Ven Ristorante
9. Al Rustichello
10. Antica Bottega di Felice & Passatelli l'Osteria del Mariani
11. Ristorante la Gardèla
12. Ristorante Osteria del Tempo Perso
13. L'Acciuga Osteria
14. Profuma di Piadina
15. La Piadina del Melarancio & Ali Kebab
16. Gastronomia Alpine
17. Supermarket
18. Papilla Gelato
19. Leonardi Dolciumi
20. Bike Rental
21. Launderette

Bike Rental: Many hotels have loaner bikes, or try **Co-op San Vitale,** in front of the train station (€1.50/hour, €12/day, Mon-Fri 7:00-19:00, also Sat-Sun 8:00-12:00 in summer, photo ID required, tel. 054-437-031).

Local Guide: Private guide **Claudia Frassineti** is excellent (€110/half-day, mobile 335-613-2996, claudia.frassineti@gmail.com).

Ravenna Walk

A visit to Ravenna can be as short as a four-hour loop from the train station. This 45-minute self-guided walk brings you from the train station to Ravenna's top draw (Basilica di San Vitale), quickly taking in a few other sights on the way. When done, you'll be oriented and can use any remaining time to visit more of Ravenna's sights.

• *Start at the train station, and walk (or pedal) directly into town on the main drag...*

Viale Farini

The station and surrounding neighborhood were bombed in World War II, when Ravenna was right on the so-called Gothic Line—the Nazis' last line of defense against an encroaching Allied surge in 1944. The architectural heritage of the 20th century is a mix of old-fashioned Italian buildings; stern, interwar, fascist structures; and postwar concrete gloom.

After a block, on the left, you'll pass the **St. John the Evangelist** church, with a rebuilt facade. This was the palace church of the fifth-century Empress Galla Placidia (the namesake of one of Ravenna's major sights, a mausoleum we'll see later on this walk). She and her children were caught at sea in a storm, prayed to St. John (the protector of sailors), and survived. In thanks, she had this church built at the site of their first safe step ashore. At least that's the story. It is true that in ancient times, the town harbor came right up to here. Historic churches are so abundant in Ravenna that we'll skip this one.

The next big building is the high school, with students' motorbikes parked in front. After that, the boulevard becomes **Via Diaz,** an arcaded pedestrian shopping street. Note that the lighter cobbles are for the bikes.

• *At the intersection with Via degli Ariani, side-trip to the right 50 yards to find the...*

Arian Baptistery

Built during the reign of the Goths (c. 526), this small octagonal building marks the center of their Arian-style Christian faith (see sidebar).

Cost and Hours: €1, daily 8:30-19:30, off-season until 16:30, tel. 0544-543-711, www.turismo.ra.it.

Visiting the Baptistery: Theodoric the Great, the Gothic king of Italy (r. 493-526), built the church next door, with this as his baptistery. Imagine the small baptismal pool that once stood beneath this gloriously decorated dome.

The mosaic-covered dome shows Christ standing waist-deep in the River Jordan, being baptized by John the Baptist (in leopard-skin robe), as the dove of the Holy Spirit descends. The body builder on the left is the personified River Jordan, next to a vase from which the river springs. Notice the realism in John's stance. The 12 apostles, dynamic, with feet in motion, proceed around the dome. The empty throne between Paul (with scroll) and Peter (with keys) is a reminder that Judgment Day will come.

The mosaic is Arian, stressing Jesus' human rather than divine nature. Jesus is naked, with his genitals only partly obscured by the water. This emphasizes his mortal body, not his divine spirit. He's a beardless youth, suggesting his recent creation by God. The descending dove spews water to purify Jesus, marking the exact moment when Arians believed Jesus' divine nature emerged. Besides heretical Arian elements, there's also the pagan river god, shown in (pagan) Roman fashion as a bearded old man with a vase and river plant.

To modern eyes, these subtle details mean little. But to Byzantine Emperor Justinian and the Nicenes, these were red flags announcing heresy. While most of Ravenna's Arian art was destroyed when Justinian took control, this ceiling is one of the rare survivors.

The adjacent church is closed to the public. It was the cathedral of the Goths, with a simple main structure surviving from the sixth century and a Renaissance portico.

• *Now, return to the pedestrian boulevard, turn right, and continue to...*

Piazza del Popolo

Marking the town center, this square was created by Ravenna's Venetian rulers in the 15th century. Today's shipping canal was once a river that flowed to about where the two columns stand. But it got mucky and full of mosquitoes. (Dante died here...of malaria.) One column was topped by a Venetian lion until 1509 when, with the support of Rome, Ravenna won its independence from Venice. Ravenna's citizens pulled down that symbol of Venetian rule and did the local equivalent of tarring and feathering it. The lion was replaced by St. Vitale (a first-century Christian martyr). The column on the left is topped by Ravenna's first bishop, St. Apollinare. Behind the twin pillars stands City Hall. To the left is a Venetian palace decorated with granite columns and capitals, plundered from a heretical Arian church that was destroyed and then used as a quarry. This square is a fine place to join the old guys on benches, watching the community parade by.

• *At the end of Piazza del Popolo, turn left through the arcade, head down Via Cairoli and walk two blocks—crossing a busy street and passing some heavy-handed fascist architecture—to find the...*

Basilica di San Francesco

Pop into this basilica to see its flooded mosaic-covered crypt below the main altar. Today's water table is about three feet above the Roman crypt's floor level—so there's a pond with goldfish over the fifth-century mosaics (insert a €1 coin to turn on the light). The interior is simple and Franciscan; the altar features a fourth-century Christian sarcophagus with Jesus in the center and the 12 apostles.

Cost and Hours: Free, daily 7:00-12:00 & 15:00-19:00 (but closed during Masses), Piazza San Francesco, tel. 054-433-256.

• *With your back to the church, cut right through the small wooded park. On your right, next to the double archway, a tall, white, domed chapel marks the...*

Tomb of Dante

After he was exiled from Florence for his political beliefs, Dante lived out the rest of his life in Ravenna. The Florentines forgave Dante posthumously and wanted to bring their famous poet's bones home to rest. To protect Dante's relics from theft by the Florentines, in 1519 Ravenna hid his bones inside the wall of the Monastery of San Francesco. There the bones lay forgotten for three centuries, until they were rediscovered and eventually placed here in 1865. (Florence's Santa Croce Church has a Dante memorial that's often mistaken for a tomb—but it's empty.)

The mausoleum is loaded with symbolism. High above the door, for example, the bronze snake eating its own tail—a symbol of eternity—suggests that Dante's soul (or, at least, his works) will have everlasting life. Capping the structure is an allegorical pinecone: A tasty pine nut hides inside the cone's lifeless exterior—a reminder of how our spirits can transcend the death of our earthly form. (And, not coincidentally, the pine tree is the symbol of Ravenna.)

Just to the right of the tomb, peer through the clever hanging fence with the pine tree city medallions (give it a jiggle) to the garden with the mound *(tumulo)* where Dante's bones were briefly hidden during World War II.

Cost and Hours: Free, daily 10:00-18:00, Nov-Feb until 16:00, Via D. Alighieri 9.

Nearby: The door to the left of the tomb leads into the peaceful twin cloisters of a former Franciscan monastery (attached to the Basilica di San Francesco, which we saw earlier). Today this com-

The Arian Heresy

Ravenna's art reflects a centuries-long battle of ideas among Europe's Christians that came to a violent head right here. As you wonder at the beauty of Ravenna's mosaics, you're also witnessing an epic clash between two different interpretations of Christianity.

Around AD 320 in Alexandria, a devout Christian priest named Arius (c. 256-336) began preaching a seemingly simple idea: Jesus, being the Son of God, was therefore created by God the Father. This idea touched off a firestorm of debate and division unmatched in Christianity until the Protestant Reformation. Arius had raised questions about the very nature of the Christian God: Is God a single entity (as the head of a monotheistic religion should be), three different persons (God the Father, Jesus Christ, and the Holy Spirit), or something in between?

To keep the peace, Roman Emperor Constantine convened a Council at Nicea (in AD 325, near modern Istanbul). Arius was accused of doubting the divinity of Christ, by making him separate from and inferior to God the Father. The Council branded Arius a heretic and burned his books. After splitting many theological hairs, they issued the Nicene Creed, which defined God as a Trinity: There was one God, existing in three persons "of the same substance." (Don't make me try to explain it further, or this book may end up getting burned by some sect somewhere.) The three-in-one Trinity became the standard throughout the Empire, and Arian sects were brutally suppressed. (Don't confuse the Arian sect with Nazi Germany's idea of an Aryan race.)

But that didn't settle the matter. Constantine's own son, a fervent Arian, sent missionaries north across the Danube to convert the barbarian Goths to Arian-style Christianity. A century later, as Rome was falling, those same Goths came knocking on Italy's doorstep. They overran Ravenna (476) and made Arian Christianity the official religion of state, though they tolerated the Nicene Christianity of their Italian subjects.

The churches the Goths built—including the Arian Baptistery and Basilica di Sant'Apollinare Nuovo—reflected their Arian faith. Arian mosaics of Jesus emphasized his humanness rather than his divinity.

In 540, the Byzantine Emperor Justinian drove out the Goths. To unite his empire, he demanded both political and theological conformity. Anything with the slightest whiff of Arianism was wiped out. Mosaics were stripped from the walls, statues defaced, and churches were renamed for saints famous for fighting heretics. In their place came art that reflected Byzantine tastes and Trinitarian theology. You'll see evidence of this shift at many of Ravenna's top sights.

Ravenna was Arianism's Waterloo. Sects were snuffed out, Trinitarians triumphed, and the Nicene Creed (in some form) is still said in many Christian churches today.

plex houses the fascinating-to-Italians **Dante Museum** (described later). It's worth a visit if you're a fan; otherwise, save your sightseeing stamina for what's coming up.

• *Turn your back to Dante's tomb and walk straight ahead until you pop out into...*

Piazza Garibaldi

With a statue of Giuseppe Garibaldi (a heroic leader in Italy's unification struggle in the mid-1800s) in the center and the stately, vivid-yellow Alighieri Theater (named for Dante) on the right, this is the humbler of Ravenna's two main squares. On the wall on your left, in a building housing Ravenna's post office, look for the plaques honoring patriots from Ravenna *(patrioti ravennati)* who died in World War II. You'll see both *morti sul patibolo nelle carceri in esilio* (died in prisons in exile) and *caduti sui campo di battaglia* (killed on the field of battle). In the summer and fall of 1944, the Nazis—steadily losing their grip on Italy—dug in near Ravenna and fought determinedly to hang on. The countryside surrounding Ravenna is dotted with several WWII cemeteries, as well as a few remaining "bailey bridges"—temporary bridges erected quickly by Allies on the march.

Next to the plaque listing the war dead is one listing the names of the Nazis' Jewish victims *(ebrei)* from Ravenna and their age at death. Notice how young many of them were.

Continue under the arcade back into Piazza del Popolo, and look at the *Il Comune di Ravenna* plaque on the towered building to your right, dedicated *ai suoi caduti per la liberta* (to those "fallen for freedom"). Those killed included *partigiani caduti in combattimento* (patriots lost in battle) and *per rappresaglia*—killed by the Nazis in retribution for Allied successes. Ravenna was ultimately liberated by mostly Canadian forces.

• *From here, you'll walk six blocks to the Basilica di San Vitale: With your back to the tower, turn and cross to the far-right corner of the piazza. Turn right and head one block up Via IV Novembre. At the old covered market (and the Max Mara shop), turn left and head down Via Cavour, Ravenna's favored street for evening strolling and shopping.*

About two blocks down Via Cavour, on the right, at #43, peek into the courtyard that holds Gastronomia Alpine, a deli selling top-quality local meats and cheeses—you could pull together a classy picnic here (see listing later, under "Eating in Ravenna").

As you approach the end of the block, the yellow Porta Adriana city gate comes into view (straight ahead). A few steps later, turn right onto Via Argentario. Halfway down this block on the left, at #22, is the ticket office for Ravenna's big sights. Buy your ticket here, then continue down the street to Ravenna's crown jewel, the Basilica di San Vitale (through the gateway at the end of this block). Of Ravenna's many impressive and important buildings from this time, the next sights are two of the finest:

RAVENNA

first the basilica itself, with its dazzling mosaics, and then, across the yard, the small but poignant Mausoleum of Galla Placidia.

▲▲▲Basilica di San Vitale

Imagine: It's AD 540. The city of Rome has been looted, the land is crawling with barbarians, and the infrastructure of Rome's thou-

sand-year empire is crumbling fast. Into this chaotic world comes the emperor of the East (Justinian), bringing order and stability, briefly reassembling the empire, and making Ravenna a beacon of civilization.

Cost and Hours: Covered by €11.50 combo-ticket that includes (and is also sold at) the Mausoleum of Galla Placidia, Basilica di Sant'Apollinare Nuovo, Archiepiscopal Museum, and Neonian Baptistery. The church is open daily 9:00-19:00, March and Oct until 17:30, Nov-Feb 9:30-17:00. Tel. 0544-541-688, www.ravennamosaici.it.

Visiting the Basilica: Step into the church, circle around to the middle of the nave, and take it all in.

The basilica—standing as a sanctuary of order in the midst of the madness after the fall of Rome—is covered with lavish **mosaics**: gold and glass chips the size of your fingernail. It's impressive enough to see a 1,400-year-old church, but it's rare to see one decorated in such brilliant mosaics, which still manage to convey their intended message: "This sense of peace and stability was brought to you by your emperor and God." The art is an intricate ensemble of images that, with the help of a medieval priest, would teach volumes.

The centerpiece, high above the altar, is God in heaven, portrayed as Christ sitting on a celestial orb, overseeing his glorious creation.

Step up to the **altar.** Position yourself to best see the side walls

flanking it. Running the show on earth is Justinian (left side), sporting both a halo and a crown to indicate that he's leader of both the Church and the State. Here Justinian brings together the military leaders and the church leaders, all united by the straight line of eyes. The bald bishop of Ravenna—the only local guy in this group—is portrayed most realistically (with a name tag above reading *Maximianus*).

On the opposite wall, facing the emperor, is his wife, Theodora, flanked by her entourage. Decked out in jewels and pearls, the former dancer who became Justinian's mistress (and then empress) carries a chalice with which to consecrate the new church.

The border inside the apse's arch, high above, is decorated with horns of plenty (cornucopia), promising prosperity in return for the people's obedience to the Church and State (Justinian and Theodora).

Back up a bit to let this space work its magic. Get in a medieval frame of mind and study the composition—with floor, walls, and ceiling all integrated into a cohesive meaning. Stand immediately under the **main dome** surrounded by scallop-shell designs, symbolizing St. James, the patron saint of pilgrims. From there the mosaic floor directs your journey to a 16th-century inlaid marble labyrinth which, if you do it right, leads you on to the altar. The lesson: The pilgrimage of faithful life on earth leads to salvation through Christ.

While the decor behind you is Baroque and of no particular artistic importance, the walls and ceilings above and in front sparkle with colorful biblical scenes told with a sixth-century exuberance. (Viennese artist Gustav Klimt sat right here around 1900 and was inspired by the glint of the light on the gold leaf.)

Now take a longitudinal, **ground-up tour** from your spot before the altar: The inlaid floor leads to the sixth-century marble altar (busy with iconography). High on the wall above that is Christ on the globe. Appreciate the symmetry. At the top of the arch, the circle with the monogram of Christ (*I* for Jesus and *X* for Christ) symbolizes perfection and eternity. Floating above the arch, two angels hold rays of sun (Christ is the origin of light). The scene is bookended by two cities: Bethlehem and Jerusalem (each the same but labeled, where Jesus was born and died). Above each city are potted grapevines producing wine, symbols of the blood of Christ.

The **ceiling** above is a festive celebration of God's creation, with 80 different birds from the sixth century—most still flying around Ravenna today. (Bird-watchers—who visit with binoculars, of course—can easily identify these by their exquisitely detailed and accurate feathers.) At the very top, all creation swirls around Christ as the sacrificial lamb, supported by four angels.

Framing the entire apse, arcing high above, is a triumphal

arch. Its 15 medallions depict 12 apostles, 2 sons of St. Vitale, and a medieval bearded Christ. Notice the realism...the eyes, the hairstyles.

The mid-sixth century was a time of transition, and many consider Ravenna's mosaics to be both the last ancient Roman and the first medieval European works of art. Standing here, we can witness a culture suddenly lurching forward out of antiquity and into the Middle Ages. Notice, for example, that the Christ who hovers above the altar is beardless (per standard ancient-Roman depiction), whereas it's the usual medieval bearded Jesus who's encircled atop the arch—and yet these mosaics were created within the same generation.

The church's **octagonal design**—clearly Eastern in origin—inspired at least two influential churches, including Hagia Sofia, the church-turned-mosque-turned-museum built 10 years later in Constantinople (today's Istanbul). Hagia Sofia, in turn, became the classic architectural model for mosques around the world. In AD 787, Emperor Charlemagne traveled to Ravenna and was so impressed with San Vitale that he returned to Aix-la-Chapelle (now Aachen, Germany) and built a new palace—the power base for his vast empire—with a San Vitale-esque chapel at its core. It still stands as part of Aachen Cathedral, making it the oldest great stone building in northern Europe.

The intricate basketlike **capitals** were built to order and shipped from Constantinople to Ravenna. The pilasters surrounding you are brick, covered by sliced marble veneers. Similar marble sheets once covered all the walls. Many were scavenged by Charlemagne to provide flooring for his grand church.

• *When you're ready, exit through the door on the left (as you face the altar) and head across the grounds to the much smaller but even older...*

▲▲Mausoleum of Galla Placidia

Just across the courtyard from the Basilica di San Vitale is a tiny, humble-looking mausoleum, with the oldest—and, to many, the most precious—mosaics in Ravenna. Ninety-five percent of the mosaics here are originals, dating from the late Roman period, when Ravenna was the capital of a declining West.

Cost and Hours: Covered by Basilica di San Vitale combo-ticket, same hours.

Visiting the Mausoleum: The Mausoleum of Galla Placidia (plah-CHEE-dee-ah) was designed to be the burial place of this daughter, sister, and mother of emperors, who died around AD 450. But Galla Placidia died in Rome and wasn't buried here. The three sarcophagi, built for the imperial family but likely only used by later Christian leaders, stand empty today. The original floor was about four feet lower, explaining the stunted feel of the interior. The art's realistic portrayal of tunics and sandals gives us a peek at the fashions of fifth-century Romans.

The little light that sneaks through the thin alabaster panels brings a glow and a twinkle to the early Christian symbolism that fills the small room. Opposite the door is St. Lawrence being martyred on a fiery grill. He's legendary for mocking his executioners, reportedly saying something like, "I'm done on this side. You can turn me over now." He was famous as an example of the strength of the feisty early Christians. Note the four Gospels clearly labeled on the bookshelf, another inspiration for these first believers as they were persecuted by the Romans.

The dome is filled with stars. Along with Mark's lion, Luke's ox, Matthew's angel, and John's eagle, the golden cross rises from the east, bringing life to all. Doves drink from fountains, symbolic of souls finding nourishment in the Word of God. In both transepts are deer, reminding worshippers of Psalms 42: "Like the thirsty deer longs for spring water, so my soul longs for you, my God."

Look toward the back of the mausoleum. Cover the light from the door with this book (or close the curtain) to see the standard Roman portrayal of Christ—beardless and as the Good Shepherd. Jesus, dressed in gold and purple like a Roman emperor, is the King of Paradise—receiving the faithful (represented by lambs). The Eastern influence (perhaps inspired by the designs on fine Persian carpets or silks) is apparent in the vault's decorative patterns.

• *Our walk is done. Got a train to catch? Head straight back to the station. If you have more time, visit the other sights included on your basilica ticket on your way: the Neonian Baptistery, the Archiepiscopal Museum, and the Basilica di Sant'Apollinare Nuovo.*

RAVENNA

More Sights in Ravenna

EAST OF PIAZZA DEL POPOLO

▲▲Basilica di Sant'Apollinare Nuovo

This austere sixth-century church has a typical early Christian-basilica floor plan and two huge and wonderfully preserved side panels. The only noteworthy sight in this part of town, it's on Via di Roma, just a short detour off the main road back to the train station.

Cost and Hours: Covered by Basilica di San Vitale combo-ticket, daily 9:00-19:00, March and Oct 9:30-17:30, Nov-Feb 10:00-17:00, tel. 0544-541-688, www.ravennamosaici.it.

Eating: You can have a quick lunch at the air-conditioned, efficient Sant'Apollinare self-serve cafeteria on the church grounds (Mon-Fri 12:00-15:00, closed Sat-Sun).

Visiting the Basilica: Head inside. Ignoring the Baroque altar from a thousand years later, you can clearly see the rectangular Roman hall of justice (basilica) floor plan—which was adopted by Christian churches and used throughout the Middle Ages.

The important art here is the decoration along the sides of the nave, just above the symmetrical arches. The one on the left side is a procession of haloed virgins, each bringing gifts to the Madonna and the Christ Child; the three wise men are at the head of the queue. Opposite, Christ is on his throne with four angels, awaiting a solemn procession of 26 martyrs.

Notice on each side how the processions lead to segments from an earlier Arian design—each about 50 years older. This basilica started (c. 500) as an Arian church—the palace church of King Theodoric of the Goths. Theodoric decorated it with scenes of himself and his royal palace amid Christ and the saints. Look for original, surviving Arian art in the front (on the left, Mary and Baby Jesus; on the right, Jesus and four angels) and in the rear (two cityscapes: *Civi Classis*—Classe; and *Palatium,* for the palace in Ravenna).

When Justinian arrived, he transformed the church in the Byzantine (and Nicene) style. If you study the arcades in the Ravenna cityscape (rear of church, above where you entered), you can see how the palace was kept while the Arian figures were erased, leaving only bits of hands and fingers on the columns and blotted-out haloes behind the curtains. On the opposite side, see three ships in the ancient harbor and a palace where golden bricks were used to cover Arian figures. The brilliant white-robed figures parading on both sides were remade in the mid-500s with a Byzantine rather than an Arian message.

The uppermost panels (hard to see without binoculars) are original Theodoric Arian: prophets (between windows), miracles of Christ (top row on the left), and scenes from the last week of Jesus' life and his Resurrection (top row on the right).

SOUTH OF PIAZZA DEL POPOLO

The first three sights described below cluster near Ravenna's modest Duomo, about a 10-minute walk from Piazza del Popolo. The last sight, the Dante Museum, is a few minutes' walk east of here, right next to the Basilica di San Francesco and Dante's tomb (both described earlier, on my self-guided walk).

▲▲Archiepiscopal Museum

This impressive museum, in Ravenna's Duomo, complements all the relatively empty buildings you've seen and contains the sixth-century Chapel of Sant'Andrea.
Built as the private prayer chapel for the Catholic bishop during Theodoric's time (c. 500), today it anchors a fine collection of Roman, Byzantine-Christian, and pagan statues, reliefs, and mosaics—all very well described.

Cost and Hours: Covered by Basilica di San Vitale combo-ticket, daily 9:00-19:00, March and Oct 9:30-17:30, Nov-Feb 10:00-17:00, tel. 0544-541-688, www.ravennamosaici.it.

Visiting the Museum: From the museum entrance on Piazza Arcivescovado, follow signs to the *Cappella di Sant'Andrea*, in Room IE. Enter the room, turn around, and look above the door to see a sixth-century mosaic showing Christ as a religious warrior, stepping triumphantly on a lion and snake (ancient symbols of evil) and carrying the cross as if it were a weapon. The book he holds reads in Latin, "I am the way, the truth, and the life." This is a strong pro-Trinity statement (Jesus, God, and the Holy Spirit are one) against the Arian heresy. The main chamber of the charming chapel is covered in rich mosaics, with lots of sixth-century symbolism and realistic portrait medallions. Topping the arch just over the door is another clean-shaven Jesus.

Exiting the chapel, turn left into Room IF to see the museum's other highlight, an exquisite sixth-century Byzantine ivory throne, decorated with intricate scenes from the life of Christ. It was carved for Bishop Maximianus, Justinian's Trinitarian appointee, the man who oversaw construction of the Basilica di San Vitale, and whose bald head appears in its mosaics. Nearby, in Room IG, is an interesting circular calendar designed to keep track of the dates for Easter between the years 532 and 626. The upstairs, worth a quick look, offers a chance for a close-up view of mosaics and more Byzantine and Venetian-era church art.

• *Exiting the museum, turn left to find the...*

▲Neonian Baptistery

Also known as the Baptistery of the Orthodox, this octagonal space dates from about the year 400. Imagine pagan adults im-mersed in the pool under glorious ceiling mosaics as they convert to Christianity. The mosaic portrays the common baptistery theme: John the Baptist baptizing Christ, with the personification of the River Jordan looking on. The scene is ringed by empty chairs, waiting to welcome you into the eternal heav-enly banquet. Twelve apostles with dancing feet—their tunics and cloaks alternating between gold and white—give the room a joyful vi-sual sense of rhythm. The acanthus

flowers dividing the apostles were the botanical inspiration for the Corinthian capital, the Roman capital of choice. Decoration on the lower walls features dark purple disks made of precious porphyry stone and a gold leafy arcade creating almond-shaped frames for the prophets.

Over the last 15 centuries, the building (being far heavier than the streets around it) has sunk about 10 feet into the mucky local soil. That's why the floor is higher than the architect planned, which messes up his intended proportion. For that reason also, the baptismal font is not original.

Cost and Hours: Covered by Basilica di San Vitale combo-ticket, daily 9:00-19:00, March and Oct 9:30-17:30, Nov-Feb 10:00-17:00, tel. 0544-541-688, www.ravennamosaici.it.

• *While you're here, consider at least popping into Ravenna's Duomo for a quick peek. From the Baptistery, walk away from the Archiepiscopal Museum and hook left to reach the front door of the...*

Duomo

Ravenna's main church is a typically big, Baroque house of worship. Like nearly everything else in this town, it's built on much older rubble. In the 18th century, to make way for the current structure, its builders razed the gigantic five-nave Basilica Ursiana—but pragmatically repurposed big chunks of the old church to build the new one. Pay close attention to the inlaid floors, made with cross-sections of columns, capitals, and other decorations from the previous church, all neatly sliced and joined together. Just before the right transept, notice the fine sixth-century marble-carved pulpit, covered with two-dimensional images of animals (typical of the Byzantine style). The Latin inscription, referring to the bishop who reconsecrated the Arian churches, reads, "Agnellus made this pulpit."

Cost and Hours: Free, Mon-Fri 7:00-12:00 & 14:30-18:30 (off-season until 17:00), Sat-Sun until 19:00.

Nearby: The free **botanical garden** (Giardino Rasponi)—with a great view of the cathedral—is a delightful spot to rest after so much sightseeing. Exiting the Duomo, turn right and walk up Via G. Rasponi. After one block, turn right on Via A. Guerrini to find the garden entrance.

Dante Museum (Museo Dantesco)

This small museum celebrates Dante Alighieri, "the Italian Shakespeare," who spent his last three years in Ravenna and now rests next door in the former Monastery of San Francesco. It was here that a 19th-century bricklayer stumbled upon the author's long-lost remains, tucked in a wooden box—now displayed in the museum—simply marked *Dantis ossa* ("Dante's bones"). The exhibit includes good descriptions, but it takes a strong background on Dante and his *Divine Comedy* to make a visit here worthwhile. If you do go in, request an English showing of the seven-minute film (theater on ground floor). Then climb to the first floor where the exhibit circles the courtyard: Be prepared to visit hell, purgatory, and paradise (or at least halls representing each of these). Outside, enjoy the two restful, grassy courtyards, one of them with modern statues of St. Francis and St. Claire.

Cost and Hours: €3, Tue-Sun 10:00-18:00, Nov-Feb until 16:00, closed Mon year-round, Via—what else?—Dante Alighieri 4, tel. 0544-215-676.

NORTHWEST OF PIAZZA DEL POPOLO

House of Stone Carpets (Domus dei Tappeti di Pietra)

Discovered in 1993, the stone mosaic floors of this sixth-century Byzantine house show both pictorial images and abstract designs. Excavations revealed many layers, dating back to the second century BC. All were peeled away and preserved elsewhere. Only the sixth-century floor (12 rooms on one level) was put back and exhibited here, very close to its original location. Because this was a private home, its art could break from the conservative norms for public art of the age. The highlight is the wonderfully realistic *Dance of the Four Seasons* (displayed on the wall on your right as you descend the stairs). Don't miss the fourth-century *Christ as a Shepherd,* which some consider the earliest portrayal of Jesus (it's on the wall facing the *Four Seasons;* part of the face was lost to modern excavations). A visit here is almost meaningless without the €2 audioguide.

Cost and Hours: €4, €7 combo-ticket includes TAMO and Rasponi Crypt (see below); daily 10:00-18:00, shorter hours and closed Mon in off-season; ask for the 10-minute English-language video—the computer-generated images help visitors envision the place in action; entrance through Church of Sant'Eufemia, on Via Barbiani just off Via Cavour near Piazza Baracca, tel. 0544-32512, www.domusdeitappetidipietra.it.

More Mosaics: The same association that runs the House of Stone Carpets also runs two other mosaic sights (all covered by the House of Stone Carpets combo-ticket): **TAMO** has little in the way of historical artifacts but tells the story of mosaic-making (daily 10:00-18:30, June-Aug until 14:00, Via Rondinelli 2); **Rasponi Crypt** displays a floor of mosaics pieced together from different sites, crazy-quilt style (same hours as TAMO except closed Mon, Piazza San Francesco 1).

NEAR RAVENNA
▲▲Church of Sant'Apollinare in Classe

The final major sight for Byzantine mosaic fans is a sixth-century church standing a few miles outside Ravenna in the suburb of Classe. It's impressive, but it comes in fourth place after the Basilica di San Vitale, Mausoleum of Galla Placidia, and Basilica di Sant'Apollinare Nuovo. On a quick day trip, it's certainly skippable.

Cost and Hours: €5, Mon-Sat 8:30-19:30, Sun from 13:00, closed during services, Via Romea Sud 224, tel. 0544-527-308, www.turismo.ra.it. If trying to see it Sunday morning, you can generally get in for free between Masses until 13:00.

Getting There: The church is three miles out of town—an easy bike ride. To go by bus, buy two local bus tickets (€1.30 each) at any tobacco shop, newsstand, or the TI, then catch bus #4 across the street from the train station (on the corner by the park; 3/hour Mon-Sat, 1/hour on Sun, 15 minutes; save second ticket for return trip). The bus also leaves from Piazza Caduti (near the TI, stop is on the corner). To return to Ravenna from the church, walk back toward town along the main road about 100 yards to find the bus shelter on the right. You could also pay for a taxi (figure around €12 one-way, or €25 round-trip if your visit is quick).

Visiting the Church: The statue of Emperor Augustus, standing in front of the church, is a reminder that Classe was a strategic navy base in Roman times. In early Christian days, Classe was a big pilgrimage destination and home to a large Christian community. Today little remains other than its church, and even that was nearly bombed-out in World War II when the Germans used its medieval tower as a lookout.

The artistic treasure here is the mosaic work in the apse, 90 percent of which is original from the sixth century. The scene is an abstract portrayal of the Transfiguration of Jesus. The cross with a tiny portrait of Christ in its center beams light. God's hand above affirms that "This is the Truth." The three lambs represent James, John, and Peter. The landscape is of pine trees, which once forested the region. And St. Apollinare, the first local bishop, is celebrated because it was he who brought Christianity to the area.

The rest of the church—its mosaics lost to time—is pretty plain. While many churches this old have settled and the bases of their columns are no longer visible, here the floor level remains unchanged, and you can admire the columns' original bases. Near the entrance, a bilingual display panel gives detailed information on the church.

Sleeping in Ravenna

IN THE PEDESTRIAN ZONE, NEAR PIAZZA DEL POPOLO

$$ Hotel Bisanzio is a business-class hotel with dated public spaces and 38 rooms in the city center (air-con, elevator, usually free on-street parking with hotel permit; Via Salara 30, tel. 054-421-7111, www.bisanziohotel.com, info@bisanziohotel.com).

$$ M Club B&B is a creative, comfortable, and stylish five-room place with an elegant breakfast room, spacious bedrooms, and thoughtful touches. Its website describes each unique room in detail (one family room, loaner bikes, Piazza Baracca 26, mobile 333-955-6466, www.m-club.it, info@m-club.it, Michael). The M Club faces the Porta Adriana gate at the far end of the old town from the train station (a 15-minute walk).

$$ Casa Masoli B&B, in an updated 17th-century building, is run with TLC by Fabio and Sandra. The six elegantly outfitted rooms have ample space and giant bathrooms in a wood-paneled Art Deco style (family rooms, air-con, library, Via G. Rossi 22, tel. 0544-217-682, mobile 335-609-9471, www.casamasoli.it, info@casamasoli.it).

$$ Villa Noctis is a hidden gem behind an enclosed courtyard, close to the covered market and the Neonian Baptistery. Proud Massimiliano's B&B has seven vogue and inviting rooms that feel luxurious without the luxe price. Two have private balconies (family rooms, air-con, sauna, garden, loaner bikes, pay parking; Via Giuseppe Pasolini 57, tel. 329-901-8590, www.villanoctis. it, info@villanoctis.it).

$ A Casa di Paola is a converted private home (Paola's mother has an apartment on the ground floor) with eight nicely decorated rooms, comfy common spaces, and a treehouse floor plan (family rooms, air-con, free drinks, loaner bikes, Via P. Costa 31, tel. 0544-39425, mobile 347-730-6386, www.acasadipaola.it, info@ acasadipaola.it). They also rent three rooms in their art-cluttered home a half-block away, at #26.

NEAR THE TRAIN STATION
These places are convenient but have less atmosphere.

$$ Hotel Italia, just 100 yards from the train station, feels like a dated chain hotel but is actually family-owned. Its 45 basic rooms lack character but provide comfort and lots of space (family rooms, air-con, elevator, loaner bikes, free parking on first-come, first-served basis, turn left out of station, Viale Pallavicini 4, tel. 0544-212-363, www.hotelitaliaravenna.com, info@hotelitaliaravenna. com).

$ Albergo I Cherubini is a last-resort budget option with 18 basic, no-frills rooms and dark hallways. Ask for a room off the street (fans, cheaper rooms with shared bathrooms, Via R. Brancaleone 42, tel. 0544-39403, www.albergoristoranteicherubini.it, info@albergoristoranteicherubini.it, Donatella).

Eating in Ravenna

Located in the cuisine-crazy Emilia-Romagna region—famous for its cheeses and *salumi*—Ravenna has more than its share of great restaurants. Emilia-Romagna, nestled between farm fields and the sea, boasts seafood that's as good as its landfood. A local staple—served at carryout stands as well as fine restaurants—is *piadina* (pee-ah-DEE-nah), unleavened flatbread served plain or with a wide variety of fillings. At the top of every pasta menu is *cappelletti* ("little hats"), small doughy raviolis of cheese in a variety of sauces. Chefs here also make ample use of *squacquerone* ("shapeless"), a soft cream cheese that, by necessity, comes in a bowl. (For more on *salumi* and other Italian treats, see the "Eating" section of the Practicalities chapter.)

RESTAURANTS
$$ Ca' de Ven ("House of Wine"), the most famous restaurant in town, is surprisingly affordable. It fills a 16th-century warehouse with communal seating and residents enjoying quality wine and traditional regional cuisine. Up front is a bar with tables under or-

nately decorated Baroque domes, with 15-foot-tall wine cabinets towering above; in back is a huge hall under rough barrel vaults. For a light meal, order one of their *piadine*. Reserve ahead for dinner, and avoid weekend evenings when it's often overwhelmed (€38 fixed-price meal, no cover, Tue-Sun 11:00-14:15 & 18:30-22:00, closed Mon, 2-minute walk from Piazza del Popolo on Via Cairoli, which turns into Via C. Ricci—look for #24, tel. 0544-30163, www.cadeven.it). You can enjoy light meals and/or a glass of fine wine at the bar.

$$ Al Rustichello, a classic trattoria just outside the Porta Adriana city gate, has cozy ambience under heavy timbers. Few diners can resist their *cappelletti,* served in the pan it was cooked in. Their *antipasti* plate is a fun, splittable starter, with enticing samples of four local dishes (Mon-Sat 19:30-22:15, also open for lunch Mon-Fri 12:30-14:15, closed Sun, Via Maggiore 21, tel. 0544-36043).

$$ Antica Bottega di Felice, behind the covered market, has a cheese-and-meat shop in front and sit-down eatery in back, serving up new interpretations of local cuisine. While the space is more functional than atmospheric, the food more than compensates (Mon-Sat 8:00-24:00, closed Sun, Via Ponte Marino 23, tel. 0544-240-170).

$$ Passatelli l'Osteria del Mariani has turned a former cinema into a fun and lively place to dine. The big screen adds to the bright, modern, and spacious atmosphere (two smaller dining areas are less charismatic), as does the open kitchen where *piadina* and pasta are made. They offer modern fare from the Emilia-Romagna region and a hearty salad bar (daily 12:00-15:00 & 19:00-24:00, Via Ponte Marino 19, tel. 0544-215-206). For a cheap light meal, drop by their bar in front, where they offer an inviting *aperitivo* (free appetizers with your drink) from 18:00 to 24:00 each evening.

$$ Ristorante la Gardèla is a local fixture—if Ravenna had a town dining room, this would be it. The fun-loving waitstaff has been here for years, and the restaurant has all the nice touches without the pretense. While there are a few tables outside and upstairs, I like the jolly main floor. Their *cappelletti* is served *in brodo* (soup) or *al ragù* (with meat sauce; €15 and €25 fixed-price meals, Fri-Wed 12:00-14:30 & 19:00-22:00, closed Thu, tucked behind the covered market at Via Ponte Marino 3, tel. 0544-217-147).

FISH AND SEAFOOD

$$$ Ristorante Osteria del Tempo Perso is a red-velvet-romantic choice for seafood, with service as warm as its color scheme, mellow jazz on the soundtrack, and a grown-up vibe. I'd ignore the forgettable outdoor seating (daily 19:30-23:00, also Sat-Sun 12:30-14:00, Via Gamba 12, tel. 0544-215-393).

$$$ L'Acciuga Osteria ("Anchovy"), hiding at the back of a little courtyard on a residential street just outside the old town center, is well-respected for its intentionally short menu of fresh seafood that changes daily. Because everything is fresh and priced by the weight, this can get expensive, but it's worth a trip for seafood lovers. The restaurant is done up like the lower holds of a submarine, but—thanks to the tasteful, dressy decor—seems stylish rather than tacky (€48 fixed-price meal, Tue-Sat 12:00-15:00 & 19:30-22:30, Sun 12:00-14:30 only, closed Mon, Viale Francesco Baracca 74, tel. 0544-212-713).

QUICK SNACK SPOTS

$ *Piadina* Stands: For the best cheap, traditional lunch in Ravenna, skip the pizza and instead grab a *piadina*. These tasty flatbread sandwiches are stuffed with a variety of local meats, vegetables, and cheeses (including *squacquerone,* described earlier), then folded over and grilled. You'll see several takeout windows in the downtown pedestrian zone selling them. Consider the popular-with-students **Profuma di Piadina** (on the way from Piazza del Popolo to the Basilica di San Francesco, at Via Cairoli 24) and **La Piadina del Melarancio** (just off Piazza del Popolo at Via IV Novembre 31). For a break from Italian food, **Ali Kebab,** across from La Piadina del Melarancio at Via IV Novembre 26, is cheap, fast, and inviting.

Local Products: Tucked into a small courtyard along the main pedestrian street, **Gastronomia Alpine,** a "gastronomic boutique," sells regional cheeses, *salumi,* country bread, and other products, treating in-the-know picnic shoppers to the bounty of the local Emilia-Romagna region (Mon-Wed 8:00-16:00, Thu-Sun until 21:00, Via Cavour 43, tel. 0544-37529). **Antica Bottega di Felice,** recommended earlier as a restaurant, also has a fine cheese and *salumi* shop up front.

Supermarkets: For lunch, assemble a picnic at the **InCoop** store at the corner of Via di Roma and Via A. Mariani (daily 8:00-20:30 except closed Sun for a few hours midday). A fine place to enjoy your feast is in the shady gardens of the Rocca Brancaleone fortress (daily until 18:00; 5-minute walk from station, follow Via Maroncelli until you see the walls).

Sweets: Bright, loud, and trendy, **Papilla Gelato** offers free dips from its chocolate fountain if you like (pricey cones, but small is big here, a block off Piazza del Popolo at Via IV Novembre 8). **Leonardi Dolciumi,** not far from the covered market, curates fine chocolates and candies from Italian producers that you can mix and match. Elisa and Sergio will even do instructive chocolate tastings (€3-5/person, 25 minutes). They also have select wines and regional gourmet products (daily 9:00-19:30, Via Pellegrino

RAVENNA

Matteucci 5A, mobile 340-9699-7947, www.leonardidolciumi. com).

Ravenna Connections

From Ravenna by Train to: Venice (roughly hourly, 3 hours), **Padua** (roughly hourly, 2.5-3.5 hours), **Florence** (about hourly, 2.5 hours by fast train, no slow train option). All of these trips require a change in either Ferrara or Bologna.

VENETIAN HISTORY

In the Middle Ages, the clever Venetian aristocracy became Europe's middlemen for East-West trade, creating a great merchant empire presided over by a series of elected dukes, called doges. By smuggling in the bones of St. Mark, Venice gained religious importance as well. But after the discovery of America and new trading routes to the Orient, Venetian power ebbed. Yet as Venice fell, her appetite for decadence grew. Throughout the 17th and 18th centuries, Venice partied on the wealth accumulated during its time as a trading power.

That's Venetian history in a seashell. Want more? Read on.

ROME FALLS, VENICE RISES (AD 500)
In AD 476, the last Roman emperor abdicated, the empire's infrastructure was crumbling, and northern Italy was crawling with

Germanic-speaking "barbarian" invaders. Hoping these Visigoths, Huns, and Lombards didn't like water, Latin-speaking mainlanders took refuge on the marshy, uninhabited islands of the Venetian lagoon.

The refugees squatted on this wet and miserable land. Eventually, they sank pilings in the mud to build on, channeled water into canals, and constructed bridges to lace together the motley collection of more than 100 natural islands that would eventually become Venice.

MEDIEVAL GROWTH (500-1000)

These first Venetians harvested salt and fish for their livelihood, and traded it on the mainland. Though Venice's islands were desolate, the area—known to the Romans as the "Seven Seas"—was strategically important. In about 540 AD, the Byzantine Emperor Justinian reconquered Italy from the barbarians and briefly reunited the Roman Empire. He established a capital at Ravenna, bringing the Venetian islands under Byzantine influence.

Soon, Venetians began to elect local rulers whom they called "doges"—the first of many who would rule for more than a thousand years. (Though "doge" is linguistically related to our word "duke," Venetian rulers were more like constitutional monarchs, elected by their fellow nobles and expected to govern according to the rule of law.) As early as 810, one doge had his seat in the settlement of Rivo Alto ("High Bank"), near today's Rialto Bridge.

Under Byzantine protection, Venetians became prosperous seagoing merchants. Acting as middlemen, they bought goods from the sophisticated Byzantine and Islamic lands to the East and sold them to consumers in the West.

Venice's merchant economy boomed while the rest of Europe languished under land-based feudalism. Charlemagne, the Holy Roman Emperor who'd conquered much of Italy (c. 800), eyed the region hungrily. But Venetians, wanting to keep their independence, deposed Charlemagne's bishop and chose one who was loyal to distant Byzantium.

To legitimize their new bishop, the Venetians managed to smuggle the holy relics of St. Mark from Egypt in 828, thus becoming a religious power overnight. To seal the city's oriental orientation, Venetian leaders had the grand St. Mark's Basilica built in a distinctly Eastern style.

Sights

- Gondolas and the network of canals
- Old crypt under San Zaccaria Church
- Santa Maria Assunta Church on Torcello Island

A SEAFARING POWER (1000-1500)

Venetian sea traders established trading outposts in Byzantine and Muslim territories to the east. They used the same alpine passes that we travel today to ship luxury goods to Western Europe. At home, a stable, constitutional government ran an efficient, state-

Venice's Empire

London
•Amsterdam
•Bruges
Paris
•Vienna
Atlantic
Ocean
Verona
Milan• ⓐ **Venice**
Genoa•
Ravenna• DALMATIA
Pisa•
Florence•
Rome•
Amalfi•
Black
Sea
Constantinople
Corfu
Aegean
Sea
To China →
Gibraltar
Mediterranean
Sea
BATTLE OF
LEPANTO
(1571)
Nafplio
Crete
Rhodes
Cyprus
HOLY
LAND
Alexandria•

■ Lands united with or linked to the
Venetian Empire over the centuries

---- Current National Borders

operated multinational corporation.
The shallow lagoon was easily defended
against attack, making fortifications
unnecessary. Grand buildings reflected
Venice's wealth.

Venetian merchants ran a prof-
itable trading triangle: timber from
Venice's mainland to Egypt for gold to
Byzantium for luxury goods to Venice.
Its merchant fleet was the biggest in
the Mediterranean, backed by powerful warships.

By the 12th century, tiny Venice
had effectively established itself as an

HISTORY

independent, self-ruling country and was running Europe's first
industrial complex, the Arsenale (1104). With more than 1,000
workers using an early form of assembly-line production, the Arsenale could produce about one warship a day. This put the "fear
of Venice" into visiting rulers. When France's King Henry III
dropped by the Arsenale, Venice entertained him with a shipbuilding spectacle: from ribs to finished product in four hours.

When Europe launched its Crusades to the Holy Land (1095-
1272), Venice transported soldiers and defended Byzantine and
Crusader ports in return for commercial privileges. This made the

eastern Mediterranean a virtual free-trade zone for a very aggressive Venetian trading community to exploit.

Wealthy Venetian nobles built lavish homes. With a natural lagoon as a defense, these were not fortified castles like the rest of Europe but luxurious *palazzi*, complete with loading docks, warehouses, and chandeliered ballrooms. The streets were paved. The government provided oil and required that streets be lit—a first in Europe.

Besides sea trade, Venice established strong local industries. Having mastered the art of making glass, Venice was on the cutting edge of the new science of grinding lenses for eyeglasses and telescopes. Understanding medicine as a chemical rather than an herbal pursuit, Venetians developed Europe's first real pharmaceutical industry. They made Europe's first affordable paper, from rags rather than from sheepskin (parchment). As the city offered the world's first copyright protection, its printing and bookmaking industry boomed. With mountains of capital and a sophisticated trade system of insurance, joint ventures, and money drafts, Venice's merchants eventually became bankers, loaning money at interest—making them early capitalists.

Rather than being ruled by a king—as was standard in feudal Europe—Venice developed a sophisticated government run by voting aristocrats. By the 13th century, Venice was fast becoming a Mediterranean superpower. During the Fourth Crusade (1204), Venetian troops joined other Crusaders in attacking and looting Christian Constantinople. The haul of booty enriched the city, enabling Venice to stand up to its former Byzantine protectors. When Venetian ships routed the fleet of their Genoan rivals at Chioggia (on the south end of the lagoon) in 1381, Venice became the undisputed master of the eastern Mediterranean. Next, they launched attacks on the mainland, conquering much of northern Italy. By 1420, Venice was at the height of its power, with mainland possessions and a powerful overseas trading empire to the east.

Sights
- Doge's Palace
- St. Mark's Basilica
- Frari Church
- Buildings decorated in ornate Venetian Gothic style
- Doge paraphernalia and city history at Correr Museum
- Glass and lace industries (including the Murano glassworks)
- Arsenale shipbuilding complex

Noteworthy Residents
Enrico Dandolo (r. 1192-1205): Doge during the Fourth Crusade,

when Venetian crusaders looted Constantinople, helping to enrich Venice.

Marco Polo (1254-1324): Traveler to faraway China whose journal, *The Book of Marvels*, was dismissed by many as fiction.

Paolo Veneziano (1310-1358): Painter who mastered the Byzantine gold-icon style, then added touches of Western realism.

Francesco Foscari (1373-1457): Doge at the peak of Venice's power, whose ill-advised wars against Milan and the Ottoman Turks started the Republic's slow fade.

Jacopo Bellini (c. 1400-1470): Father of painting family. His training in Renaissance Florence brought 3-D realism to Venice.

Gentile Bellini (c. 1429-1507): Elder son of painting family, known for straightforward, historical scenes of Venice.

RENAISSANCE AND SEEDS OF DECLINE (1500-1600)

In 1500, Venice was a commercial powerhouse—among the six biggest cities in Europe. Of its estimated 180,000 citizens, nearly

1,000 were of Rockefeller-esque wealth and power. Europe's richest city-state poured money into the arts. Titian, Tintoretto, Sansovino, the Bellini family, and Palladio called Venice home. St. Mark's Square became the gathering place for merchants and nobles from Venice's vast trading empire. Across Europe, Venice had a reputation as a luxury-loving, exotic, cosmopolitan playground.

But Venice's power had started to wane. The seeds had been sown in the 15th century. In 1492, Columbus sailed the ocean blue, and began to trade with a World that was New. In 1498, Vasco da Gama circled Africa's Cape of Good Hope, finding a new sea route to eastern markets. Venice's monopoly was broken.

On the Italian mainland, Venice became locked in draining wars against its rival Milan. Meanwhile, Ottomans were expanding in the East, encroaching on Venice's former dominions. Venetians and Ottomans became wary trade partners, sometimes dealing peacefully but sometimes battling over strategic ports. In 1453, the Ottomans took Constantinople, and Venice suddenly lost one of its best customers. Venice (and its European allies) scored a temporary victory over the Ottomans at the Battle of Lepanto (1571), but Venice's navy suffered major damage. Spain, England, and Holland, with their oceangoing vessels, emerged as superior traders in a more global economy.

HISTORY

Church Architecture

History comes to life when you visit a centuries-old church. Even if you wouldn't know your apse from a hole in the ground, learning a few simple terms will enrich your experience. Of course, not every church has every feature. It's worth noting that a "cathedral" (*duomo* in Italian) isn't a type of church architecture, but rather a designation for a church that's a governing center for a local bishop.

Aisles: The long, generally low-ceilinged arcades that flank the nave.

Altar: The raised area with a ceremonial table (often adorned with candles or a crucifix), where the priest prepares and serves the bread and wine for Communion.

Apse: The space beyond the altar, generally bordered with small chapels.

Barrel Vault: A continuous round-arched ceiling that resembles an upside-down "U."

Choir: A cozy area, often screened off, located within the church nave and near the high altar, where services are sung in a more intimate setting.

Cloister: Covered hallways bordering a square or rectangular open-air courtyard, traditionally where monks and nuns got fresh air.

Facade: The exterior of the church's main (west) entrance, usually highly decorated.

Groin Vault: An arched ceiling formed where two equal barrel vaults meet at right angles. Also: a medieval jock strap.

Narthex: The area (portico or foyer) between the main entry and the nave.

Nave: The long, central section of the church (running west to east, from the entrance to the altar) where the congregation sits or stands through the service.

Transept: In a traditional cross-shaped floor plan, the transept is one of the two parts forming the "arms" of the cross. The transept runs north-south, perpendicularly crossing the east-west nave.

West Portal: The main entry to the church (on the west end, opposite the main altar).

Sights
- St. Mark's Square facades and other work by Sansovino
- Palladio's classical facades (San Giorgio Maggiore and Il Redentore churches)
- Masterpiece paintings by Titian, Giovanni Bellini, Giorgione, and Tintoretto (Accademia, Frari Church, Doge's Palace, San Zaccaria Church, Correr Museum, Scuola San Rocco)
- Jewish Ghetto and Jewish Museum

Noteworthy Residents
Giovanni Bellini (c. 1430-1516): The most famous son in the painting family, whose glowing, colorful, 3-D Madonna-and-Childs started the Venetian Renaissance. Teacher of Titian and Giorgione.

Vittore Carpaccio (c. 1460-1525): Painter of realistic, secular scenes and the impressive Scuola Dalmata di San Giorgio.

Giorgione (c. 1477-1511): Innovative painter whose moody realism influenced Bellini (his teacher) and Titian (his friend and fellow painter).

Jacopo Sansovino (1486-1570): Renaissance architect who redid the face of Venice (especially St. Mark's Square), introducing sober, classical columns and arches to a city previously full of ornate Gothic.

Titian (Tiziano Vecellio, c. 1490-1576): Premier Venetian Renaissance painter. Master of many styles, from teenage Madonnas to sober state portraits to exuberant mythological scenes to centerfold nudes.

Andrea Palladio (1508-1580): Influential architect whose classical style was much imitated around the world, resulting in villas, government buildings, and banks that look like Greek temples.

Tintoretto (Jacopo Robusti, c. 1518-1594): Painter of dramatic religious scenes, using strong 3-D, diagonal compositions, twisting poses, sharp contrast of light and shadow, and bright, "black velvet" colors (late Renaissance/Mannerist style).

Paolo Veronese (1528-1588): Painter of big, colorful canvases, capturing the exuberance and luxury of Renaissance Venice.

ELEGANT DECLINE (1600-1800)
New trade routes, new European powers, and belligerent Ottomans drained Venice's economy and shrank its commercial empire. At home, however, Venice's reputation for luxury—and even decadence—still made it a popular tourist destination for Europe's gentry. In some ways, this is the period that most defines Venice: the city of Baroque monuments, masked balls at Carnevale, velvet-dressed nobles at opera debuts, and the roguish debauchery of Casanova.

Venice's empire dwindled economically and politically. In 1669, its last major outpost, Crete, fell to the Ottomans. Several devastating plagues gutted the population at home. The once-enlightened government gained a nasty reputation for corruption and for locking away dissidents in the dank prisons of the Doge's Palace. In 1797, Napoleon Bonaparte rolled into Venice and toppled the final doge. A thousand-year era of independent rule was over.

Sights

- Ca' Rezzonico (Museum of 18th-Century Venice)
- La Salute Church
- Masks of the Carnevale tradition
- Old cafés (e.g., the Florian and the Quadri, both on St. Mark's Square)
- La Fenice Opera House
- Baroque interiors in many churches
- Canova sculptures (Correr Museum, Frari Church)
- G. B. Tiepolo paintings (Accademia, Doge's Palace, Ca' Rezzonico)
- Paintings of Canaletto, Guardi, and G. D. Tiepolo (Ca' Rezzonico)

Noteworthy Residents

Claudio Monteverdi (1567-1643): The composer and *maestro di capella* at St. Mark's Basilica who wrote in a budding new medium—opera.

Baldassare Longhena (1598-1682): Architect of the Baroque La Salute Church.

Antonio Vivaldi (1678-1741): Composer of *The Four Seasons* ("Dah dunt-dunt-duh dutta dah-ah-ah").

G. B. Tiepolo (Giovanni Battista, 1696-1770): Painter of mythological subjects in colorful Rococo ceilings.

Giovanni Antonio Canal, a.k.a. Canaletto (1697-1768): Painter of photo-realist Venice views.

Carlo Goldoni (1707-1793): Comic playwright who brought refinement to commedia dell'arte buffoonery.

Francesco Guardi (1712-1793): Painter of proto-Impressionist Venice views.

Giacomo Casanova (1725-1798): Gambler, womanizer, and adventurer whose exaggerated memoirs inspired Romantics.

HISTORY

G. D. Tiepolo (Giovanni Domenico, 1727-1804): Painter son of the famous G. B. Tiepolo.

Lorenzo Da Ponte (1749-1838): Mozart's librettist, who popularized Venice's sophisticated and decadent high society.

Antonio Canova (1757-1822): Neoclassical sculptor whose beautiful polished-white statues were especially popular in Napoleon's France.

MODERN VENICE (1800 TO THE PRESENT)

After Napoleon's defeat at Waterloo, the European allies placed Venice under Austrian rule. Sophisticated Venetians chafed against their Viennese masters. However, Venice was still a key stop on any traveler's Grand Tour, and Europe's young aristocrats visited the city to "complete" their education. Venice and Italy became a political backwater as Austrian and French influence dominated.

In 1866, when Prussia dealt Austria a humiliating military defeat, rebellious Venetians seized the moment to join Italy's independence movement, and annexed themselves to the newly unified, democratic nation of Italy.

Venice joined the Industrial Revolution only reluctantly. A two-mile railroad causeway was built to connect the island city with the mainland during the Austrian period (1846). This was later paralleled by a highway for cars (1932). On the mainland, unbridled industrialization produced pollution (mainly sulfuric acid) that threatened Venice's stone monuments. In 1966, Venice suffered a disastrous flood, which prompted many plans and projects to control future flooding—some have been enacted, while others are still on the drawing board.

Inside Venice proper, however, there has been little new building for centuries. Today, Venice remains a museum piece for

foreigners—one increasingly threatened by mainland pollution, climate change, floods, and hordes of tourists. In the 2000s, Venice—ever an obligatory destination—became a hugely popular stop for cruise ships. Local and UNESCO regulations try to preserve Venice as a cultural landmark. When Venice's venerable La Fenice Opera House burned down in 1996, it was rebuilt right away. Recent repairs to the Rialto Bridge have been largely funded by the Diesel fashion line, whose owner pledged €5 million in response to the city's pleas for sponsorship (but only in return for advertising space on the scaffolding). While keeping up with what's new, Venice remains a historic wonderland. Venice is timeless—a place where visitors can easily blink away elements of the modern world and find themselves transported back in time.

Sights
- Correr Museum's Risorgimento wing
- Statue of Daniele Manin (between St. Mark's Square and Rialto Bridge)
- Motorized vaporetti and taxis
- Train station (1954)
- Peggy Guggenheim Collection
- Biennale International Art Exhibition (held in odd years)
- Pollution from the mainland city of Mestre
- Calatrava Bridge (2008)
- Stazione Marittima cruise port
- Burger King and KFC

Noteworthy Residents
Daniele Manin (1804-1857): Rebel who led 1848 Venetian revolt against the city's Austrian rulers, eventually allowing Venice to join a united, democratic, modern Italy.

Peggy Guggenheim (1898-1979): American-born art collector, gallery owner, and friend of modern art and artists.

For more on the history of Venice and on Europe throughout the centuries, consider Europe 101: History and Art for the Traveler, *written by Rick Steves and Gene Openshaw (available at www.ricksteves.com).*

HISTORY

PRACTICALITIES

This chapter covers the practical skills of European travel: how to get tourist information, pay for things, sightsee efficiently, find good-value accommodations, eat affordably but well, use technology wisely, and get between destinations smoothly. For more information on these topics, see www.ricksteves.com/travel-tips.

Tourist Information

Before your trip, scan the website of the Italian national tourist office (www.italia.it) for a wealth of travel information. If you have a specific question, try contacting one of their US offices (New York: Tel. 212/245-5618, newyork@enit.it; Chicago: Tel. 312/644-9335, chicago@enit.it; Los Angeles: Tel. 310/820-1898, losangeles@enit.it).

In Venice, TIs are generally understaffed and not very helpful. For more on their services and locations, see page 13.

Travel Tips

Emergency and Medical Help: For any emergency service—ambulance, police, or fire—call **112** from a mobile phone or landline. Operators, who generally speak English, will deal with your request or route you to the right emergency service. If you get sick, do as the locals do and go to a pharmacist for advice. Or ask at your hotel for help—they'll know the nearest medical and emergency services. For the hospital and first-aid help, see page 15.

ETIAS Registration: Beginning in 2021, US and Canadian citizens may be required to register online with the European Travel Information and Authorization System (ETIAS) before entering certain European countries (quick and easy process, $8 fee, valid 3 years). A useful private website with more details is www.schengenvisainfo.com/etias.

Theft or Loss: To replace a passport, you'll need to go in person to an embassy (see below). If your credit and debit cards disappear, cancel and replace them (see "Damage Control for Lost Cards," later). File a police report, either on the spot or within a day or two; you'll need it to submit an insurance claim for lost or stolen rail passes or electronics, and it can help with replacing your passport or credit and debit cards. For more information, see www.ricksteves.com/help.

US Embassies and Consulates: Embassy in Rome—tel. 06-46741 for 24-hour emergency line, tel. 06-4674-2420 for non-emergencies, by appointment only (Via Vittorio Veneto 121). Consulates in Milan—tel. 02-290-351 (Via Principe Amedeo 2/10); Florence—tel. 055-266-951 (Lungarno Vespucci 38); and Naples—tel. 081-583-8111 (Piazza della Repubblica). For all, see http://it.usembassy.gov.

Canadian Embassies and Consulates: Rome—tel. 06-854-442-911 (Via Zara 30); Milan—tel. 02-626-94238 (Piazza Cavour 3). For both, see www.italy.gc.ca.

Time Zones: Italy, like most of continental Europe, is generally six/nine hours ahead of the East/West Coasts of the US. The exceptions are the beginning and end of Daylight Saving Time: Europe "springs forward" the last Sunday in March (two weeks after most of North America), and "falls back" the last Sunday in October (one week before North America). For a handy time converter, use the world clock app on your phone or download one (see www.timeanddate.com).

Business Hours: Traditionally, Italy used the siesta plan, with people generally working from about 9:00 to 13:00 and from 15:30-16:00 to 19:00-19:30, Monday through Saturday. Siesta hours are no longer required by law, so many shops stay open through lunch or later into the evening, especially larger stores in tourist areas. In

Venice, some stores and restaurants close on Sunday, or at least one other day per week.

Watt's Up? Europe's electrical system is 220 volts, instead of North America's 110 volts. Most electronics (laptops, smartphones, cameras) and new hair dryers convert automatically, so you won't need a converter, but you will need an adapter plug with two round prongs, sold inexpensively at travel stores in the US. Sockets in Italy and Switzerland only accept plugs with slimmer prongs: Don't buy an adapter with the thicker ("Schuko" style) prongs—it won't work. Avoid bringing older appliances that don't automatically convert voltage; instead, buy a cheap replacement in Europe.

Discounts: Discounts for sights are generally not listed in this book. Italy's national museums generally offer free admission to children under 18, but some discounts are available only for citizens of the European Union (EU). However, Venice's city museums (run by the Fondazione Musei Civici Venezia, or MUVE) all offer youth and senior discounts to Americans and others who are not citizens of the EU—bring an ID. These museums include the Doge's Palace, Correr Museum, Clock Tower on St. Mark's Square, Ca' Rezzonico, Ca' Pesaro, Palazzo Mocenigo Costume Museum, Murano's Glass Museum, and Burano's Lace Museum.

Online Translation Tips: Google's Chrome browser instantly translates websites; Translate.google.com is also handy. The Google Translate app converts spoken or typed English into most European languages (and vice versa) and can also translate text it "reads" with your smartphone's camera.

Money

Here's my basic strategy for using money in Europe:
- Upon arrival, head for a cash machine (ATM) at the airport and withdraw some local currency, using a debit card with low international transaction fees.
- In general, pay for bigger expenses with a credit card and use cash for smaller purchases and tips. Use a debit card only for cash withdrawals.
- Keep your cards and cash safe in a money belt.

PLASTIC VERSUS CASH
Although credit cards are widely accepted in Europe, cash is sometimes the only way to pay for cheap food, bus fare, taxis, tips, and local guides. Some businesses (especially smaller ones, such as B&Bs and mom-and-pop cafés and shops) may charge you extra for using a credit card—or might not accept credit cards at all. Having cash on hand helps you out of a jam if your card randomly doesn't work.

PRACTICALITIES

Exchange Rate

1 euro (€) = about $1.20

To convert prices in euros to dollars, add about 20 percent: €20 = about $24, €50 = about $60. (Check www.oanda.com for the latest exchange rates.) Just like the dollar, one euro is broken down into 100 cents. Coins range from €0.01 to €2, and bills from €5 to €200 (bills over €50 are rarely used).

I use my credit card to book and pay for hotel reservations, to buy advance tickets for events or sights, and to cover most other expenses. It can also be smart to use plastic near the end of your trip, to avoid another visit to the ATM.

WHAT TO BRING

I pack the following and keep it all safe in my money belt.

Debit Card: Use this at ATMs to withdraw local cash.

Credit Card: Handy for bigger transactions (at hotels, shops, restaurants, travel agencies, car-rental agencies, and so on), payment machines, and online purchases.

Backup Card: Some travelers carry a third card (debit or credit; ideally from a different bank), in case one gets lost, demagnetized, eaten by a temperamental machine, or simply doesn't work.

A Stash of Cash: I carry $100-200 in US dollars as a cash backup, which comes in handy in an emergency (such as when the banks go on strike or if your ATM card gets eaten by the machine).

What NOT to Bring: Resist the urge to buy euros before your trip or you'll pay the price in bad stateside exchange rates. Wait until you arrive to withdraw money. I've yet to see a European airport that didn't have plenty of ATMs.

BEFORE YOU GO

Use this pre-trip checklist.

Know your cards. Debit cards from any major US bank will work in any standard European bank's ATM (ideally, use a debit card with a Visa or MasterCard logo). As for credit cards, Visa and MasterCard are universal, American Express is less common, and Discover is unknown in Europe.

Know your PIN. Make sure you know the numeric, four-digit PIN for all of your cards, both debit and credit. Request it if you don't have one, as it may be required for some purchases in Europe (see "Using Credit Cards," later), and allow time to receive the information by mail.

Report your travel dates. Let your bank know that you'll be using your debit and credit cards in Europe, and when and where you're headed.

Adjust your ATM withdrawal limit. Find out how much you can take out daily and ask for a higher daily withdrawal limit if you want to get more cash at once. Note that European ATMs will withdraw funds only from checking accounts; you're unlikely to have access to your savings account.

Ask about fees. For any purchase or withdrawal made with a card, you may be charged a currency conversion fee (1-3 percent) and/or a Visa or MasterCard international transaction fee (less than 1 percent). If you're getting a bad deal, consider getting a new debit or credit card. Reputable no-fee cards include those from Capital One, as well as Charles Schwab debit cards. Most credit unions and some airline loyalty cards have low or no international transaction fees.

IN EUROPE
Using Cash Machines
European cash machines have English-language instructions and work just like they do at home—except they spit out local currency instead of dollars, calculated at the day's standard bank-to-bank rate.

In most places, ATMs are easy to locate—in Italy ask for a *bancomat*. When possible, withdraw cash from a bank-run ATM located just outside that bank. Ideally use the machine during the bank's opening hours so you can go inside for help if your card is munched.

If your debit card doesn't work, try a lower amount—your request may have exceeded your withdrawal limit or the ATM's limit. If you still have a problem, try a different ATM or come back later—your bank's network may be temporarily down.

Avoid "independent" ATMs, such as Travelex, Euronet, Moneybox, Your Cash, Cardpoint, and Cashzone. These have high fees, can be less secure than a bank ATM, and may try to trick users with "dynamic currency conversion" (see next page).

Exchanging Cash
Avoid exchanging money in Europe; it's a big rip-off. In a pinch, you can always find exchange desks at major train stations or airports—convenient but with crummy rates. Anything over 5 percent for a transaction is piracy. Banks generally do not exchange money unless you have an account with them.

Using Credit Cards
Despite some differences between European and US cards, there's little to worry about: US credit cards generally work fine in Eu-

PRACTICALITIES

rope. I've been inconvenienced a few times by self-service payment machines that wouldn't accept my card, but it's never caused me serious trouble (I carry cash just in case).

European cards use chip-and-PIN technology; most chip cards issued in the US instead have a signature option. Some European card readers will accept your card as-is while others may generate a receipt for you to sign or prompt you to enter your PIN (so it's important to know the code for each of your cards). If a cashier is present, you should have no problems.

At self-service payment machines (transit-ticket kiosks, parking, etc.), results are mixed, as US cards may not work in some unattended transactions. If your card won't work, look for a cashier who can process your card manually—or pay in cash.

Drivers Beware: Be aware of potential problems using a US credit card to fill up at an unattended gas station, enter a parking garage, or exit a toll road. Always carry cash as a backup and be prepared to move on to the next gas station if necessary. When approaching a toll plaza, use the "cash" lane.

Dynamic Currency Conversion

If merchants offer to convert your purchase price into dollars (called dynamic currency conversion, or DCC), refuse this "service." You'll pay extra for the expensive convenience of seeing your charge in dollars. If an ATM offers to "lock in" or "guarantee" your conversion rate, choose "proceed without conversion." Other prompts might state, "You can be charged in dollars: Press YES for dollars, NO for euros." Always choose the local currency.

Security Tips

Pickpockets target tourists. Keep your cash, credit cards, and passport secure in your money belt, and carry only a day's spending money in your front pocket or wallet.

Before inserting your card into an ATM, inspect the front. If anything looks crooked, loose, or damaged, it could be a sign of a card-skimming device. When entering your PIN, carefully block other people's view of the keypad.

Don't use a debit card for purchases. Because a debit card pulls funds directly from your bank account, potential charges incurred by a thief will stay on your account while the fraudulent use is investigated by your bank.

To access your accounts online while traveling, be sure to use a secure connection (see the "Tips on Internet Security" sidebar, later).

Damage Control for Lost Cards

If you lose your credit or debit card, report the loss immediately to the respective global customer-assistance centers. With a mobile phone, call these 24-hour US numbers: Visa (tel. +1 303/967-1096), MasterCard (tel. +1 636/722-7111), and American Express (tel. +1 336/393-1111). From a landline, you can call these US numbers collect by going through a local operator. European toll-free numbers can be found at the websites for Visa and MasterCard.

You'll need to provide the primary cardholder's identification-verification details (such as birth date, mother's maiden name, or Social Security number). You can generally receive a temporary card within two or three business days in Europe (see www.ricksteves.com/help for more).

If you report your loss within two days, you typically won't be responsible for unauthorized transactions on your account, although many banks charge a liability fee.

TIPPING

Tipping in Italy isn't as automatic and generous as it is in the US. For special service, tips are appreciated, but not expected. As in the US, the proper amount depends on your resources, tipping philosophy, and the circumstances, but some general guidelines apply.

Restaurants: In Italy, a service charge *(servizio)* is usually built into your check (look at the bill carefully). If it is included, there's no need to leave an extra tip. If it's not included, it's common to leave about €1 per person (a bit more at finer restaurants) or to round up the bill. For more details on restaurant tipping, see page 435.

Taxis: For a typical ride, round up your fare a bit (for instance, if the fare is €4.50, pay €5). If the cabbie hauls your bags and zips you to the airport to help you catch your flight, you might want to toss in a little more. But if you feel like you're being driven in circles or otherwise ripped off, skip the tip.

Services: In general, if someone in the tourism or service industry does a super job for you, a small tip of a euro or two is appropriate...but not required. If you're not sure whether (or how much) to tip, ask a local for advice.

GETTING A VAT REFUND

Wrapped into the purchase price of your Italian souvenirs is a Value-Added Tax (VAT) of about 22 percent. You're entitled to get most of that tax back if you purchase more than €155 (about $170) worth of goods at a store that participates in the VAT-refund scheme. Typically, you must ring up the minimum at a single retailer—you can't add up your purchases from various shops to reach the required amount. (If the store ships the goods to your US home, VAT is not assessed on your purchase.)

Getting your refund is straightforward...and worthwhile if you spend a significant amount on souvenirs.

Get the paperwork. Have the merchant completely fill out the necessary refund document. You'll have to present your passport. Get the paperwork done before you leave the store to ensure you'll have everything you need (including your original sales receipt).

Get your stamp at the border or airport. Process your VAT document at your last stop in the European Union (such as at the airport) with the customs agent who deals with VAT refunds. Arrive an additional hour before you need to check in to allow time to find the customs office—and wait. Some customs desks are positioned before airport security; confirm the location before going through security.

It's best to keep your purchases in your carry-on. If your item isn't allowed as carry-on (such as a knife), pack it in your checked bag and alert the check-in agent. You'll be sent (with your tagged bag) to a customs desk outside security; someone will examine your bag, stamp your paperwork, and put your bag on the belt. You're not supposed to use your purchased goods before you leave. If you show up at customs wearing your new Italian leather shoes, officials might look the other way—or deny you a refund.

Collect your refund. You can claim your VAT refund from refund companies such as Global Blue or Planet with offices at major airports, ports, or border crossings (either before or after security, probably strategically located near a duty-free shop). These services (which extract a 4 percent fee) can refund your money in cash immediately or credit your card. Otherwise, mail the stamped refund documents to the address given by the shop where you made your purchase.

CUSTOMS FOR AMERICAN SHOPPERS

You can take home $800 worth of items per person duty-free, once every 31 days. Many processed and packaged foods are allowed, including vacuum-packed cheeses, dried herbs, jams, baked goods, candy, chocolate, oil, vinegar, mustard, and honey. Fresh fruits and vegetables and most meats are not allowed, with exceptions for some canned items. As for alcohol, you can bring in one liter duty-free (it can be packed securely in your checked luggage, along with any other liquid-containing items).

To bring alcohol (or liquid-packed foods) in your carry-on bag on your flight home, buy it at a duty-free shop at the airport. You'll increase your odds of getting it onto a connecting flight if it's packaged in a "STEB"—a secure, tamper-evident bag. But stay away from liquids in opaque, ceramic, or metallic containers, which usually cannot be successfully screened (STEB or no STEB).

For details on allowable goods, customs rules, and duty rates, visit http://help.cbp.gov.

Sightseeing

Sightseeing can be hard work. Use these tips to make your visits to Venice's finest sights meaningful, fun, efficient, and painless.

MAPS AND NAVIGATION TOOLS

A good map is essential for efficient navigation while sightseeing. The maps in this book are concise and simple, designed to help you locate recommended destinations, sights, and local TIs, where you can pick up more in-depth maps.

You can also use a mapping app on your mobile device. Be aware that pulling up maps or looking up turn-by-turn walking directions on the fly usually requires a data connection: To use this feature, it's smart to get an international data plan. With Google Maps or City Maps 2Go, it's possible to download a map while online, then go offline and navigate without incurring data-roaming charges, though you can't search for an address or get real-time walking directions. A handful of other apps—including Apple Maps and Navmii—also allow you to use maps offline.

PLAN AHEAD

Set up an itinerary that allows you to fit in all your must-see sights. For a one-stop look at opening hours, see "Venice at a Glance" on page 34 (also see the "Daily Reminder" on page 14). Most sights keep stable hours, but you can easily confirm the latest by checking with the TI or visiting museum websites. Or call sights in the morning and ask: "Are you open today?" (*"Aperto oggi?"*; ah-PER-toh OH-jee) and "What time do you close?" (*"A che ora chiude?"*; ah kay OH-rah kee-OO-day).

Don't put off visiting a must-see sight—you never know when a place will close unexpectedly for a holiday, strike, or restoration. Many museums are closed or have reduced hours at least a few days a year, especially on holidays such as Christmas, New Year's *(Capo-danno)*, Italian Liberation Day (April 25), and Labor Day (May 1). A list of holidays is in the appendix; check for possible closures during your trip. In summer, some sights may stay open late. In the off-season, hours may be shorter.

Going at the right time helps avoid crowds. This book offers tips on the best times to see specific sights. Try visiting popular sights very early or very late. Evening visits (when possible) are usually peaceful, with fewer crowds. Late-morning is usually the worst time to visit a popular sight.

If you plan to hire a local guide, reserve ahead by email. Popular guides can get booked up.

Study up. To get the most out of the self-guided tours and sight descriptions in this book, read them before you visit.

RESERVATIONS, ADVANCE TICKETS, AND PASSES

Given how precious your vacation time is, I recommend getting reservations for any must-see sight that offers them. If you plan to visit Padua's Scrovegni Chapel, make reservations in advance (see page 330). Reservations are also required for the view terrace at Venice's Fondaco dei Tedeschi mall (see page 43). You might also consider reserving an entry slot for St. Mark's Basilica or to tour the Clock Tower on St. Mark's Square in Venice (see page 77).

To deal with lines, many popular sights sell advance tickets that guarantee admission at a certain time of day (for example, Venice's St. Mark's Basilica), or that allow you to skip entry lines. Either way, it's worth giving up some spontaneity to book in advance. While hundreds of tourists sweat in long ticket-buying lines, those who've booked ahead are assured of getting in. In some cases, getting a ticket in advance simply means buying your ticket earlier on the same day. But for other sights, you may need to book weeks or even months in advance. As soon as you're ready to commit to a certain date, book it.

The advance-purchase price may be less expensive than what you would pay on-site (my listings include the online price, if available). And many museums offer convenient mobile ticketing. Simply buy your ticket online and send it to your phone, eliminating the need for a paper ticket.

Booking a guided tour can help you avoid lines at many popular sights. So can knowing what days to avoid. Italian state museums are free to enter (and often very crowded) one or two days a month; the specific day varies in peak season (in low season, it's the first Sun). Check museum websites for specifics and avoid free entry days when possible.

AT SIGHTS

Here's what you can typically expect:

Entering: You may not be allowed to enter if you arrive too close to closing time. And guards start ushering people out well before the actual closing time, so don't save the best for last.

Many sights have a security check. Allow extra time for these lines. Some sights require you to check daypacks and coats. (If you'd rather not check your daypack, try carrying it tucked under your arm like a purse as you enter.)

Photography: If the museum's photo policy isn't clearly posted, ask a guard. Generally, taking photos without a flash or tripod is allowed. Some sights ban selfie sticks; others ban photos altogether.

Audioguides and Apps: Many sights rent audioguides with excellent recorded descriptions in English. If you bring your own earbuds, you can often enjoy better sound. If you don't mind being tethered to your travel partner, you'll save money by bringing a Y-jack and sharing one audioguide. Museums and sights often offer free apps that you can download to your mobile device (check their websites). And, I've produced free, downloadable audio tours for my Grand Canal Cruise, as well as my tours of Venice's St. Mark's Square, St. Mark's Basilica, and Frari Church; look for the 🎧 in this book. For more on my audio tours, see page 8.

Temporary Exhibits: Museums may show special exhibits in addition to their permanent collection. Some exhibits are included in the entry price, while others come at an extra cost (which you may have to pay even if you don't want to see the exhibit).

Expect Changes: Artwork can be on tour, on loan, out sick, or shifted at the whim of the curator. Pick up a floor plan as you enter, and ask the museum staff if you can't find a particular item. Say the title or artist's name, or point to the photograph in this book and ask, *"Dov'è?"* (doh-VEH, meaning "Where is?").

Dates for Artwork: It helps to know the terms. Art historians and Italians refer to centuries by dropping a thousand years. The Trecento (300s), Quattrocento (400s), and Cinquecento (500s) were the 1300s, 1400s, and 1500s. The Novecento (900s) means modern art (the 1900s). In Italian museums, art is dated with *sec* for *secolo* (century, often indicated with Roman numerals), AC (*avanti Cristo,* or BC), and DC (*dopo Cristo,* or AD). OK?

Services: Important sights usually have a reasonably priced on-site café or cafeteria (handy places to rejuvenate during a long visit). The WCs at sights are free and generally clean.

Before Leaving: At the gift shop, scan the postcard rack or thumb through a guidebook to be sure that you haven't overlooked something that you'd like to see. Every sight or museum offers more than what is covered in this book. Use the information I provide as an introduction—not the final word.

FIND RELIGION

Churches offer some amazing art (usually free), a cool respite from heat, and a welcome seat.

A modest dress code—no bare shoulders or shorts for anyone, even kids—is enforced at larger churches—such as the Duomo in both Florence and Siena, Venice's St. Mark's Basilica and Frari Church, and the Vatican's St. Peter's—but is often overlooked elsewhere. If you're caught by surprise, you can sometimes improvise, using maps to cover your shoulders and a jacket for your knees. A few major churches let you borrow or buy disposable ponchos to cover up in a pinch. (I wear a super-lightweight pair of long pants rather than shorts for my hot and muggy Italian sightseeing.) If your heart's set on seeing a certain church, err on the side of caution and dress appropriately.

Some churches have coin-operated audioboxes that describe the art and history; just set the dial on English, put in your coins, and listen. Coin boxes near a piece of art illuminate the art. I pop in a coin whenever I can, to improve my experience (and photos), as a small contribution to that church, and as a courtesy to other visitors enjoying this great art. Whenever possible, let there be light.

Sleeping

Extensive and opinionated listings of good-value rooms are a major feature of this book's Sleeping sections. Rather than list accommodations scattered throughout a town, I choose hotels in my favorite neighborhoods that are convenient to your sightseeing.

My recommendations run the gamut, from dorm beds to fancy rooms with all of the comforts. I like places that are clean, central, relatively quiet at night (except for the singing of gondoliers), reasonably priced, friendly, small enough to have a hands-on owner or manager, and run with a respect for Italian traditions. I'm more impressed by a handy location and a fun-loving philosophy than flat-screen TVs and a fancy gym. Most of my recommendations fall short of perfection. But if I can find a place with most of these features, it's a keeper.

Book your accommodations as soon as your itinerary is set, especially if you want to stay at one of my top listings or if you'll be traveling during busy times. See the appendix for a list of major holidays and festivals in Italy.

RATES AND DEALS

I've categorized my recommended accommodations based on price, indicated with a dollar-sign rating (see sidebar). The price ranges suggest an estimated cost for a one-night stay in high season in a standard double room with a private toilet and shower, including breakfast, and assume you're booking directly with the hotel (not through a booking site, which extracts a commission). Room prices can fluctuate significantly with demand and amenities (size, views, room class, and so on), but relative price categories remain constant. The city of Venice levies a tax on hotel rooms to generate income for infrastructure and restoration projects. This tax is generally not reflected in the price ratings in this book, and must

Sleep Code

Hotels are classified based on the average price of a standard double room with breakfast in high season.

$$$$	**Splurge:** Most rooms over €170
$$$	**Pricier:** €130-170
$$	**Moderate:** €90-130
$	**Budget:** €50-90
¢	**Backpacker:** Under €50
RS%	**Rick Steves discount**

Unless otherwise noted, credit cards are accepted, hotel staff speak basic English, and free Wi-Fi is available. Comparison-shop by checking prices at several hotels (on each hotel's own website, on a booking site, or by email). For the best deal, *book directly with the hotel.* Ask for a discount if paying in cash; if the listing includes **RS%,** request a Rick Steves discount.

be paid in cash at checkout. It varies from €1 to €5 per person, per night, depending on how many stars the hotel has.

Room rates are especially volatile at hotels that use "dynamic pricing" to set rates. Prices can skyrocket during festivals and conventions, while business hotels can have deep discounts on weekends when demand plummets. Of the many hotels I recommend, it's difficult to say which will be the best value on a given day—until you do your homework.

Booking Direct: Once your dates are set, compare prices at several hotels. You can do this by checking Hotels.com, Booking.com, and hotel websites. Then book directly with the hotel itself. Contact small family-run hotels directly by phone or email. When you go direct, the owner avoids the commission paid to booking sites, thereby leaving enough wiggle room to offer you a discount, a nicer room, or a free breakfast (if it's not already included). If you prefer to book online or are considering a hotel chain, it's to your advantage to use the hotel's website.

Booking directly also increases the chances that the hotelier will be able to accommodate any special needs or requests (such as shifting your reservation). Going through a middleman makes it more difficult for the hotel to adjust your booking.

Getting a Discount: Some hotels extend a discount to those who pay cash or stay longer than three nights. And some accommodations offer a special discount for Rick Steves readers, indicated in this guidebook by the abbreviation **"RS%."** Discounts vary: Ask for details when you reserve. Generally, to qualify for this discount, you must book direct (not through a booking site), mention this book when you reserve, show this book upon arrival, and sometimes pay cash or stay a certain number of nights. In some

Using Online Services to Your Advantage

From booking services to user reviews, online businesses play a greater role in travelers' planning than ever before. Take advantage of their pluses—and be wise to their downsides.

Booking Sites

Booking websites such as Booking.com and Hotels.com offer one-stop shopping for hotels. While convenient for travelers, they present a real problem for independent, family-run hotels. Without a presence on these sites, small hotels become almost invisible. But to be listed, a hotel must pay a sizeable commission... and promise that its own website won't undercut the price on the booking-service site.

Here's the work-around: Use the big sites to research what's out there, then book directly with the hotel by email or phone, in which case hotel owners are free to give you whatever price they like. Ask for a room without the commission mark-up (or ask for a free breakfast if not included, or a free upgrade). If you do book online, be sure to use the hotel's website. The price will likely be the same as via a booking site, but your money goes to the hotel, not agency commissions.

As a savvy consumer, remember: When you book with an online booking service, you're adding a middleman who takes roughly 20 percent. To support small, family-run hotels whose world is more difficult than ever, book direct.

Short-Term Rental Sites

Rental juggernaut Airbnb (along with other short-term rental sites) allows travelers to rent rooms and apartments directly from locals, often providing more value than a cookie-cutter hotel. Airbnb fans appreciate feeling part of a real neighborhood and getting into a daily routine as "temporary Europeans." Depending on the host, Airbnb can provide an opportunity to get to know a

cases, you may need to enter a discount code (which I've provided in the listing) in the booking form on the hotel's website. Rick Steves discounts apply to readers with either print or digital books. Understandably, discounts do not apply to promotional rates.

TYPES OF ACCOMMODATIONS
Hotels

The double rooms in Venice listed in this book will range from about €90 (very simple, toilet and shower down the hall) to €400 (plush Grand Canal views and maximum plumbing), with most clustered around €140-180 (with private bathrooms).

Some hotels can add an extra bed (for a small charge) to turn a double into a triple; some offer larger rooms for four or more people local person, while keeping the money spent on your accommo-dations in the community.

Critics view Airbnb as a threat to "traditional Europe," saying it creates unfair, unqualified competition for established guest-house owners. In some places, the lucrative Airbnb market has forced traditional guesthouses out of business and is driving property values out of range for locals. Some cities have cracked down, requiring owners to occupy rental properties part of the year (and staging disruptive "inspections" that inconvenience guests).

As a lover of Europe, I share the worry of those who see resi-dents nudged aside by tourists. But as an advocate for travelers, I appreciate the value and cultural intimacy Airbnb provides.

User Reviews

User-generated review sites and apps such as Yelp and TripAdvi-sor can give you a consensus of opinions about everything from hotels and restaurants to sights and nightlife. If you scan reviews of a restaurant or hotel and see several complaints about noise or a rotten location, you've gained insight that can help in your decision-making.

But as a guidebook writer, my sense is that there is a big difference between the uncurated information on a review site and the vetted listings in a guidebook. A user-generated review is based on the limited experience of one person, who stayed at just one hotel in a given city and ate at a few restaurants there. A guidebook is the work of a trained researcher who forms a well-developed basis for comparison by visiting many restaurants and hotels year after year.

Both types of information have their place, and in many ways, they're complementary. If something is well reviewed in a guide-book and it also gets good online reviews, it's likely a winner.

(I call these "family rooms" in the listings). If there's space for an extra cot, they'll cram it in for you. In general, a triple room is cheaper than the cost of a double and a single. Three or four people can economize by requesting one big room.

Arrival and Check-In: Hotels and B&Bs are sometimes lo-cated on the higher floors of a multipurpose building with a se-cured door. In that case, look for your hotel's name on the buttons by the main entrance. When you ring the bell, you'll be buzzed in.

Hotel elevators are common, though some older buildings still lack them. You may have to climb a flight of stairs to reach the el-evator (if so, you can ask the front desk for help carrying your bags up). Elevators are typically very small—pack light, or you may need to send your bags up without you.

Keep Cool

If you're visiting Italy in the summer, you'll want an air-conditioned room. Most hotel air-conditioners come with a control stick that generally has similar symbols and features: fan icon (click to toggle through wind power, from light to gale); temperature control (20 degrees Celsius is comfortable); louver icon (choose steady airflow or waves); snowflake and sunshine icons (cold air or heat); and clock ("O" setting: run X hours before turning off; "I" setting: wait X hours to start). When you leave your room for the day, turning off the air-conditioning is good form.

The EU requires that hotels collect your name, nationality, and ID number. When you check in, the receptionist will normally ask for your passport and may keep it for anywhere from a couple of minutes to a couple of hours. If you're not comfortable leaving your passport at the desk for a long time, ask when you can pick it up. Or, if you packed a color copy of your passport, you can generally leave that rather than the original.

If you're arriving in the morning, your room probably won't be ready. Check your bag safely at the hotel and dive right into sightseeing.

In Your Room: Most hotel rooms have a TV, telephone, and free Wi-Fi (although in old buildings with thick walls, the Wi-Fi signal might be available only in the lobby). Simpler places rarely have a room phone. Pricier hotels usually come with a small fridge stocked with beverages, called a *frigo bar* (FREE-goh bar; pay for what you use).

More pillows and blankets are usually in the closet or available on request. Towels and linens aren't always replaced every day. Some hotels use lightweight "waffle," or very thin, tablecloth-type towels; these take less water and electricity to launder and are preferred by many Italians.

Nearly all places offer private bathrooms, which have a tub or shower, a toilet, and a bidet (which Italians use for quick sponge baths). The cord over the tub or shower is not a clothesline. You pull it when you've fallen and can't get up.

Double beds are called *matrimoniale*, even though hotels aren't interested in your marital status. Twins are *due letti singoli*.

Breakfast and Meals: Italian hotels typically include breakfast in their room prices. If breakfast is optional, you may want to skip it. While convenient, it's usually pricey for what you get: a simple continental buffet with (at its most generous) bread, croissants, ham, cheese, yogurt, and unlimited *caffè latte*. A picnic in your room followed by a coffee at the corner café can be lots cheaper.

Checking Out: While it's customary to pay for your room upon departure, it can be a good idea to settle your bill the day before, when you're not in a hurry and while the manager's in.

Hotelier Help: Hoteliers can be a good source of advice. Most know their city well, and can assist you with everything from public transit and airport connections to finding a good restaurant, the nearest launderette, or a late-night pharmacy.

Hotel Hassles: Even at the best places, mechanical breakdowns occur: Sinks leak, hot water turns cold, toilets may gurgle or smell, the Wi-Fi goes out, or the air-conditioning dies when you need it most. Report your concerns clearly and calmly at the front desk.

If you suspect night noise will be a problem, ask for a quiet room in the back or on an upper floor. In Venice, a canalside room sounds romantic, but in reality you might be sleeping next to a busy, noisy, boat- and gondola-clogged "street." The quietest Venetian rooms will probably face a courtyard. Once you see your room, consider the potential problem of night noise. Don't hesitate to ask for a quieter room.

To guard against theft in your room, keep valuables out of sight. Some rooms come with a safe, and other hotels have safes at the front desk. I've never bothered using one and, in a lifetime of travel, I've never had anything stolen out of my room.

For more complicated problems, don't expect instant results. Above all, keep a positive attitude. Remember, you're on vacation. If your hotel is a disappointment, spend more time out enjoying the place you came to see.

Bed-and-Breakfasts

B&Bs can offer good-value accommodations in excellent locations. Usually converted family homes or apartments, they can range from humble rooms with communal kitchens to high-end boutique accommodations with extra amenities. Boutique B&Bs can be an especially good option, as they are typically less expensive than a big hotel, but often newer and nicer, with more personal service. Because the B&B scene is constantly changing, it's smart to supplement this book's recommendations with your own research.

Be aware that B&Bs can suffer from absentee management. The proprietors often live off-site (or even in another town) and may be around only when they are expecting guests. Clearly communicate your arrival time, and after checking in, be sure you have your host's telephone number in case you need to reach them.

Short-Term Rentals

A short-term rental—whether an apartment, house, or room in a local's home—is an increasingly popular alternative, especially if

PRACTICALITIES

Making Hotel Reservations

Reserve your rooms as soon as you've pinned down your travel dates. For busy national holidays, it's wise to reserve far in advance (see the appendix).

Requesting a Reservation: For family-run hotels, it's generally best to book your room directly via email or phone. For business-class and chain hotels, or if you'd rather book online, reserve directly through the hotel's official website (not a booking website). Almost all of my recommended hotels take reservations in English.

Here's what the hotelier wants to know:
- Type(s) of rooms you want and size of your party
- Number of nights you'll stay
- Your arrival and departure dates, written European-style as day/month/year (for example, 18/06/21 or 18 June 2021);
- Special requests (en suite bathroom, cheapest room, twin beds vs. double bed, quiet room)
- Applicable discounts (such as a Rick Steves reader discount, cash discount, or promotional rate)

Confirming a Reservation: Most places will request a credit-card number to hold your room. If you're using an online reservation form, make sure it's secure by looking for the *https* or a lock icon at the top of your browser. If the hotel's website doesn't have a secure form where you can enter the number directly, it's best to share that confidential info via a phone call.

Canceling a Reservation: If you must cancel, it's courteous—and smart—to do so with as much notice as possible, especially for

you plan to settle in one location for several nights. For stays longer than a few days, you can usually find a rental that's comparable to—and even cheaper than—a hotel room with similar amenities. Plus, you'll get a behind-the-scenes peek into how locals live.

Many places require a minimum stay and have strict cancellation policies. And you're generally on your own: There's no hotel reception desk, breakfast, or daily cleaning service.

Finding Accommodations: Websites such as Airbnb, FlipKey, Booking.com, and the HomeAway family of sites (HomeAway, VRBO, and VacationRentals) let you browse a wide range of properties. Alternatively, rental agencies such as InterhomeUSA.com or RentaVilla.com, which list more carefully selected accommodations that might cost more, can provide more personalized service.

Before you commit, be clear on the location. I like to virtually "explore" the neighborhood using the Street View feature on Google Maps. Also consider the proximity to public transportation, and how well connected the property is with the rest of the city. Ask about amenities (elevator, air-conditioning, laundry, Wi-

From:	rick@ricksteves.com
Sent:	Today
To:	info@hotelcentral.com
Subject:	Reservation request for 19-22 July

Dear Hotel Central,

I would like to stay at your hotel. Please let me know if you have a room available and the price for:
• 2 people
• Double bed and en suite bathroom in a quiet room
• Arriving 19 July, departing 22 July (3 nights)

Thank you!
Rick Steves

smaller family-run places. Cancellation policies can be strict; read the fine print before you book. Many discount deals require pre-payment, with no cancellation refunds.

Reconfirming a Reservation: Always call or email to reconfirm your room reservation a few days in advance. For B&Bs or very small hotels, I call again on my day of arrival to tell my host what time to expect me (especially important if arriving late—after 17:00).

Phoning: For tips on calling hotels overseas, see page 450.

Fi, parking, etc.). Reviews from previous guests can help identify trouble spots.

Think about the kind of experience you want: Just a key and an affordable bed...or a chance to get to know a local? There are typically two kinds of hosts: those who want minimal interaction with their guests, and hosts who are friendly and may want to interact with you. Read the promotional text and online reviews to help shape your decision.

Confirming and Paying: Many places require you to pay the entire balance before your trip. It's easiest and safest to pay through the site where you found the listing. Be wary of owners who want to take your transaction offline; this gives you no recourse if things go awry. Never agree to wire money (a key indicator of a fraudulent transaction).

Apartments or Houses: If you're staying in one place for four or more nights, it's worth considering an apartment or rental house (shorter stays aren't worth the hassle of arranging key pickup, buying groceries, etc.). Apartment or house rentals can be especially cost-effective for groups and families. European apartments, like hotel rooms, tend to be small by US standards. But they often come with laundry machines and small, equipped kitchens *(cucinetta)*, making it easier and cheaper to dine in.

Rooms in Private Homes: Renting a room in someone's home is a good option for those traveling alone, as you're more likely to find true single rooms—with just one single bed, and a price to match. Beds range from air-mattress-in-living-room basic to plush-B&B-suite posh. Some places allow you to book for a single night. While you can't expect your host to also be your tour guide—or even to provide you with much info—some may be interested in getting to know the travelers who come through their home.

Other Options: Swapping homes with a local works for people with an appealing place to offer (don't assume where you live is not interesting to Europeans). Good places to start are HomeExchange.com and LoveHomeSwap.com. To sleep for free, Couchsurfing.com is a vagabond's alternative to Airbnb. It lists millions of outgoing members, who host fellow "surfers" in their homes.

Hostels

A hostel provides cheap beds in dorms where you sleep alongside strangers for about €25-30 per night. Travelers of any age are welcome if they don't mind dorm-style accommodations and meeting other travelers. Most hostels offer kitchen facilities, guest computers, Wi-Fi, and a self-service laundry. Hostels almost always provide bedding, but the towel's up to you (though you can usually rent one for a small fee). Family and private rooms are often available.

Independent hostels tend to be easygoing, colorful, and informal (no membership required; www.hostelworld.com). You may pay slightly less by booking directly with the hostel. **Official hostels** are part of Hostelling International (HI) and share a booking site (www.hihostels.com). HI hostels typically require that you be a member or else pay a bit more per night.

Eating

The Italians are masters of the art of fine living. That means eating long and well. Lengthy, multicourse meals and endless hours sitting in outdoor cafés are the norm. Americans eat on their way to an evening event and complain if the check is slow in coming. For Italians, the meal is an end in itself, and only rude servers rush you.

A highlight of your Italian adventure will be this country's cafés, cuisine, and wines. Trust me: This is sightseeing for your palate. Even if you liked dorm food and are sleeping in cheap hotels, your taste buds will relish an occasional first-class splurge. You can

---

Restaurant Code

Eateries in this book are categorized according to the average cost of a typical main course. Drinks, desserts, and splurge items can raise the price considerably.

$$$$	**Splurge:** Most main courses over €20
$$$	**Pricier:** €15-20
$$	**Moderate:** €10-15
$	**Budget:** Under €10

Pizza by the slice and other takeaway food is **$**; a basic trattoria or sit-down pizzeria is **$$**; a casual but more upscale restaurant is **$$$**; and a swanky splurge is **$$$$**.

---

eat well without going broke. But be careful: You're just as likely to blow a small fortune on a disappointing meal as you are to dine wonderfully for €25. Rely on my recommendations in the various Eating sections throughout this book.

In general, Italians eat meals a bit later than we do. At 7:00 or 8:00, they have a light breakfast (coffee—usually cappuccino or espresso—and a pastry, often standing up at a café). Lunch (between 13:00 and 15:00) is traditionally the largest meal of the day. Then they eat a late, light dinner (around 20:00-21:30, or maybe earlier in winter). To bridge the gap, people drop into a bar in the late afternoon for a *spuntino* (snack) and aperitif.

RESTAURANT PRICING

I've categorized my recommended eateries based on the average price of a typical main course, indicated with a dollar-sign rating (see sidebar). Obviously, expensive specialties, fine wine, appetizers, and dessert can significantly increase your final bill.

The categories also indicate the personality of a place: **Budget** eateries include street food, takeaway, order-at-the-counter shops, basic cafeterias, and bakeries selling sandwiches. **Moderate** eateries are nice (but not fancy) sit-down restaurants, ideal for a straightforward, fill-the-tank meal. Most of my listings fall in this category—great for a good taste of local cuisine at a reasonable price.

Pricier eateries are a notch up, with more attention paid to the setting, presentation, and (often inventive) cuisine. **Splurge** eateries are dress-up-for-a-special-occasion swanky—typically with an elegant setting, polished service, pricey and intricate cuisine, and an expansive (and expensive) wine list.

PRACTICALITIES

BREAKFAST

Italian breakfasts, like Italian bath towels, can be small: The basic, traditional version is coffee and a roll with butter and marmalade. Many places have yogurt and juice (the delicious red orange juice—*spremuta d'arancia rossa*—is made from Sicilian blood oranges), and possibly also cereal, cold cuts and sliced cheese, and eggs (typically hard-boiled; scrambled or fried eggs are less common). Small budget hotels may leave a basic breakfast in your room (stale croissant, roll, jam, yogurt, coffee).

If you want to skip your hotel breakfast, consider browsing for a morning picnic at a local open-air market. Or do as the Italians do: Stop into a bar or café to drink a cappuccino and munch a *cornetto* (croissant) while standing at the bar. While the *cornetto* is the most common pastry, you'll find a range of *pasticcini* (pastries, sometimes called *dolci*—sweets). Look for *otto* (an 8-shaped pastry, often filled with custard, jam, or chocolate), *sfoglia* (filo-dough crust that's fruit-filled, like a turnover), or *ciambella* (doughnut filled with custard or chocolate)—or ask about local specialties.

ITALIAN RESTAURANTS

While *ristorante* is self-explanatory, you'll also see other types of Italian eateries. A trattoria and an osteria (which can be more casual) are both generally family-owned places serving home-cooked meals, often at moderate prices. A *locanda* is an inn, a *cantina* is a wine cellar, and a *birreria* is a brewpub. *Pizzerie*, *rosticcerie* (delis), *tavola calda* ("hot table") bars, *enoteche* (wine bars), and other alternatives are explained later.

I look for restaurants that are convenient to your hotel and sightseeing. When restaurant-hunting, choose a spot filled with locals, not the place with the big neon signs boasting, "We speak English and accept credit cards." Restaurants parked on famous squares and canals generally serve bad food at high prices to tourists. Venturing even a block or two off the main drag leads to higher-quality food for less than half the price of the tourist-oriented places. Locals eat better at lower-rent locales. Family-run places operate without hired help and can offer cheaper meals.

Most restaurant kitchens close between their lunch and dinner service. Good restaurants don't reopen for dinner before 19:00. If you arrive at opening time, most restaurants will be empty and available—the main push of customers arrives later. Small restaurants with a full slate of reservations for 20:30 or 21:00 often will accommodate walk-in diners willing to eat a quick, early meal, but you aren't expected to linger.

When you want the bill, mime-scribble on your raised palm or request it: *"Il conto, per favore."* You may have to ask more than once. If you're in a hurry, request the check when you receive the last item you order.

Cover and Tipping

Avoid surprises when eating out by familiarizing yourself with two common Italian restaurant charges: *coperto* and *servizio*. You won't encounter them in all restaurants, but both charges, if assessed, by law must be listed on the menu.

The *coperto* (cover), sometimes called *pane e coperto* (bread and cover), is a minor fee (€1.50-3/person) covering the cost of the typical basket of bread, oil, salt, cutlery, and linens found on your table. It's not negotiable, even if you don't eat the bread. And it's not a tip (it goes to the owner)—think of it as entitling you to use the table for as long as you like.

The *servizio* (a 10- to 15-percent service charge) is similar to the mandatory gratuity that American restaurants often add for groups of six or more. You can consider it a "tourist tax," as you're most likely to encounter it in locations with lots of tourists. Because the service charge is sometimes built into your bill, look carefully at your check to see if you've already paid a tip—don't leave any tip beyond this.

If there is no *servizio* on the bill, a common **tip** at a simple restaurant or pizzeria is €1 per person at the table (or simply round up the bill). At a finer restaurant, leave a few euro per person. Don't leave the tip on the table; hand it directly to the server to make sure he or she receives it. Be prepared to tip with cash/coins, as credit/debit card receipts won't have a tip line as in the US.

Italian Menu Courses

A full Italian meal consists of multiple courses (all described below). For most travelers, it's simply too much food—and the euros can add up in a hurry. To avoid overeating (and to stretch your budget), share dishes. A good rule of thumb is for each person to order any two courses. For example, a couple can order and share one *antipasto,* one *primo,* one *secondo,* and one dessert; or two *antipasti* and two *primi;* or whatever combination appeals.

Small groups can mix *antipasti* and *primi* family-style (skipping *secondi*). If you do this right, you can eat well in better places for less than the cost of a tourist *menù* in a cheap place.

Some touristy restaurants serve a *piatto unico,* with smaller portions of each course on one dish (for instance, a meat, starch, and vegetable).

PRACTICALITIES

Antipasto: An appetizer such as bruschetta, grilled veggies, deep-fried tasties, thin-sliced meat (prosciutto or carpaccio), or a plate of olives, cold cuts, and cheeses. To get a sampler plate of cold cuts and cheeses in a restaurant, ask for *affettato misto* (mixed cold cuts), *antipasto misto* (cold cuts, cheeses, and marinated vegetables), or *tagliere* (a sampler "board"). This could make a light meal in itself.

Primo piatto: A "first dish" generally consisting of pasta but also rice or soup. If you think of pasta when you think of Italian food, you can dine well here without ever going beyond the *primo.*

Secondo piatto: A "second dish," equivalent to our main course, of meat or fish/seafood. Italians freely admit the *secondo* is the least interesting part of their cuisine.

Contorno: A vegetable side dish may come with the *secondo* but more often must be ordered separately. Typical *contorni* are *insalata mista,* spinach, roasted potatoes, or grilled veggies. This can be an interesting, if overlooked, part of the menu. Vegetarians can skip the *secondo* and order several *contorni* to make a meal.

Dolce: No meal is complete without a sweet. On most menus you'll find typical Italian desserts such as tiramisu and *panna cotta* as well as local favorites.

Ordering Tips

Seafood and steak may be sold by weight and priced by the *etto* (100 grams, 3.5 ounces) or the kilo (1,000 grams, 2.2 pounds). The abbreviation *s.q. (secondo quantità)* indicates an item is priced by weight (often used at antipasto buffets). Unless the menu indicates a fillet *(filetto),* fish is usually served whole with the head and tail. However, you can always ask your server to select a small fish and fillet it for you. Sometimes, especially for steak, restaurants require a minimum order of four or five *etti* (which diners can share). Make sure you're clear on the price before ordering.

Some special dishes come in larger quantities meant to be shared by two people. The shorthand way of showing this on a menu is "X2" (for two), but the price listed could indicate the cost per person.

In a traditional restaurant, if you order a pasta dish and a side salad—but no main course—the server will bring the salad after the pasta (Italians prefer it this way, believing that it enhances digestion). If you want the salad with your pasta, specify *insieme* (een-see-EH-meh; together).

Because pasta and bread are both starches, Italians consider them redundant. If you order only a pasta dish, bread may not come with it; you can request it, but you may be charged extra. On the other hand, if you order a vegetable antipasto or a meat *secondo,* bread is often provided to balance the ingredients.

At places with counter service—such as at a bar or a freeway rest-stop diner—you'll order and pay at the *cassa* (cashier). Take your receipt to the counter to claim your food.

Fixed-Price Meals and Ordering à la Carte

You can save by getting a fixed-priced meal, which is frequently exempt from cover and service charges. Avoid the cheapest ones (often called a *menù turistico*). Look instead for a genuine *menù del giorno* (menu of the day), which offers diners a choice of appetizer, main course, and dessert. It's worth paying a little more for an inventive fixed-price meal that shows off the chef's creativity.

While fixed-price meals can be easy and convenient, galloping gourmets prefer to order à la carte with the help of a menu translator. When going to an especially good restaurant with an approachable staff, I like to find out what they're eager to serve. Sometimes I'll simply say, *"Mi faccia felice"* (Make me happy) and set a price limit.

BUDGET EATING

Italy offers many budget options for hungry travelers.

Self-service cafeterias offer the basics without add-on charges. Travelers on a hard-core budget equip their room with a pantry stocked at the market (fruits and veggies are remarkably cheap), or pick up a sandwich or *döner kebab,* then dine in at picnic prices. Bars and cafés are also good places to grab a meal on the go.

Pizzerias

Pizza is cheap and readily available. Stop by a pizza shop for stand-up or takeout (many pizza places sell whole pies meant for one person; *pizza al taglio* means "by the slice"). Supermarkets usually have a pizza counter, too.

Some shops feature *pizza rustica*—thick pizza baked in a large rectangular pan and sold by weight. If you simply ask for a piece, you may wind up with a gigantic slab and be charged top euro. Instead, clearly indicate how much you want: 100 grams, or *un etto,* is a hot and cheap snack; 200 grams, or *due etti,* makes a light meal. Or show the size with your hands—*tanto così* (TAHN-toh koh-ZEE; this much). They'll often helpfully cut it up into smaller pieces. If you want your pizza warm, say *"sì"* when they ask if you want it heated up (*riscaldare;* ree-skahl-DAH-ray). For a rundown of common types of pizza, see that section, later.

Bars/Cafés

Italian "bars" are not taverns, but inexpensive cafés. These neighborhood hangouts serve coffee, mini pizzas *(pizzette),* sandwiches, and drinks from the cooler. This budget choice is the Italian equivalent of English pub grub. In Venice, *cicchetti* bars serve a fun assortment of appetizer-sized plates (see the Eating in Venice chapter for recommendations).

Many bars are small—if you can't find a table, you'll need to stand or find a ledge to sit on outside. Most charge extra for table service. To get food to go, say, *"da portar via"* (for the road) or *"da portar canale"* (for the canal). All bars have a WC *(toilette, bagno)* in the back, and customers—and the discreet public—can use it.

Food: For quick meals, bars usually have trays of cheap, premade sandwiches (*panini,* on a baguette; *piadini,* on flatbread; or *tramezzini,* on crustless white bread)—some are delightful grilled. (Others have too much mayo.) In bigger cities, they'll have a variety of salads ready to serve up from under the glass counter. To save time for sightseeing and room for dinner, stop by a bar for a light lunch, such as a ham-and-cheese sandwich (called *toast*); have it grilled twice if you want it really hot.

Prices and Paying: You'll notice a two- or three-tiered pricing system. Drinking a cup of coffee while standing at the bar is cheaper than drinking it at an indoor table (you'll pay still more at an outdoor table). Many places have a *lista dei prezzi* (price list) with two columns—*al bar* and *al tavolo* (table)—posted somewhere by the bar or cash register. If you're on a budget, don't sit down without first checking out the financial consequences. Ask, "Same price if I sit or stand?" by saying, *"Costa uguale al tavolo o al banco?"* (KOH-stah oo-GWAH-lay ahl TAH-voh-loh oh ahl BAHN-koh). Throughout Italy, you can get cheap coffee at the bar of any establishment, no matter how fancy, and pay the same low, government-regulated price (generally a euro or less if you stand).

If the bar isn't busy, you can probably just order and pay when you leave. Otherwise: 1) Decide what you want; 2) find out the price by checking the price list on the wall, the prices posted near the food, or by asking the barista; 3) pay the cashier; and 4) give the receipt to the barista (whose clean fingers handle no dirty euros) and tell him or her what you want.

Tavola Calda Bars and *Rosticcerie*

For a fast and cheap lunch, find an Italian variation on the corner deli: a *rosticceria* (specializing in roasted meats and accompanying *antipasti*) or a *tavola calda* bar (a "hot table" point-and-shoot cafeteria with a buffet spread of meat and vegetables; sometimes called *tavola fredda*, or "cold table," in the north). For a healthy light meal, ask for a mixed plate of vegetables with a hunk of mozzarella (*piatto misto di verdure con mozzarella;* pee-AH-toh MEE-stoh dee vehr-DOO-ray). Don't be limited by what's displayed. If you'd like a salad with a slice of cantaloupe and a hunk of cheese, they'll whip that up for you in a snap. Belly up to the bar; with a pointing finger, you can assemble a fine meal. If something's a mystery, ask for *un assaggio* (oon ah-SAH-joh) to get a little taste. To have your choices warmed up, ask for them to be heated (*riscaldare;* ree-skahl-DAH-ray).

Wine Bars

Wine bars (*enoteche;* sometimes called *bacari* in Venice) are a popular, fast, and inexpensive option for lunch. Surrounded by the office crowd, you can get a salad, a plate of meats (cold cuts) and cheeses, and a glass of good wine (see blackboards for the day's selection and price per glass). A good *enoteca* aims to impress visitors with its wine, and will generally feature excellent-quality ingredients for the simple dishes it offers with the wine (though the prices add up—be careful with your ordering to keep this a budget choice). For more on Italian cocktails and wines, see page 447.

Aperitivo Buffets

The Italian term *aperitivo* means a predinner drink, but it's also used to describe their version of what we might call happy hour: a light buffet that many bars serve to customers during the predinner hours (typically around 18:00 or 19:00 until 21:00). The drink itself may not be cheap (typically around €8-12), but bars lay out an enticing array of meats, cheeses, grilled vegetables, and other *antipasti*-type dishes, and you're welcome to nibble to your heart's content while you nurse your drink. While it's intended as an appetizer course before heading out for a full dinner, light eaters could discreetly turn this into a small meal. Bars advertising *"apericena"* (*cena* means dinner) tend to have buffets hearty enough to pass as dinner. Drop by a few bars around this time to scope out their buffets before choosing.

Markets, Groceries, and Delis: Assembling a Picnic

Picnicking saves lots of euros and is a great way to sample regional specialties. A picnic can even be an adventure in high cuisine. Be daring. Try the fresh ricotta, *presto* pesto, shriveled olives, and any regional specialties the locals are excited about.

Markets: For the most colorful experience, gather your ingredients in the morning at a produce market. Towns big and small have markets selling everything imaginable for a fantastic picnic, including cheese, meat, bread, sweets, and prepared foods. You'll often find street-food stalls tucked into the marketplace as well (note that many stalls close in the early afternoon).

Groceries and Delis: Another budget option is to visit a supermarket (look for the Conad, Carrefour, and Co-op chains), *alimentari* (neighborhood grocery), or *salumeria* (delicatessen) to pick up cold cuts, cheeses, and other picnic supplies. Some grocery stores, *salumerie,* and any *paninoteca* or *focacceria* (sandwich shop) can make a sandwich to order. Just point to what you want, and they'll stuff it into a *panino*. Almost every grocery store has a deli case with prepared items like stuffed peppers, lasagna, olives, or chicken, all usually sold by weight; if you want it reheated, remember the word *riscaldare* (ree-skahl-DAH-ray). And *rosticcerie* sell cheap food to go—you'll find options such as lasagna, rotisserie chicken, and sides including roasted potatoes and spinach. For more on *salumi* and cheeses, see those sections, later.

Ordering: A typical picnic for two might be fresh rolls, *un etto* (quarter-pound) of cheese, and *un etto* of meat (sometimes ordered by the slice—*fetta*—or piece—*pezzo*). For two people, I might get *un etto* of prosciutto and *due pezzi* of bread. Add two tomatoes, three carrots, two apples, yogurt, and a liter box of juice. Total cost: about €10.

If ordering *antipasti* (such as grilled or marinated veggies) at a deli counter, you can ask for *una porzione* in a takeaway container *(contenitore).* Use gestures to show exactly how much you want. To set a price limit on what you order, say *"Da __ euro, per favore."*

The word *basta* (BAH-stah; enough) works as a question or as a statement.

Shopkeepers are happy to sell small quantities of produce, but it's customary to let the merchant choose for you. Say *"per oggi"* (pehr OH-jee; for today) and he or she will grab you something ready to eat. To avoid being overcharged, know the cost per kilo, study the weighing procedure, and do the arithmetic. Remember that a kilo is 2.2 pounds.

ITALIAN CUISINE STAPLES

Much of your Italian eating experience will likely involve the big five: pizza, pasta, *salumi*, cheese, and gelato. For a look at cuisine you'll likely find in Venice, see the sidebar on page 272. For more food help, try a menu translator, such as the *Rick Steves Italian Phrase Book & Dictionary*, which has a menu decoder and plenty of useful phrases for navigating the culinary scene.

Pizza

Here are some of the pizzas you might see at restaurants or at a pizzeria. Note that if you ask for pepperoni on your pizza, you'll get *peperoni* (green or red peppers, not sausage); request *diavola*, *salsiccia piccante*, or *salame piccante* instead (the closest thing in Italy to American pepperoni).

Bianca: White pizza with no tomatoes

Capricciosa: Prosciutto, mushrooms, olives, and artichokes—literally the chef's "caprice"

Funghi: Mushrooms

Margherita: Tomato sauce, mozzarella, and basil—the red, white, and green of the Italian flag

Marinara: Tomato sauce, oregano, garlic, no cheese

Napoletana: Mozzarella, anchovies, and tomato sauce

Ortolana or *vegetariana:* "Greengrocer-style," with vegetables

Quattro formaggi: Four different cheeses

Quattro stagioni: Different toppings on each of the four quarters

Pasta

While we think of pasta as a main dish, in Italy it's considered a *primo piatto*—first course. There are more than 600 varieties of Italian pasta, and each is specifically used to highlight a certain sauce, meat, or regional ingredient. Most pastas in Italy are made fresh.

Italian pasta falls into two broad categories: *pasta lunga* (long pasta) and *pasta corta* (short pasta).

Pasta lunga can be round, such as *capellini* (thin "little hairs"), *vermicelli* ("little worms"), and *bucatini* (long and hollow), or it can be flat, such as *linguine* (narrow "little tongues"), *fettuccine* (wider

Eating with the Seasons Across Italy

Italian cooks love to serve fresh produce and seafood at its tastiest. Each region in Italy has its seasonal specialties, which you'll see displayed in open-air markets. To get a plate of the freshest veggies at a fine restaurant, request *"Un piatto di verdure della stagione, per favore."* ("A plate of seasonal vegetables, please.") Italians take fresh, seasonal ingredients so seriously that a restaurant cooking with frozen ingredients *(congelato)* must note it on the menu. Here are a few examples of what's fresh when:

April-May: Calamari (Venice), romanesco (similar to cauliflower), fava beans (Rome), green beans, artichokes

April-May and Sept-Oct: Black truffles

April-June: Asparagus, zucchini flowers, zucchini

May-June: Mussels, cantaloupe, loquats, strawberries

May-Aug: Eggplant, clams

July-Sept: Figs

Oct-Nov: Mushrooms, white truffles, persimmons, chestnuts

Nov-Feb: Radicchio (Venice), cardoon (wild artichoke), puntarelle (chicory shoots; Rome)

"small ribbons"), *tagliatelle* (even wider), and *pappardelle* (very wide, best with meat sauces).

The most common *pasta corta* are tubes, such as *penne, rigatoni, ziti, manicotti,* and *cannelloni;* they come either *lisce* (smooth) or *rigate* (grooved—better to catch and cling to sauce). Many short pastas are named for their shapes, such as *conchiglie* (shells), *farfalle* (butterflies), or *cavatappi* (corkscrews).

Here's a list of common pasta toppings and sauces. On a menu, these terms are usually preceded by *alla* (in the style of) or *in* (in):

Aglio e olio: Garlic and olive oil

Alfredo: Butter, cream, and parmesan

Amatriciana: Pork cheek, *pecorino romano* cheese, and tomato

Arrabbiata: "Angry," spicy tomato sauce with chili peppers

Bolognese: Meat and tomato sauce

Boscaiola: Mushrooms and sausage

Burro e salvia: Butter and sage

Cacio e pepe: Pecorino romano cheese and ground pepper

Carbonara: Bacon, egg, cheese, and pepper

PRACTICALITIES

Carrettiera: Spicy and garlicky, with olive oil and little tomatoes
Diavola: "Devil-style," spicy hot
Frutti di mare: Seafood
Genovese: Basil ground with *parmigiano* cheese, garlic, pine nuts, and olive oil; a.k.a. pesto
Gricia: Cured pork cheek and *pecorino romano* cheese
Marinara: Usually tomato, often with garlic and onions, but can also be a seafood sauce ("sailor's style")
Norma: Tomato, eggplant, and ricotta cheese
Pajata: Calf intestines (also called *pagliata*)
Pescatora: Seafood ("fisherman style")
Pomodoro: Tomato only
Puttanesca: "Harlot-style" tomato sauce with anchovies, olives, and capers
Ragù: Meaty tomato sauce
Scoglio: Mussels, clams, and tomatoes
Sorrentina: "Sorrento-style," with tomatoes, basil, and mozzarella (usually over gnocchi)
Sugo di lepre: Rich sauce made of wild hare
Tartufi: Truffles (also called *tartufate*)
Umbria: Sauce of anchovies, garlic, tomatoes, and truffles
Vongole: Clams and spices

Salumi

Salumi (cured meats), also called *affettati* (sliced meats), are an Italian staple. While most American cold cuts are cooked, in Italy they're far more commonly cured by air-drying, salting, and smoking. (Don't worry; these so-called "raw" meats are safe to eat, and you can really taste the difference.)

The two most familiar types of *salumi* are *salame* and *prosciutto*. *Salame* is an air-dried, sometimes-spicy sausage that comes in many varieties. When Italians say *"prosciutto,"* they usually mean *prosciutto crudo*—the raw ham that air-cures on the hock and is then thinly sliced. Produced mainly in the north of Italy, *prosciutto* can be either *dolce* (sweet) or *salato* (salty). Purists say the best is *prosciutto di Parma*.

Other *salumi* may be less familiar:
Bresaola: Air-cured beef
Capocollo: Peppery pork shoulder (also called *coppa*)
Culatello: High quality, slow-cured prosciutto
Finocchiona: *Salame* with fennel seeds
Guanciale: Tender pork cheek
Lonzino: Cured pork loin
Mortadella: A finely ground pork loaf, similar to our bologna
Pancetta: Salt-cured, peppery pork-belly meat, similar to bacon
Salame di Sant'Olcese: What we'd call "Genoa salami"

Salame piccante: Spicy hot, similar to pepperoni

Speck: Smoked pork shoulder

If you've got a weak stomach, avoid *testa in cassetta* (head-cheese—organs in aspic) and *lampredotto* (cow stomach).

Cheese

When it comes to cheese *(formaggio)*, you're probably already familiar with most of these Italian favorites:

Asiago: Hard cow cheese that comes either *mezzano* (young, firm, and creamy) or *stravecchio* (aged, pungent, and granular)

Burrata: A creamy mozzarella

Fontina: Semihard, nutty, Gruyère-style mountain cheese

Gorgonzola: Pungent, blue-veined cheese, either *dolce* (creamy) or *stagionato* (aged and hard)

Mascarpone: Sweet, buttery, spreadable dessert cheese

Mozzarella di bufala: Made from the milk of water buffaloes

Parmigiano-reggiano: Hard, crumbly, sharp, aged cow cheese with more nuanced flavor than American parmesan; *grana padano* is a less expensive variation

Pecorino: Either *fresco* (fresh, soft, and mild) or *stagionato* (aged and sharp, sometimes called *pecorino romano*)

Provolone: Rich, firm, aged cow cheese

Ricotta: Soft, airy cheese made by "recooking" leftover whey

Scamorza: Similar to mozzarella, but often smoked

Gelato

American ice cream and Italian gelato are similar but decidedly not the same. Gelato is denser and creamier (even though it has less butterfat than ice cream), and connoisseurs swear it's more flavorful.

A key to gelato appreciation is sampling liberally and choosing flavors that go well together. At a *gelateria*, ask, as Italians do, for a taste: *"Un assaggio, per favore?"* (oon ah-SAH-joh pehr fah-VOH-ray). You can also ask what flavors go well together: *"Quali gusti stanno bene insieme?"* (KWAH-lee GOO-stee STAH-noh BEH-nay een-see-EH-may).

Most *gelaterie* clearly display prices and sizes. But in the textbook *gelateria* scam, the tourist orders two or three flavors—and the clerk selects a fancy, expensive chocolate-coated waffle cone, piles it high with huge scoops, and cheerfully charges the tourist €10. To avoid rip-offs, point to the price or say what you want—for instance, a €3 cup: *"Una coppetta da tre euro"* (OO-nah koh-PEH-tah dah tray eh-OO-roh).

The best *gelaterie* display signs reading *artiginale, nostra produzione,* or *produzione propia,* indicating that the gelato is made on the premises. Seasonal flavors are also a good sign, as are mellow hues (avoid colors that don't appear in nature). Gelato stored in covered metal tins (rather than white plastic) is more likely to be homemade. Gourmet gelato shops are popping up all over Italy, selling exotic flavors. Unless it's a gelato emergency, avoid the chain called Grom—it's the Starbucks of gelato in Italy.

Gelato variations or alternatives include *sorbetto* (sorbet—made with fruit, but no milk or eggs); *granita* or *grattachecca* (a cup of slushy ice with flavored syrup); and *cremolata* (a gelato-*granita* float).

Classic gelato flavors include:

After Eight: Chocolate and mint
Bacio: Chocolate hazelnut, named for Italy's popular "kiss" candies
Cassata: With dried fruits
Cioccolato: Chocolate
Crema: Vanilla
Croccantino: "Crunchy," with toasted peanut bits
Fior di latte: Sweet milk
Fragola: Strawberry
Macedonia: Mixed fruits
Malaga: Similar to rum raisin
Riso: With actual bits of rice mixed in
Stracciatella: Vanilla with chocolate shreds
Tartufo: Super chocolate
Zabaione: Named for the egg yolk-and-Marsala wine dessert
Zuppa inglese: Sponge cake, custard, chocolate, and cream

BEVERAGES

Italian bars serve great drinks—hot, cold, sweet, caffeinated, or alcoholic.

Water, Juice, and Cold Drinks

Italians are notorious water snobs. At restaurants, your server just can't understand why you wouldn't want good water to go with your good food. It's customary and never expensive to order a *litro* or *mezzo litro* (half-liter) of bottled water. *Acqua leggermente effervescente* (lightly carbonated water) is a mealtime favorite. Or simply ask for *con gas* if you want fizzy water and *senza gas* if you prefer still water. You can ask for *acqua del rubinetto* (tap water) in restaurants, but your server may give you a funny look. Chilled bottled water—still *(naturale)* or carbonated *(frizzante)*—is sold cheap in stores. Half-liter bottles of mineral water are available everywhere for about €1. (I refill my water bottle with tap water.)

Juice is *succo*, and *spremuta* means freshly squeezed. Order *una spremuta* (don't confuse it with *spumante*, sparkling wine)—it's usually orange juice *(arancia)*, and from February through April it's almost always made from Sicilian blood oranges *(arance rosse)*.

In grocery stores, you can get a liter of O.J. for the price of a Coke or coffee. Look for *100% succo* or *senza zucchero* (without sugar) on the label—or be surprised by something diluted and sugary sweet. Hang on to your water bottles. Buy juice in cheap liter boxes, then drink some and store the extra in your water bottle.

Tè freddo (iced tea) is usually from a can—sweetened and flavored with lemon or peach. Lemonade is *limonata*.

Coffee and Other Hot Drinks

The espresso-based style of coffee so popular in the US was born in Italy. If you ask for *"un caffè,"* you'll get a shot of espresso in a little cup—the closest thing to American-style drip coffee is a *caffè americano*. Most Italian coffee drinks begin with espresso, to which they add varying amounts of hot water and/or steamed or foamed milk. Milky drinks, like cappuccino or *caffè latte,* are served to locals before noon and to tourists any time of day (to an Italian, cappuccino is a morning drink; they believe having milk after a big meal or anything with tomato sauce impairs digestion). If they add any milk after lunch, it's just a splash, in a *caffè macchiato*. Italians like their coffee only warm—to get it very hot, request *"Molto caldo, per favore"* (MOHL-toh KAHL-doh pehr fah-VOH-ray). Any coffee drink is available decaffeinated—ask for it *decaffeinato* (deh-kah-feh-NAH-toh).

If you want a hot drink other than coffee, *cioccolato* is hot chocolate, and *tè* is hot tea.

Cappuccino: Espresso with foamed milk on top (*cappuccino freddo* is iced cappuccino)

Caffè latte: Espresso mixed with hot milk, no foam, in a tall glass (ordering just a "latte" gets you only milk)

Caffè macchiato: Espresso "marked" with a splash of milk, in a small cup

Latte macchiato: Layers of hot milk and foam, "marked" by an espresso shot, in a tall glass. Note that if you order simply a *"macchiato,"* you'll probably get a *caffè macchiato*.

Caffè corto/lungo: Concentrated espresso diluted with a tiny bit of hot water, in a small cup

Caffè americano: Espresso diluted with even more hot water, in a larger cup

Caffè corretto: Espresso "corrected" with a shot of liqueur (normally *grappa, amaro,* or *sambuca*)

Marocchino: "Moroccan" coffee with espresso, foamed milk, and cocoa powder; the similar *mocaccino* has chocolate instead of cocoa

Caffè freddo: Sweet and iced espresso

Caffè hag: Instant decaf

Ordering Wine

To order a glass of red or white wine, say, *"Un bicchiere di vino rosso/bianco."* House wine comes in a carafe; choose from a quarter-liter pitcher (8.5 oz, *un quarto*), half-liter pitcher (17 oz, *un mezzo*), or one-liter pitcher (34 oz, *un litro*). When ordering, have some fun, gesture like a local, and you'll have no problems speaking the language of the *enoteca. Salute!*

English	Italian
wine	*vino* (VEE-noh)
house wine	*vino della casa* (VEE-noh DEH-lah KAH-zah)
glass	*bicchiere* (bee-kee-EH-ray)
bottle	*bottiglia* (boh-TEEL-yah)
carafe	*caraffa* (kah-RAH-fah)
red	*rosso* (ROH-soh)
white	*bianco* (bee-AHN-koh)
rosé	*rosato* (roh-ZAH-toh)
sparkling	*spumante/frizzante* (spoo-MAHN-tay/ freed-ZAHN-tay)
dry	*secco* (SEH-koh)
fruity	*fruttato* (froo-TAH-toh)
full-bodied	*corposo/pieno* (kor-POH-zoh/pee-EH-noh)
sweet	*dolce* (DOHL-chay)

Alcoholic Beverages

Beer: While Italy is traditionally considered wine country, in recent years there's been a huge and passionate growth in the production of craft beer *(birra artigianale)*. Even in small towns, you'll see microbreweries slinging their own brews. You'll also find local brews (Peroni and Moretti), as well as imports such as Heineken. Italians drink mainly lager beers. Beer on tap is *alla spina*. Get it *piccola* (33 cl, 11 oz), *media* (50 cl, about a pint), or *grande* (a liter). A *lattina* (lah-TEE-nah) is a can and a *bottiglia* (boh-TEEL-yah) is a bottle.

Cocktails and Spirits: Italians appreciate both *aperitivi* (palate-stimulating cocktails) and *digestivi* (after-dinner drinks designed to aid digestion). Popular *aperitivo* options include Campari (carmine-red bitters with herbs and orange peel), Aperol (bright orange bitters with herbal, citrusy undertones), Americano (vermouth with bitters, brandy, and lemon peel), Cynar (bitters flavored with artichoke), and Punt e Mes (sweet red vermouth and red wine). Widely used vermouth brands include Cinzano and Martini.

Digestivo choices are usually either strong herbal bitters or something sweet. Many restaurants have their own secret recipe for a bittersweet herbal brew called *amaro;* popular commercial brands are Fernet Branca and Montenegro. If your tastes run sweeter, try

PRACTICALITIES

any of these flavored liqueurs: *amaretto* (almond), Frangelico (hazelnut), *limoncello* (lemon), *nocino* (walnut), *sambuca* (anise), or a sweet Marsala wine. *Grappa* is a brandy distilled from grape skins and stems; *stravecchio* is an aged, mellower variation.

Wine: The ancient Greeks who colonized Italy more than 2,000 years ago called it Oenotria—land of the grape. Centuries later, Galileo wrote, "Wine is light held together by water." Wine *(vino)* is certainly a part of the Italian culinary trinity—grape, olive, and wheat. (I'd add gelato.) Ideal conditions for grapes (warm climate, well-draining soil, and an abundance of hillsides) make the Italian peninsula a paradise for grape growers, winemakers, and wine drinkers. For regional wines produced near Venice, see the sidebar on page 272.

Even if you're clueless about wine, the information on an Italian wine label can help you choose something decent. Terms you may see on the bottle include *classico* (from a defined, select area), *annata* (year of harvest), *vendemmia* (harvest), and *imbottigliato dal produttore all'origine* (bottled by producers).

In general, Italy designates its wines by one of four official categories:

Vino da Tavola (VDT) is table wine, the lowest grade, made from grapes grown anywhere in Italy. It's often inexpensive, but Italy's wines are so good that, for many people, a basic *vino da tavola* is just fine with a meal. Many restaurants, even modest ones, take pride in their house wine *(vino della casa)*, bottling their own or working with wineries.

Denominazione di Origine Controllata (DOC) meets national standards for high-quality wine. Made from grapes grown in a defined area, it's usually quite affordable and can be surprisingly good. Hundreds of wines have earned the DOC designation.

Denominazione di Origine Controllata e Guarantita (DOCG), the highest grade, meets national standards for the highest-quality wine (made with grapes from a defined area whose quality is "guaranteed"). These wines can be identified by the pink or green label on the neck...and the scary price tag on the shelf. They're generally a good bet if you want a quality wine, but you don't know anything else about the winemaker. (*Riserva* indicates a DOC or DOCG wine that's been aged for even longer than required.)

Indicazione Geografica Tipica (IGT) is a broad group of wines that don't meet the standard for DOC or DOCG status, but have been designated as "typical" of a particular region.

Hurdling the Language Barrier

Many Italians—especially those in the tourist trade and in big cities—speak English. Still, you'll get better treatment if you learn and use Italian pleasantries. In smaller, nontouristy towns, Italian is the norm. Italians have an endearing habit of talking to you even if they know you don't speak their language—and yet, thanks to gestures and thoughtfully simplified words, it somehow works. Don't stop them to tell them you don't understand every word—just go along for the ride. For a list of survival phrases, see the appendix.

Note that Italian is pronounced much like English, with a few exceptions, such as: c followed by e or i is pronounced ch (to ask, *"Per centro?"* "To the center?"—you say, pehr CHEHN-troh). In Italian, ch followed by e or i is pronounced like the hard c in Chianti (*chiesa*—church—is pronounced kee-AY-zah). Adding a vowel to the English word often gets you close to the Italian one. Give it your best shot. Italians appreciate your efforts.

For more tips on hurdling the language barrier, consider the *Rick Steves Italian Phrase Book* (available at www.ricksteves.com).

Staying Connected

One of the most common questions I hear from travelers is, "How can I stay connected in Europe?" The short answer is: more easily and cheaply than you might think.

The simplest solution is to bring your own device—mobile phone, tablet, or laptop—and use it just as you would at home (following the money-saving tips below, such as getting an international plan or connecting to free Wi-Fi whenever possible). Another option is to buy a European SIM card for your US mobile phone. Or you can use European landlines and computers to connect. Each of these options is described next, and more details are at www.ricksteves.com/phoning. For a very practical one-hour talk covering tech issues for travelers, see www.ricksteves.com/mobile-travel-skills.

USING A MOBILE PHONE IN EUROPE

Here are some budget tips and options.

Sign up for an international plan. To stay connected at a lower cost, sign up for an international service plan through your carrier. Most providers offer a simple bundle that includes calling, messaging, and data. Your normal plan may already include international coverage (T-Mobile's does).

Before your trip, call your provider or check online to confirm

How to Dial

International Calls

Whether phoning from a US landline or mobile phone, or from a number in another European country, here's how to make an international call. I've used one of my recommended Florence hotels as an example (tel. 055-213-154).

Initial Zero: Drop the initial zero from international phone numbers—except when calling Italy.

Mobile Tip: If using a mobile phone, the "+" sign can replace the international access code (for a "+" sign, press and hold "0").

US/Canada to Europe

Dial 011 (US/Canada international access code), country code (39 for Italy), and phone number.

▶ To call the Florence hotel from home, dial 011-39-055-213-154.

Country to Country Within Europe

Dial 00 (Europe international access code), country code, and phone number.

▶ To call the Florence hotel from Germany, dial 00-39-055-213-154.

Europe to the US/Canada

Dial 00, country code (1 for US/Canada), and phone number.

▶ To call from Europe to my office in Edmonds, Washington, dial 00-1-425-771-8303.

Domestic Calls

To call within Italy (from one Italian landline or mobile phone to another), simply dial the phone number, including the initial 0 if there is one.

▶ To call the Florence hotel from Rome, dial 055-213-154.

---

that your phone will work in Europe, and research your provider's international rates. Activate the plan a day or two before you leave, then remember to cancel it when your trip's over.

Use free Wi-Fi whenever possible. Unless you have an unlimited-data plan, you're best off saving most of your online tasks for Wi-Fi. You can access the internet, send texts, and even make voice calls over Wi-Fi.

Most accommodations in Europe offer free Wi-Fi, but some—especially expensive hotels—charge a fee. Many cafés (including Starbucks and McDonald's) have free hotspots for customers; look for signs offering it and ask for the Wi-Fi password when you buy something. You'll also often find Wi-Fi at TIs, city squares, major museums, public-transit hubs, airports, and aboard trains and buses.

More Dialing Tips

Italian Phone Numbers: Italian phone numbers vary in length; a hotel can have, say, an eight-digit phone number. Italy's landlines start with 0; mobile lines start with 3.

More Phoning Help: See www.howtocallabroad.com.

European Country Codes		Ireland & N. Ireland	353/44
Austria	43	Italy	39
Belgium	32	Latvia	371
Bosnia-Herzegovina	387	Montenegro	382
Croatia	385	Morocco	212
Czech Republic	420	Netherlands	31
Denmark	45	Norway	47
Estonia	372	Poland	48
Finland	358	Portugal	351
France	33	Russia	7
Germany	49	Slovakia	421
Gibraltar	350	Slovenia	386
Great Britain	44	Spain	34
Greece	30	Sweden	46
Hungary	36	Switzerland	41
Iceland	354	Turkey	90

Minimize the use of your cellular network. The best way to make sure you're not accidentally burning through data is to put your device in "airplane" mode (which also disables phone calls and texts), turn your Wi-Fi back on, and connect to networks as needed. When you need to get online but can't find Wi-Fi, simply turn on your cellular network (or turn off airplane mode) just long enough for the task at hand.

Even with an international data plan, wait until you're on Wi-Fi to Skype, download apps, stream videos, or do other megabyte-greedy tasks. Using a navigation app such as Google Maps over a cellular network can take lots of data, so do this sparingly or offline.

Limit automatic updates. By default, your device constantly checks for a data connection and updates apps. It's smart to disable these features so your apps will only update when you're on Wi-Fi. Also change your device's email settings from "auto-retrieve" to "manual" (or from "push" to "fetch").

Use Wi-Fi calling and messaging apps. Skype, WhatsApp, FaceTime, and Google Hangouts are great for making free or low-cost calls or sending texts over Wi-Fi worldwide. Just log on to a Wi-Fi network, then connect with any of your friends or family members who use the same service. If you buy credit in advance, with some of these services you can call or text anywhere for just pennies.

Some apps, such as Apple's iMessage, will use the cellular network for texts if Wi-Fi isn't available: To avoid this possibility, turn off the "Send as SMS" feature.

Buy a European SIM Card. If you anticipate making a lot of local calls or need a local phone number, or if your provider's international data rates are expensive, consider buying a SIM card in Europe to replace the one in your (unlocked) US phone or tablet.

In Italy, buy SIM cards at mobile-phone shops. You'll be required to register the SIM card with your passport as an antiterrorism measure (which may mean you can't use the phone for the first hour or two).

There are no roaming charges when using a European SIM card in other EU countries, though to be sure you get this "roam-like-at-home" pricing, ask if this feature is included when you buy your SIM card.

WITHOUT A MOBILE PHONE

It's less convenient but possible to travel in Europe without a mobile device. You can make calls from your hotel and check email or get online using public computers.

Most **hotels** charge a fee for placing calls—ask for rates before you dial. You can use a prepaid international phone card (*carta telefonica prepagata internazionale*—usually available at newsstands, tobacco shops, and train stations) to call out from your hotel. Dial the toll-free access number, enter the card's PIN code, then dial the number.

You'll only see **public pay phones** in a few post offices and train stations. Most don't take coins but instead require insertable phone cards, which you can buy at a newsstand, convenience store, or post office. Except for emergencies, they're not worth the hassle.

Some hotels have **public computers** in their lobbies for guests to use; otherwise you may find them at public libraries (ask your hotelier or the TI for the nearest location). On a European keyboard, use the "Alt Gr" key to the right of the space bar to insert the extra symbol that appears on some keys. If you can't

---

Tips on Internet Security

Make sure that your device is running the latest versions of its operating system, security software, and apps. Next, ensure that your device and key programs (like email) are password-protected. On the road, use only secure, password-protected Wi-Fi hotspots. Ask the hotel or café staff for the specific name of their Wi-Fi network, and make sure you log on to that exact one.

If you must access your financial info online, use a banking app rather than accessing your account via a browser. A cellular connection is more secure than Wi-Fi. Avoid logging onto personal finance sites on a public computer.

Never share your credit-card number (or any other sensitive information) online unless you know that the site is secure. A secure site displays a little padlock icon, and the URL begins with *https* (instead of the usual *http*).

---

locate a special character (such as @), simply copy and paste it from a web page.

MAIL

You can mail one package per day to yourself worth up to $200 duty-free from Europe to the US (mark it "personal purchases"). If you're sending a gift to someone, mark it "unsolicited gift." For details, visit www.cbp.gov, select "Travel," and search for "Know Before You Visit." The Italian postal service works fine, but for quick transatlantic delivery (in either direction), consider services such as DHL (www.dhl.com).

Transportation

If your trip will cover more of Italy than just Venice, you may need to take a long-distance train or bus, rent a car, or fly. Buses are an alternative to trains (and may be your only option for reaching some small Italian towns), but they are generally slower and less efficient. Renting a car is great for touring the countryside outside of Venice. I give some specifics on trains, buses, and flights here. For more detailed information on transportation throughout Europe, including trains, flying, buses, renting a car, and driving, see www.ricksteves.com/transportation.

TRAINS

To travel by train affordably within Italy, you can simply buy tickets as you go. For travelers ready to lock in dates and times weeks or months in advance, buying nonrefundable tickets online can cut

PRACTICALITIES

costs in half. Note that the Italy rail pass is generally not a good value, but if your travel extends beyond Italy, there are multicountry rail passes that might be worth checking into. For advice on figuring out the smartest train-ticket or rail-pass options for your trip, visit the Trains & Rail Passes section of my website at www.ricksteves.com/rail.

Types of Trains

Most trains in Italy are operated by the state-run **Trenitalia** company (www.trenitalia.com, a.k.a. Ferrovie dello Stato Italiane, abbreviated FS). Ticket prices depend on the speed of the train, so it helps to know the different types of trains: pokey Regionale (R or REG); medium-speed Regionale Veloce (RV); fast InterCity (IC) and EuroCity (EC); and super-fast Frecce trains. All Frecce trains, many EuroCity and InterCity trains, and most international trains require reservations.

Regional trains offer only open seating (no assigned seats); all other classes of service come with an assigned seat. If you're traveling with a rail pass, you'll need to reserve a seat for any service but regional trains (see "Rail Passes," later).

A private train company called **Italo** (www.italotreno.it) runs fast trains on major routes in Italy. Italo is focused on two corridors: Venice-Padua-Bologna-Florence-Rome-Salerno and Turin-Milan-Bologna-Florence-Rome-Naples. They also run a useful Milan-Venice train. Italo has fewer departures than Trenitalia but offers discounts for tickets booked well in advance. In Naples, Milan, and Rome, some departures use secondary stations—pay attention to which station you need. Italo does not accept rail passes, but is a worthy alternative for point-to-point tickets.

Both train companies have call centers for answering general questions (**Trenitalia:** daily 7:00-24:00, tel. 06-6847-5475; **Italo:** daily 6:00-23:00, tel. 06-8937-1892).

Be aware that Trenitalia and Italo don't cooperate at all. If you buy a ticket for one train line, it's not valid on the other. Even if you're just looking for schedule information, the company you ask will most likely ignore the other's options.

Another private train company, **Thello,** runs night trains between Paris and Venice (www.thello.com).

Schedules

Check schedules at www.trenitalia.it and www.italotreno.it (domestic journeys only) or use their smartphone apps; for international trips, use www.bahn.com (Germany's excellent all-Europe schedule website). At the train station, the easiest way to check schedules is at a ticket machine. Enter the desired date, time, and destination to see all your options. Printed schedules are also posted at the station (yellow posters show departures—*partenze;* white posters show arrivals).

Schedules list the time of departure *(ora),* the type of train *(treni),* and service classes offered *(classi servizi)*—first- and second-class cars, dining car, *cuccetta* berths, and whether you need reservations (usually denoted by an R in a box). The train's destination *(principali fermate destinazioni)* is shown, along with intermediate stops, and notes such as "also stops in..." *(ferma anche a...),* "doesn't stop in..." *(non ferma a...),* "stops in every station" *(ferma in tutte le stazioni),* "delayed..." *(ritardo...),* and so on.

Note that for today's trains on the station reader boards, your destination may be listed as an intermediate stop. For example, if you're going from Venice to Verona, scan the schedule and you'll notice that many trains that terminate in Milan or Torino also stop in Verona en route (but are also more expensive than Regional train tickets or require a seat reservation with a rail pass). The reader board also lists the track *(binario)* the train departs from. If you're not sure, confirm the *binario* with a ticket seller or railway official, or check monitors on the platform.

Point-to-Point Tickets

Train tickets are a good value in Italy. Typical fares are shown on the map on page 460, though ticket prices can vary for the same journey, mainly depending on the time of day, the speed of the train, and advance discounts.

Classes of Service: Frecce and Italo trains each offer several classes of service (e.g., Standard, Premium, Business, Executive) where all seats are reserved. Other trains offer standard first- and second-class seating (with first class costing up to 50 percent more than second). Buying up gives you a little more elbow room, a snack, or perhaps a better chance at seating a group together, if you're buying on short notice.

Advance Discounts: Ticket price levels are Base (full fare, easily changeable or partly refundable before scheduled departure), Economy (one schedule change allowed before departure, for a fee), and Super Economy or Low Cost (sells out quickly, no refunds or exchanges). For example, traveling Standard class from Venice to Florence on the fastest train costs €57 for a Base fare, €43 for an Economy fare, or €33 at the Super Economy rate.

PRACTICALITIES

Italy's Public Transportation

Discounted fares typically sell out several weeks before departure. Fares labeled *servizi abbonati* are available only for locals with monthly passes—not tourists. Regional trains don't offer advance discounts or seat assignments, so there's little need to buy those tickets in advance.

Speed vs. Savings: For point-to-point tickets, you'll pay more the faster you go. Spending a modest amount of extra time in transit can save money. On longer, mainline routes, fast trains save more time and provide most of the service. On routes like Verona-Padua-Venice, Regionale and Regionale Veloce trains cost considerably less than IC and Frecce express trains, and are only a little slower. For more on regional versus express trains in northern Italy, see page 315.

Age-Based Discounts: Discounts for kids don't usually beat the Super Economy rate described above. If the cheapest tickets are no longer available, look for deals like "Bimbi Gratis" and "Offerta Famiglia." Other discounts for youths and seniors require purchase of a separate card (€40 Carta Verde for ages 12-26, €30 Carta Argento for ages 60 and over), but the ticket discount is so minor (10-15 percent respectively for domestic travel), it's not worth it for most.

Buying Point-to-Point Tickets

You can buy tickets online, with a smartphone app, at train station ticket windows, from ticket machines, or at travel agencies. For long-haul runs or travel on a busy weekend or holiday, it can be cheaper to buy tickets in advance. But because most Italian trains run frequently and there's no deadline to buy tickets, for the most part I prefer to keep my travel plans flexible by purchasing tickets as I go. (You can buy tickets for several trips when you are ready to commit.)

It's easy to buy tickets **online** at Trenitalia.com or ItaloTreno.it. On either website, choose English and be sure to read the pricing info, as many of the cheaper tickets are not refundable or changeable. You can keep the ticket on your mobile device (either as a PDF or in a "ticketless" format with a booking code), or you can print it out.

Or download the Trenitalia or Italo app to your **smartphone**—both have English versions. If using the Trenitalia app to buy tickets, do so as a guest (a log-in isn't necessary—or possible—if you don't live in Italy).

If you instead go to the train station to buy tickets, you can avoid ticket-office lines by using the ticket machines in station halls. You'll be able to easily purchase tickets for travel within Italy, make seat reservations, and even book a *cuccetta* (koo-CHEH-tah; overnight berth). If you do use the ticket windows (e.g., to buy international tickets), be sure you're in the correct line. Key terms: *biglietti* (general tickets), *prenotazioni* (reservations), *nazionali* (domestic), and *internazionali*.

Trenitalia's **ticket machines** are user-friendly and found in all but the tiniest stations in Italy. You can pay with cash (change given when indicated) or by debit or credit card (even for small amounts, but you may need to enter your PIN). Select English, then your destination. If you don't immediately see the city you're traveling to, keep keying in the spelling until it's listed. You can choose from first- and second-class seats, request tickets for more than one traveler, and pick seats, when applicable. Don't select a discount rate without being sure that you meet the criteria (for example, Americans are not eligible for certain EU or resident discounts).

To buy tickets at the station for **Italo** trains, look for a dedicated service counter (in most major stations) or a red ticket machine labeled *Italo*.

Some **international tickets** can't be bought online or from machines; for these tickets and anything else that requires a real person, you must go to a ticket window at the station. A good alternative, though, is to drop by a local travel agency. Agencies sell domestic and international tickets and make reservations. They charge a small fee, but the language barrier (and the lines) can be smaller than at the station's ticket windows.

Rail Passes

The single-country Eurail Italy Pass may save you money if you take several long train rides or prefer first-class travel, but for most people it's not a good value. Most train travelers in Italy take relatively short rides on the Milan-Venice-Florence-Rome circuit. For these trips, it can be cheaper to buy point-to-point tickets. Remember that rail passes are valid only on Trenitalia trains (not on Italo or Thello trains).

Furthermore, a rail pass doesn't offer much hop-on convenience in Italy, since even with a rail pass, seat reservations are required for InterCity, EuroCity, and Frecce trains (€5-10 each; make seat reservations at station ticket machines or windows). Most regional trains (such as Florence-Pisa-Cinque Terre service) don't require (or offer) reservations. Reservations for berths on overnight trains cost extra and aren't covered by rail passes.

If you're also traveling by train in other countries, consider a Eurail Global Pass. Although it covers most of Europe, prices can work for trips as short as three travel days or as long as three months. For more info, see the sidebar.

PRACTICALITIES

Rail Pass or Point-to-Point Tickets?

Will you be better off buying a rail pass or point-to-point tickets? It pays to know your options and choose what's best for your itinerary.

Rail Passes

A Eurail Italy Pass lets you travel by train in Italy for three to eight days (consecutively or not) within a one-month period. Italy is also covered (along with most of Europe) by the classic Eurail Global Pass.

Discounted rates are offered for seniors (age 60 and up) and youths (ages 12-27). Up to two kids (ages 4-11) can travel free with each adult-rate pass (but not with senior rates). All rail passes offer a choice of first or second class for all ages.

Rail passes are best purchased outside Europe (through travel agents or Rick Steves' Europe). For more on rail passes, including current prices, visit RickSteves.com/rail.

Point-to-Point Tickets

Italian train tickets are relatively cheap, and most include seat reservations, making them the best deal for most travelers. Use this map to add up approximate pay-as-you-go fares for your itinerary, and compare that to the price of a rail pass plus reservations. Keep in mind that significant discounts on point-to-point tickets may be available with advance purchase.

Map shows approximate costs, in US dollars, for one-way, second-class tickets on faster trains.

Train Tips

Validating Tickets: If your ticket includes a seat reservation on a specific train *(biglietto con prenotazione)*, you're all set and can just get on board. The same is true for any ticket bought online or with the Trenitalia or Italo smartphone apps (whether open or reserved seating); these tickets are considered already validated.

An open ticket (generally for a *regionale* train) bought from a ticket desk or machine must be validated (date-stamped) before you board (the ticket may say *da convalidare* or *convalida*). To validate it, before getting on the train, stamp your ticket in the machine near the platform (usually marked *convalida biglietti* or *vidimazione*). Once you validate a ticket, you must complete your trip within the timeframe stamped on the ticket (usually about four hours). If you forget to validate your ticket, go right away to the train conductor—before he comes to you—or you'll pay a fine.

Getting a Seat: If you're taking an unreserved *regionale* train that originates at your departure point (e.g., you're catching the Venice-Verona train in Venice), arriving at least 15 minutes before the departure time will help you snare a seat.

Baggage Storage: Many Italian stations have *deposito bagagli* where you can safely leave your bag for a standardized but steep price (€6/5 hours, €12/12 hours, €17/24 hours, payable when you pick up the bag, double-check closing hours; they may ask to photocopy your passport). Due to security concerns, no Italian stations have lockers.

Theft Concerns: In big cities, exercise caution and prudence at train stations to avoid thieves and con artists. Homeless and marginalized people lurk around the station trying to skim tips (or worse) from unsuspecting tourists. If someone helps you to find your train or carry your bags, be aware that they are not an official porter; they are simply hoping for some cash. And if someone other than a uniformed railway employee tries to help you use the ticket machines, politely refuse.

Italian trains are famous for their thieves. Never leave a bag unattended. Police do ride the trains, cutting down on theft. Still, for an overnight trip, I'd feel safe only in a *cuccetta* (a bunk in a special sleeping car with an attendant who keeps track of who comes and goes while you sleep—approximately €40 or more).

Strikes: Strikes, which are common, generally last a day (often a Friday). Train employees will simply explain, *"Sciopero"* (SHOH-peh-roh, strike). But in actuality, a minimum amount of "essential" main-line service is maintained (by law) during strikes. When a strike is pending, travel agencies, savvy hoteliers, and remaining station personnel can check to see when the strike will go into effect and which trains will continue to run. Revised schedules may be posted online and in Italian at stations. See www.trenitalia.com, choose English, then "Information and Contacts," and then "In Case of Strike."

If your train is cancelled, your reserved-seat ticket will likely be accepted on any similar train running that day (either earlier or later than the original departure time) but you won't have a seat assignment. Tickets for cancelled trains should also be exchangeable without penalty ahead of the original departure time, or can be refunded (have an agent mark it "unused," and check refund deadlines). A rail pass works on any train still operating, but partially used rail passes can't be refunded—so make full use of any pass you have to continue your trip.

BUSES

You can usually get anywhere you want in Italy by bus, as long as you're not in a hurry and plan ahead using bus schedules (pick up at local TIs or bus stations). For reaching small towns, buses are sometimes the only option if you don't have a car.

Long-distance buses are catching on in Italy as an alternative to the train. They are usually cheaper, modern, and often (unlike trains) have free Wi-Fi. They're especially useful on routes poorly served by train. Some of the operators you'll see are Megabus (www.megabus.com), Flixbus (https://global.flixbus.com), and Marozzi (www.marozzivt.it). In general, orange buses are local city buses, and blue buses are for long distances.

Larger towns have a (usually chaotic) long-distance bus station *(stazione degli autobus)*, with ticket windows and several stalls (usually labeled *corsia, stallo,* or *binario*)—but to save time, buy your ticket at a travel agent or online, and print it out. Smaller towns—where buses are more useful—often have a central bus stop *(fermata)*, likely along the main road or on the main square, and maybe several more scattered around town. In small towns, buy bus tickets at newsstands or tobacco shops (with the big *T* signs). When buying your ticket, confirm the departure point *("Dov'è la fermata?")*.

Before boarding, confirm the destination with the driver. You are expected to stow big backpacks underneath the bus (open the luggage compartment yourself if it's closed). Upon arrival, double-check that the posted schedule lists your next destination and departure time.

Traveling by bus on Sundays and holidays can be problematic; even from large cities, schedules are sparse, departing buses are jam-packed, and ticket offices are often closed. Plan ahead and buy your ticket in advance. Most travel agencies book bus (and train) tickets for a small fee.

PRACTICALITIES

TAXIS AND RIDE-BOOKING SERVICES

Most Italian taxis are reliable and cheap. In many cities, two people can travel short distances by cab for little more than the cost of bus or subway tickets. If you like ride-booking services such as Uber, their apps usually work in Europe just like they do in the US: Request a car on your mobile phone (connected to Wi-Fi or data), and the fare is automatically charged to your credit card. In Italy, however, Uber faces legal challenges, and may not be consistently available.

FLIGHTS

To compare flight costs and times, begin with an online travel search engine: Kayak is the top site for flights to and within Europe, easy-to-use Google Flights has price alerts, and Skyscanner includes many inexpensive flights within Europe. To avoid unpleasant surprises, before you book be sure to read the small print about refunds, changes, and the costs for "extras" such as reserving a seat, checking a bag, or printing a boarding pass.

Flights to Europe: Start looking for international flights about four to six months before your trip, especially for peak-season travel. Depending on your itinerary, it can be efficient and no more expensive to fly into one city and out of another. If your flight requires a connection in Europe, see my hints on navigating Europe's top hub airports at www.ricksteves.com/hub-airports.

Flights Within Europe: Flying between European cities is surprisingly affordable. Before buying a long-distance train or bus ticket, check the cost of a flight on one of Europe's airlines, whether a major carrier or a no-frills outfit like Easyjet or Ryanair. Be aware that flying with a discount airline can have drawbacks, such as minimal customer service and time-consuming treks to secondary airports.

Flying to the US and Canada: Because security is extra tight for flights to the US, be sure to give yourself plenty of time at the airport. Charge your electronic devices before you board in case security checks require you to turn them on (see www.tsa.gov for the latest rules).

Resources from Rick Steves

Begin Your Trip at RickSteves.com

My mobile-friendly **website** is *the* place to explore Europe in preparation for your trip. You'll find thousands of fun articles, videos, and radio interviews; a wealth of money-saving tips for planning your dream trip; travel news dispatches; a video library of my travel talks; my travel blog; my latest guidebook updates

PRACTICALITIES

(www.ricksteves.com/update); and my free Rick Steves Audio Europe app. You can also follow me on Facebook, Instagram, and Twitter.

Our **Travel Forum** is a well-groomed collection of message boards, where our travel-savvy community answers questions and shares their personal travel experiences—and our well-traveled staff chimes in when they can be helpful (www.ricksteves.com/forums).

Our **online Travel Store** offers bags and accessories that I've designed to help you travel smarter and lighter. These include my popular carry-on bags (which I live out of four months a year), money belts, totes, toiletries kits, adapters, guidebooks, and planning maps (www.ricksteves.com/shop).

Our website can also help you find the perfect **rail pass** for your itinerary and your budget, with easy, one-stop shopping for rail passes, seat reservations, and point-to-point tickets (www.ricksteves.com/rail).

Rick Steves' Tours, Guidebooks, TV Shows, and More

Small Group Tours: Want to travel with greater efficiency and less stress? We offer more than 40 itineraries reaching the best destinations in this book...and beyond. Each year about 30,000 travelers join us on about 1,000 Rick Steves bus tours. You'll enjoy great guides and a fun bunch of travel partners (with small groups of 24 to 28 travelers). You'll find European adventures to fit every vacation length. For all the details, and to get our tour catalog, visit www.ricksteves.com/tours or call us at 425/608-4217.

Books: *Rick Steves Venice* is just one of many books in my series on European travel, which includes country and city guidebooks, Snapshots (excerpted chapters from bigger guides), Pocket guides (full-color little books on big cities), "Best Of" guidebooks (condensed, full-color country guides), and my budget-travel skills handbook, *Rick Steves Europe Through the Back Door*. A complete list of my titles—including phrase books, cruising guides, and more—appears near the end of this book.

TV Shows and Travel Talks: My public television series, *Rick Steves' Europe*, covers Europe from top to bottom with over 100 half-hour episodes—and we're working on new shows every year (watch full episodes at my website for free). My free online video library, Rick Steves Classroom Europe, offers a searchable database of short video clips on European history, culture, and geography (http://classroom.ricksteves.com). And to raise your travel I.Q., check out the video versions of our popular classes (covering most European countries as well as travel skills, packing smart, cruising, tech for travelers, European art, and travel as a political act—www.ricksteves.com/travel-talks).

Radio: My weekly public radio show, *Travel with Rick Steves,* features interviews with travel experts from around the world. It airs on 400 public radio stations across the US, or you can hear it as a podcast. A complete archive of programs is available at www.ricksteves.com/radio.

Audio Tours on My Free App: I've produced dozens of free, self-guided audio tours of the top sights in Europe. For those tours and other audio content, get my free **Rick Steves Audio Europe app,** an extensive online library organized by destination. For more on my app, see page 8.

APPENDIX

Holidays and Festivals

This list includes selected festivals in Venice, plus national holidays observed throughout Italy. Many sights and banks close on national holidays—keep this in mind when planning your itinerary. Before planning a trip around a festival, verify the dates with the festival website, the tourist office (www.veneziaunica.it or www.italia.it), or my "Upcoming Holidays and Festivals in Italy" web page (www.ricksteves.com/europe/italy/festivals).

In Venice, hotels get booked up on Carnevale, Easter weekend, Liberation Day/St. Mark's Day, Labor Day, Feast of the Ascension Day, the Feast and Regatta of the Redeemer, the Historical Regatta, All Saint's Day, the Feast of our Lady of Good Health, Christmas, and New Year's Eve, and on Fridays and Saturdays year-round. Some hotels require you to book the full three-day weekend around a holiday.

Jan 1	New Year's Day
Jan 6	Epiphany
Feb	Carnevale: Feb 8-25, 2020
April	Easter weekend (Good Friday-Easter Monday): April 10-13, 2020; April 2-5, 2021

April 25	Italian Liberation Day, St. Mark's Day (Venetian patron saint)
May 1	Labor Day
May	Feast of the Ascension Day: May 21, 2020; May 13, 2021
Late May-Early June	Vogalonga Regatta
June 2	Anniversary of the Republic
June	Feast of Corpus Christi: June 11, 2020; June 3, 2021
Early July	Murano Regatta
July (third weekend)	Feast and Regatta of the Redeemer (Festa del Redentore)
Aug 15	Feast of the Assumption (Ferragosto)
Sept (first weekend)	Historical Regatta
Mid-Sept	Burano Regatta
Nov 1	All Saints' Day
Nov 21	Feast of Our Lady of Good Health (Santa Maria della Salute)
Dec 8	Feast of the Immaculate Conception
Dec 25	Christmas
Dec 26	St. Stephen's Day

FESTIVALS IN VENICE

Venice's most famous festival is **Carnevale,** the celebration Americans call Mardi Gras (February; www.carnevale.venezia.it). In Carnevale's heyday—the 1600s and 1700s—you could do pretty much anything with anybody from any social class if you were wearing a mask. These days, tourists and Venetians—from kids to businessmen—gather for parades, parties, and masquerade balls. In drawing such big crowds, Carnevale has nearly been a victim of its own success, driving away many Venetians (who skip out on the craziness to go skiing in the Dolomites). Unless you're interested in joining the fun, any other day this time of year will be much less chaotic, and less expensive. For more on Carnevale, see the sidebar on page 6.

Every year, the city hosts the **Venice Biennale International Art Exhibition,** a world-class contemporary fair, alternating between art in odd years (the main event) and architecture in even years (much smaller). The exhibition spreads over the Arsenale and Giardini park. When the Biennale focuses on visual art, representatives from 80-plus nations offer the latest in contemporary art forms: video, digital art, performance art, and photography, along with painting and sculpture (take vaporetto #1 or #2 to Giardini-Biennale; for details and an events calendar, see www.labiennale.org). The actual exhibition usually runs from June through November, but other events loosely connected with the Biennale—film, dance, theater—are held throughout the year (starting as early as February) in various venues on the island.

Other typically Venetian festival days filling the city's hotels with visitors and its canals with decked-out boats are **Feast of the Ascension Day, Feast and Regatta of the Redeemer** (with spectacular fireworks show Sat night), and the **Historical Regatta** (old-time boats and pageantry). **Vogalonga** is a colorful regatta that attracts more than 1,500 human-powered watercraft; teams of often-costumed participants follow a 20-mile course through the canals and lagoon (www.vogalonga.it). Crowds soar and vaporetti run limited schedules during these events. Smaller regattas include the **Murano Regatta** and the **Burano Regatta.**

Venice's patron saint, **St. Mark,** is commemorated every April 25. Venetian men celebrate the day by presenting roses to the women in their lives (mothers, wives, and lovers).

Every November 21 is the **Feast of Our Lady of Good Health.** On this local "Thanksgiving," a bridge is built over the Grand Canal so that the city can pile into La Salute Church and remember how Venice survived the gruesome plague of 1630. On this day, Venetians eat smoked lamb from Dalmatia (which was the cargo of the first ship admitted when the plague lifted). Festivities around the church include stands selling candles, sweets, and novelties for kids.

Books and Films

To learn more about Italy past and present, and specifically Venice, check out a few of these books or films. For kids' recommendations, see the Venice with Children chapter.

Nonfiction

The City of Falling Angels (John Berendt, 2005). A best-selling author slowly solves the real-life mystery of a 1996 fire that destroyed Venice's La Fenice Opera House.

A History of Venice (John Julius Norwich, 1977). English Lord Norwich's engaging account spans more than a century, from Venice's fifth-century origins to the arrival of Napoleon.

Italian Journey (Johann Wolfgang von Goethe, 1786). In his 18th-century collection of writings, Goethe describes his travels to Rome, Venice, Sicily, and Naples.

A Literary Companion to Venice (Ian Littlewood, 1992). Seven detailed walking tours show Venice's impact on writers such as Byron, Goethe, James, Proust, Lawrence, and Pound.

The Science of Saving Venice (Caroline Fletcher and Jane da Mosto, 2004). This readable introduction to the ecology of Venice's lagoon asks if Venice can survive in the 21st century.

Venice: Lion City (Garry Wills, 2001). One of America's greatest historians tackles the provocative history of Venice in the 15th and 16th centuries.

Venice Observed (Mary McCarthy, 1963). This snappy and engaging memoir details the Venetian ethos through the eyes of a sharply critical writer.

Venice: The Tourist Maze (Robert C. Davis and Garry R. Marvin, 2004). This history of tourism in Venice warns how the city is now being loved to death.

A Venetian Affair (Andrea di Robilant, 2003). Based on letters found in a palazzo, this is a true love story between an aristocrat and an illegitimate girl in 18th-century Venice.

The Venetian Empire: A Sea Voyage (Jan Morris, 1990). Morris brings a maritime empire to life in this book that illustrates the city's place on a larger historical canvas.

Fiction

The Aspern Papers and Other Stories (Henry James, 1894). An American editor travels to Venice in search of letters written to his mistress. Other James works about Italy include *Italian Hours* and *Daisy Miller*.

Death at La Fenice (Donna Leon, 1992). This chilling Venetian mystery and the others in Leon's Commissario Brunetti series reveal more about "real" Italy than many memoirs do.

Death in Venice and Other Tales (Thomas Mann, 1912). The centerpiece of this collection is an eloquent classic that explores obsession, beauty, and death in plague-ridden Venice (also a 1971 film).

The Glassblower of Murano (Marina Fiorato, 2009). A 17th-century glassblower reveals the secrets of his trade to the French, which has repercussions for his descendants in the 21st century.

Invisible Cities (Italo Calvino, 1972). Marco Polo tells of the fantastical cities he's seen...or is he just describing the many facets of his beloved Venice?

The Merchant of Venice (William Shakespeare, 1598). In addition to *Merchant*, other Shakespearean plays set in Italy include *Romeo and Juliet* (Verona), *Much Ado About Nothing* (Sicily), *The Two Gentlemen of Verona*, and *The Taming of the Shrew* (Padua).

The Passion (Jeanette Winterson, 1987). Set in the Napoleonic era, this is both a complex love story and a work of magical realist fiction.

The Rossetti Letter (Christi Phillips, 2007). Shifting between past and present, this novel explores the legacy of a mysterious courtesan in 17th-century Venice.

Film and TV

Bread and Tulips (2000). A harassed Italian housewife left behind by her family at a roadside café discovers beauty, love, and her true self in Venice.

Casanova (2005). This comic romp, set in 18th-century Venice, stars the late Heath Ledger as the master of *amore*.

Dangerous Beauty (1998). A 16th-century prostitute accused of witchcraft confronts the impossible choices for women in Venetian society.

Don't Look Now (1973). Venice is both threatening and beautiful when a couple (Donald Sutherland and Julie Christie)—grieving the death of their daughter—encounter what may be her ghost.

Letters to Juliet (2010). A would-be writer comes to Verona and discovers a 50-year-old letter left at a statue of Juliet—sparking several unexpected romances.

Summertime (1955). Director David Lean's film follows a melancholy Ohio schoolteacher (Katharine Hepburn) who travels to Venice looking for romance and finds more than antiques in Rossano Brazzi's shop.

The Wings of the Dove (1997). Based on the Henry James novel, this romantic drama is a tale of desire that takes full advantage of its Venetian locale.

Conversions and Climate

Numbers and Stumblers

- Europeans write a few of their numbers differently than we do. 1 = 1, 4 = 4, 7 = 7.
- In Europe, dates appear as day/month/year, so Christmas 2021 is 25/12/21.
- Commas are decimal points and decimals are commas. A dollar and a half is $1,50, one thousand is 1.000, and there are 5.280 feet in a mile.
- When counting with fingers, start with your thumb. If you hold up your first finger to request one item, you'll probably get two.
- What Americans call the second floor of a building is the first floor in Europe.
- On escalators and moving sidewalks, Europeans keep the left "lane" open for passing. Keep to the right.

Metric Conversions

A **kilogram** equals 1,000 grams (about 2.2 pounds). One hundred **grams** (a common unit at markets) is about a quarter-pound. One **liter** is about a quart, or almost four to a gallon.

A **kilometer** is six-tenths of a mile. To convert kilometers to miles, cut the kilometers in half and add back 10 percent of the original (120 km: 60 + 12 = 72 miles). One **meter** is 39 inches—just over a yard.

1 foot = 0.3 meter	1 square yard = 0.8 square meter
1 yard = 0.9 meter	1 square mile = 2.6 square kilometers
1 mile = 1.6 kilometers	1 ounce = 28 grams
1 centimeter = 0.4 inch	1 quart = 0.95 liter
1 meter = 39.4 inches	1 kilogram = 2.2 pounds
1 kilometer = 0.62 mile	32°F = 0°C

Roman Numerals

In the US, you'll see Roman numerals—which originated in ancient Rome—used for copyright dates, clocks, and the Super Bowl. In Italy, you're likely to observe these numbers chiseled on statues and buildings. If you want to do some numeric detective work, here's how: In Roman numerals, as in ours, the highest numbers (thousands, hundreds) come first, followed by smaller numbers. Many numbers are made by combining numerals into sets: V = 5, so VIII = 8 (5 plus 3). Roman numerals follow a subtraction principle for multiples of fours (4, 40, 400, etc.) and nines (9, 90, 900, etc.); the number four, for example, is written as IV (1 subtracted from 5), rather than IIII. The number nine is IX (1 subtracted from 10).

Big numbers such as dates can look daunting at first. The easiest way to handle them is to read the numbers in discrete chunks. For example, Michelangelo was born in MCDLXXV. Break it down: M (1,000) + CD (100 subtracted from 500, or 400) + LXX (50 + 10 + 10, or 70) + V (5) = 1475. It was a very good year.

M = 1000	XL = 40
CM = 900	X = 10
D = 500	IX = 9
CD = 400	V = 5
C = 100	IV = 4
XC = 90	I = duh
L = 50	

Clothing Sizes

When shopping for clothing, use these US-to-European comparisons as general guidelines (but note that no conversion is perfect).

Women: For pants and dresses, add 36 in Italy (US 10 = Italian 46). For blouses and sweaters, add 8 for most of Europe (US 32 = European 40). For shoes, add 30-31 (US 7 = European 37/38).

Men: For shirts, multiply by 2 and add about 8 (US 15 = European 38). For jackets and suits, add 10. For shoes, add 32-34.

Children: Clothing is sized by height—in centimeters (2.5 cm = 1 inch), so a US size 8 roughly equates to 132-140. For shoes up to size 13, add 16-18, and for sizes 1 and up, add 30-32.

Venice's Climate

First line, average daily high; second line, average daily low; third line, average days without rain. For more detailed weather statistics for destinations in this book (as well as the rest of the world), check www.wunderground.com.

J	F	M	A	M	J	J	A	S	O	N	D
42°	46°	53°	62°	70°	76°	81°	80°	75°	65°	53°	46°
33°	35°	41°	49°	56°	63°	66°	65°	61°	53°	44°	37°
25	21	24	21	23	22	24	24	25	24	21	23

Fahrenheit and Celsius Conversion

Europe takes its temperature using the Celsius scale, while we opt for Fahrenheit. For a rough conversion from Celsius to Fahrenheit, double the number and add 30. For weather, remember that 28°C is 82°F—perfect. For health, 37°C is just right. At a launderette, 30°C is cold, 40°C is warm (usually the default setting), 60°C is hot, and 95°C is boiling. Your air-conditioner should be set at about 20°C.

Packing Checklist

Whether you're traveling for five days or five weeks, you won't need more than this. Pack light to enjoy the sweet freedom of true mobility.

Clothing

- [ ] 5 shirts: long- & short-sleeve
- [ ] 2 pairs pants (or skirts/capris)
- [ ] 1 pair shorts
- [ ] 5 pairs underwear & socks
- [ ] 1 pair walking shoes
- [ ] Sweater or warm layer
- [ ] Rainproof jacket with hood
- [ ] Tie, scarf, belt, and/or hat
- [ ] Swimsuit
- [ ] Sleepwear/loungewear

Money

- [ ] Debit card(s)
- [ ] Credit card(s)
- [ ] Hard cash (US $100-200)
- [ ] Money belt

Documents

- [ ] Passport
- [ ] Tickets & confirmations: flights, hotels, trains, rail pass, car rental, sight entries
- [ ] Driver's license
- [ ] Student ID, hostel card, etc.
- [ ] Photocopies of important documents
- [ ] Insurance details
- [ ] Guidebooks & maps

Toiletries Kit

- [ ] Basics: soap, shampoo, toothbrush, toothpaste, floss, deodorant, sunscreen, brush/comb, etc.
- [ ] Medicines & vitamins
- [ ] First-aid kit
- [ ] Glasses/contacts/sunglasses
- [ ] Sewing kit
- [ ] Packet of tissues (for WC)
- [ ] Earplugs

Electronics

- [ ] Mobile phone
- [ ] Camera & related gear
- [ ] Tablet/ebook reader/laptop
- [ ] Headphones/earbuds
- [ ] Chargers & batteries
- [ ] Phone car charger & mount (or GPS device)
- [ ] Plug adapters

Miscellaneous

- [ ] Daypack
- [ ] Sealable plastic baggies
- [ ] Laundry supplies: soap, laundry bag, clothesline, spot remover
- [ ] Small umbrella
- [ ] Travel alarm/watch
- [ ] Notepad & pen
- [ ] Journal

Optional Extras

- [ ] Second pair of shoes (flip-flops, sandals, tennis shoes, boots)
- [ ] Travel hairdryer
- [ ] Picnic supplies
- [ ] Water bottle
- [ ] Fold-up tote bag
- [ ] Small flashlight
- [ ] Mini binoculars
- [ ] Small towel or washcloth
- [ ] Inflatable pillow/neck rest
- [ ] Tiny lock
- [ ] Address list (to mail postcards)
- [ ] Extra passport photos

Italian Survival Phrases

English	Italian	Pronunciation
Good day.	*Buongiorno.*	bwohn-**jor**-noh
Do you speak English?	*Parla inglese?*	**par**-lah een-**gleh**-zay
Yes. / No.	*Sì. / No.*	see / noh
I (don't) understand.	*(Non) capisco.*	(nohn) kah-**pees**-koh
Please.	*Per favore.*	pehr fah-**voh**-ray
Thank you.	*Grazie.*	**graht**-see-ay
You're welcome.	*Prego.*	**preh**-go
I'm sorry.	*Mi dispiace.*	mee dee-spee-**ah**-chay
Excuse me.	*Mi scusi.*	mee **skoo**-zee
(No) problem.	*(Non) c'è problema.*	(nohn) cheh proh-**bleh**-mah
Good.	*Va bene.*	vah **beh**-nay
Goodbye.	*Arrivederci.*	ah-ree-veh-**dehr**-chee
one / two	*uno / due*	**oo**-noh / **doo**-ay
three / four	*tre / quattro*	tray / **kwah**-troh
five / six	*cinque / sei*	**cheeng**-kway / **seh**-ee
seven / eight	*sette / otto*	**seh**-tay / **oh**-toh
nine / ten	*nove / dieci*	**noh**-vay / dee-**ay**-chee
How much is it?	*Quanto costa?*	**kwahn**-toh **koh**-stah
Write it?	*Me lo scrive?*	may loh **skree**-vay
Is it free?	*È gratis?*	eh **grah**-tees
Is it included?	*È incluso?*	eh een-**kloo**-zoh
Where can I buy / find...?	*Dove posso comprare / trovare...?*	**doh**-vay **poh**-soh kohm-**prah**-ray / troh-**vah**-ray
I'd like / We'd like...	*Vorrei / Vorremmo...*	voh-**reh**-ee / voh-**reh**-moh
...a room.	*...una camera.*	**oo**-nah **kah**-meh-rah
...a ticket to _____.	*...un biglietto per _____.*	oon beel-**yeh**-toh pehr _____
Is it possible?	*È possibile?*	eh poh-**see**-bee-lay
Where is...?	*Dov'è...?*	doh-**veh**
...the train station	*...la stazione*	lah staht-see-**oh**-nay
...the bus station	*...la stazione degli autobus*	lah staht-see-**oh**-nay **dehl**-yee ow-toh-boos
...tourist information	*...informazioni per turisti*	een-for-maht-see-**oh**-nee pehr too-**ree**-stee
...the toilet	*...la toilette*	lah twah-**leh**-tay
men	*uomini / signori*	**woh**-mee-nee / seen-**yoh**-ree
women	*donne / signore*	**doh**-nay / seen-**yoh**-ray
left / right	*sinistra / destra*	see-**nee**-strah / **deh**-strah
straight	*sempre dritto*	**sehm**-pray **dree**-toh
What time does this open / close?	*A che ora apre / chiude?*	ah kay **oh**-rah **ah**-pray / kee-**oo**-day
At what time?	*A che ora?*	ah kay **oh**-rah
Just a moment.	*Un momento.*	oon moh-**mehn**-toh
now / soon / later	*adesso / presto / tardi*	ah-**deh**-soh / **preh**-stoh / **tar**-dee
today / tomorrow	*oggi / domani*	**oh**-jee / doh-**mah**-nee

In an Italian Restaurant

English	Italian	Pronunciation
I'd like...	Vorrei...	voh-**reh**-ee
We'd like...	Vorremmo...	vor-**reh**-moh
...to reserve...	...prenotare...	preh-noh-**tah**-ray
...a table for one / two.	...un tavolo per uno / due.	oon **tah**-voh-loh pehr **oo**-noh / **doo**-ay
Is this seat free?	È libero questo posto?	eh **lee**-beh-roh **kweh**-stoh **poh**-stoh
The menu (in English), please.	Il menù (in inglese), per favore.	eel meh-**noo** (een een-**gleh**-zay) pehr fah-**voh**-ray
service (not) included	servizio (non) incluso	sehr-**veet**-see-oh (nohn) een-**kloo**-zoh
cover charge	pane e coperto	**pah**-nay ay koh-**pehr**-toh
to go	da portar via	dah **por**-tar **vee**-ah
with / without	con / senza	kohn / **sehnt**-sah
and / or	e / o	ay / oh
menu (of the day)	menù (del giorno)	meh-**noo** (dehl **jor**-noh)
specialty of the house	specialità della casa	speh-chah-lee-**tah deh**-lah **kah**-zah
first course (pasta, soup)	primo piatto	**pree**-moh pee-**ah**-toh
main course (meat, fish)	secondo piatto	seh-**kohn**-doh pee-**ah**-toh
side dishes	contorni	kohn-**tor**-nee
bread	pane	**pah**-nay
cheese	formaggio	for-**mah**-joh
sandwich	panino	pah-**nee**-noh
soup	zuppa	**tsoo**-pah
salad	insalata	een-sah-**lah**-tah
meat	carne	**kar**-nay
chicken	pollo	**poh**-loh
fish	pesce	**peh**-shay
seafood	frutti di mare	**froo**-tee dee **mah**-ray
fruit / vegetables	frutta / legumi	**froo**-tah / lay-**goo**-mee
dessert	dolce	**dohl**-chay
tap water	acqua del rubinetto	**ah**-kwah dehl roo-bee-**neh**-toh
mineral water	acqua minerale	**ah**-kwah mee-neh-**rah**-lay
milk	latte	**lah**-tay
(orange) juice	succo (d'arancia)	**soo**-koh (dah-**rahn**-chah)
coffee / tea	caffè / tè	kah-**feh** / teh
wine	vino	**vee**-noh
red / white	rosso / bianco	**roh**-soh / bee-**ahn**-koh
glass / bottle	bicchiere / bottiglia	bee-kee-**eh**-ray / boh-**teel**-yah
beer	birra	**bee**-rah
Cheers!	Cin cin!	cheen cheen
More. / Another.	Di più. / Un altro.	dee pew / oon **ahl**-troh
The same.	Lo stesso.	loh **steh**-soh
The bill, please.	Il conto, per favore.	eel **kohn**-toh pehr fah-**voh**-ray
Do you accept credit cards?	Accettate carte di credito?	ah-cheh-**tah**-tay **kar**-tay dee **kreh**-dee-toh
tip	mancia	**mahn**-chah
Delicious!	Delizioso!	day-leet-see-oh-**oh**-zoh

For more user-friendly Italian phrases, check out *Rick Steves Italian Phrase Book & Dictionary* or *Rick Steves French, Italian & German Phrase Book.*

INDEX

INDEX

MAP INDEX

Start your trip at

Our website enhances this book and turns

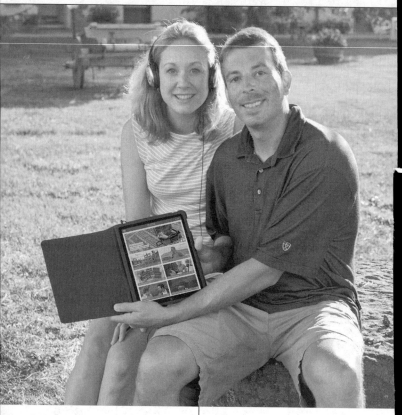

Explore Europe

At ricksteves.com you can browse through thousands of articles, videos, photos and radio interviews, plus find a wealth of money-saving travel tips for planning your dream trip. And with our mobile-friendly website, you can easily access all this great travel information anywhere you go.

TV Shows

Preview the places you'll visit by watching entire half-hour episodes of Rick Steves' Europe (choose from all 100 shows) on-demand, for free.

ricksteves.com

your travel dreams into affordable reality

Radio Interviews

Enjoy ready access to Rick's vast library of radio interviews covering travel tips and cultural insights that relate specifically to your Europe travel plans.

Travel Forums

Learn, ask, share! Our online community of savvy travelers is a great resource for first-time travelers to Europe, as well as seasoned pros.

Travel News

Subscribe to our free Travel News e-newsletter, and get monthly updates from Rick on what's happening in Europe.

Classroom Europe

Check out our free resource for educators with 300+ short video clips from the Rick Steves' Europe TV show.

Audio Europe™

Rick Steves has

Experience maximum Europe

Save time and energy

This guidebook is your independent-travel toolkit. But for all it delivers, it's still up to you to devote the time and energy it takes to manage the preparation and logistics that are essential for a happy trip. If that's a hassle, there's a solution.

Rick Steves Tours

A Rick Steves tour takes you to Europe's most interesting places with great

great tours, too!

with minimum stress

guides and small groups of 28 or less. We follow Rick's favorite itineraries, ride in comfy buses, stay in family-run hotels, and bring you intimately close to the Europe you've traveled so far to see. Most importantly, we take away the logistical headaches so you can focus on the fun.

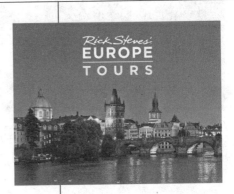

travelers—nearly half of them repeat customers—along with us on four dozen different itineraries, from Ireland to Italy to Athens. Is a Rick Steves tour the right fit for your travel dreams? Find out at ricksteves.com, where you can also request Rick's latest tour catalog. Europe is best

Join the fun

This year we'll take thousands of free-spirited experienced with happy travel partners. We hope you can join us.

A Guide for Every Trip

BEST OF GUIDES

Full-color guides in an easy-to-scan format. Focused on top sights and experiences in the most popular European destinations

Best of England
Best of Europe
Best of France
Best of Germany
Best of Ireland
Best of Italy
Best of Scotland
Best of Spain

COMPREHENSIVE GUIDES

City, country, and regional guides printed on Bible-thin paper. Packed with detailed coverage for a multi-week trip exploring iconic sights and venturing off the beaten path

Amsterdam & the Netherlands
Barcelona
Belgium: Bruges, Brussels,
   Antwerp & Ghent ·
Berlin
Budapest
Croatia & Slovenia
Eastern Europe
England
Florence & Tuscany
France
Germany
Great Britain
Greece: Athens & the Peloponnese
Iceland
Ireland
Istanbul
Italy
London
Paris
Portugal
Prague & the Czech Republic
Provence & the French Riviera
Rome
Scandinavia
Scotland
Sicily
Spain
Switzerland
Venice
Vienna, Salzburg & Tirol

HE BEST OF ROME

ne, Italy's capital, is studded with
nan remnants and floodlit-fountain
res. From the Vatican to the Colos-
n, with crazy traffic in between, Rome
nderful, huge, and exhausting. The
ds, the heat, and the weighty history

of the Eternal City where Caesars walked
can make tourists wilt. Recharge by taking siestas, gelato breaks, and after-dark
walks, strolling from one atmospheric
square to another in the refreshing evening air.

POCKET GUIDES

Compact color guides for shorter trips

Amsterdam	Paris
Athens	Prague
Barcelona	Rome
Florence	Venice
Italy's Cinque Terre	Vienna
London	
Munich & Salzburg	

SNAPSHOT GUIDES

Focused single-destination coverage

Basque Country: Spain & France
Copenhagen & the Best of Denmark
Dublin
Dubrovnik
Edinburgh
Hill Towns of Central Italy
Krakow, Warsaw & Gdansk
Lisbon
Loire Valley
Madrid & Toledo
Milan & the Italian Lakes District
Naples & the Amalfi Coast
Nice & the French Riviera
Normandy
Northern Ireland
Norway
Reykjavík
Rothenburg & the Rhine
Sevilla, Granada & Southern Spain
St. Petersburg, Helsinki & Tallinn
Stockholm

CRUISE PORTS GUIDES

Reference for cruise ports of call

Mediterranean Cruise Ports
Scandinavian & Northern European
  Cruise Ports

Complete your library with...

TRAVEL SKILLS & CULTURE

*Study up on travel skills and gain
insight on history and culture*

Europe 101
Europe Through the Back Door
Europe's Top 100 Masterpieces
European Christmas
European Easter
European Festivals
For the Love of Europe
Travel as a Political Act

PHRASE BOOKS & DICTIONARIES

French
French, Italian & German
German
Italian
Portuguese
Spanish

PLANNING MAPS

Britain, Ireland & London
Europe
France & Paris
Germany, Austria & Switzerland
Iceland
Ireland
Italy
Spain & Portugal

Credits

RESEARCHERS

For help with this edition, Rick and Gene relied on...

Trish Feaster

As a high-school Spanish teacher, Trish regularly led student trips in Europe, sharing her passions for language, history, culture, and cuisine. She now combines her love of teaching and travel as a Rick Steves' Europe tour guide, guidebook researcher, and language instructor. When not working in Europe, she binge-watches favorite shows, practices archery, and perfects her chocolate and caramel chip cookie recipe in her hometown of San Diego. You can follow Trish and her journeys at TheTravelphile.com.

Robert Wright

Raised in Memphis, Robert funded his first dream trip to Europe in 1998 by selling his entire Star Wars collection—proof that where there's a will, there's a way. He fell in love with Spain and Portugal and constantly returned, all while living for 14 years in Argentina. Robert recently married a *sevillano* and moved to Spain. He loves the Italian origins of certain Spanish traditions, like elaborate Nativity scenes that decorate parish churches and homes...even his.

PHOTO CREDITS

Avalon Travel
Hachette Book Group
1700 Fourth Street
Berkeley, CA 94710

Text © 2019 by Rick Steves' Europe, Inc. All rights reserved.
Maps © 2019 by Rick Steves' Europe, Inc. All rights reserved.

Printed in Canada by Friesens
First printing November 2019

ISBN: 978-1-64171-170-8

For the latest on Rick's talks, guidebooks, tours, public television series, and public radio show, contact Rick Steves' Europe, 130 Fourth Avenue, Edmonds, WA 98020, 425/771-8303, www.ricksteves.com, rick@ricksteves.com.

Rick Steves' Europe
Managing Editor: Jennifer Madison Davis
Assistant Managing Editor: Cathy Lu
Special Publications Manager: Risa Laib
Editors: Glenn Eriksen, Julie Fanselow, Tom Griffin, Suzanne Kotz, Rosie Leutzinger, Jessica Shaw, Carrie Shepherd
Editorial & Production Assistant: Megan Simms
Editorial Intern: Maxwell Eberle
Researchers: Trish Feaster, Robert Wright
Graphic Content Director: Sandra Hundacker
Maps & Graphics: David C. Hoerlein, Lauren Mills, Mary Rostad
Digital Asset Coordinator: Orin Dubrow

Avalon Travel
Senior Editor and Series Manager: Madhu Prasher
Editors: Jamie Andrade, Sierra Machado
Copy Editor: Maggie Ryan
Proofreader: Lisa Theobald
Indexer: Stephen Callahan
Production & Typesetting: Lisi Baldwin, Rue Flaherty
Cover Design: Kimberly Glyder Design
Maps & Graphics: Kat Bennett, Mike Morgenfeld

Let's Keep on Travelin'

Your trip doesn't need to end.

Follow Rick on social media!